ORIENTAL·LITERATURE

INDIA

THE TAJ-MAHAL.

The Taj was built by the Emperor Shah Jehan as a mausoleum for the Empress Mumtazi Mahal, who died in giving birth to the Princess Jehanava. Designed by Isâ Mohammed, it was commenced in the year 1630 and was not completed until 1647. During those seventeen years twenty thousand workmen were employed. It cost about two million dollars. It is one of the most magnificent public buildings in India.

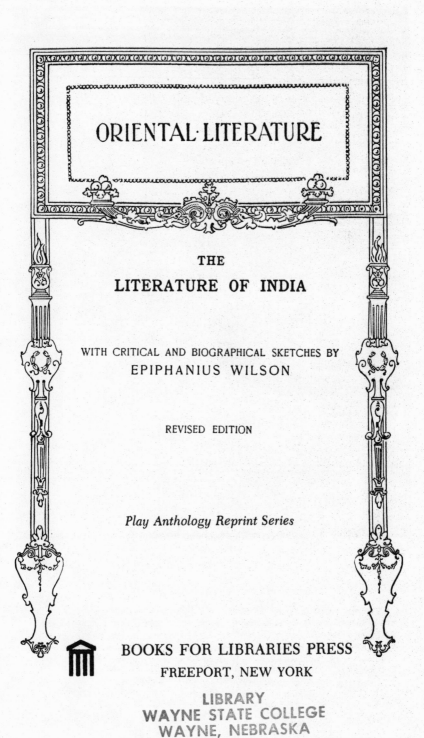

ORIENTAL·LITERATURE

THE

LITERATURE OF INDIA

WITH CRITICAL AND BIOGRAPHICAL SKETCHES BY
EPIPHANIUS WILSON

REVISED EDITION

Play Anthology Reprint Series

BOOKS FOR LIBRARIES PRESS
FREEPORT, NEW YORK

First Published 1900
Reprinted 1971

INTERNATIONAL STANDARD BOOK NUMBER:
0-8369-8226-6

LIBRARY OF CONGRESS CATALOG CARD NUMBER:
79-174765

PRINTED IN THE UNITED STATES OF AMERICA
BY
NEW WORLD BOOK MANUFACTURING CO., INC.
HALLANDALE, FLORIDA 33009

CONTENTS

THE BOOK OF GOOD COUNSELS

iii

202961

CONTENTS

SAKOONTALÁ

POEMS BY TORU DUTT

SAGOON TE

POEMS BY TOM BLYT

ILLUSTRATIONS

THE BOOK OF GOOD COUNSELS

—

SELECTED FROM

THE HITOPADEŚA

[Translated from the Sanscrit by Sir Edwin Arnold]

TRANSLATOR'S PREFACE

A STORY-BOOK from the Sanscrit at least possesses the minor merit of novelty. The " perfect language " has been hitherto regarded as the province of scholars, and few of these even have found time or taste to search its treasures. And yet among them is the key to the heart of modern India—as well as the splendid record of her ancient Gods and glories. The hope of Hindostan lies in the intelligent interest of England. Whatever avails to dissipate misconceptions between them, and to enlarge their intimacy, is a gain to both peoples; and to this end the present volume aspires, in an humble degree, to contribute.

The "Hitopadeśa" is a work of high antiquity, and extended popularity. The prose is doubtless as old as our own era; but the intercalated verses and proverbs compose a selection from writings of an age extremely remote. The " Mahabharata " and the textual Veds are of those quoted; to the first of which Professor M. Williams (in his admirable edition of the " Nala," 1860) assigns a date of 350 B.C., while he claims for the "Rig-Veda" an antiquity as high as B.C. 1300. The "Hitopadeśa " may thus be fairly styled " The Father of all Fables "; for from its numerous translations have come Æsop and Pilpay, and in later days Reineke Fuchs. Originally compiled in Sanscrit, it was rendered, by order of Nushiraván, in the sixth century, A.D., into Persic. From the Persic it passed, A.D. 850, into the Arabic, and thence into Hebrew and Greek. In its own land it obtained as wide a circulation. The Emperor Acbar, impressed with the wisdom of its maxims and the ingenuity of its apologues, commended the work of translating it to his own Vizir, Abdul Fazel. That minister accordingly put the book into a familiar style, and published it with explanations, under the title of the " Criterion of Wisdom." The Emperor had also suggested the abridgment of the long series

3

of shlokes which here and there interrupt the narrative, and the
Vizir found this advice sound, and followed it, like the present
Translator. To this day, in India, the " Hitopadeśa," under
other names (as the " Anvári Suhaili *), retains the delighted
attention of young and old, and has some representative in all
the Indian vernaculars. A work so well esteemed in the East
cannot be unwelcome to Western readers, who receive it here,
a condensed but faithful transcript of sense and manner.

As often as an Oriental allusion, or a name in Hindoo
mythology, seemed to ask some explanation for the English
reader, notes have been appended, bearing reference to the
page. In their compilation, and generally, acknowledgment is
due to Professor Johnson's excellent version and edition of
the " Hitopadeśa," and to Mr. Muir's " Sanscrit Texts."

A residence in India, and close intercourse with the Hindoos,
has given the author a lively desire to subserve their advancement. No one listens now to the precipitate ignorance which
would set aside as " heathenish " the high civilization of this
great race; but justice is not yet done to their past development
and present capacities. If the wit, the morality, and the philosophy of these " beasts of India " (so faithfully rendered by
Mr. Harrison Weir,) surprise any vigorous mind into further
exploration of her literature, and deeper sense of our respon-
sibility in her government, the author will be repaid.

EDWIN ARNOLD.

* " The lights of Canopus," a Persian paraphrase; as the " Khirad Afroz," " the
lamp of the Understanding," is in Hindustani.

THE BOOK OF GOOD COUNSELS

INTRODUCTION

Honor to Gunesh, God of Wisdom

This book of Counsel read, and you shall see,
Fair speech and Sanscrit lore, and Policy.

ON the banks of the holy river Ganges there stood a city named Pataliputra. The King of it was a good King and a virtuous, and his name was Sudarsana. It chanced one day that he overheard a certain person reciting these verses—

"Wise men, holding wisdom highest, scorn delights, as false as fair,
Daily live they as Death's fingers twined already in their hair.

Truly, richer than all riches, better than the best of gain,
Wisdom is, unbought, secure—once won, none loseth her again.

Bringing dark things into daylight, solving doubts that vex the mind,
Like an open eye is Wisdom—he that hath her not is blind."

Hearing these the King became disquieted, knowing that his own sons were gaining no wisdom, nor reading the Sacred Writings,[1] but altogether going in the wrong way; and he repeated this verse to himself—

"Childless art thou? dead thy children? leaving thee to want and dool?
Less thy misery than his is, who is father to a fool."

And again this—

"One wise son makes glad his father, forty fools avail him not:—
One moon silvers all that darkness which the silly stars did dot."

---

[1] The Vedas are the holy books of India. They are four in number: The Rig-Veda, Yajur-Veda, Sama-Veda, and Atharva-Veda.

" And it has been said," reflected he—

" Ease and health, obeisant children, wisdom, and a fair-voiced wife—
Thus, great King! are counted up the five felicities of life.
For the son the sire is honored; though the bow-cane bendeth true,
Let the strained string crack in using, and what service shall it do?"

" Nevertheless," mused the King, " I know it is urged that human efforts are useless: as, for instance—

" That which will not be, will not be—and what is to be, will be:—
Why not drink this easy physic, antidote of misery?"

" But then that comes from idleness, with people who will not do what they should do. Rather,

" Nay! and faint not, idly sighing, ' Destiny is mightiest,'
Sesamum holds oil in plenty, but it yieldeth none unpressed.
Ah! it is the Coward's babble, ' Fortune taketh, Fortune gave;'
Fortune! rate her like a master, and she serves thee like a slave."

" For indeed,

" Twofold is the life we live in—Fate and Will together run:—
Two wheels bear life's chariot onward—will it move on only one?"

" And

" Look! the clay dries into iron, but the potter moulds the clay:—
Destiny to-day is master—Man was master yesterday."

" So verily,

" Worthy ends come not by wishing. Wouldst thou? Up, and win it, then!
While the hungry lion slumbers, not a deer comes to his den."

Having concluded his reflections, the Raja gave orders to assemble a meeting of learned men. Then said he—
" Hear now, O my Pundits! Is there one among you so wise that he will undertake to give the second birth of Wisdom to these my sons, by teaching them the Books of Policy; for they have never yet read the Sacred Writings, and are altogether going in the wrong road; and ye know that

" Silly glass, in splendid settings, something of the gold may gain;
And in company of wise ones, fools to wisdom may attain."

Then uprose a great Sage, by name Vishnu-Sarman, learned in the principles of Policy as is the angel of the planet Jupiter himself, and he said—

"My Lord King, I will undertake to teach these princes Policy, seeing they are born of a great house; for—

"Labors spent on the unworthy, of reward the laborer balk;
Like the parrot, teach the heron twenty times, he will not talk."

"But in this royal family the offspring are royal-minded, and in six moons I will engage to make your Majesty's sons comprehend Policy."

The Raja replied, with condescension:—

"On the eastern mountains lying, common things shine in the sun,
And by learned minds enlightened, lower minds may show as one."

"And you, worshipful sir, are competent to teach my children the rules of Policy."

So saying, with much graciousness, he gave the Princes into the charge of Vishnu-Sarman; and that sage, by way of introduction, spake to the Princes, as they sat at ease on the balcony of the palace, in this wise:—

"Hear now, my Princes! for the delectation of your Highnesses, I purpose to tell the tale of the Crow, the Tortoise, the Deer, and the Mouse."

"Pray, sir," said the King's sons, "let us hear it."

Vishnu-Sarman answered—

"It begins with the Winning of Friends; and this is the first verse of it:—

"Sans way or wealth, wise friends their purpose gain—
The Mouse, Crow, Deer, and Tortoise make this plain."

THE WINNING OF FRIENDS

" Sans way or wealth, wise friends their purpose gain—
The Mouse, Crow, Deer, and Tortoise make this plain."

" HOWEVER was that?" asked the Princes.
Vishnu-Sarman replied:—

" On the banks of the Godavery there stood a large silk-cotton-tree, and thither at night, from all quarters and regions, the birds came to roost. Now once, when the night was just spent, and his Radiance the Moon, Lover of the white lotus, was about to retire behind the western hills, a Crow who perched there, 'Light o' Leap' by name, upon awakening, saw to his great wonder a fowler approaching—a second God of Death. The sight set him reflecting, as he flew off uneasily to follow up the man's movements, and he began to think what mischief this ill-omened apparition foretold.

" For a thousand thoughts of sorrow, and a hundred things of dread,
By the wise unheeded, trouble day by day the foolish head."

And yet in this life it must be that

" Of the day's impending dangers, Sickness, Death, and Misery,
One will be; the wise man waking, ponders which that one will be."

Presently the fowler fixed a net, scattered grains of rice about, and withdrew to hide. At this moment " Speckle-neck," King of the Pigeons, chanced to be passing through the sky with his Court, and caught sight of the rice-grains. Thereupon the King of the Pigeons asked of his rice-loving followers, 'How can there possibly be rice-grains lying here in an unfrequented forest? We will see into it, of course, but We like not the look of it—love of rice may ruin us, as the Traveller was ruined.

" All out of longing for a golden bangle,
The Tiger, in the mud, the man did mangle."

" How did that happen?" asked the Pigeons.

8

The Story of the Tiger and the Traveller

"Thus," replied Speckle-neck: "I was pecking about one day in the Deccan forest, and saw an old tiger sitting newly bathed on the bank of a pool, like a Brahman, and with holy kuskus-grass [2] in his paws.

'Ho! ho! ye travellers,' he kept calling out, 'take this golden bangle!'

Presently a covetous fellow passed by and heard him.

'Ah!' thought he, 'this is a bit of luck—but I must not risk my neck for it either.

" Good things come not out of bad things; wisely leave a longed-for ill.
    Nectar being mixed with poison serves no purpose but to kill."

'But all gain is got by risk, so I will see into it at least;'" then he called out, 'Where is thy bangle?'

The Tiger stretched forth his paw and exhibited it.

'Hem!' said the Traveller, 'can I trust such a fierce brute as thou art?'

'Listen,' replied the Tiger, 'once, in the days of my cub-hood, I know I was very wicked. I killed cows, Brahmans, and men without number—and I lost my wife and children for it—and haven't kith or kin left. But lately I met a virtuous man who counselled me to practise the duty of almsgiving—and, as thou seest, I am strict at ablutions and alms. Besides, I am old, and my nails and fangs are gone—so who would mistrust me? and I have so far conquered selfishness, that I keep the golden bangle for whoso comes. Thou seemest poor! I will give it thee. Is it not said,

'Give to poor men, son of Kûnti—on the wealthy waste not wealth;
    Good are simples for the sick man, good for nought to him in health.'

'Wade over the pool, therefore, and take the bangle.'

Thereupon the covetous Traveller determined to trust him, and waded into the pool, where he soon found himself plunged in mud, and unable to move.

'Ho! ho!' says the Tiger, 'art thou stuck in a slough? stay, I will fetch thee out!'

So saying he approached the wretched man and seized him —who meanwhile bitterly reflected—

[2] Used in many religious observances by the Hindoos.

' Be his Scripture-learning wondrous, yet the cheat will be a cheat;
  Be her pasture ne'er so bitter, yet the cow's milk will be sweet.'

And on that verse, too—

' Trust not water, trust not weapons; trust not clawed nor horned
      things;
  Neither give thy soul to women, nor thy life to Sons of Kings.'

And those others—

' Look! the Moon, the silver roamer, from whose splendor darkness
      flies
  With his starry cohorts marching, like a crowned king through the
      skies.
  All the grandeur, all the glory, vanish in the Dragon's jaw;
  What is written on the forehead, that will be, and nothing more.'

Here his meditations were cut short by the Tiger devouring
him. "And that," said Speckle-neck, " is why we counselled
caution."

"Why, yes!" said a certain pigeon, with some presumption,
"but you've read the verse—

> ' Counsel in danger; of it
>   Unwarned, be nothing begun.
>   But nobody asks a Prophet
>   Shall the risk of a dinner be run?'

Hearing that, the Pigeons settled at once; for we know that

> " Avarice begetteth anger; blind desires from her begin;
>   A right fruitful mother is she of a countless spawn of sin."

And again,

' Can a golden Deer have being? yet for such the Hero pined:—
  When the cloud of danger hovers, then its shadow dims the mind.'

Presently they were caught in the net. Thereat, indeed, they
all began to abuse the pigeon by whose suggestion they had
been ensnared. It is the old tale!

> " Be second and not first!—the share's the same
>   If all go well. If not, the Head's to blame."

And we should remember that

" Passion will be Slave or Mistress: follow her, she brings to woe;
  Lead her, 'tis the way to Fortune. Choose the path that thou wilt go."

When King Speckle-neck heard their reproaches, he said, " No, no! it is no fault of his.

' When the time of trouble cometh, friends may ofttimes irk us most:
　For the calf at milking-hour the mother's leg is tying-post.'

' And in disaster, dismay is a coward's quality; let us rather rely on fortitude, and devise some remedy. How saith the sage?

" In good fortune not elated, in ill-fortune not dismayed,
　Ever eloquent in council, never in the fight affrayed—
　Proudly emulous of honor, steadfastly on wisdom set;
　Perfect virtues in the nature of a noble soul are met.
　Whoso hath them, gem and glory of the three wide worlds[3] is he;
　Happy mother she that bore him, she who nursed him on her knee."

" Let us do this now directly," continued the King: " at one moment and with one will, rising under the net, let us fly off with it: for indeed

' Small things wax exceeding mighty, being cunningly combined:—
　Furious elephants are fastened with a rope of grass-blades twined.'

" And it is written, you know,

' Let the household hold together, though the house be ne'er so small;
　Strip the rice-husk from the rice-grain, and it groweth not at all.'

Having pondered this advice, the Pigeons adopted it; and flew away with the net. At first the fowler, who was at a distance, hoped to recover them, but as they passed out of sight with the snare about them he gave up the pursuit. Perceiving this, the Pigeons said,

" What is the next thing to be done, O King? "

" A friend of mine," said Speckle-neck, " lives near in a beautiful forest on the Gundaki. Golden-skin is his name— the King of the Mice—he is the one to cut these bonds."

Resolving to have recourse to him, they directed their flight to the hole of Golden-skin—a prudent monarch, who dreaded danger so much that he had made himself a palace with a hundred outlets, and lived always in it. Sitting there he heard the descent of the pigeons, and remained silent and alarmed.

" Friend Golden-skin," cried the King, " have you no welcome for us? "

　　　　　[3] Heaven, earth, and the lower regions.

"Ah, my friend!" said the Mouse-king, rushing out on recognizing the voice, " is it thou art come, Speckle-neck! how delightful!—But what is this?" exclaimed he, regarding the entangled net.

"That," said King Speckle-neck, "is the effect of some wrong-doing in a former life—

> ' Sickness, anguish, bonds, and woe
> Spring from wrongs wrought long ago.' [4]

Golden-skin, without replying, ran at once to the net, and began to gnaw the strings that held Speckle-neck.

" Nay! friend, not so," said the King, "cut me first these meshes from my followers, and afterwards thou shalt sever mine."

" I am little," answered Golden-skin, " and my teeth are weak —how can I gnaw so much? No! no! I will nibble your strings as long as my teeth last, and afterwards do my best for the others. To preserve dependents by sacrificing oneself is nowhere enjoined by wise moralists; on the contrary—

> ' Keep wealth for want, but spend it for thy wife,
> And wife, and wealth, and all to guard thy life.'

" Friend," replied King Speckle-neck, " that may be the rule of policy, but I am one that can by no means bear to witness the distress of those who depend on me, for—

> ' Death, that must come, comes nobly when we give
> Our wealth, and life, and all, to make men live.'

And you know the verse,

> ' Friend, art thou faithful? guard mine honor so!
> And let the earthy rotting body go.' "

When King Golden-skin heard this answer his heart was charmed, and his fur bristled up for pure pleasure. " Nobly spoken, friend," said he, " nobly spoken! with such a tenderness for those that look to thee, the Sovereignty of the Three Worlds might be fitly thine." So saying he set himself to cut

---

[4] The Hindoo accounts for the origin of evil by this theory of a series of existences continued until the balance is just, and the soul has purified itself. Every fault must have its expiation and every higher faculty its development; pain and misery being signs of the ordeals in the trial, which is to end in the happy re-absorption of the emancipated spirit.

all their bonds. This done, and the pigeons extricated, the King of the Mice [5] gave them his formal welcome. " But, your Majesty," he said, "this capture in the net was a work of destiny; you must not blame yourself as you did, and suspect a former fault. Is it not written—

> ' Floating on his fearless pinions, lost amid the noonday skies,
> Even thence the Eagle's vision kens the carcase where it lies;
> But the hour that comes to all things comes unto the Lord of Air,
> And he rushes, madly blinded, to his ruin in the snare.' "

With this correction Golden-skin proceeded to perform the duties of hospitality, and afterwards, embracing and dismissing them, the pigeons left for such destination as they fancied, and the King of the Mice retired again into his hole.

Now Light o' Leap, the Crow, had been a spectator of the whole transaction, and wondered at it so much that at last he called out, " Ho! Golden-skin, thou very laudable Prince, let me too be a friend of thine, and give me thy friendship."

" Who art thou? " said Golden-skin, who heard him, but would not come out of his hole.

" I am the Crow Light o' Leap," replied the other.

" How can I possibly be on good terms with thee? " answered Golden-skin with a laugh; " have you never read—

> ' When Food is friends with Feeder, look for Woe,
> The Jackal ate the Deer, but for the Crow.'

" No! how was that? "

" I will tell thee," replied Golden-skin :—

The Story of the Jackal, Deer, and Crow

" Far away in Behar there is a forest called Champak-Grove,[6] and in it had long lived in much affection a Deer and a Crow. The Deer, roaming unrestrained, happy and fat of carcase, was one day descried by a Jackal. ' Ho! ho! ' thought the Jackal on observing him, ' if I could but get this soft meat for a meal! It might be—if I can only win his confidence.' Thus reflecting he approached, and saluted him.

[5] The mouse, as vehicle of Gunesh, is an important animal in Hindoo legend.
[6] The champak is a bushy tree, bearing a profusion of star-like blossoms with golden centres, and of the most pleasing perfume.

' Health be to thee, friend Deer ! '

' Who art thou ? ' said the Deer.

' I'm Small-wit, the Jackal,' replied the other. ' I live in the wood here, as the dead do, without a friend; but now that I have met with such a friend as thou, I feel as if I were beginning life again with plenty of relations. Consider me your faithful servant.'

' Very well,' said the Deer; and then, as the glorious King of Day, whose diadem is the light, had withdrawn himself, the two went together to the residence of the Deer. In that same spot, on a branch of Champak, dwelt the Crow Sharp-sense, an old friend of the Deer. Seeing them approach together, the Crow said,

' Who is this number two, friend Deer ? '

' It is a Jackal,' answered the Deer, ' that desires our acquaintance.'

' You should not become friendly to a stranger without reason,' said Sharp-sense. ' Don't you know ? '

> " To folks by no one known house-room deny :—
> The Vulture housed the Cat, and thence did die."

' No ! how was that ? ' said both.

' In this wise,' answered the Crow.

The Story of the Vulture, the Cat, and the Birds

" On the banks of the Ganges there is a cliff called Vulture-Crag, and thereupon grew a great fig-tree. It was hollow, and within its shelter lived an old Vulture, named Grey-pate, whose hard fortune it was to have lost both eyes and talons. The birds that roosted in the tree made subscriptions from their own store, out of sheer pity for the poor fellow, and by that means he managed to live. One day, when the old birds were gone, Long-ear, the Cat, came there to get a meal of the nestlings; and they, alarmed at perceiving him, set up a chirruping that roused Grey-pate.

' Who comes there ? ' croaked Grey-pate.

" Now Long-ear, on espying the Vulture, thought himself undone; but as flight was impossible, he resolved to trust his destiny and approach.

My lord,' said he, ' I have the honor to salute thee.'

'Who is it?' said the Vulture.

'I am a Cat.'

'Be off, Cat, or I shall slay thee,' said the Vulture.

'I am ready to die if I deserve death,' answered the Cat; 'but let what I have to say be heard.'

'Wherefore, then, comest thou?' said the Vulture.

'I live,' began Long-ear, 'on the Ganges, bathing, and eating no flesh, practising the moon-penance,[7] like a Bramacharya. The birds that resort thither constantly praise your worship to me as one wholly given to the study of morality, and worthy of all trust; and so I came here to learn law from thee, Sir, who art so deep gone in learning and in years. Dost thou, then, so read the law of strangers as to be ready to slay a guest? What say the books about the householder?—

'Bar thy door not to the stranger, be he friend or be he foe,
For the tree will shade the woodman while his axe doth lay it low.'

And if means fail, what there is should be given with kind words, as—

'Greeting fair, and room to rest in; fire, and water from the well—
Simple gifts—are given freely in the house where good men dwell,'—

and without respect of person—

'Young, or bent with many winters; rich, or poor, whate'er thy guest,
Honor him for thine own honor—better is he than the best.'

Else comes the rebuke—

'Pity them that ask thy pity: who art thou to stint thy hoard,
When the holy moon shines equal on the leper and the lord!'

And that other, too,

'When thy gate is roughly fastened, and the asker turns away,
Thence he bears thy good deeds with him, and his sins on thee doth lay

For verily,

'In the house the husband ruleth, men the Brahmans "master" call;
Agni is the Twice-born Master—but the guest is lord of all.'

---

[7] A religious observance. The devotee commences the penance at the full moon with an allowance of fifteen mouthfuls for his food, diminishing this by one mouthful each day, till on the fifteenth it is reduced to one. As the new moon increases, his allowance ascends to its original proportion.

" To these weighty words Grey-pate answered,
' Yes! but cats like meat, and there are young birds here,
and therefore I said, go.'
' Sir,' said the Cat (and as he spoke he touched the ground,
and then his two ears, and called on Krishna to witness to his
words), ' I that have overcome passion, and practised the
moon-penance, know the Scriptures; and howsoever they
contend, in this primal duty of abstaining from injury they
are unanimous. Which of them sayeth not—

> ' He who does and thinks no wrong—
> He who suffers, being strong—
> He whose harmlessness men know—
> Unto Swerga such doth go.'

" And so, winning the old Vulture's confidence, Long-ear,
the Cat, entered the hollow tree and lived there. And day after
day he stole away some of the nestlings, and brought them
down to the hollow to devour. Meantime the parent birds,
whose little ones were being eaten, made an inquiry after them
in all quarters; and the Cat, discovering this fact, slipped out
from the hollow, and made his escape. Afterwards, when the
birds came to look closely, they found the bones of their young
ones in the hollow of the tree where Grey-pate lived; and the
birds at once concluded that their nestlings had been killed
and eaten by the old Vulture, whom they accordingly executed.
That is my story, and why I warned you against unknown ac-
quaintances."
" Sir," said the Jackal, with some warmth, " on the first day
of your encountering the Deer you also were of unknown
family and character: how is it, then, that your friendship
with him grows daily greater? True, I am only Small-wit,
the Jackal, but what says the saw?—

> " In the land where no wise men are, men of little wit are lords;
> And the castor-oil's a tree, where no tree else its shade affords."

The Deer is my friend; condescend, sir, to be my friend also."
' Oh!' broke in the Deer, ' why so much talking? We'll
all live together, and be friendly and happy—

> ' Foe is friend, and friend is foe,
> As our actions make them so.'

"Very good," said Sharp-sense; "as you will;" and in the morning each started early for his own feeding-ground (returning at night). One day the Jackal drew the Deer aside, and whispered, 'Deer, in one corner of this wood there is a field full of sweet young wheat; come and let me show you.' The Deer accompanied him, and found the field, and afterwards went every day there to eat the green corn, till at last the owner of the ground spied him and set a snare. The Deer came again very shortly, and was caught in it, and (after vainly struggling) exclaimed, 'I am fast in the net, and it will be a net of death to me if no friend comes to rescue me!' Presently Small-wit, the Jackal, who had been lurking near, made his appearance, and standing still, he said to himself, with a chuckle, 'O ho! my scheme bears fruit! When he is cut up, his bones, and gristle, and blood, will fall to my share and make me some beautiful dinners.' The Deer, here catching sight of him, exclaimed with rapture, 'Ah, friend, this is excellent! Do but gnaw these strings, and I shall be at liberty. How charming to realize the saying!—

'That friend only is the true friend who is near when trouble comes;
That man only is the brave man who can bear the battle-drums;
Words are wind; deed proveth promise: he who helps at need is kin;
And the leal wife is loving though the husband lose or win.'

And is it not written—

'Friend and kinsman—more their meaning than the idle-hearted mind.
Many a friend can prove unfriendly, many a kinsman less than kind:
He who shares his comrade's portion, be he beggar, be he lord,
Comes as truly, comes as duly, to the battle as the board—
Stands before the king to succor, follows to the pile to sigh—
He is friend, and he is kinsman—less would make the name a lie.'

"Small-wit answered nothing, but betook himself to examining the snare very closely.

'This will certainly hold,' muttered he; then, turning to the Deer, he said, 'Good friend, these strings, you see, are made of sinew, and to-day is a fast-day, so that I cannot possibly bite them. To-morrow morning, if you still desire it, I shall be happy to serve you.'

When he was gone, the Crow, who had missed the Deer upon returning that evening, and had sought for him everywhere, discovered him; and seeing his sad plight, exclaimed—

' How came this about, my friend? '

' This came,' replied the Deer, ' through disregarding a friend's advice.'

' Where is that rascal Small-wit? ' asked the Crow.

' He is waiting somewhere by,' said the Deer, ' to taste my flesh.'

' Well,' sighed the Crow, ' I warned you; but it is as in the true verse—

> ' Stars gleam, lamps flicker, friends foretell of fate;
> The fated sees, knows, hears them—all too late.'

And then, with a deeper sigh, he exclaimed, ' Ah, traitor Jackal, what an ill deed hast thou done! Smooth-tongued knave—alas!—and in the face of the monition too—

> ' Absent, flatterers' tongues are daggers—present, softer than the silk;
> Shun them! 'tis a jar of poison hidden under harmless milk;
> Shun them when they promise little! Shun them when they promise much!
> For, enkindled, charcoal burneth—cold, it doth defile the touch.'

" When the day broke, the Crow (who was still there) saw the master of the field approaching with his club in his hand.

' Now, friend Deer,' said Sharp-sense on perceiving him, ' do thou cause thyself to seem like one dead: puff thy belly up with wind, stiffen thy legs out, and lie very still. I will make a show of pecking thine eyes out with my beak; and whensoever I utter a croak, then spring to thy feet and betake thee to flight.'

The Deer thereon placed himself exactly as the Crow suggested, and was very soon espied by the husbandman, whose eyes opened with joy at the sight.

' Aha! ' said he, ' the fellow has died of himself,' and so speaking, he released the Deer from the snare, and proceeded to gather and lay aside his nets. At that instant Sharp-sense uttered a loud croak, and the Deer sprang up and made off. And the club which the husbandman flung after him in a rage struck Small-wit, the Jackal (who was close by), and killed him. Is it not said, indeed?—

> ' In years, or moons, or half-moons three,
> Or in three days—suddenly,
> Knaves are shent—true men go free.'

"Thou seest, then," said Golden-skin, "there can be no friendship between food and feeder."

"I should hardly," replied the Crow, "get a large breakfast out of your worship; but as to that indeed you have nothing to fear from me. I am not often angry, and if I were, you know—

'Anger comes to noble natures, but leaves there no strife or storm:
Plunge a lighted torch beneath it, and the ocean grows not warm.'

"Then, also, thou art such a gad-about," objected the King.

"Maybe," answered Light o' Leap; " but I am bent on winning thy friendship, and I will die at thy door of fasting if thou grantest it not. Let us be friends! for

'Noble hearts are golden vases—close the bond true metals make;
Easily the smith may weld them, harder far it is to break.
Evil hearts are earthen vessels—at a touch they crack a-twain,
And what craftsman's ready cunning can unite the shards again?'

And then, too,

'Good men's friendships may be broken, yet abide they friends at heart;
Snap the stem of Luxmee's lotus, and its fibres will not part.'

"Good sir," said the King of the Mice, "your conversation is as pleasing as pearl necklets or oil of sandal-wood in hot weather. Be it as you will"—and thereon King Golden-skin made a treaty with the Crow, and after gratifying him with the best of his store reëntered his hole. The Crow returned to his accustomed perch:—and thenceforward the time passed in mutual presents of food, in polite inquiries, and the most unrestrained talk. One day Light o' Leap thus accosted Golden-skin:—

"This is a poor place, your Majesty, for a Crow to get a living in. I should like to leave it and go elsewhere."

"Whither wouldst thou go?" replied the King; they say,

'One foot goes, and one foot stands,
When the wise man leaves his lands.'

"And they say, too," answered the Crow,

'Over-love of home were weakness; wheresoe'er the hero come,
Stalwart arm and steadfast spirit find or win for him a home.

Little recks the awless lion where his hunting jungles lie—
When he enters it be certain that a royal prey shall die.'

"I know an excellent jungle now."

"Which is that?" asked the Mouse-king.

"In the Nerbudda woods, by Camphor-water," replied the Crow. "There is an old and valued friend of mine lives there —Slow-toes his name is, a very virtuous Tortoise; he will regale me with fish and good things."

"Why should I stay behind," said Golden-skin, "if thou goest? Take me also."

Accordingly, the two set forth together, enjoying charming converse upon the road. Slow-toes perceived Light o' Leap a long way off, and hastened to do him the guest-rites, extending them to the Mouse upon Light o' Leap's introduction.

"Good Slow-toes," said he, "this is Golden-skin, King of the Mice—pay all honor to him—he is burdened with virtues—a very jewel-mine of kindnesses. I don't know if the Prince of all the Serpents, with his two thousand tongues, could rightly repeat them." So speaking, he told the story of Speckle-neck. Thereupon Slow-toes made a profound obeisance to Golden-skin, and said, "How came your Majesty, may I ask, to retire to an unfrequented forest?"

"I will tell you," said the King. "You must know that in the town of Champaka there is a college for the devotees. Unto this resorted daily a beggar-priest, named Chudakarna, whose custom was to place his begging-dish upon the shelf, with such alms in it as he had not eaten, and go to sleep by it; and I, so soon as he slept, used to jump up, and devour the meal. One day a great friend of his, named Vinakarna, also a mendicant, came to visit him; and observed that while conversing, he kept striking the ground with a split cane, to frighten me. 'Why don't you listen?' said Vinakarna. 'I am listening!' replied the other; 'but this plaguy mouse is always eating the meal out of my begging-dish.' Vinakarna looked at the shelf and remarked, 'However can a mouse jump as high as this? There must be a reason, though there seems none. I guess the cause —the fellow is well off and fat.' With these words Vinakarna snatched up a shovel, discovered my retreat, and took away all my hoard of provisions. After that I lost strength daily, had scarcely energy enough to get my dinner, and, in fact, crept

about so wretchedly, that when Chudakarna saw me he fell to
quoting—

'Very feeble folk are poor folk; money lost takes wit away:—
All their doings fail like runnels, wasting through the summer day.'

"Yes!" I thought, "he is right, and so are the sayings—

'Wealth is friends, home, father, brother—title to respect and fame;
Yea, and wealth is held for wisdom—that it should be so is shame.'
'Home is empty to the childless; hearts to them who friends deplore:—
Earth unto the idle-minded; and the three worlds to the poor.'

'I can stay here no longer; and to tell my distress to another
is out of the question—altogether out of the question!—

'Say the sages, nine things name not: Age, domestic joys and woes,
Counsel, sickness, shame, alms, penance; neither Poverty disclose.
Better for the proud of spirit, death, than life with losses told;
Fire consents to be extinguished, but submits not to be cold.'

'Verily he was wise, methought also, who wrote—

'As Age doth banish beauty,
    As moonlight dies in gloom,
As Slavery's menial duty
    Is Honor's certain tomb;
As Hari's name and Hara's
    Spoken, charm sin away,
So Poverty can surely
    A hundred virtues slay.'

'And as to sustaining myself on another man's bread, that,' I
mused, 'would be but a second door of death. Say not the
books the same?—

'Half-known knowledge, present pleasure purchased with a future woe,
And to taste the salt of service—greater griefs no man can know.'

'And herein, also—

'All existence is not equal, and all living is not life;
Sick men live; and he who, banished, pines for children, home, and
        wife;
And the craven-hearted eater of another's leavings lives,
And the wretched captive waiting for the word of doom survives;
But they bear an anguished body, and they draw a deadly breath,
And life cometh to them only on the happy day of death.'

Yet, after all these reflections, I was covetous enough to make one more attempt on Chudakarna's meal, and got a blow from the split cane for my pains. 'Just so,' I said to myself, 'the soul and organs of the discontented want keeping in subjection. I must be done with discontent:—

'Golden gift, serene Contentment! have thou that, and all is had;
  Thrust thy slipper on, and think thee that the earth is leather-clad.'

'All is known, digested, tested; nothing new is left to learn
  When the soul, serene, reliant, Hope's delusive dreams can spurn.'

'And the sorry task of seeking favor is numbered in the miseries of life—

'Hast thou never watched, a-waiting till the great man's door unbarred?
. Didst thou never linger parting, saying many a last sad word?
  Spak'st thou never word of folly, one light thing thou wouldst recall?
  Rare and noble hath thy life been! fair thy fortune did befall!'

'No!' exclaimed I, 'I will do none of these; but, by retiring into the quiet and untrodden forest, I will show my discernment of real good and ill. The holy Books counsel it—

'True Religion!—'tis not blindly prating what the priest may prate,
  But to love, as God hath loved them, all things, be they small or great;
  And true bliss is when a sane mind doth a healthy body fill;
  And true knowledge is the knowing what is good and what is ill.'

" So came I to the forest, where, by good fortune and this good friend, I met much kindness; and by the same good fortune have encountered you, Sir, whose friendliness is as Heaven to me. Ah! Sir Tortoise,

'Poisonous though the tree of life be, two fair blossoms grow thereon:
  One, the company of good men; and sweet songs of Poet's, one.'

" King!" said Slow-toes, "your error was getting too much, without giving. Give, says the sage—

'Give, and it shall swell thy getting; give, and thou shalt safer keep:
  Pierce the tank-wall; or it yieldeth, when the water waxes deep.'

And he is very hard upon money-grubbing: as thus—

  'When the miser hides his treasure in the earth, he doeth well;
    For he opens up a passage that his soul may sink to hell.'

And thus—

' He whose coins are kept for counting, not to barter nor to give,
   Breathe he like a blacksmith's bellows, yet in truth he doth not live.'

It hath been well written, indeed,

' Gifts, bestowed with words of kindness, making giving doubly dear:—
   Wisdom, deep, complete, benignant, of all arrogancy clear;
   Valor, never yet forgetful of sweet Mercy's pleading prayer;
   Wealth, and scorn of wealth to spend it—oh! but these be virtues
      rare! '

" Frugal one may be," continued Slow-toes; " but not a nig-
gard like the Jackal—

> ' The Jackal-knave, that starved his spirit so,
>   And died of saving, by a broken bow.'

" Did he, indeed," said Golden-skin; " and how was that?"
" I will tell you," answered Slow-toes :—

The Story of the Dead Game and the Jackal

" In a town called ' Well-to-Dwell ' there lived a mighty
hunter, whose name was ' Grim-face.' Feeling a desire one day
for a little venison, he took his bow, and went into the woods;
where he soon killed a deer. As he was carrying the deer home,
he came upon a wild boar of prodigious proportions. Laying
the deer upon the earth, he fixed and discharged an arrow and
struck the boar, which instantly rushed upon him with a roar
louder than the last thunder, and ripped the hunter up. He
fell like a tree cut by the axe, and lay dead along with the boar,
and a snake also, which had been crushed by the feet of the
combatants. Not long afterwards, there came that way, in his
prowl for food, a Jackal, named ' Howl o' Nights,' and cast
eyes on the hunter, the deer, the boar, and the snake lying dead
together. ' Aha! ' said he, ' what luck! Here's a grand dinner
got ready for me! Good fortune can come, I see, as well as ill
fortune. Let me think :—the man will be fine pickings for a
month; the deer with the boar will last two more; the snake
will do for to-morrow; and, as I am very particularly hungry,
I will treat myself now to this bit of meat on the bow-
horn.' So saying, he began to gnaw it asunder, and the bow-

string slipping, the bow sprang back, and resolved Howl o'
Nights into the five elements by death. That is my story,"
continued Slow-toes, " and its application is for the wise :—

'Sentences of studied wisdom, nought avail they unapplied;
  Though the blind man hold a lantern, yet his footsteps stray aside.'

The secret of success, indeed, is a free, contented, and yet en-
terprising mind. How say the books thereon?—

'Wouldst thou know whose happy dwelling Fortune entereth unknown?
His, who careless of her favor, standeth fearless in his own;
His, who for the vague to-morrow barters not the sure to-day—
Master of himself, and sternly steadfast to the rightful way:
Very mindful of past service, valiant, faithful, true of heart—
Unto such comes Lakshmi [8] smiling—comes, and will not lightly part.'

What indeed," continued Slow-toes, " is wealth, that we should
prize it, or grieve to lose it?—

  'Be not haughty, being wealthy; droop not, having lost thine all;
  Fate doth play with mortal fortunes as a girl doth toss her ball.'

It is unstable by nature. We are told—

'Worldly friendships, fair but fleeting, shadows of the clouds at noon,
Women, youth, new corn, and riches—these be pleasures passing soon.'

And it is idle to be anxious; the Master of Life knows how to
sustain it. Is it not written?—

'For thy bread be not o'er thoughtful—God for all hath taken thought:
When the babe is born, the sweet milk to the mother's breast is brought.

He who gave the swan her silver, and the hawk her plumes of pride,
And his purples to the peacock—He will verily provide.'

Yes, verily," said Slow-toes, " wealth is bad to handle, and better left alone; there is no truer saying than this—

    'Though for good ends, waste not on wealth a minute;
    Mud may be wiped, but wise men plunge not in it.'

Hearing the wisdom of these monitions, Light o' Leap broke
out, 'Good Slow-toes! thou art a wise protector of those that
come to thee; thy learning comforts my enlightened friend, as

        [8] The wife of Vishnoo, Goddess of beauty and abundance.

elephants drag elephants from the mire.' And thus, on the best of terms, wandering where they pleased for food, the three lived there together.

One day it chanced that a Deer named Dapple-back, who had seen some cause of alarm in the forest, came suddenly upon the three in his flight. Thinking the danger imminent, Slow-toes dropped into the water, King Golden-skin slipped into his hole, and Light o' Leap flew up into the top of a high tree. Thence he looked all round to a great distance, but could discover nothing. So they all came back again, and sat down together. Slow-toes welcomed the Deer.

'Good Deer,' said he, 'may grass and water never fail thee at thy need. Gratify us by residing here, and consider this forest thine own.'

'Indeed,' answered Dapple-back, 'I came hither for your protection, flying from a hunter; and to live with you in friendship is my greatest desire.'

'Then the thing is settled,' observed Golden-skin.

'Yes! yes!' said Light o' Leap, 'make yourself altogether at home!'

So the Deer, charmed at his reception, ate grass and drank water, and laid himself down in the shade of a Banyan-tree to talk. Who does not know?—

> 'Brunettes, and the Banyan's shadow,
>   Well-springs, and a brick-built wall,
> Are all alike cool in the summer,
>   And warm in the winter—all.'

'What made thee alarmed, friend Deer?' began Slow-toes. 'Do hunters ever come to this unfrequented forest?'

'I have heard,' replied Dapple-back, 'that the Prince of the Kalinga country, Rukmangada, is coming here. He is even now encamped on the Cheenab River, on his march to subjugate the borders; and the hunters have been heard to say that he will halt to-morrow by this very lake of "Camphor-water." Don't you think, as it is dangerous to stay, that we ought to resolve on something?'

'I shall certainly go to another pool,' exclaimed Slow-toes.

'It would be better,' answered the Crow and Deer together.

'Yes!' remarked the King of the Mice, after a minute's thought; 'but how is Slow-toes to get across the country in

time? Animals like our amphibious host are best in the water;
on land he might suffer from his own design, like the merchant's son—

> ' The merchant's son laid plans for gains,
>   And saw his wife kissed for his pains.'

' How came that about?' asked all.
" I'll tell you," answered Golden-skin.

The Prince and the Wife of the Merchant's Son

" In the country of Kanouj there was a King named Virasena,
and he made his son viceroy of a city called Virapoora. The
Prince was rich, handsome, and in the bloom of youth. Passing through the streets of his city one day, he observed a very
lovely woman, whose name was Lávanyavati—i.e., the Beautiful—the wife of a merchant's son. On reaching his palace, full
of her charms and of passionate admiration for them, he despatched a message to her, and a letter, by a female attendant:
—who wonders at it?—

> ' Ah! the gleaming, glancing arrows of a lovely woman's eye!
>   Feathered with her jetty lashes, perilous they pass us by:—
>   Loosed at venture from the black bows of her arching brow they part,
>   All too penetrant and deadly for an undefended heart.'

Now Lávanyavati, from the moment she saw the Prince, was
hit with the same weapon of love that wounded him; but upon
hearing the message of the attendant, she refused with dignity
to receive his letter.
' I am my husband's,' she said, ' and that is my honor; for—

> ' Beautiful the Koïl[9] seemeth for the sweetness of his song,
>   Beautiful the world esteemeth pious souls for patience strong;
>   Homely features lack not favor when true wisdom they reveal,
>   And a wife is fair and honored while her heart is firm and leal.'

What the lord of my life enjoins, that I do.'
' Is such my answer?' asked the attendant.
' It is,' said Lávanyavati.
Upon the messenger reporting her reply to the Prince, he
was in despair.

---

[9] The black or Indian cuckoo.

'The God of the five shafts has hit me,' he exclaimed, 'and only her presence will cure my wound.'

'We must make her husband bring her, then,' said the messenger.

'That can never be,' replied the Prince.

'It can,' replied the messenger—

> 'Fraud may achieve what force would never try:—
> The Jackal killed the Elephant thereby.'

'How was that?' asked the Prince.

The Slave related:—

The Story of the Old Jackal and the Elephant

" In the forest of Brahma[10] lived an Elephant, whose name was 'White-front.' The Jackals knew him, and said among themselves, 'If this great brute would but die, there would be four months' food for us, and plenty, out of his carcase.' With that an old Jackal stood up, and pledged himself to compass the death of the Elephant by his own wit. Accordingly, he sought for 'White-front,' and, going up to him, he made the reverential prostration of the eight members, gravely saluting him.

'Divine creature,' said he, 'vouchsafe me the regard of one look.'

'Who art thou?' grunted the Elephant, 'and whence comest thou?'

'I am only a Jackal,' said the other; 'but the beasts of the forest are convinced that it is not expedient to live without a king, and they have met in full council, and despatched me to acquaint your Royal Highness that on you, endowed with so many lordly qualities, their choice has fallen for a sovereign over the forest here; for—

> 'Who is just, and strong, and wise?
> Who is true to social ties?
> He is formed for Emperies.

Let your Majesty, therefore, repair thither at once, that the moment of fortunate conjunction may not escape us.' So say-

---

[10] A grove where the Vedas are read and expounded.

ing he led the way, followed at a great pace by White-front, who was eager to commence his reign.

"Presently the Jackal brought him upon a deep slough, into which he plunged heavily before he could stop himself.

'Good master Jackal,' cried the Elephant, 'what's to do now? I am up to my belly in this quagmire.'

'Perhaps your Majesty,' said the Jackal, with an impudent laugh, 'will condescend to take hold of the tip of my brush with your trunk, and so get out.'

'Then White-front, the Elephant, knew that he had been deceived; and thus he sank in the slime, and was devoured by the Jackals. Hence,' continued the attendant, 'is why I suggested stratagem to your Highness.'

Shortly afterwards, by the Slave's advice, the Prince sent for the merchant's son (whose name was Charudatta), and appointed him to be near his person; and one day, with the same design, when he was just come from the bath, and had on his jewels, he summoned Charudatta, and said—

"I have a vow to keep to Gauri—bring hither to me every evening for a month some lady of good family, that I may do honor to her, according to my vow; and begin to-day."

Charudatta in due course brought a lady of quality, and, having introduced her, retired to watch the interview. The Prince, without even approaching his fair visitor, made her the most respectful obeisances, and dismissed her with gifts of ornaments, sandal-wood, and perfumes, under the protection of a guard. This made Charudatta confident, and longing to get some of these princely presents he brought his own wife next evening. When the Prince recognized the charming Lávan-yavati—the joy of his soul—he sprang to meet her, and kissed and caressed her without the least restraint. At sight of this the miserable Charudatta stood transfixed with despair—the very picture of wretchedness '——

'And you too, Slow-toes—but where is he gone?' abruptly asked King Golden-skin.

Now Slow-toes had not chosen to wait the end of the story, but was gone before, and Golden-skin and the others followed him up in some anxiety. The Tortoise had been painfully travelling along, until a hunter, who was beating the wood for game, had overtaken him. The fellow, who was very hungry, picked him up, fastened him on his bow-stick, and set off for home; while the Deer, the Crow, and the Mouse, who had witnessed the capture, followed them in terrible concern. 'Alas!' cried the Mouse-king, 'he is gone!—and such a friend!

> 'Friend! gracious word!—the heart to tell is ill able
> Whence came to men this jewel of a syllable.'

'Let us,' continued he to his companions, 'let us make one attempt, at least, to rescue Slow-toes before the hunter is out of the wood!'

'Only tell us how to do it,' replied they.

'Do thus,' said Golden-skin: 'let Dapple-back hasten on to the water, and lie down there and make himself appear dead; and do you, Light o' Leap, hover over him and peck about his body. The hunter is sure to put the Tortoise down to get the venison, and I will gnaw his bonds.'

'The Deer and the Crow started at once; and the hunter, who was sitting down to rest under a tree and drinking water, soon caught sight of the Deer, apparently dead. Drawing his wood-knife, and putting the Tortoise down by the water, he hastened to secure the Deer, and Golden-skin, in the meantime, gnawed asunder the string that held Slow-toes, who instantly dropped into the pool. The Deer, of course, when the hunter got near, sprang up and made off, and when he returned to the tree the Tortoise was gone also. "I deserve this," thought he—

> 'Whoso for greater quits his gain,
> Shall have his labor for his pain;
> The things unwon unwon remain,
> And what was won is lost again.'

And so lamenting, he went to his village. Slow-toes and his friends, quit of all fears, repaired together to their new habitations, and there lived happily.

Then spake the King Sudarsana's sons, "We have heard every word, and are delighted; it fell out just as we wished."

"I rejoice thereat, my Princes," said Vishnu-Sarman; "may it also fall out according to this my wish—

> "Lakshmi give you friends like these!
> Lakshmi keep your lands in ease!
> Set, your sovereign thrones beside,
> Policy, a winsome bride!
> And He, whose forehead-jewel is the moon
> Give peace to us and all—serene and soon."

THE PARTING OF FRIENDS

T HEN spake the Royal Princes to Vishnu-Sarman, "Reverend Sir! we have listened to the 'Winning of Friends,' we would now hear how friends are parted."

"Attend, then," replied the Sage, "to 'the Parting of Friends,' the first couplet of which runs in this wise—

'The Jackal set—of knavish cunning full—
At loggerheads the Lion and the Bull.'

"How was that?" asked the sons of the Rajah.

Vishnu-Sarman proceeded to relate:—

The Story of the Lion, the Jackals, and the Bull

"In the Deccan there is a city called Golden-town, and a wealthy merchant lived there named Well-to-do. He had abundant means, but as many of his relations were even yet richer, his mind was bent upon outdoing them by gaining more. Enough is never what we have—

'Looking down on lives below them, men of little store are great;
Looking up to higher fortunes, hard to each man seems his fate.'

And is not wealth won by courage and enterprise?—

'As a bride, unwisely wedded, shuns the cold caress of eld,
So, from coward souls and slothful, Lakshmi's favors turn repelled.'

'Ease, ill-health, home-keeping, sleeping, woman-service, and content—
In the path that leads to greatness these be six obstructions sent.'

And wealth that increases not, diminishes—a little gain is so far good—

'Seeing how the soorma wasteth, seeing how the ant-hill grows,
Little adding unto little—live, give, learn, as life-time goes.'

'Drops of water falling, falling, falling, brim the chatty o'er;
Wisdom comes in little lessons—little gains make largest store.'

30

Moved by these reflections Well-to-do loaded a cart with wares
of all kinds, yoked two bulls to it, named Lusty-life and Roarer,
and started for Kashmir to trade. He had not gone far upon
his journey when in passing through a great forest called
Bramble-wood, Lusty-life slipped down and broke his fore-
leg. At sight of this disaster Well-to-do fell a-thinking, and
repeated—

> 'Men their cunning schemes may spin—
> God knows who shall lose or win.'

Comforting himself with such philosophy, Well-to-do left
Lusty-life there, and went on his way. The Bull watched him
depart, and stood mournfully on three legs, alone in the forest.
'Well, well,' he thought, 'it is all destiny whether I live or
die:—

> 'Shoot a hundred shafts, the quarry lives and flies—not due to death;
> When his hour is come, a grass-blade hath a point to stop his breath.'

As the days passed by, and Lusty-life picked about in the
tender forest grass, he grew wonderfully well, and fat of carcase, and happy, and bellowed about the wood as though it
were his own. Now, the reigning monarch of the forest was
King Tawny-hide the Lion, who ruled over the whole country
absolutely, by right of having deposed everybody else. Is not
might right?—

> 'Robes were none, nor oil of unction, when the King of Beasts was
>   crowned:—
> 'Twas his own fierce roar proclaimed him, rolling all his kingdom
>   round.'

One morning, his Majesty, being exceedingly thirsty, had repaired to the bank of the Jumna to drink water, and just as he
was about to lap it, the bellow of Lusty-life, awful as the
thunder of the last day, reached the imperial ears. Upon catching the sound the King retreated in trepidation to his own lair,
without drinking a drop, and stood there in silence and alarm
revolving what it could mean. In this position he was observed by the sons of his minister, two jackals named Karataka
and Damanaka, who began to remark upon it.

'Friend Karataka,' said the last, 'what makes our royal master slink away from the river when he was dying to drink?'

'Why should we care?' replied Karataka. 'It's bad enough
to serve him, and be neglected for our pains—

'Oh, the bitter salt of service!—toil, frost, fire, are not so keen:—
Half such heavy penance bearing, tender consciences were clean.'

'Nay, friend! never think thus,' said Damanaka—

> 'What but for their vassals,
>   Elephant and man—
> Swing of golden tassels,
>   Wave of silken fan—
> But for regal manner
>   That the "Chattra"[11] brings,
> Horse, and foot, and banner—
>   What would come of kings?'

'I care not,' replied Karataka; 'we have nothing to do with
it, and matters that don't concern us are best left alone. You
know the story of the Monkey, don't you?'—

> 'The Monkey drew the sawyer's wedge, and died:—
> Let meddlers mark it, and be edified.'

'No!' said Damanaka. 'How was it?'
'In this way,' answered Karataka:—

The Story of the Monkey and the Wedge

"In South Behar, close by the retreat of Dhurmma, there
was an open plot of ground, upon which a temple was in course
of erection, under the management of a man of the Káyeth
caste, named Subhadatta. A carpenter upon the works had
partly sawed through a long beam of wood, and wedged it
open, and was gone away, leaving the wedge fixed. Shortly
afterwards a large herd of monkeys came frolicking that way,
and one of their number, directed doubtless by the Angel of
death, got astride the beam, and grasped the wedge, with his
tail and lower parts dangling down between the pieces of the
wood. Not content with this, in the mischief natural to
monkeys, he began to tug at the wedge; till at last it yielded
to a great effort and came out; when the wood closed upon

11 The white umbrella borne above the heads of Indian rajahs.

him, and jammed him all fast. So perished the monkey, miserably crushed; and I say again—

> 'Let meddlers mark it, and be edified.'

'But surely,' argued Damanaka, 'servants are bound to watch the movements of their masters!'

'Let the prime minister do it, then,' answered Karataka; 'it is his business to overlook things, and subordinates shouldn't interfere in the department of their chief. You might get ass's thanks for it—

> 'The Ass that hee-hawed, when the dog should do it,
> For his lord's welfare, like an ass did rue it.'

Damanaka asked how that happened, and Karataka related:—

The Story of the Washerman's Jackass

" There was a certain Washerman at Benares, whose name was Carpúrapataka, and he had an Ass and a Dog in his courtyard; the first tethered, and the last roaming loose. Once on a time, when he had been spending his morning in the society of his wife, whom he had just married, and had fallen to sleep in her arms, a robber entered the house, and began to carry off his goods. The Ass observed the occupation of the thief, and was much concerned.

'Good Dog,' said he, 'this is thy matter: why dost thou not bark aloud, and rouse the master?'

'Gossip Ass,' replied the Dog, 'leave me alone to guard the premises. I can do it, if I choose; but the truth is, this master of ours thinks himself so safe lately that he clean forgets me, and I don't find my allowance of food nearly regular enough. Masters will do so; and a little fright will put him in mind of his defenders again.'

'Thou scurvy cur!' exclaimed the Ass—

> 'At the work-time, asking wages—is it like a faithful herd?'

'Thou extreme Ass!' replied the Dog.

> 'When the work's done, grudging wages—is that acting like a lord?'

'Mean-spirited beast,' retorted the Ass, 'who neglectest thy master's business! Well, then, I at least will endeavor to arouse him; it is no less than religion,

'Serve the Sun with sweat of body; starve thy maw to feed the flame;
Stead thy lord with all thy service; to thy death go, quit of blame.'

So saying, he put forth his very best braying. The Washerman sprang up at the noise, and missing the thief, turned in a rage upon the Ass for disturbing him, and beat it with a cudgel to such an extent that the blows resolved the poor animal into the five elements of death. 'So that,' continued Karataka, 'is why I say, Let the prime minister look to him. The hunting for prey is our duty—let us stick to it, then. And this,' he said, with a meditative look, 'need not trouble us to-day; for we have a capital dish of the royal leavings.'

'What!' said Damanaka, rough with rage, 'dost thou serve the King for the sake of thy belly? Why take any such trouble to preserve an existence like thine?—

'Many prayers for him are uttered whereon many a life relies;
'Tis but one poor fool the fewer when the gulping Raven dies.'

For assisting friends, and defeating enemies also, the service of kings is desirable. To enter upon it for a mere living makes the thing low indeed. There must be dogs and elephants; but servants need not be like hungry curs, while their masters are noble. What say the books?

'Give thy Dog the merest mouthful, and he crouches at thy feet,
Wags his tail, and fawns, and grovels, in his eagerness to eat;
Bid the Elephant be feeding, and the best of fodder bring;
Gravely—after much entreaty—condescends that mighty king.'

'Well, well!' said Karataka; 'the books are nothing to us, who are not councillors.'

'But we may come to be,' replied Damanaka; 'men rise, not by chance or nature, but by exertions—

'By their own deeds men go downward, by them men mount upward all,
Like the diggers of a well, and like the builders of a wall.'

Advancement is slow—but that is in the nature of things—

'Rushes down the hill the crag, which upward 'twas so hard to roll:
So to virtue slowly rises—so to vice quick sinks the soul.'

'Very good,' observed Karataka; 'but what is all this talk
about?'

'Why! don't you see our Royal Master there, and how he
came home without drinking? I know he has been horribly
frightened,' said Damanaka.

'How do you know it?' asked the other.

'By my perception—at a glance!' replied Damanaka; 'and
I mean to make out of this occasion that which shall put his
Majesty at my disposal.'

'Now,' exclaimed Karataka, 'it is thou who art ignorant
about service—

> 'Who speaks unasked, or comes unbid,
> Or counts on favor—will be chid.'

'I ignorant about service!' said Damanaka; 'no, no, my
friend, I know the secret of it—

> 'Wise, modest, constant, ever close at hand,
> Not weighing but obeying all command,
> Such servant by a Monarch's throne may stand.'

'In any case, the King often rates thee,' remarked Karataka,
'for coming to the presence unsummoned.'

'A dependent,' replied Damanaka, 'should nevertheless
present himself; he must make himself known to the great
man, at any risk—

> 'Pitiful, that fearing failure, therefore no beginning makes,
> Who forswears his daily dinner for the chance of stomach-aches?'

and besides, to be near is at last to be needful;—is it not said—

> 'Nearest to the King is dearest, be thy merit low or high;
> Women, creeping plants, and princes, twine round that which groweth
> nigh.'

'Well,' inquired Karataka, 'what wilt thou say, being come
to him?'

'First,' replied Damanaka, 'I will discover if his Majesty
is well affected to me.'

'How do you compass that?' asked the other.

'Oh, easily! by a look, a word,' answered Damanaka; 'and
that ascertained, I will proceed to speak what will put him at
my disposal.'

'I can't see how you can venture to speak,' objected the other, 'without an opportunity—

> 'If Vrihaspati, the Grave,
> 　Spoke a sentence out of season,
> Even Vrihaspati would have
> 　Strong rebuke for such unreason.'

'Pray don't imagine I shall speak unseasonably,' interrupted Damanaka; 'if that is all you fear, I will start at once.'

'Go, then,' said Karataka; 'and may you be as lucky as you hope.'

"Thereupon Damanaka set out for the lair of King Tawny-hide; putting on, as he approached it, the look of one greatly disconcerted. The Rajah observed him coming, and gave permission that he should draw near; of which Damanaka availing himself, made reverential prostration of the eight members and sat down upon his haunches.

'You have come at last, then, Sir Jackal!' growled his Majesty.

'Great Monarch!' humbly replied Damanaka, 'my service is not worthy of laying at your imperial feet, but a servant should attend when he can perform a service, and therefore I am come—

> 'When Kings' ears itch, they use a straw to scratch 'em;
> When Kings' foes plot, they get wise men to match 'em.'

'H'm!' growled the Lion.

'Your Majesty suspects my intellect, I fear,' continued the Jackal, 'after so long an absence from your Majesty's feet; but, if I may say so, it is still sound.'

'H'm!' growled the Lion again.

'A king, may it please your Majesty, should know how to estimate his servants, whatever their position—

> 'Pearls are dull in leaden settings, but the setter is to blame;
> Glass will glitter like the ruby, dulled with dust—are they the same?

> 'And a fool may tread on jewels, setting in his crown mere glass;
> Yet, at selling, gems are gems, and fardels but for fardels pass.'

'Servants, gracious liege! are good or bad as they are entertained. Is it not written?—

'Horse and weapon, lute and volume, man and woman, gift of speech,
Have their uselessness or uses in the One who owneth each.'

'And if I have been traduced to your Majesty as a dull fellow,
that hath not made me so—

'Not disparagement nor slander kills the spirit of the brave;
Fling a torch down, upward ever burns the brilliant flame it gave.'

'Accept then, Sire, from the humblest of your slaves his very
humble counsel—for

'Wisdom from the mouth of children be it overpast of none;
What man scorns to walk by lamplight in the absence of the sun?'

'Good Damanaka,' said King Tawny-hide, somewhat appeased, 'how is it that thou, so wise a son of our first minister,
hast been absent all this while from our Court? But now
speak thy mind fearlessly: what wouldst thou?'

'Will your Majesty deign to answer one question?' said
Damanaka. 'Wherefore came He back from the river without
drinking?'

'Hush!' whispered the King, 'thou hast hit right upon my
trouble. I knew no one unto whom I might confide it; but
thou seemest a faithful fellow, and I will tell thee. Listen,
then,' continued his Majesty in an agitated whisper, 'there is
some awful beast that was never seen before in this wood here;
and we shall have to leave it, look you. Did you hear by
chance the inconceivable great roar he gave? What a strong
beast it must be to have such a voice!'

'May it please your Majesty, I did hear the noise,' said the
Jackal, 'and there is doubtless cause for terrible apprehension
therein; but take comfort, my Liege, he is no minister who
bids thee prepare for either war or resignation. All will go
well, and your Majesty will learn by this difficulty which be
your best servants.'

'Good Jackal,' said Tawny-hide, 'I am horribly frightened
about it.'

'I can see that,' thought Damanaka; but he only said, 'Fear
nothing, my liege, while thy servant survives.'

'What shall I do?' asked the King.

'It is well to encourage those who can avert disaster. If

your Majesty condescended now to bestow some favor on Karataka and the other——'

'It shall be done,' said the Rajah; and, summoning the other Jackals, he gave them and Damanaka a magnificent gift of flesh, and they left the presence, undertaking to meet the threatened danger.

'But, brother,' began Karataka, 'haven't we eaten the King's dinner without knowing what the danger is which we are to meet, and whether we can obviate it?'

'Hold thy peace,' said Damanaka, laughing; 'I know very well what the danger is! It was a bull, aha! that bellowed— a bull, my brother—whose beef you and I could pick, much more the King our master.'

'And why not tell him so?' asked Karataka.

'What! and quiet his Majesty's fears! And where would our splendid dinner have been then? No, no, my friend—

> 'Set not your lord at ease; for, doing that,
> Might starve you as it starved " Curd-ear " the Cat.'

'Who was Curd-ear, the Cat?' inquired Karataka. Damanaka related:—

The Story of the Cat Who Served the Lion

" Far away in the North, on a mountain named ' Thousand-Crags,' there lived a lion called ' Mighty-heart '; and he was much annoyed by a certain mouse, who made a custom of nibbling his mane while he lay asleep in his den. The Lion would wake in a great rage at finding the ends of his magnificent mane made ragged, but the little mouse ran into his hole, and he could never catch it. After much consideration he went down to a village, and got a Cat named Curd-ear to come to his cave with much persuasion. He kept the Cat royally on all kinds of dainties, and slept comfortably without having his mane nibbled, as the mouse would now never venture out. Whenever the Lion heard the mouse scratching about, that was always a signal for regaling the Cat in a most distinguished style. But one day, the wretched mouse being nearly starved, he took courage to creep timidly from his hole, and was directly pounced upon by Curd-ear and killed. After that the Lion heard no more of the mouse, and quite left off his regular entertainments of the Cat. No!" concluded Damanaka, " we will keep our mouse alive for his Majesty."

So conversing, the Jackals went away to find Lusty-life the
Bull, and upon discovering him, Karataka squatted down with
great dignity at the foot of a tree, while Damanaka approached
to accost him.

' Bull,' said Damanaka, ' I am the warder of this forest under
the King Tawny-hide, and Karataka the Jackal there is his
General. The General bids thee come before him, or else instantly depart from the wood. It were better for thee to obey,
for his anger is terrible.'

' Thereupon Lusty-life, knowing nothing of the country customs, advanced at once to Karataka, made the respectful prostration of the eight members, and said timidly, ' My Lord General! what dost thou bid me do?—

' Strength serves Reason. Saith the Mahout, when he beats the brazen
    drum,
  "Ho! ye elephants, to this work must your mightinesses come." '

' Bull,' answered Karataka, ' thou canst remain in the wood
no longer unless thou goest directly to lay thyself at our Royal
master's imperial feet.'

' My Lord,' replied the Bull, ' give me a guarantee of safety,
and I will go.'

' Bull,' said Karataka, ' thou art foolish; fear nothing—

  " When the King of Chedi cursed him,
      Krishna scorned to make reply;
    Lions roar the thunder quiet,
      Jackals'-yells they let go by."

Our Lord the King will not vouchsafe his anger to thee;
knowest thou not—

' Mighty natures war with mighty: when the raging tempests blow,
  O'er the green rice harmless pass they, but they lay the palm-trees low.'

' So the Jackals, keeping Lusty-life in the rear, went towards
the palace of King Tawny-hide; where the Rajah received
them with much graciousness, and bade them sit down.

' Have you seen him?' asked the King.

' We have seen him, your Majesty,' answered Damanaka;
' it is quite as your Majesty expected—the creature has enor-

mous strength, and wishes to see your Majesty. Will you be
seated, Sire, and prepare yourself—it will never do to appear
alarmed at a noise.'

'Oh, if it was only a noise,' began the Rajah.

'Ah, but the cause, Sire! that was what had to be found
out; like the secret of Swing-ear the Spirit.'

'And who might Swing-ear be?' asked the King.

The Story of the Terrible Bell

"A goblin, your Majesty," responded Damanaka, "it
seemed so, at least, to the good people of Brahmapoora. A
thief had stolen a bell from the city, and was making off with
that plunder, and more, into the Sri-parvata hills, when he
was killed by a tiger. The bell lay in the jungle till some
monkeys picked it up, and amused themselves by constantly
ringing it. The townspeople found the bones of the man, and
heard the noise of the bell all about the hills; so they gave out
that there was a terrible devil there, whose ears rang like bells
as he swung them about, and whose delight was to devour men.
Every one, accordingly, was leaving the town, when a peasant
woman named Karála, who liked belief the better for a little
proof, came to the Rajah.

'Highness!' she observed, 'for a consideration I could settle this Swing-ear.'

'You could!' exclaimed the Rajah.

'I think so!' repeated the woman.

'Give her a consideration forthwith,' said the Rajah.

"Karála, who had her own ideas upon the matter, took the
present and set out. Being come to the hills, she made a circle,
and did homage to Gunputtee,[12] without whom nothing pros-
pers. Then, taking some fruit she had brought, such as monkeys love extremely, she scattered it up and down in the wood,
and withdrew to watch. Very soon the monkeys finding the
fruit, put down the bell, to do justice to it, and the woman picking it up, bore it back to the town, where she became an object
of uncommon veneration. We, indeed," concluded Damanaka,
"bring you a Bull instead of a bell—your Majesty shall now
see him!"

"Thereupon Lusty-life was introduced, and, the interview

[12] The deity of prudence.

passing off well, he remained many days in the forest on excellent terms with the Lion.

'One day another Lion, named 'Stiff-ears,' the brother of King Tawny-hide, came to visit him. The King received him with all imaginable respect, bade him be seated, and rose from his throne to go and kill some beasts for his refreshment.

'May it please your Majesty,' interposed the Bull, 'a deer was slain to-day—where is its flesh?'

'Damanaka and his brother know best,' said the King.

'Let us ascertain if there be any,' suggested the Bull.

'It is useless,' said the King, laughing—'they leave none.'

'What!' exclaimed the Bull, 'have those Jackals eaten a whole deer?'

'Eaten it, spoiled it, and given it away,' answered Tawny-hide; 'they always do so.'

'And this without your Majesty's sanction?' asked the Bull.

'Oh! certainly not with my sanction,' said the King.

'Then,' exclaimed the Bull, 'it is too bad: and in Ministers too!—

> 'Narrow-necked to let out little, big of belly to keep much,
> As a flagon is—the Vizir of a Sultan should be such.'

'No wealth will stand such waste, your Majesty—

> 'He who thinks a minute little, like a fool misuses more;
> He who counts a cowry nothing, being wealthy, will be poor.'

'A king's treasury, my liege, is the king's life.'

'Good brother,' observed Stiff-ears, who had heard what the Bull said, 'these Jackals are your Ministers of Home and Foreign Affairs—they should not have direction of the Treasury. They are old servants, too, and you know the saying—

> 'Brahmans, soldiers, these and kinsmen—of the three set none in charge:
> For the Brahman, tho' you rack him, yields no treasure small or large;
> And the soldier, being trusted, writes his quittance with his sword,
> And the kinsman cheats his kindred by the charter of the word;
> But a servant old in service, worse than any one is thought,
> Who, by long-tried license fearless, knows his master's anger nought.'

Ministers, my royal brother, are often like obstinate swellings that want squeezing, and yours must be kept in order.'

'They are not particularly obedient, I confess,' said Tawny-hide.

' It is very wrong,' replied Stiff-ears; ' and if you will be advised by me—as we have banqueted enough to-day—you will appoint this grain-eating and sagacious Bull your Superintendent of Stores.'

' It shall be so,' exclaimed the King.

' Lusty-life was accordingly appointed to serve out the provisions, and for many days Tawny-hide showed him favor beyond all others in the Court.

" Now the Jackals soon found that food was no longer so freely provided by this arrangement as before, and they met to consult about it.

' It is all our own fault,' said Damanaka, ' and people must suffer for their own mistakes. You know who said—

> " I that could not leave alone
> ' Streak-o'-Gold,' must therefore moan.
> She that took the House-wife's place
> Lost the nose from off her face.
> Take this lesson to thy heart—
> Fools for folly suffer smart."

' No! ' said Karataka, ' how was it? ' Damanaka related:—

The Story of the Prince and the Procuress

" In the city of ' Golden-Streets ' there reigned a valorous King, named Vira-vikrama, whose officer of justice was one day taking away to punishment a certain Barber, when he was stopped by a strolling mendicant, who held him by the skirts, and cried out, ' Punish not this man—punish them that do wrong of their own knowledge.' Being asked his meaning, he recited the foregoing verses, and, being still further questioned, he told this story—

" I am Prince Kandarpa-ketu, son of the King of Ceylon. Walking one day in my summer-garden, I heard a merchant-captain narrating how that out at sea, deep under water, on the fourteenth day of the moon, he had seen what was like nothing but the famous tree of Paradise, and sitting under it a lady of most lustrous beauty, bedecked with strings of pearls like Lukshmi herself, reclining, with a lute in her hands, on what appeared to be a golden couch crusted all over with precious

stones. At once I engaged the captain and his ship, and steered
to the spot of which he told me. On reaching it I beheld the
beautiful apparition as he had described it, and, transported
with the exquisite beauty of the lady, I leapt after her into the
sea. In a moment I found myself in a city of gold; and in an
apartment of a golden palace, surrounded by young and beautiful girls, I found the Sea-queen. She perceived my approach,
and sent an attendant with a courteous message to meet me.
In reply to my questions, I learned that the lady was the Princess Ratnamanjari, daughter of the King of All the Spirits—
and how she had made a vow that whoever should first come
to see her golden city, with his own eyes, should marry her.
So I married her by the form called Gundharva, or 'Union by
mutual consent,' and spent many and happy days in her delightful society. One day she took me aside, and said, 'Dear
Prince! all these delights, and I myself, are thine to enjoy;
only that picture yonder, of the Fairy Streak-o'-Gold, that thou
must never touch!' For a long time I observed this injunc-
tion; at last, impelled by resistless curiosity, I laid my hand
on the picture of 'Streak-o'-Gold.' In one instant her little
foot, lovely as the lotus-blossom, advanced from out of the
painting, and launched me through sea and air into my own
country. Since that I have been a miserable wanderer; and
passing through this city, I chanced to lodge at a Cowkeeper's
hut, and saw the truth of this Barber's affair. The herdsman
returned at night with his cattle, and found his wife talking
with the wife of the Barber, who is no better than a bawd.
Enraged at this, the man beat his wife, tied her to the milking-
post, and fell asleep. In the dead of the night the Barber's wife
came back, and said to the woman, 'He, whom thou knowest,
is burnt with the cruel fire of thine absence, and lies nigh to
death; go therefore and console him, and I will tie myself to
the post until thou returnest.' This was done, and the Cowkeeper presently awoke. 'Ah! thou light thing!' he said jeer-
ingly, 'why dost not thou keep promise, and meet thy gallant?'
The Barber's wife could make no reply; whereat becoming incensed, the man cried out, 'What! dost thou scorn to speak to
me? I will cut thy nose off!' And so he did, and then lay
down to sleep again. Very soon the Cowkeeper's wife came
back and asked if 'all was well.' 'Look at my face!' said the
Barber's wife, 'and you will see if all is well.' The woman

could do nothing but take her place again, while the Barber's wife, picking up the severed nose, and at a sad loss how to account for it, went to her house. In the morning, before it was light, the Barber called to her to bring his box of razors, and she bringing one only, he flung it away in a passion. 'Oh, the knave!' she cried out, directly, aloud, 'Neighbors, neighbors! he has cut my nose off!' and so she took him before the officers. The Cowkeeper, meantime, wondering at his wife's patience, made some inquiry about her nose; whereto she replied, 'Cruel wretch! thou canst not harm a virtuous woman. If Yama and the seven guardians of the world know me chaste, then be my face unmaimed!' The herdsman hastened to fetch a light, and finding her features unaltered, he flung himself at her feet, and begged forgiveness. For,

'Never tires the fire of burning, never wearies death of slaying,
Nor the sea of drinking rivers, nor the bright-eyed of betraying.'

Thereupon the King's officer dismissed Kandarpa-ketu, and did justice by setting the Barber free, shaving the head of the Barber's wife, and punishing the Cowkeeper's.

'That is my story,' concluded Damanaka, 'and thence I said that we had no reason to complain.'

'Well, but we must do something,' said Karataka.

'Yes! How shall we break the friendship of the King with the Bull?' asked the other.

'It is very strong,' observed Karataka.

'But we can do it,' replied the other.

'What force would fail to win, fraud can attain:—
The Crow despatched the Serpent by a chain.'

'How did that occur?' asked Karataka.
Damanaka related:—

The Story of the Black Snake and the Golden Chain

" A pair of Crows had their abode in a certain tree, the hollow of which was occupied by a black snake, who had often devoured their young. The Hen-bird, finding herself breeding again, thus addressed her mate: 'Husband, we must leave this tree; we shall never rear young ones while this black snake lives here! You know the saw—

'From false friends that breed thee strife,
From a house with serpents rife,
Saucy slaves and brawling wife—
Get thee out, to save thy life.'

'My dear,' replied the Crow, 'you need not fear; I have put up with him till I am tired. Now I will put an end to him.'

'How can you fight with a great black snake like that?' said the Hen-bird.

'Doubt nothing,' answered the other—

'He that hath sense hath strength; the fool is weak:—
The Lion proud died by the Hare so meek.'

'How came that about?' asked the Hen-Crow.

'Thus,' replied her mate:—

The Story of the Lion and the Old Hare

"On the Mandara mountain there lived a Lion named Fierce-of-heart, and he was perpetually making massacre of all the wild animals. The thing grew so bad that the beasts held a public meeting, and drew up a respectful remonstrance to the Lion in these words:—

"Wherefore should your Majesty thus make carnage of us all? If it may please you, we ourselves will daily furnish a beast for your Majesty's meal." The Lion responded, "If that arrangement is more agreeable to you, be it so"; and from that time a beast was allotted to him daily, and daily devoured. One day it came to the turn of an old hare to supply the royal table, who reflected to himself as he walked along, "I can but die, and I will go to my death leisurely."

"Now Fierce-of-heart, the lion, was pinched with hunger, and seeing the Hare so approaching he roared out, "How darest thou thus delay in coming?"

'Sire,' replied the Hare, 'I am not to blame. I was detained on the road by another lion, who exacted an oath from me to return when I should have informed your Majesty.'

'Go,' exclaimed King Fierce-of-heart in a rage; 'show me, instantly, where this insolent villain of a lion lives.'

"The Hare led the way accordingly till he came to a deep well, whereat he stopped, and said, 'Let my lord the King come hither and behold him.' The Lion approached, and beheld his own reflection in the water of the well, upon which, in his passion, he directly flung himself, and so perished."

"I have heard your story," said the Hen-Crow, "but what plan do you propose?"

"My dear," replied her mate, "the Rajah's son comes here every day to bathe in the stream. When he takes off his gold anklet, and lays it on the stone, do thou bring it in thy beak to the hollow of the tree, and drop it in there." Shortly after the Prince came, as was his wont, and taking off his dress and ornaments, the Hen-Crow did as had been determined; and while the servants of the Prince were searching in the hollow, there they found the Black Snake, which they at once dispatched.

'Said I not well,' continued Damanaka, 'that stratagem excels force?'

'It was well said,' replied Karataka; 'go! and may thy path be prosperous!'

'With that Damanaka repaired to the King, and having done homage, thus addressed him:—

"Your Majesty, there is a dreadful thing on my mind, and I am come to disclose it."

'Speak!' said the King, with much graciousness.

'Your Majesty,' said the Jackal, 'this Bull has been detected of treason. To my face he has spoken contemptuously of the three prerogatives of the throne,[13] unto which he aspires.'

"At these words King Tawny-hide stood aghast.

'Your Majesty,' continued Damanaka, 'has placed him above us all in the Court. Sire! he must be displaced!—

'Teeth grown loose, and wicked-hearted ministers, and poison-trees,
    Pluck them by the roots together; 'Tis the thing that giveth ease.'

'Good Jackal,' said the King, after some silence; 'this is indeed dreadful; but my regard for the Bull is very great, and it is said—

'Long-tried friends are friends to cleave to—never leave thou these
    i' the lurch:—
What man shuns the fire as sinful for that once it burned a church?'

[13] Regal authority derives its rights from three sources: Power, Prescription or continuance, and Wisdom.

'That is written of discarding old servants, may it please
your Majesty,' observed Damanaka; 'and this Bull is quite a
stranger.'

'Wondrous strange!' replied the Lion; 'when I have advanced and protected him that he should plot against me!'

'Your Majesty,' said the Jackal, 'knows what has been written—

'Raise an evil soul to honor, and his evil bents remain;
  Bind a cur's tail ne'er so straightly, yet it curleth up again.'

'How, in sooth, should Trust and Honor change the evil nature's root?
  Though one watered them with nectar, poison-trees bear deadly fruit.'

I have now at least warned your Majesty: if evil comes, the
fault is not mine.'

'It will not do to condemn the Bull without inquiry,' mused
the King; then he said aloud, 'shall we admonish him, think
you, Damanaka?'

'No, no, Sire!' exclaimed the Jackal, eagerly; 'that would
spoil all our precautions—

'Safe within the husk of silence guard the seed of counsel so
  That it break not—being broken, then the seedling will not grow.'

What is to be done must be done with despatch. After censur-
ing his treason, would your Majesty still trust the traitor?—

'Whoso unto ancient fondness takes again a faithless friend,
  Like she-mules that die conceiving, in his folly finds his end.'

'But wherein can the Bull injure me?' asked Tawny-hide;
'tell me that!'

'Sire,' replied the Jackal, how can I tell it?—

'Ask who his friends are, ere you scorn your foe;
  The Wagtail foiled the sea, that did not so.'

'How could that be?' demanded King Tawny-hide.

'The Jackal related:—

The Story of the Wagtail and the Sea

" On the shore of the Southern Sea there dwelt a pair of Wagtails. The Hen-bird was about to lay, and thus addressed her mate :—

' Husband, we must look about for a fit place to lay my eggs.'

' My dear,' replied the Cock-bird, ' will not this spot do? '

' This spot! ' exclaimed the Hen; ' why, the tide overflows it.'

' Good dame,' said the Cock, ' am I so pitiful a fellow that the Sea will venture to wash the eggs out of my nest? '

' You are my very good Lord,' replied the Hen, with a laugh; ' but still there is a great difference between you and the Sea.'

" Afterwards, however, at the desire of her mate, she consented to lay her eggs on the sea-beach. Now the Ocean had overheard all this, and, bent upon displaying its strength, it rose and washed away the nest and eggs. Overwhelmed with grief, the Hen-bird flew to her mate, and cried :—

' Husband, the terrible disaster has occurred! My eggs are gone! '

' Be of good heart! my Life,' answered he.

" And therewith he called a meeting of fowls, and went with them into the presence of Gurud, the Lord of the birds. When the Master of the Mighty Wing had listened to their complaint, he conveyed it to the knowledge of the God Narayen, who keeps, and kills, and makes alive the world. The almighty mandate given, Gurud bound it upon his forehead, and bore it to the Ocean, which, so soon as it heard the will of Narayen, at once gave back the eggs.

' How, indeed,' concluded Damanaka, ' should I judge of the Bull's power, not knowing who supports him? '

' By what signs, then,' asked the King, ' may I conclude him a traitor? '

' If he comes into the presence with his horns lowered for goring, as one that expects the fight. That,' replied the Jackal, ' will convince your Majesty.'

' Thereupon Damanaka the Jackal withdrew, and betook himself towards the Bull, upon perceiving whom he approached slowly, with all the air of one greatly distressed.

' Good master Jackal,' said Lusty-life, ' what goes amiss with thee? '

'All goes amiss with such as serve wicked masters,' replied the Jackal.

'But what ails thee?' asked the Bull.

'Alas!' answered the Jackal, 'what can I say in such a strait!—

> 'Even as one who grasps a serpent, drowning in the bitter sea,
> Death to hold and death to loosen—such is life's perplexity.'

'And therewithal the Jackal heaved a deep sigh, and squatted down.

'But, good friend,' said the Bull, 'at least tell me what is in thy mind.'

'Bull,' began Damanaka, 'it is a King's secret, and should not be spoken; but thou didst come here upon my safeguard, and as I hope for the life to come, I will tell thee of what touches thee so nearly. Listen!—the heart of the King is turned against thee! he hath sworn secretly that he will kill thee and feast upon thy flesh.'

'Then Lusty-life the Bull was sorely troubled, and he fell a-musing thus—

> "Woman's love rewards the worthless—kings of knaves exalters be;
> Wealth attends the selfish niggard, and the cloud rains on the sea."

'Can this be the Jackal's doing?' he reflected. Going with honest folk will not make one honest—

> 'Many a knave wins fair opinions standing in fair company,
> As the sooty soorma pleases, lighted by a brilliant eye.'

Then he said aloud, 'wherein can I have angered the King? Do kings hate without cause? I can tell nothing, except that there is no happiness which abides long—

> 'Where the azure lotus[14] blossoms, there the alligators hide;
> In the sandal-tree are serpents. Pain and pleasure live allied.'

I thought his Majesty noble as the sandal-tree; but that, indeed, is not wholly noble—

> 'Rich the sandal—yet no part is but a vile thing habits there;
> Snake and wasp haunt root and blossom; on the boughs sit ape and bear.'

[14] The lotus resembles the water-lily, but is more varied in form and color.

'Bull,' said Damanaka, 'I knew the King of old for one whose tongue was honey and whose heart was poison.'

'But how very hard!' said the Bull, 'that he, being a lion, should attack me, an innocent eater of grass!'

'It is very hard!' said the Jackal.

'Who can have set him against me?' asked the Bull.

'Being so, it cannot be bettered,' replied the Jackal, 'whoever did it—

> 'As a bracelet of crystal, once broke, is not mended;
> So the favor of princes, once altered, is ended.'

'Yes,' said the Bull, 'and a king incensed is terrible—

'Wrath of kings, and rage of lightning—both be very full of dread;
But one falls on one man only—one strikes many victims dead.'

Still, I can but die—and I will die fighting! When death is certain, and no hope left but in battle, that is the time for war.'

'It is so,' said the Jackal.

'Having weighed all this, Lusty-life inquired of the Jackal by what signs he might conclude the King's hostile intentions.

'If he glowers upon thee,' answered Damanaka, 'and awaits thee with ears pricked, tail stiffened, paw upraised, and muzzle agape, then thou mayest get thee to thy weapons like a Bull of spirit, for

'All men scorn the soulless coward who his manhood doth forget:—
On a lifeless heap of ashes fearlessly the foot is set.'

'Then Damanaka the Jackal returned to the Lion, and said to him:—

'If it please your Majesty, the traitor is now coming; let your Majesty be on your guard, with ears pricked and paw upraised.'

'The Bull meanwhile approached, and observing the hostile attitude of King Tawny-hide, he also lowered his horns, and prepared for the combat. A terrible battle ensued, and at the last King Tawny-hide slew Lusty-life the Bull. Now when the Bull was dead, the Lion was very sorrowful, and as he sat on his throne lamenting, he said—

'I repent me of this deed!—

> 'As when an Elephant's life-blood is spilt,
> Another hath the spoils—mine is the guilt.'

'Sire,' replied the Jackal, 'a King over-merciful is like a Brahman that eats all things equally. May all your Majesty's enemies perish as did this Bull.'

"Thus endeth," said the Sage Vishnu-Sarman, "the 'Parting of Friends.'"

"We are gratified exceedingly thereby," replied the Sons of the King.

"Let me then close it thus," said their Preceptor—

> 'So be friendship never parted,
> But among the evil-hearted;
> Time's sure step drag, soon or later,
> To his judgment, such a Traitor;
> Lady Lukshmi, of her grace,
> Grant good fortune to this place;
> And you, Royal boys! and boys of times to be,
> In this fair fable-garden wander free.'

WAR

WHEN the next day of instruction was come, the King's sons spake to the Sage, Vishnu-Sarman.

"Master," said they, "we are Princes, and the sons of Princes, and we earnestly desire to hear thee discourse upon War."

"I am to speak on what shall please you," replied Vishnu-Sarman. "Hear now, therefore, of 'War,' whose opening is thus:—

> 'Between the peoples of Peacock and Swan [15]
> War raged; and evenly the contest ran,
> Until the Swans to trust the Crows began.'

'And how was all that?' asked the sons of the Rajah. Vishnu-Sarman proceeded to relate—

The Battle of the Swans and Peacocks

"In the Isle of Camphor there is a lake called 'Lotus-water,' and therein a Swan-Royal, named 'Silver-sides,' had his residence. The birds of the marsh and the mere had elected him King, in full council of all the fowls—for a people with no ruler is like a ship that is without a helmsman. One day King Silver-sides, with his courtiers, was quietly reposing on a couch of well-spread lotus-blossoms, when a Crane, named 'Long-bill,' who had just arrived from foreign parts, entered the presence with an obeisance, and sat down.

'What news from abroad, Long-bill?' asked his Majesty.

'Great news, may it please you,' answered the Crane, 'and therefore have I hastened hither. Will your Majesty hear me?'

'Speak!' said King Silver-sides.

[15] The peacock is wild in most Indian jungles. The swan is a species of flamingo of a white color. The voice and gait of a beautiful woman are likened by the Hindoo poets to those of the swan.

52

'You must know, my Liege,' began the Crane, 'that over all the birds of the Vindhya mountains in Jambudwipa a Peacock is King, and his name is 'Jewel-plume.' I was looking for food about a certain burnt jungle there, when some of his retainers discovered me, and asked my name and country. 'I am a vassal of King Silver-sides, Lord of the Island of Camphor,' I replied, 'and I am travelling in foreign lands for my pleasure.' Upon that the birds asked me which country, my own or theirs, and which King, appeared to me superior. 'How can you ask?' I replied; 'the island of Camphor is, as it were, Heaven itself, and its King a heaven-born ruler. To dwellers in a barren land like yours how can I describe them? Come for yourselves, and see the country where I live.' Thereupon, your Majesty, the birds were exceedingly offended, as one might expect—

'Simple milk, when serpents drink it, straightway into venom turns;
And a fool who heareth counsel all the wisdom of it spurns.'

For, indeed, no reflecting person wastes time in admonishing blockheads—

'The birds that took the apes to teaching,
Lost eggs and nests in pay for preaching.'

'How did that befall?' asked the King.
The Crane related:—

The Story of the Weaver-Birds and the Monkeys

"In a nullah that leads down to the Nerbudda river there stood a large silk-cotton tree, where a colony of weaver-birds had built their hanging nests, and lived snugly in them, whatever the weather. It was in the rainy season, when the heavens are overlaid with clouds like indigo-sheets, and a tremendous storm of water was falling. The birds looked out from their nests, and saw some monkeys, shivering and starved with the cold, standing under a tree. 'Twit! twit! you Monkeys,' they began to chirrup. 'Listen to us!—

'With beaks we built these nests, of fibres scattered;
You that have hands and feet, build, or be spattered.'

On hearing that the Monkeys were by no means pleased. 'Ho!
ho!' said they, 'the Birds in their snug nests are jeering at
us; wait till the rain is over.' Accordingly, so soon as the
weather mended, the Monkeys climbed into the tree, and broke
all the birds' eggs and demolished every nest. I ought to have
known better,' concluded the Crane, 'than to have wasted my
suggestions on King Jewel-plume's creatures.'

'But what did they say?' asked Silver-sides.

'They said, Rajah,' answered the Crane, 'who made that
Swan of thine a King?'

'And what was your reply?' asked Silver-sides.

'I demanded,' replied the Crane, 'who made a King of that
Peacock of theirs. Thereupon they were ready to kill me for
rage; but I displayed my very best valor. Is it not written—

> 'A modest manner fits a maid,
>   And Patience is a man's adorning;
> But brides may kiss, nor do amiss,
>   And men may draw, at scathe and scorning.'

'Yet a man should measure his own strength first,' said the
Rajah, smiling; 'how did you fare against King Jewel-plume's
fellows?'

'Very scurvily,' replied Long-bill. "Thou rascal Crane,"
they cried, "dost thou feed on his soil, and revile our Sovereign? That is past bearing!" And thereat they all pecked
at me. Then they began again: "Thou thick-skulled Crane!
that King of thine is a goose—a web-footed lord of littleness
—and thou art but a frog in a well to bid us serve him—him
forsooth!—

> 'Serving narrow-minded masters dwarfs high natures to their size:—
> Seen before a convex mirror, elephants do show as mice.'

Bad kings are only strong enough to spoil good vassals—as a
fiction once was mightier than a herd of elephants. You know
it, don't you?—

> 'Mighty may prove things insignificant:—
> A tale of moonshine turned an elephant.'

'No! how was that?' I asked.
The birds related—

The Story of the Old Hare and the Elephants

" Once on a time, very little rain had fallen in the due season; and the Elephants being oppressed with thirst, thus accosted their leader :—' Master, how are we to live? The small
creatures find something to wash in, but we cannot, and we
are half dead in consequence; whither shall we go then, and
what shall we do?' Upon that the King of the Elephants led
them away a little space; and showed them a beautiful pool
of crystal water, where they took their ease. Now it chanced
that a company of Hares resided on the banks of the pool, and
the going and coming of the elephants trampled many of them
to death, till one of their number named Hard-head grumbled
out, ' This troop will be coming here to water every day, and
every one of our family will be crushed.' ' Do not disquiet
yourself,' said an old buck named Good-speed, ' I will contrive
to avert it,' and so saying, he set off, bethinking himself on his
way how he should approach and accost a herd of elephants;
for,

' Elephants destroy by touching, snakes with point of tooth beguile;
Kings by favor kill, and traitors murder with a fatal smile.'

' I will get on the top of a hill,' he thought, ' and address the
Elephants thence.'

" This being done, and the Lord of the herd perceiving him,
it was asked of the Hare, ' Who art thou? and whence comest
thou?'

' I am an ambassador from his Godship the Moon,' replied
Good-speed.

' State your business,' said the Elephant-king.

' Sire,' began the Hare, ' an ambassador speaks the truth
safely by charter of his name. Thus saith the Moon, then:
" These hares were the guardians of my pool, and thine elephants in coming thither have scared them away. This is not
well. Am I not Sasanka, whose banner bears a hare, and are
not these hares my votaries? " '

' Please your worship,' said the Elephant-king with much
trepidation, ' we knew nothing of this; we will go there no
more.'

' It were well,' said the sham ambassador, ' that you first

made your apologies to the Divinity, who is quaking with rage in his pool, and then went about your business.'

'We will do so,' replied the Elephant with meekness; and being led by night to the pool, in the ripples of which the image of the Moon was quivering, the herd made their prostrations; the Hare explaining to the Moon that their fault was done in ignorance, and thereupon they got their dismissal.'

'Nay,' I said, 'my Sovereign is no fiction, but a great King and a noble, and one that might govern the Three Worlds, much more a kingdom.'

'Thou shalt talk thy treason in the presence,' they cried; and therewith I was dragged before King Jewel-plume.

'Who is this?' asked the Rajah.

'He is a servant of King Silver-sides, of the Island of Camphor,' they replied; 'and he slights your Majesty, on your Majesty's own land.'

'Sirrah Crane!' said the Prime Minister, a Vulture, 'who is chief officer in that court?'

'A Brahmany Goose,' I answered, 'named "Know-all"; and he does know every possible science.'

'Sire,' broke in a Parrot, 'this Camphor-isle and the rest are poor places, and belong to Jambudwipa. Your Majesty has but to plant the royal foot upon them.'

'Oh! of course,' said the King.

'Nay,' said I, 'if talking makes your Majesty King of Camphor-island, my Liege may be lord of Jambudwipa by a better title.'

'And that?' said the Parrot.

'Is fighting!' I responded.

'Good!' said the King, with a smile; 'bid your people prepare for war.'

'Not so,' I replied; 'but send your own ambassador.'

'Who will bear the message?' asked the Rajah. 'He should be loyal, dexterous, and bold.'

'And virtuous,' said the Vulture, 'and therefore a Brahman:—

'Better Virtue marked a herald than that noble blood should deck;
Shiva reigns forever Shiva while the sea-wave stains his neck.'

'Then let the Parrot be appointed,' said the Rajah.

'I am your Majesty's humble servant,' replied the Parrot;

'but this Crane is a bad character, and with the bad I never
like to travel. The ten-headed Ravana carried off the wife of
Ramchundra! It does not do,

> 'With evil people neither stay nor go;
> The Heron died for being with the Crow.'

'How did that befall?' asked the King. The Parrot related:—

The Story of the Heron and the Crow

' The high-road to Oogein is a very unshaded and sultry one;
but there stands upon it one large Peepul-tree, and therein a
Crow and a Heron had their residence together. It was in the
hot weather that a tired traveller passed that way, and, for
the sake of the shade, he laid his bow and arrows down, and
dropped asleep under the tree. Before long the shadow of
the tree shifted, and left his face exposed to the glare; which
the Heron perceiving, like the kindly bird he was, perched on
the Peepul-tree, and spread his wings out so as to cast a
shadow on the traveller's face. There the poor fellow, weary
with his travel, continued to sleep soundly, and snored away
comfortably with open mouth. The sight of his enjoyment
was too much for the malevolent Crow, who, perching over him,
dropped an unwelcome morsel into the sleeper's mouth, and
straightway flew off. The traveller, starting from his slumber, looked about, and, seeing no bird but the Heron, he fitted
an arrow and shot him dead. No!' concluded the Parrot, ' I
like the society of honest folk.'

' But why these words, my brother?' I said; 'his Majesty's
herald is to me even as his Majesty.'

' Very fine!' replied the Parrot; ' but—

> 'Kindly courtesies that issue from a smiling villain's mouth
> Serve to startle, like a flower blossoming in time of drouth.'

Needs must that thou art a bad man; for by thy talk war will
have arisen, which a little conciliation had averted:—

> ' Conciliation!—weapon of the wise!
> Wheedled therewith, by woman's quick device,
> The Wheelwright let his ears betray his eyes.'

'How came that about?' asked the King. The Parrot related:—

The Story of the Appeased Wheelwright

"There was a Wheelwright in Shri-nuggur, whose name was 'Heavy-head.' He had good reason to suspect the infidelity of his wife, but he had no absolute proof of it. One day he gave out that he should go to a neighboring town, and he started accordingly; but he went a very little way, and then returning, hid himself in his wife's chamber. She being quite satisfied that he was really gone away, invited her gallant to pass the evening with her, and began to spend it with him in unrestrained freedom. Presently, by chance, she detected the presence of her husband, and her manner instantly changed.

'Life of my soul! what ails you?' said her lover; 'you are quite dull to-night.'

'I am dull,' she replied, 'because the lord of my life is gone. Without my husband the town is a wilderness. Who knows what may befall him, and whether he will have a nice supper?'

'Trouble thyself no more about the quarrelsome dullard,' said her gallant.

'Dullard, quotha!' exclaimed the wife. 'What matter what he is, since he is my all? Knowest thou not—

'Of the wife the lord is jewel, though no gems upon her beam;
  Lacking him, she lacks adornment, howsoe'er her jewels gleam?'

Thou, and the like of thee, may serve a whim, as we chew a betel-leaf and trifle with a flower; but my husband is my master, and can do with me as he will. My life is wrapped up in him—and when he dies, alas! I will certainly die too. Is it not plainly said—

'Hairs three-crore, and half-a-crore hairs, on a man so many grow—
  And so many years to Swerga shall the true wife surely go?'

And better still is promised; as herein—

'When the faithful wife,[16] embracing tenderly her husband dead,
  Mounts the blazing pile beside him, as it were the bridal-bed;
  Though his sins were twenty thousand, twenty thousand times o'er-
    told,
  She shall bring his soul to splendor, for her love so large and bold.'

[16] By such a death as that alluded to, she earns the title of Sati. the "excellent."

All this the Wheelwright heard. 'What a lucky fellow I am,' he thought, ' to have a wife so virtuous,' and rushing from his place of concealment, he exclaimed in ecstasy to his wife's gallant, ' Sir! saw you ever truer wife than mine? '

' When the story was concluded,' said Long-bill, ' the King, with a gracious gift of food, sent me off before the Parrot; but he is coming after me, and it is now for your Majesty to determine as it shall please you.'

' My Liege,' observed the Brahmany-goose with a sneer, ' the Crane has done the King's business in foreign parts to the best of his power, which is that of a fool.'

" Let the past pass," replied the King, " and take thought for the present."

" Be it in secret, then, your Majesty," said the Brahmany-goose—

'Counsel unto six ears spoken, unto all is notified:—
When a King holds consultation, let it be with one beside.'

Thereupon all withdrew, but the Rajah and the Minister.

' What think you? ' said Silver-sides.

' That the Crane has been employed to bring this about,' replied the other.

' What shall we do? ' asked the King.

' Despatch two spies—the first to inform and send back the other, and make us know the enemy's strength or weakness. They must be such as can travel by land and water, so the Crane will serve for one, and we will keep his family in pledge at the King's gate. The other must be a very reserved character; as it is said—

'Sick men are for skilful leeches—prodigals for prisoning—
Fools for teachers—and the man who keeps a secret, for a King.'

' I know such a one,' said his Majesty, after a pause.

' It is half the victory,' responded the Minister.

At this juncture a chamberlain entered with a profound obeisance, and announced the arrival from Jambudwipa of the Parrot.

' Let him be shown to a reception-room,' commanded the Goose, in reply to a look from the King. ' He shall presently have audience.'

'War is pronounced, then,' said the King, as the attendant withdrew.

'It is offered, my Liege; but must not be rashly accepted,' replied the other—

> 'With gift, craft, promise, cause thy foe to yield;
> When these have failed thee, challenge him a-field.'

To gain time for expedients is the first point. Expedients are good for great and little matters equally, like

> 'The subtle wash of waves, that smoothly pass,
> But lay the tree as lowly as the grass.'

Let his Excellency the Parrot, then, be cajoled and detained here, while we place our fort in condition to be useful. Is it not said—

> 'Ten true bowmen on a rampart fifty's onset may sustain;
> Fortalices keep a country more than armies in the plain?'

And your Majesty,' continued the Goose, ' will recall the points of a good fortress—

> 'Build it strong, and build it spacious, with an entry and retreat;
> Store it well with wood and water, fill its garners full with wheat.'

'Whom, then, shall we entrust with this work?' asked King Silver-sides.

'The Paddy-bird[17] is a good bird, and a skilful,' replied his Minister.

'Let him be summoned!' said the King. And upon the entrance of the Paddy-bird, the superintendence of the fortress was committed to him, and accepted with a low prostration.

'As to the fort, Sire!' remarked the Paddy-bird, ' it exists already in yonder large pool; the thing is to store the island in the middle of it with provisions—

> 'Gems will no man's life sustain;
> Best of gold is golden grain.'

'Good!' said King Silver-sides; ' let it be looked to.' Thereupon, as the Paddy-bird was retiring, the Usher entered

---

[17] The common Indian crane; a graceful white bird, seen everywhere in the interior of Hindoostan.

again, and making prostration, said: 'May it please your Majesty, the King of all the Crows, Night-cloud by name, has just arrived from Singhala-dwipa, and desires to lay his homage at your Majesty's feet.'

'He is a wise bird, and a far-travelled,' said the King; 'I think we must give him audience.'

'Nevertheless, Sire,' interrupted the Goose, 'we must not forget that he is a land-bird, and therefore not to be received as a water-fowl. Your royal memory doubtless retains the story of

'The Jackal's fate, who being colored blue,
Leaving his party, left his own life too.'

'No! How was that?' asked King Silver-sides. The Goose related—

The Story of the Dyed Jackal

"A Jackal once on a time, as he was prowling about the suburbs of a town, slipped into an indigo-tank; and not being able to get out he laid himself down so as to be taken for dead. The dyer presently coming and finding what seemed a dead Jackal, carried him into the jungle and then flung him away. Left to himself, the Jackal found his natural color changed to a splendid blue. 'Really,' he reflected, 'I am now of a most magnificent tint; why should I not make it conduce to my elevation?' With this view, he assembled the other Jackals, and thus harangued them:—

'Good people, the Goddess of the Wood, with her own divine hand, and with every magical herb of the forest, has anointed me King. Behold the complexion of royalty!—and henceforward transact nothing without my imperial permission."

"The Jackals, overcome by so distinguished a color, could do nothing but prostrate themselves and promise obedience. His reign, thus begun, extended in time to the lions and tigers; and with these high-born attendants he allowed himself to despise the Jackals, keeping his own kindred at a distance, as though ashamed of them. The Jackals were indignant, but an old beast of their number thus consoled them:—

"Leave the impudent fellow to me. I will contrive his ruin. These tigers and the rest think him a King, because he is colored blue; we must show them his true colors. Do this,

now!—in the evening-time come close about him, and set up
a great yell together—he is sure to join in, as he used to do—

'Hard it is to conquer nature: if a dog were made a King,
  Mid the coronation trumpets, he would gnaw his sandal-string.'

And when he yells the Tigers will know him for a Jackal and
fall upon him.'

'The thing befell exactly so, and the Jackal,' concluded the
Minister, 'met the fate of one who leaves his proper party.'

'Still,' said the King, 'the Crow has come a long way, and
we might see him, I think.'

'Admit the Parrot first, Sire,' said the Goose; 'the fort has
been put in order and the spy despatched.'

"Thereupon a Court was called, and the Parrot introduced,
followed by Night-cloud, the Crow.   A seat was offered to the
parrot, who took it, and, with his beak in the air, thus delivered
his mission:—

'King Silver-sides!—My master, the King Jewel-plume,
Lord of Lords, bids thee, if life and lands be dear to thee, to
come and make homage at his august feet; and failing this
to get thee gone from Camphor-island.'

'S'death!' exclaimed the Rajah, 'is there none that will
silence this traitor?'

'Give the sign, your Majesty,' said the Crow, starting up,
and I will despatch this audacious bird.'

'Sir,' said the Goose, 'be calm! and Sire, deign to listen—

''Tis no Council where no Sage is—'tis no Sage that fears not Law;
'Tis no Law which Truth confirms not—'tis no Truth which Fear
    can awe.'

An ambassador must speak unthreatened—

'Though base be the Herald, nor hinder nor let,
    For the mouth of a king is he;
  The sword may be whet, and the battle set,
    But the word of his message is free.'

Thereat the Rajah and Night-cloud resumed their compo-
sure; and the Parrot took his departure, escorted by the Minister, and presented with complimentary gifts of gold and
jewels. On reaching the palace of Jewel-plume, the King demanded his tidings, and inquired of the country he had visited.

' War must be prepared, may it please you,' said the Parrot:
' the country is a country of Paradise.'

' Prepare for war, then!' said the King.

' We must not enter on it in the face of destiny,' interposed
the Vulture-Minister, whose title was ' Far-sight.'

' Let the Astrologer then discover a favorable conjuncture
for the expedition, and let my forces be reviewed meantime,'
said the King.

' We must not march without great circumspection,' observed Far-sight.

' Minister!' exclaimed the King, ' you chafe me. Say, however, with what force we should set out.'

' It should be well selected, rather than unwieldy,' replied the
Vulture—

' Better few and chosen fighters than of shaven crowns a host,
For in headlong flight confounded, with the base the brave are lost.'

And its commanders must be judiciously appointed; for it is
said—

' Ever absent, harsh, unjustly portioning the captured prey—
These, and cold or laggard leaders make a host to melt away.'

' Ah!' interrupted the Rajah, ' what need of so much talk?
We will go, and, if Váchaspati please, we will conquer.'

Shortly afterwards the Spy returned to Camphor-island.
' King Silver-sides,' he cried, ' the Rajah, Jewel-plume, is on
his way hither, and has reached the Ghauts. Let the fort be
manned, for that Vulture is a great minister; and I have
learned, too, that there is one among us who is in his pay.'

' King!' said the Goose, ' that must be the Crow.'

' But whence, then, did he show such willingness to punish
the Parrot?' objected his Majesty. ' Besides, war was declared long after the Crow came to Court.'

' I misdoubt him,' said the Minister, ' because he is a
stranger.'

' But strangers surely may be well-disposed,' replied the
King. ' How say the books?—

' Kind is kin, howe'er a stranger—kin unkind is stranger shown;
Sores hurt, though the body breeds them—drugs relieve, though des-
ert-grown.'

Have you never heard of King Sudraka and the unknown Servant, who gave his son's life for the King?

'Never,' answered the Goose.

The Story of the Faithful Rajpoot

"I will tell you the tale," said the King, "as I heard it from 'Lilyflower,' daughter of the Flamingo 'White-flag,' of whom I was once very fond:—A soldier presented himself one morning at King Sudraka's gate, and bade the porter procure an audience for 'Vira-vara, a Rajpoot,'[18] who sought employment. Being admitted to the presence, he thus addressed the King:—

'If your Highness needs an attendant, behold one!'

'What pay do you ask?' inquired the King.

'Five hundred pieces of gold a day,' said Vira-vara.

'And your accoutrements?' asked the King.

'Are these two arms, and this sabre, which serve for a third,' said Vira-vara, rolling up his sleeve.

'I cannot entertain you,' rejoined his Majesty; and thereupon the Rajpoot made salaam, and withdrew. Then said the Ministers, 'If it please your Majesty, the stipend is excessive, but give him pay for four days, and see wherein he may deserve it.' Accordingly, the Rajpoot was recalled, and received wages for four days, with the complimentary betel.—Ah! the rare betel! Truly say the wise of it—

'Betel-nut is bitter, hot, sweet, spicy, binding, alkaline—
A demulcent—an astringent—foe to evils intestine;
Giving to the breath a fragrance—to the lips a crimson red;
A detergent, and a kindler of Love's flame that lieth dead.
Praise the gods for the good Betel!—these be thirteen virtues given,
Hard to meet in one thing blended, even in their happy heaven.'

'Now the King narrowly watched the spending of Vira-vara's pay, and discovered that he bestowed half in the service of the Gods and the support of Brahmans, a fourth part in relieving the poor, and reserved a fourth for his sustenance and recreation. This daily division made, he would take his stand with his sabre at the gate of the palace; retiring only upon receiving the royal permission.

[18] A man of military caste.

'It was on the fourteenth night of the dark half of the month that King Sudraka heard below a sound of passionate sobbing. 'Ho! there,' he cried, ' who waits at the gate? '

' I,' replied Vira-vara, ' may it please you.'

' Go and learn what means this weeping,' said the King.

' I go, your Majesty, answered the Rajpoot, and therewith departed.

' No sooner was he gone than the King repented him of sending one man alone into a night so dark that a bodkin might pierce a hole in it, and girding on his scimitar, he followed his guard beyond the city gates. When Vira-vara had gone thus far he encountered a beautiful and splendidly dressed lady who was weeping bitterly; and accosting her, he requested to know her name, and why she thus lamented.

' I am the Fortune of the King Sudraka,' answered she; ' a long while I have lived happily in the shadow of his arm; but on the third day he will die, and I must depart, and therefore lament I.'

' Can nothing serve, Divine Lady, to prolong thy stay? ' asked the Rajpoot.

' It might be,' replied the Spirit, ' if thou shouldst cut off the head of thy first-born Shaktidhar, that hath on his body the thirty-two auspicious marks of greatness. Were his head offered to the all-helpful Durga, the Rajah should live a hundred years, and I might tarry beside him.'

' So speaking, she disappeared, and Vira-vara retraced his steps to his own house and awoke his wife and son. They arose, and listened with attention until Vira-vara had repeated all the words of the vision. When he had finished, Shaktidhar exclaimed, ' I am thrice happy to be able to save the state of the King. Kill me, my father, and linger not; to give my life in such a cause is good indeed.' ' Yes,' said the Mother, ' it is good, and worthy of our blood; how else should we deserve the King's pay? ' Being thus agreed, they repaired together at once to the temple of the Goddess Durga, and having paid their devotions and entreated the favor of the deity on behalf of the King, Vira-vara struck off his son's head, and laid it as an offering upon the shrine. That done, Vira-vara said, ' My service to the King is accomplished, and life without my boy is but a burden,' and therewith he plunged his sword in his own breast and fell dead. Overpowered with grief for her husband and child, the mother also withdrew the twice-blooded weapon, and slew herself with it on the bodies of Vira-vara and Shaktidhar.

'All this was heard and seen by King Sudraka, and he stood aghast at the sad sight. 'Woe is me!' he exclaimed—

> 'Kings may come, and Kings may go;
> What was I, to bring these low?
> Souls so noble, slain for me,
> Were not, and will never be!'

What reck I of my realm, having lost these?' and thereat he drew his scimitar to take his own life also. At that moment there appeared to him the Goddess, who is Mistress of all men's fortunes. 'Son,' said she, staying his lifted hand, 'forbear thy rash purpose, and bethink thee of thy kingdom.'

"The Rajah fell prostrate before her, and cried—'O Goddess! I am done with life and wealth and kingdom! If thou hast compassion on me, let my death restore these faithful ones to life; anywise I follow the path they have marked.' 'Son,' replied the Goddess, 'thine affection is pleasing to me: be it as thou wilt! The Rajpoot and his house shall be rendered alive to thee.' Then the King departed, and presently saw Vira-vara return, and take up again his station as before at the palace-gate.

'Ho! there, Vira-vara!' cried the King, 'what meant the weeping?'

'Let your Majesty rest well!' answered the Rajpoot, 'it was a woman who wept, and disappeared on my approach.' This answer completed the Rajah's astonishment and delight; for we know—

> 'He is brave whose tongue is silent of the trophies of his sword;
> He is great whose quiet bearing marks his greatness well assured.'

So when the day was come, he called a full council, and, declaring therein all the events of the night, he invested the faithful guard with the sovereignty of the Carnatic.

"Thus, then," concluded King Silver-sides, "in entertaining strangers a man may add to his friends."

"It may well be," replied the Goose; "but a Minister should advise what is expedient, and not what is pleasing in sentiment :—

'When the Priest, the Leech, the Vizir of a King his flatterers be,
Very soon the King will part with health, and wealth, and piety.'

'Let it pass, then,' said Silver-sides, 'and turn we to the
matter in hand. King Jewel-plume is even now pitched under
the Ghauts. What think you?'

'That we shall vanquish him,' replied the Goose; 'for he
disregards, as I learn, the counsel of that great statesman, the
Vulture Far-sight; and the wise have said—

'Merciless, or money-loving, deaf to counsel, false of faith,
Thoughtless, spiritless, or careless, changing course with every breath,
Or the man who scorns his rival—if a prince should choose a foe,
Ripe for meeting and defeating, certes he would choose him so.'

He is marching without due preparation; let us send the Paddy-bird at the head of a force and attack him on his march."

Accordingly the Paddy-bird, setting out with a force of
water-fowl, fell upon the host of the Peacock-king, and did
immense execution. Disheartened thereat, King Jewel-plume
summoned Far-sight, his Minister, and acknowledged to him
his precipitation.

'Wherefore do you abandon us, my father?' he said. 'Correct for us what has been done amiss.'

'My Liege,' replied the Vulture, 'it has been well observed—

'By the valorous and unskilful great achievements are not wrought;
Courage, led by careful Prudence, unto highest ends is brought.'

You have set Strength in the seat of Counsel, your Majesty,
and he hath clumsily spoiled your plans. How indeed could it
fall otherwise? for—

'Grief kills gladness, winter summer, midnight-gloom the light of day,
Kindnesses ingratitude, and pleasant friends drive pain away;
Each ends each, but none of other surer conquerors can be
Than Impolicy of Fortune—of Misfortune Policy.'

I have said to myself, 'My Prince's understanding is affected
—how else would he obscure the moonlight of policy with the
night-vapors of talk;' in such a mood I cannot help him—

'Wisdom answers all who ask her, but a fool she cannot aid;
Blind men in the faithful mirror see not their reflection made.'

And therefore I have been absent.'

'My father!' said the King, joining his palms in respect, 'mine is all the fault! Pardon it, and instruct me how to withdraw my army without further loss.'

Then the Vulture's anger melted, and he reflected—

"Where the Gods are, or thy Gúrú—in the face of Pain and Age,
  Cattle, Brahmans, Kings, and Children—reverently curb thy rage.'

And with a benignant smile, he answered the King thus, ' Be of good heart, my Liege; thou shalt not only bring the host back safely, but thou shalt first destroy the castle of King Silver-sides.'

'How can that be, with my diminished forces?' asked the Rajah.

'It will come to pass!' answered the Vulture. 'Break up to-day for the blockade of the fort.'

Now, when this was reported by the spies to King Silver-sides, he was greatly alarmed. 'Good Goose!' said he, 'what is to be done? Here is the King of the Peacocks at hand, to blockade us—by his Minister's advice, too.'

'Sire,' replied the Goose, 'separate the efficient and the inefficient in your force; and stimulate the loyalty of the first, with a royal bounty of gold and dresses, as each may seem to merit. Now is the time for it—

' Oh, my Prince! on eight occasions prodigality is none—
  In the solemn sacrificing, at the wedding of a son,
  When the glittering treasure given makes the proud invader bleed,
  Or its lustre bringeth comfort to the people in their need,
  Or when kinsmen are to succor, or a worthy work to end,
  Or to do a mistress honor, or to welcome back a friend.'

'But is this expenditure needed?' said the King.

'It is needed, my Liege,' said the Goose, 'and it befits a Monarch; for—

' Truth, munificence, and valor, are the virtues of a King;
  Royalty, devoid of either, sinks to a rejected thing.'

'Let it be incurred then!' replied the King.

At this moment Night-cloud, the Crow, made his appearance. 'Deign me one regard, Sire,' said he, 'the insolent enemy is at our gates; let your Majesty give the word, and I will go forth and show my valor and devotion to your Crown.'

' It were better to keep our cover,' said the Goose. ' Wherefore else builded we this fortalice? Is it not said?—

> ' Hold thy vantage!—alligators on the land make none afraid;
> And the lion's but a jackal that hath left his forest-shade.'

But go, your Majesty, and encourage our warriors." Thereupon they repaired to the Gateway of the Fort, and all day the battle raged there.

It was the morning after, when King Jewel-plume spake thus to his Minister the Vulture—" Good sir, shall thy promise be kept to us?'

' It shall be kept, your Majesty,' replied the Vulture; ' storm the fort!'

' We will storm it!' said the Peacock-king. The sun was not well-risen accordingly when the attack was made, and there arose hot fighting at all the four gates. It was then that the traitorous Crows, headed by their Monarch, Night-cloud, put fire to every dwelling in the citadel, and raised a shout of ' The Fort is taken! it is taken!' At this terrible sound the soldiers of the Swan-king forsook their posts, and plunged into the pool.

Not thus King Silver-sides:—retiring coolly before the foe, with his General the Paddy-bird, he was cut off and encircled by the troopers of King Jewel-plume, under the command of his Marshal, the Cock.

' My General,' said the King, ' thou shalt not perish for me. Fly! I can go no farther. Fly! I bid thee, and take counsel with the Goose that Crest-jewel, my son, be named King!'

' Good my Lord,' replied the Paddy-bird, ' speak not thus! Let your Majesty reign victorious while the sun and moon endure. I am governor of your Majesty's fortress, and if the enemy enter it he shall but do so over my body; let me die for thee, my Master!—

> ' Gentle, generous, and discerning; such a Prince the Gods do give!'

' That shalt thou not,' replied the Rajah—

> ' Skilful, honest, and true-hearted; where doth such a Vassal live?'

' Nay! my royal Lord, escape!' cried the Paddy-bird; a king's life is the life of his people—

> ' The people are the lotus-leaves, their monarch is the sun—
> When he doth sink beneath the waves they vanish every one.

When he doth rise they rise again with bud and blossom rife,
To bask awhile in his warm smile, who is their lord and life.'

' Think no more of me.' At this instant the Cock rushing
forward, inflicted a wound with his sharp spurs on the person
of the King; but the Paddy-bird sprang in front of him, and
receiving on his body the blows designed for the Rajah, forced
him away into the pool.   Then turning upon the Cock, he
despatched him with a shower of blows from his long bill; and
finally succumbed, fighting in the midst of his enemies.   Thus
the King of the Peacocks captured the fortress; and marched
home with all the treasure in it, amid songs of victory.

Then spake the Princes: " In that army of the Swans
there was no soldier like the Paddy-bird, who gave his own
life for the King's."

" There be nowhere many such," replied Vishnu-Sarman;
" for

' All the cows bring forth are cattle—only now and then is born
An authentic lord of pastures, with his shoulder-scratching horn.' [19]

" It is well spoken," said the Princes.

" But for him that dares to die so," added the Sage, " may
an eternal heaven be reserved, and may the lustrous Angels
of Paradise, the Apsaras, conduct him thither! Is it not so
declared, indeed?—

' When the soldier in the battle lays his life down for his king,
Unto Swerga's perfect glory such a deed his soul shall bring.'

" It is so declared," said the Rajah's sons.

" And now, my Princes," concluded Vishnu-Sarman, " you
have listened to ' War.' "

" We have listened, and are gratified," replied the sons of
the King.

" Let me end then," said their Preceptor, " with this—

' If the clouds of Battle lower
When ye come into your power,
Durga grant the foes that dare you
Bring no elephants to scare you;
Nor the thunderous rush of horses,
Nor the footmen's steel-fringed forces:
But overblown by Policy's strong breath,
Hide they in caverns from the avenging death.'

[19] Large branching horns which reach backward and rub upon his shoulders.

PEACE

WHEN the time came for resuming instruction, the King's sons said to Vishnu-Sarman, "Master, we have heard of War, we would now learn somewhat of the treaties which follow war." "It is well asked," replied the Sage; "listen therefore to 'Peace,' which hath this commencement—

> 'When those great Kings their weary war did cease,
> The Vulture and the Goose concluded Peace.'

'How came that?' asked the Princes.
Vishnu-Sarman related:—

The Treaty Between the Peacocks and the Swans

"So soon as King Jewel-plume had retreated, the first care of King Silver-sides was the discovery of the treason that had cost him the fort.

'Goose,' he said to his Minister, 'who put the fire to our citadel, think you? Was it an enemy or an inmate?'

'Sire,' replied the Goose, 'Night-cloud and his followers are nowhere to be seen—it must needs be his work.'

'It must needs be,' sighed the King, after a pause; 'but what ill-fortune!'

'If it please your Majesty, no,' replied the Minister; 'it is written—

> "'Tis the fool who, meeting trouble, straightway destiny reviles;
> Knowing not his own misdoing brought his own mischance the whiles."

You have forgotten the saying—

> 'Who listens not, when true friends counsel well,
> Must fall, as once the foolish Tortoise fell.'

'I never heard it,' said the King. 'How was that?' The Goose related—

71

The Story of the Tortoise and the Geese

"There is a pool in South Behar called the 'Pool of the Blue Lotus,' and two Geese had for a long time lived there. They had a friend in the pool who was a Tortoise, and he was known as 'Shelly-neck.' It chanced one evening that the Tortoise overheard some fishermen talking by the water. 'We will stop here to-night,' they said, 'and in the morning we will catch the fish, the tortoises, and such like.' Extremely alarmed at this, the Tortoise repaired to his friends the Geese, and reported the conversation.

'What ever am I to do, Gossips?' he asked.

'The first thing is to be assured of the danger,' said the Geese.

'I am assured,' exclaimed the Tortoise; 'the first thing is to avoid it: don't you know?—

'Time-not-come' and 'Quick-at-peril,' these two fishes 'scaped the net;
'What-will-be-will-be,' he perished, by the fishermen beset.'

'No,' said the Geese, 'how was it?' Shelly-neck related:—

The Story of Fate and the Three Fishes

"It was just such a pool as this, and on the arrival at it of just such men as these fishermen, that three fishes, who had heard their designs, held consultation as to what should be done.

'I shall go to another water,' said "Time-not-come," and away he went.

'Why should we leave unless obliged?' asked "Quick-at-peril." 'When the thing befalls I shall do the best I can—

'Who deals with bad dilemmas well, is wise.
The merchant's wife, with womanly device,
Kissed—and denied the kiss—under his eyes.'

'How was that?' asked the other fish. Quick-at-peril related:—

The Story of the Unabashed Wife

" There was a trader in Vikrama-poora, who had a very beautiful wife, and her name was Jewel-bright. The lady was as unfaithful as she was fair, and had chosen for her last lover one of the household servants. Ah! woman-kind!—

> ' Sex, that tires of being true,
> Base and new is brave to you!
> Like the jungle-cows ye range,
> Changing food for sake of change.'

Now it befell one day that as Jewel-bright was bestowing a kiss on the mouth of the servant, she was surprised by her husband; and seeing him she ran up hastily and said, ' My lord, here is an impudent varlet! he eats the camphor which I procured for you; I was actually smelling it on his lips as you entered.' The servant catching her meaning, affected offence. ' How can a man stay in a house where the mistress is always smelling one's lips for a little camphor?' he said; and thereat he was for going off, and was only constrained by the good man to stay, after much entreaty. ' Therefore,' said Quick-at-peril, ' I mean to abide here, and make the best I can of what befalls, as she did.'

' Yes, yes,' said What-will-be-will-be, ' we all know

> ' That which will not be will not be, and what is to be will be:—
> Why not drink this easy physic, antidote of misery?'

' When the morning came, the net was thrown, and both the fishes inclosed. Quick-at-peril, on being drawn up, feigned himself dead; and upon the fisherman's laying him aside, he leaped off again into the water. As to What-will-be-will-be, he was seized and forthwith dispatched.—And that,' concluded the Tortoise, ' is why I wish to devise some plan of escape.'

' It might be compassed if you could go elsewhere,' said the Geese, ' but how can you get across the ground?'

' Can't you take me through the air?' asked the Tortoise.

' Impossible!' said the Geese.

' Not at all!' replied the Tortoise; ' you shall hold a stick across in your bills, and I will hang on to it by my mouth— and thus you can readily convey me.'

' It is feasible,' observed the Geese, ' but remember,

'Wise men their plans revolve, lest ill befall;
The Herons gained a friend, and so, lost all.'

'How came that about?' asked the Tortoise. The Geese related:—

The Story of the Herons and the Mongoose

"Among the mountains of the north there is one named Eagle-cliff, and near it, upon a fig-tree, a flock of Herons had their residence. At the foot of the tree, in a hollow, there lived a serpent; and he was constantly devouring the nestlings of the Herons. Loud were the complaints of the parent birds, until an old Heron thus advised them:—'You should bring some fishes from the pool, and lay them one by one in a line from the hole of yonder Mongoose to the hollow where the Serpent lives. The Mongoose will find him when it comes after the fish, and if it finds him it will kill him.' The advice seemed good, and was acted upon; but in killing the Snake the Mongoose overheard the cry of the young Herons; and climbing the tree daily, he devoured all that the Snake had left. Therefore,' concluded the Geese, 'do we bid you look well into your plan: if you should open your mouth, for instance, as we carry you, you will drop and be killed.'

'Am I a fool,' cried the Tortoise, 'to open my mouth? Not I! Come now, convey me!'

'Thereupon the Geese took up the stick; the Tortoise held fast with his mouth, and away they flew. The country people, observing this strange sight, ran after.

'Ho! ho!' cried one, 'look at the flying Tortoise!'

'When he falls we'll cook and eat him here,' said another.

'No; let us take him home for dinner!' cried a third.

'We can light a fire by the pool, and eat him,' said the first.

'The Tortoise heard these unkind remarks in a towering passion. 'Eat me!—eat ashes!' he exclaimed, opening his mouth—and down he fell directly, and was caught by the countrymen.—Said I not well,' concluded the Goose-Minister, 'that to scorn counsel is to seek destruction?'

'You have well said,' replied King Silver-sides, disconsolately.

'Yes, your Majesty,' interposed the Crane, who was just returned, ' if the Fort had been cleared, Night-cloud could not have fired it, as he did, by the Vulture's instigation.'

' We see it all,' sighed the King, ' but too late ! '

> ' Whoso trusts, for service rendered, or fair words, an enemy,
> Wakes from folly like one falling in his slumber from a tree.'

' I witnessed Night-cloud's reception,' continued the Crane. ' King Jewel-plume showed him great favor, and was for anointing him Rajah of Camphor-island.'

' Hear you that, my Liege?' asked the Goose.

' Go on; I hear ! ' said Silver-sides.

' To that the Vulture demurred,' continued the Crane:— ' " favor to low persons," he said, " was like writing on the sea-sand. To set the base-born in the seat of the great was long ago declared impolitic—

> ' Give mean men power, and give thy throat to the knife;
> The Mouse, made Tiger, sought his master's life.'

' How was that?' asked King Jewel-plume. The Vulture related—

The Story of the Recluse and the Mouse

" In the forest of the Sage Gautama there dwelt a Recluse named Mighty-at-Prayer. Once, as he sat at his frugal meal, a young mouse dropped beside him from the beak of a crow, and he took it up and fed it tenderly with rice grains. Some time after the Saint observed a cat pursuing his dependent to devour it, whereupon he changed the mouse into a stout cat. The cat was a great deal harassed by dogs, upon which the Saint again transformed it into a dog. The dog was always in danger of the tigers, and his protector at last gave him the form of a tiger—considering him all this while, and treating him withal, like nothing but a mouse. The country-folk passing by would say, ' That a tiger ! not he; it is a mouse the Saint has transformed.' And the mouse being vexed at this, reflected, ' So long as the Master lives, this shameful story of my origin will survive ! ' With this thought he was about to take the Saint's life, when he, who knew his purpose, turned the ungrateful beast by a word to his original shape. Besides,

your Majesty," continued the Vulture, " it may not be so easy
to take in Camphor-island—

> ' Many fine fishes did the old Crane kill,
> But the Crab matched him, maugre all his bill.'

' How came that to pass?' asked Jewel-plume.
' The Vulture related:—

The Story of the Crane and the Crab

" There was an old Crane at a mere called Lily-water, in
Malwa, who stood one day in the shallows with a most dejected
look and drooping bill. A Crab observed him and called out,
' Friend Crane! have you given up eating, that you stand
there all day?' ' Nay, sir!' replied the old Crane; ' I love my
dish of fish, but I have heard the fishermen say that they mean
to capture every one that swims in this water; and as that destroys my hope of subsistence, I am resigning myself to death.'
All this the fishes overheard. ' In this matter certainly,' they
said, ' his interest is ours; we ought to consult him; for it
is written—

> ' Fellow be with kindly foemen, rather than with friends unkind;
> Friend and foeman are distinguished not by title but by mind.'

Thereupon they repaired to him: ' Good Crane,' they said,
' what course is there for safety?'
' Course of safety there is,' replied the Crane, ' to go elsewhere; and I will carry you one by one to another pool, if you
please.'
' Do so,' said the trembling fishes.
" The Crane accordingly took one after another, and having
eaten them returned with the report that he had safely deposited each. Last of all, the Crab requested to be taken; and
the Crane, coveting his tender flesh, took him up with great
apparent respect. On arriving at the spot, which was covered
with fish-bones, the Crab perceived the fate reserved for him;
and turning round he fastened upon the Crane's throat and tore
it so that he perished.'
' Well, but,' said King Jewel-plume, ' we can make Night-
cloud viceroy here, to send over to Vindhya all the productions
of Camphor-isle!'

' Then the Vulture Far-sight laughed a low laugh and said—

' Who, ere he makes a gain has spent it,
Like the pot-breaker will repent it.'

' What was that?' asked the King. Far-sight related:—

The Story of the Brahman and the Pans

" There was a Brahman in the city of Vána, whose name was
Deva Sarman. At the equinoctial feast of the Dussera, he obtained for his duxina-gift a dish of flour, which he took into
a potter's shed; and there lay down in the shade among the
pots, staff in hand. As he thus reclined he began to meditate,
' I can sell this meal for ten cowrie-shells, and with them I can
purchase some of these pots and sell them at an advance. With
all that money I shall invest in betel-nuts and body-cloths and
make a new profit by their sale; and so go on trafficking till
I get a lakh of rupees—what's to prevent me? Then I shall
marry four wives—and one at least will be beautiful and young,
and she shall be my favorite. Of course the others will be
jealous; but if they quarrel, and talk, and trouble me I will
belabor them like this—and this '—and therewith he flourished
his staff to such a purpose as to smash his meal-dish and break
several of the potter's jars. The potter, rushing out, took him
by the throat, and turned him off; and so ended his specula-
tions. I smiled, my Liege,' concluded the Vulture, ' at your
precipitancy, thinking of that story.'

' Tell me, then, my Father, what should be done,' said the
King.

' Tell me first, your Majesty, what took the fortress:
strength or stratagem?'

' It was a device of yours,' said the King.

' It is well,' replied the Minister, ' and my counsel now is
to return before the rainy season, while we can return; and
to make peace. We have won renown and taken the enemy's
stronghold; let it suffice. I speak as a faithful adviser; and
it is written—

' Whoso setting duty highest, speaks at need unwelcome things,
Disregarding fear and favor, such a one may succor kings.'

Oh, my Liege! war is uncertain! Nay, it may ruin victor and
vanquished—

> ' Sunda the strong, and giant Upasunda,
> Contending, like the lightning and the thunder,
> Slew each the other. Learn, the while you wonder.'

' Tell me that,' said the King of the Peacocks.
' The Vulture related—

The Duel of the Giants

" Long ago, my Liege, there were two Daityas named Sunda
and Upasunda, the which with penance and fasting worshipped
that God who wears the moon for his forehead-jewel; desiring to win his favor, and thereby the lordship of the Three
Worlds. At last the God, propitiated by their devotion, spake
thus unto them :—
' I grant a boon unto ye—choose what it shall be.'
' And they, who would have asked dominion, were suddenly
minded of Saraswati—who reigns over the hearts and thoughts
of men—to seek a forbidden thing.
' If,' said they, ' we have found favor, let the Divinity give
us his own cherished Parvati, the Queen of Heaven!'
' Terribly incensed was the God, but his word had passed,
and the boon must be granted; and Parvati the Divine was delivered up to them. Then those two world-breakers, sick at
heart, sin-blinded, and afire with the glorious beauty of the
Queen of Life—began to dispute, saying one to another: ' Mine
is she! mine is she!' At the last they called for an umpire,
and the God himself appeared before them as a venerable
Brahman.
' Master,' said they, ' tell us whose she is, for we both won
her by our might.'
' Then spake that Brahman :—

> ' Brahmans for their lore have honor; Kshattriyas for their bravery;
> Vaisyas for their hard-earned treasure; Sudras for humility.'

Ye are Kshattriyas—and it is yours to fight; settle, then, this
question by the sword.'
' Thereupon they agreed that he spoke wisely, and drew and
battled; and being of equal force, they fell at the same mo-

ment by an exchange of blows. Good my Lord,' concluded
the Minister, ' peace is a better thing than war.'

' But why not say so before?' asked Jewel-plume.

' I said it at the first,' replied the Minister. ' I knew King
Silver-sides for a just King, upon whom it was ill to wage
battle. How say the Scriptures?—

' Seven foemen of all foemen, very hard to vanquish be:
 The Truth-teller, the Just-dweller, and the man from passion free,
 Subtle, self-sustained, and counting frequent well-won victories,
 And the man of many kinsmen—keep the peace with such as these.'

The Swan-king has friends and kinsmen, my Liege:—

 ' And the man with many kinsmen answers with them all attacks;
 As the bambu, in the bambus safely sheltered, scorns the axe.'

' My counsel then is that peace be concluded with him,' said
the Vulture.

' All this King Silver-sides and his Minister the Goose heard
attentively from the Crane.

' Go again!' said the Goose to Long-bill, ' and bring us news
of how the Vulture's advice is received.'

' Minister!' began the King, upon the departure of the
Crane, ' tell me as to this peace, who are they with whom it
should not be concluded?'

' They be twenty, namely——'

' Tarry not to name them,' said the King; ' and what be the
qualities of a good ally?'

' Such should be learned in Peace and War,' replied the
Goose, ' in marching and pitching, and seasonably placing an
army in the field; for it is said—

 ' He who sets his battle wisely, conquers the unwary foe;
 As the Owl, awaiting night-time, slew the overweening Crow.'

Counsel, my Liege, is quintuple—Commencing, providing, di-
viding, repelling, and completing.'

' Good!' said the King.

' Power is triple,' continued the Goose, ' being of Kings, of
counsels, and of constant effort.'

' It is so!' said the King.

' And expedients, my Liege,' continued the Goose, ' are quadruple, and consist of conciliation, of gifts, of strife-stirring, and of force of arms; for thus it is written—

> 'Whoso hath the gift of giving wisely, equitably, well;
> Whoso, learning all men's secrets, unto none his own will tell;
> Whoso, ever cold and courtly, utters nothing that offends,
> Such a one may rule his fellows unto Earth's extremest ends.'

'Then King Jewel-plume would be a good ally,' observed the Swan-king.

'Doubtless!' said the Goose, 'but elated with victory, he will hardly listen to the Vulture's counsel; we must make him do it.'

'How?' asked the King.

'We will cause our dependent, the King of Ceylon, Strong-bill the Stork, to raise an insurrection in Jambudwipa.'

'It is well-conceived,' said the King. And forthwith a Crane, named Pied-body, was dismissed with a secret message to that Rajah.

'In course of time the first Crane, who had been sent as a spy, came back, and made his report. He related that the Vulture had advised his Sovereign to summon Night-cloud, the Crow, and learn from him regarding King Silver-sides' intentions. Night-cloud attended accordingly.

'Crow!' asked King Jewel-plume, 'what sort of a Monarch is the Rajah Silver-sides?'

'Truthful, may it please you,' replied the Crow; 'and therewithal noble as Yudisthira himself.'

'And his Minister, the Goose?'

'Is a Minister unrivalled, my Liege,' said the Crow-king.

'But how then didst thou so easily deceive them?'

'Ah! your Majesty,' said the Crow, 'there was little credit in that. Is it not said?—

> 'Cheating them that truly trust you, 'tis a clumsy villainy!
> Any knave may slay the child who climbs and slumbers on his knee.'

Besides, the Minister detected me immediately. It was the King whose innate goodness forbade him to suspect evil in another:—

> 'Believe a knave, thyself scorning a lie,
> And rue it, like the Brahman, by and by.'

'What Brahman was that?' asked the King. Night-cloud replied:—

The Story of the Brahman and the Goat

"A Brahman that lived in the forest of Gautama, your Majesty. He had purveyed a goat to make pooja, and was returning home with it on his shoulder when he was descried by three knaves. 'If we could but obtain that goat,' said they, 'it would be a rare trick'; and they ran on, and seated themselves at the foot of three different trees upon the Brahman's road. Presently he came up with the first of them, who addressed him thus: 'Master! why do you carry that dog on your shoulder?' 'Dog!' said the Brahman, 'it is a goat for sacrifice!' With that he went on a coss, and came to the second knave; who called out—'What doest thou with that dog, Master?' The Brahman laid his goat upon the ground, looked it all over, took it up again upon his back, and walked on with his mind in a whirl; for—

'The good think evil slowly, and they pay
A price for faith—as witness "Crop-ear" may.'

'Who was Crop-ear?' asked the King of the Peacocks.

The Story of the Camel, the Lion, and His Court

"A Camel, may it please you," replied Night-cloud, "who strayed away from a kafila, and wandered into the forest. A Lion, named 'Fierce-fangs,' lived in that forest; and his three courtiers, a Tiger, a Jackal, and a Crow, met the Camel, and conducted him to their King. His account of himself was satisfactory, and the Lion took him into his service under the name of Crop-ear. Now it happened that the rainy season was very severe, and the Lion became indisposed, so that there was much difficulty in obtaining food for the Court. The courtiers resolved accordingly to prevail on the Lion to kill the Camel; 'for what interest have we,' they said, 'in this browser of thistles?'

'What, indeed!' observed the Tiger; 'but will the Rajah kill him after his promise of protection, think you?'

Vol. III.—6

' Being famished he will,' said the Crow. ' Know you not?—

' Hunger hears not, cares not, spares not; no boon of the starving beg;
   When the snake is pinched with craving, verily she eats her egg.'

Accordingly they repaired to the Lion.

' Hast brought me food, fellow?' growled the Rajah.

' None, may it please you,' said the Crow.

' Must we starve, then?' asked his Majesty.

' Not unless you reject the food before you, Sire,' rejoined
the Crow.

' Before me! how mean you?'

' I mean,' replied the Crow (and he whispered it in the
Lion's ear), ' Crop-ear, the Camel!'

' Now!' said the Lion, and he touched the ground, and afterwards both ears, as he spoke, ' I have given him my pledge
for his safety, and how should I slay him?'

' Nay, Sire! I said not slay,' replied the Crow; ' it may be
that he will offer himself for food. To that your Majesty
would not object?'

' I am parlous hungry,' muttered the Lion.

' Then the Crow went to find the Camel, and, bringing all
together before the King under some pretence or other, he thus
addressed him:—

' Sire! our pains are come to nothing: we can get no food,
and we behold our Lord falling away,

> ' Of the Tree of State the root
> Kings are—feed what brings the fruit.'

Take me, therefore, your Majesty, and break your fast upon
me."

' Good Crow,' said the Lion, ' I had liefer die than do so.'

' Will your Majesty deign to make a repast upon me?' asked
the Jackal.

' On no account!' replied the Lion.

' Condescend, my Lord,' said the Tiger, ' to appease your
hunger with my poor flesh.'

' Impossible!' responded the Lion.

' Thereupon Crop-ear, not to be behind in what seemed safe,
made offer of his own carcase, which was accepted before he
had finished; the Tiger instantly tearing his flank open, and
all the rest at once devouring him.

' The Brahman,' continued Night-cloud, ' suspected nothing more than did the Camel; and when the third knave had broken his jest upon him for bearing a dog, he threw it down, washed himself clean of the contamination, and went home; while the knaves secured and cooked his goat.'

' But, Night-cloud,' asked the Rajah, ' how couldst thou abide so long among enemies, and conciliate them?'

' It is easy to play the courtier for a purpose,' said Night-cloud—

' Courtesy may cover malice; on their heads the woodmen bring,
  Meaning all the while to burn them, logs and fagots—oh, my King!
  And the strong and subtle river, rippling at the cedar's foot,
  While it seems to lave and kiss it, undermines the hanging root.'

Indeed, it has been said—

> ' A wise man for an object's sake
> His foe upon his back will take,
> As with the Frogs once did the Snake.'

' How was that?' asked the Peacock-King. The Crow related:—

The Story of the Frogs and the Old Serpent

" In a deserted garden there once lived a Serpent, ' Slow-coil' by name; who had reached an age when he was no longer able to obtain his own food. Lying listlessly by the edge of a pond, he was descried by a certain Frog, and interrogated—

' Have you given up caring for food, Serpent?'

' Leave me, kindly Sir,' replied the subtle reptile; ' the griefs of a miserable wretch like me cannot interest your lofty mind.'

' Let me at least hear them,' said the Frog, somewhat flattered.

' You must know, then, gracious Sir,' began the Serpent, ' that it is now twenty years since here, in Brahmapoora, I bit the son of Kaundinya, a holy Brahman; of which cruel bite he died. Seeing his boy dead, Kaundinya abandoned himself to despair, and grovelled in his distress upon the ground. Thereat came all his kinsmen, citizens of Brahmapoora, and sat down with him, as the manner is—

' He who shares his brother's portion, be he beggar, be he lord,
  Comes as truly, comes as duly, to the battle as the board;

Stands before the King to succor, follows to the pile to sigh;
He is friend and he is kinsman—less would make the name a lie.'

Then spoke a twice-passed Brahman,[20] Kapila by name, 'O
Kaundinya! thou dost forget thyself to lament thus. Hear
what is written—

'Weep not! Life the hired nurse is, holding us a little space;
Death, the mother who doth take us back into our proper place.'

'Gone, with all their gauds and glories: gone, like peasants, are the
    Kings,
Whereunto the world is witness, whereof all hei record rings.'

What, indeed, my friend, is this mortal frame, that we should
set store by it?—

'For the body, daily wasting, is not seen to waste away,
Until wasted, as in water set a jar of unbaked clay.'

'And day after day man goeth near and nearer to his fate,
As step after step the victim thither where its slayers wait.'

Friends and kinsmen—they must all be surrendered! Is it
not said—

'Like as a plank of drift-wood
    Tossed on the watery main,
Another plank encountered,
    Meets—touches—parts again;
So tossed, and drifting ever,
    On life's unresting sea,
Men meet, and greet, and sever,
    Parting eternally.'

Thou knowest these things, let thy wisdom chide thy sorrow,
saying—

'Halt, traveller! rest i' the shade: then up and leave it!
Stay, Soul! take fill of love; nor losing, grieve it!'

But in sooth a wise man would better avoid love; for—

'Each beloved object born
Sets within the heart a thorn,
Bleeding, when they be uptorn.'

[20] A young Brahman, being invested with the sacred thread, and having concluded his studies, becomes of the second order: a householder.

And it is well asked—

> 'When thine own house, this rotting frame, doth wither,
> Thinking another's lasting—goest thou thither?'

What will be, will be; and who knows not—

> 'Meeting makes a parting sure,
> Life is nothing but death's door.'

For truly—

> 'As the downward-running rivers never turn and never stay,
> So the days and nights stream deathward, bearing human lives away.'

And though it be objected that—

> 'Bethinking him of darkness grim, and death's unshunnèd pain,
> A man strong-souled relaxes hold, like leather soaked in rain.'

Yet is this none the less assured, that—

> 'From the day, the hour, the minute,
> Each life quickens in the womb;
> Thence its march, no falter in it,
> Goes straight forward to the tomb.'

Form, good friend, a true idea of mundane matters; and bethink thee that regret is after all but an illusion, an ignorance—

> 'An 'twere not so, would sorrow cease with years?
> Wisdom sees aright what want of knowledge fears.'

'Kaundinya listened to all this with the air of a dreamer. Then rising up he said, 'Enough! the house is hell to me—I will betake me to the forest.'

'Will that stead you?' asked Kapila; 'nay—

> 'Seek not the wild, sad heart! thy passions haunt it;
> Play hermit in thine house with heart undaunted;
> A governed heart, thinking no thought but good,
> Makes crowded houses holy solitude.'

To be master of one's self—to eat only to prolong life—to yield to love no more than may suffice to perpetuate a family —and never to speak but in the cause of truth, this,' said Kapila, 'is armor against grief. What wouldst thou with a hermit's life—prayer and purification from sorrow and sin in holy streams? Hear this!—

> ' Away with those that preach to us the washing off of sin—
> Thine own self is the stream for thee to make ablutions in:
> In self-restraint it rises pure—flows clear in tide of truth,
> By widening banks of wisdom, in waves of peace and ruth.
> Bathe there, thou son of Pandu! with reverence and rite,
> For never yet was water wet could wash the spirit white.'

Resign thyself to loss. Pain exists absolutely. Ease, what is it but a minute's alleviation?'

' It is nothing else,' said Kaundinya: ' I will resign myself!' Thereupon,' the Serpent continued, ' he cursed me with the curse that I should be a carrier of frogs, and so retired—and here remain I to do according to the Brahman's malediction.'

' The Frog, hearing all this, went and reported it to Web-foot the Frog-King, who shortly came himself for an excursion on the Serpent. He was carried delightfully, and constantly employed the conveyance. But one day observing the Serpent to be sluggish, he asked the reason.

' May it please you,' explained the Serpent, 'your slave has nothing to eat.'

' Eat a few of my frogs,' said the King. ' I give you leave.'

' I thank your Majesty!' answered the Serpent, and forthwith he began to eat the frogs, until the pond becoming clear, he finished with their monarch himself. ' I also,' said Night-cloud, ' stooped to conquer, but King Silver-sides is a good King, and I would your Majesty were at peace with him.'

' Peace!' cried King Jewel-plume, ' shall I make peace with my vassal! I have vanquished him—let him serve me!'

" At this moment the Parrot came in. ' Sire!' said he, breathlessly, ' the Stork Strong-bill, Rajah of Ceylon, has raised the standard of revolt in Jambudwipa, and claims the country.'

' What! what!' cried the King in a fury.

' Excellent good, Goose!' muttered the Minister. ' This is thy work!'

' Bid him but await me!' exclaimed the King, ' and I will tear him up like a tree!'

' Ah, Sire,' said the Minister—

> ' Thunder for nothing, like December's cloud,
> Passes unmarked: strike hard, but speak not loud.'

We cannot march without making peace first; our rear will be attacked.'

' Must it be so?' asked the King.

' My Liege, it must,' replied the Vulture.

' Make a peace then,' said the King, ' and make an end.'

' It is well,' observed the Minister, and set out for the Court of the King Silver-sides. While he was yet coming, the Crane announced his approach.

' Ah!' said the Swan-King, ' this will be another designing spy from the enemy.'

' Misdoubt him not!' answered the Goose, smiling, ' it is the Vulture Far-sight, a spirit beyond suspicion. Would your Majesty be as the Swan that took the stars reflected in the pool for lily-buds, and being deceived, would eat no lily-shoots by day, thinking them stars?'

' Not so! but treachery breeds mistrust,' replied the Rajah; is it not written—

' Minds deceived by evil natures, from the good their faith withhold;
  When hot conjee once has burned them, children blow upon the cold.'

' It is so written, my Liege,' said the Minister. ' But this one may be trusted. Let him be received with compliments and a gift.'

' Accordingly the Vulture was conducted, with the most profound respect, from the fort to the King's audience-hall, where a throne was placed for him.

' Minister,' said the Goose, ' consider us and ours at thy disposal.'

' So consider us,' assented the Swan-King.

' I thank you,' said Far-sight; ' but—

> ' With a gift the miser meet;
> Proud men by obeisance greet;
> Women's silly fancies soothe;
> Give wise men their due—the truth.'

' I am come to conclude a peace, not to claim your kingdom. By what mode shall we conclude it?'

' How many modes be there?' asked King Silver-sides.

' Sixteen,' replied the Vulture.

' Are the alliances numbered therein?' asked the King.

'No! these be four,' answered the Vulture, 'namely—of mutual help—of friendship—of blood—and of sacrifice.'

'You are a great diplomatist!' said the King. 'Advise us which to choose!'

'There is no Peace like the Golden "Sangata," which is made between good men, based on friendly feeling, and preceded by the Oath of Truth,' replied the Vulture.

'Let us make that Peace!' said the Goose. Far-sight accordingly, with fresh presents of robes and jewels, accompanied the Goose to the camp of the Peacock-King. The Rajah, Jewel-plume, gave the Goose a gracious audience, accepted his terms of Peace, and sent him back to the Swan-King, loaded with gifts and kind speeches. The revolt in Jambudwipa was suppressed, and the Peacock-King retired to his own kingdom.

"And now," said Vishnu-Sarman, "I have told your Royal Highnesses all. Is there anything remaining to be told?"

"Reverend Sir!" replied the Princes, "there is nothing. Thanks to you, we have heard and comprehended the perfect cycle of kingly duty, and are content."

"There remains but this, then," said their Preceptor:—

> 'Peace and Plenty, all fair things,
> Grace the realm where ye reign Kings;
> Grief and loss come not anigh you,
> Glory guide and magnify you;
> Wisdom keep your statesmen still
> Clinging fast, in good or ill,
> Clinging, like a bride new-wed,
> Unto lips, 'and breast, and head:
> And day by day, that these 'fair things befall,
> The Lady Lukshmi give her grace to all.'

CHOICE EXAMPLES OF ORIENTAL PRINTING AND ENGRAVING.

THE MIRACLE OF THE ELEPHANT.

Fac-simile of an old Chinese print.

In this characteristic Chinese picture the child Buddha is represented in the act of throwing an elephant over seven fences. An annotator to Fà-hien's "Travels" alludes to the incident in these words: "Nanda, coming that way, saw the carcass [of the elephant] lying in the road, and pulled it to one side; but the Bodhisattva [Buddha], seeing it there, took it by the tail, and tossed it over seven fences and ditches, when the force of its fall made a great ditch."

NALA AND DAMAYANTI

[*Selected from the "Mahâbhârata." Translation by Sir Edwin Arnold*]

INTRODUCTION

THE "Mahâbhârata" is the oldest epic in Sanscrit literature, and is sevenfold greater in bulk than the "Iliad" and "Odyssey" taken together. This remarkable poem contains almost all the history of ancient India, so far as it can be recovered, together with inexhaustible details of its political, social, and religious life—in fact, the antique Hindoo world stands epitomized in it. The Old Testament is not more interwoven with the Jewish race, nor the New Testament with the civilization of Christendom, nor even the Koran with the records and destinies of Islam, than is this great Sanscrit poem with the unchanging and teeming population of Hindostan. The stories, songs, and ballads, the genealogies, the nursery tales and religious discourses, the art, the learning, the philosophy, the creeds, the modes of thought, the very phrases and daily ideas of the Hindoo people are taken from this poem. Their children are named after its heroes; so are their cities, streets, and even cattle. It is the spiritual life of the Hindoo people. It is personified, worshipped, and cited as being something divine. To read, or even to listen, is to the devout Hindoo sufficiently meritorious to bring prosperity to the fireside in this world, and happiness in the world to come.

The western world has as yet only received the "Mahâbhârata" in fragments—mere specimens, bearing to those vast treasures of Sanscrit literature such small proportion as cabinet samples of ore have to the riches of a mine. Such knowledge as we have of the great Indian epics is largely due to Sir William Jones, and the host of translators who followed him.

In its present shape the "Mahâbhârata" contains some two hundred thousand verses. The style is forcible, often terse and nervous: the action is well sustained, and the whole effect produced is that of a poem written in commemoration of actual

91

conflict between members of rival clans who lived somewhere southeast of the Punjab. In portrayal of character the Hindoo poem somewhat resembles its Grecian counterpart—the "Iliad"; the noble devotion and chivalric character of its chief hero, Arjuna, reminds us of Hector—and the wily, sinful, Duryodhana, is a second Ulysses. The "Mahâbhârata" was probably begun in the third or fourth century B.C., and completed soon after the beginning of the Christian era.

The "Bhârata" war is a war between rival cousins of the house of Bhârata, a race of heroes mentioned in the Rig-veda collection. Duryodhana deprives his cousin Yudhisthira of his throne by inducing him to squander his fortune, kingdom, family, and self—and then banishes Yudhisthira and the latter's four brothers for twelve years. The gambling was conducted in an unfair manner, and the cousins feel that their banishment was the result of treachery, although pretended to be mercy in lieu of death. When the twelve years are over they collect armies of sympathizers, and on the Sacred Plain of the Kurus (the Holy Land of India) the great war is fought out. The good prevails, Duryodhana is slain, and Yudhisthira recovers his kingdom. This story is told so graphically that the "Mahâbhârata" still has the charm that comes from plot and action, as well as that of poetic beauty.

A concluding passage of this great poem says: "The reading of this ' Mahâbhârata ' destroys all sin and produces virtue, so much so that the pronunciation of a single shloka is sufficient to wipe away much guilt. It has bound human beings in a chain, of which one end is life and the other death. If a man reads the ' Mahâbhârata ' and has faith in its doctrines, he is free from all sin and ascends to heaven after his death."

The present selection is the episode of Nala and Damayanti. It is one of the most charming of the "Mahâbhârata" stories, and its Oriental flavor and delicacy have been well preserved by the translator, Sir Edwin Arnold.

L. F. C.

THE MAHÂBHÂRATA

NALA AND DAMAYANTI

Part I

A PRINCE there was, named Nala, Virasen's noble breed,
Goodly to see, and virtuous; a tamer of the steed;
    As Indra 'midst the gods, so he of kings was kingliest
      one,
Sovereign of men, and splendid as the golden, glittering sun;
Pure, knowing scripture, gallant; ruling nobly Nishadh's
    lands;
Dice-loving, but a proud, true chief of her embattled bands;
By lovely ladies lauded; free, trained in self-control;
A shield and bow; a Manu on earth; a royal soul!
And in Vidarbha's city the Raja Bhima dwelled;
Save offspring, from his perfect bliss no blessing was withheld;
For offspring, many a pious rite full patiently he wrought,
Till Damana the Brahman unto his house was brought.
Him Bhima, ever reverent, did courteously entreat,
Within the Queen's pavilion led him, to rest and eat;
Whereby that sage, grown grateful, gave her—for joy of joys—
A girl, the gem of girlhood, and three brave lusty boys—
Damana, Dama, Dânta, their names:—Damayanti she;
No daughter more delightful, no sons could goodlier be.
Stately and bright and beautiful did Damayanti grow;
No land there was which did not the Slender-waisted know;
A hundred slaves her fair form decked with robe and orna-
    ment—
Like Sachi's self to serve her a hundred virgins bent;
And 'midst them Bhima's daughter, in peerless glory dight,
Gleamed as the lightning glitters against the murk of night;
Having the eyes of Lakshmi, long-lidded, black, and bright—

Nay—never Gods, nor Yakshas, nor mortal men among
Was one so rare and radiant e'er seen, or sued, or sung
As she, the heart-consuming, in heaven itself desired.
And Nala, too, of princes the Tiger-Prince, admired
Like Kama was; in beauty an embodied lord of love:
And ofttimes Nala praised they all other chiefs above
In Damayanti's hearing; and oftentimes to him,
With worship and with wonder, her beauty they would limn;
So that, unmet, unknowing, unseen, in each for each
A tender thought of longing grew up from seed of speech;
And love (thou son of Kunti!) those gentle hearts did reach.

  Thus Nala—hardly bearing in his heart
Such longing—wandered in his palace-woods,
And marked some water-birds, with painted plumes,
Disporting.   One, by stealthy steps, he seized;
But the sky-traveller spake to Nala this:—
" Kill me not, Prince, and I will serve thee well.
For I, in Damayanti's ear, will say
Such good of Nishadh's lord, that nevermore
Shall thought of man possess her, save of thee."

  Thereat the Prince gladly gave liberty
To his soft prisoner, and all the swans
Flew, clanging, to Vidarbha—a bright flock—
Straight to Vidarbha, where the Princess walked;
And there, beneath her eyes, those wingèd ones
Lighted.   She saw them sail to earth, and marked—
Sitting amid her maids—their graceful forms;
While those for wantonness 'gan chase the swans,
Which fluttered this and that way through the grove:
Each girl with tripping feet her bird pursued,
And Damayanti, laughing, followed hers;
Till—at the point to grasp—the flying prey
Deftly eluding touch, spake as men speak,
Addressing Bhima's daughter:—
                              " Lady dear!

Loveliest Damayanti! Nala dwells
In near Nishadha: oh, a noble Prince,
Not to be matched of men; an Aswin he,
For goodliness.   Incomparable maid!
Wert thou but wife to that surpassing chief,
Rich would the fruit grow from such lordly birth,

Such peerless beauty.   Slender-waisted one,
Gods, men, and Gandharvas have we beheld,
But never none among them like to him.
As thou art pearl of princesses, so he
Is crown of princes; happy would it fall,
One such perfection should another wed."
    And when she heard that bird (O King of men!)
The Princess answered: " Go, dear swan, and tell
This same to Nala; " and the egg-born said,
" I go "—and flew; and told the Prince of all.
    But Damayanti, having heard the bird,
Lived fancy-free no more; by Nala's side
Her soul dwelt, while she sat at home distraught,
Mournful and wan, sighing the hours away,
With eyes upcast, and passion-laden looks;
So that, eftsoons, her limbs failed, and her mind—
With love o'erweighted—found no rest in sleep,
No grace in company, no joy at feasts.
Nor night nor day brought peace; always she heaved
Sigh upon sigh, till all her maidens knew—
By glance and mien and moan—how changed she was,
Her own sweet self no more.   Then to the King
They told how Damayanti loved the Prince.
Which thing when Bhima from her maidens heard,
Deep pondering for his child what should be done,
And why the Princess was beside herself,
That lord of lands perceived his daughter grown,
And knew that for her high Swayamvara
The time was come.
                        So, to the Rajas all
The King sent word: " Ye Lords of Earth, attend
Of Damayanti the Swayamvara."
And when these learned of her Swayamvara,
Obeying Bhima, to his court they thronged—
Elephants, horses, cars—over the land
In full files wending, bearing flags and wreaths
Of countless hues, with gallant companies
Of fighting men.   And those high-hearted chiefs
The strong-armed King welcomed with worship fair,
As fitted each, and led them to their seats.
    Now at that hour there passed towards Indra's heaven,

Thither from earth ascending, those twain saints—
The wise, the pure, the mighty-minded ones,
The self-restrained—Narad and Parvata.
The mansion of the Sovereign of the Gods
In honor entered they; and he, the Lord
Of Clouds, dread Indra, softly them salutes,
Inquiring of their weal, and of the world
Wherethrough their name was famous, how it fares.
　Then Narad said: "Well is it, Lord of Gods,
With us, and with our world; and well with those
Who rule the peoples, O thou King in Heaven!"
　But He that slew the Demons spake again:—
"The princes of the earth, just-minded, brave,
Those who, in battle fearing not to fall,
See death on the descending blade, and charge
Full front against it, turning not their face—
Theirs is this realm eternal, as to me
The cow of plenty, Kâmadhuk, belongs.
Where be my Kshatriya warriors? Wherefore now
See I none coming of those slaughtered lords,
Chiefs of mankind, our always honored guests?"
　And unto Indra Narad gave reply:—
"King of the Air! no wars are waged below;
None fall in fight, to enter here. The Lord
Of high Vidarbha hath a daughter, famed
For loveliness beyond all earthly maids,
The Princess Damayanti, far-renowned.
Of her, dread Sakra! the Swayamvara
Shall soon befall, and thither now repair
The kings and princes of all lands, to woo—
Each for himself—this pearl of womanhood.
For oh, thou Slayer of the Demons, all
Desire the maid."
　　　　　　　Drew round, while Narad spake,
The Masters, th' Immortals, pressing in
With Agni and the Greatest, near the throne,
To listen to the speech of Narada;
Whom having heard, all cried delightedly,
"We, too, will go." Thereupon those high gods,
With chariots, and with heavenly retinues,
Sped to Vidarbha, where the kings were met.

And Nala, knowing of this kingly tryst,
Went thither joyous, heart-full with the thought
Of Damayanti.
        Thus it chanced the gods
Beheld the Prince wending along his road,
Goodly of mien, as is the Lord of Love.
The world's Protectors saw him, like a sun
For splendor; and, in very wonder, paused
Some time irresolute, so fair he was;
Then in mid-sky their golden chariots stayed,
And through the clouds descending called to him:—
"Abo! Nala of Nishadha! Noblest Prince,
Be herald for us; bear our message now."
  "Yea!" Nala made reply, "this will I do"—
And then—palm unto palm in reverence pressed—
Asked: "Shining Ones, who are ye? Unto whom,
And what words bearing, will ye that I go?
Deign to instruct me what it is ye bid."
Thus the Prince spake, and Indra answered him:—
"Thou seest th' immortal gods. Indra am I,
And this is Agni, and the other here,
Varuna, Lord of Waters; and beyond,
Yama, the King of Death, who parteth souls
From mortal frames. To Damayanti go;
Tell our approach. Say this: 'The world's dread lords,
Wishful to see thee, come; desiring thee—
Indra, Varuna, Agni, Yama, all.
Choose of these powers to which thou wilt be given.'"
But Nala, hearing that, joined palms again,
And cried: "Ah, send me not, with one accord
For this, most mighty Gods! How should a man
Sue for another, being suitor too?
How bear such errand? Have compassion, Gods!"
  Then spake they: "Yet thou saidst, 'This shall I do,'
Nishadha's Prince! and wilt thou do it not,
Forswearing faith? Nay, but depart, and soon!"
  So bid, but lingering yet again, he said:—
"Well guarded are the gates; how shall I find
Speech with her?"
             "Thou shalt find," Indra replied.
And, lo! upon that word Nala was brought

To Damayanti's chamber.   There he saw
Vidarbha's glory, sitting 'mid her maids,
In majesty and grace surpassing all;
So exquisite, so delicate of form,
Waist so fine-turned, such limbs, such lighted eyes,
The moon hath meaner radiance than she.
Love at the sight of that soft smiling face
Sprang to full passion, while he stood and gazed.
Yet, faith and duty urging, he restrained
His beating heart; but when those beauteous maids
Spied Nala, from their cushions they uprose,
Startled to see a man, yet startled more
Because he showed so heavenly bright and fair.
In wondering pleasure each saluted him,
Uttering no sound, but murmuring to themselves:—
"Aho! the grace of him; aho! the brilliance;
Aho! what glorious strength lives in his limbs!
What is he?   Is he God, Gandharva, Yaksha?"
But this unspoken, for they dared not breathe
One syllable, all standing shyly there
To see him, and to see his youth so sweet.
Yet, softly glancing back to his soft glance,
The Princess, presently, with fluttering breath,
Accosted Nala, saying: "Fairest Prince,
Who by thy faultless form hath filled my heart
With sudden joy, coming as come the gods,
Unstayed, I crave to know thee, who thou art;
How didst thou enter? how wert thou unseen?
Our palace is close-guarded, and the King
Hath issued mandates stern."
                                        Tenderly spake
The Prince, replying to those tender words:—
"Most lovely! I am Nala.   I am come
A herald of the gods unto thee here.
The gods desire thee, the immortal Four—
Indra, Varuna, Yama, Agni.   Choose,
O Brightest! one from these to be thy lord.
By their help is it I have entered in
Unseen; none could behold me at thy gates,
Nor stay me, passing; and to speak their will
They sent me, fairest one and best.   Do thou,

Knowing the message, judge as seemeth well."
    She bowed her head, hearing the great gods named,
And then, divinely smiling, said to him:—
" Pledge thyself faithfully to me, and I
Will seek, O Raja, only how to pay
That debt with all I am, with all I have;
For I and mine are thine—in full trust thine.
Make me that promise, Prince. Thy gentle name—
Sung by the swan—first set my thoughts afire;
And for thy sake—only for thee—sweet Lord,
The kings were summoned hither. If, alas!
Fair Prince, thou dost reject my sudden love,
So proffered, then must poison, flame, or flood,
Or knitted cord, be my sad remedy."
    So spake Vidarbha's Pride; and Nala said:—
" With gods so waiting—with the world's dread lords
Hastening to woo, canst thou desire a man?
Bethink! I, unto these, that make and mar,
These all-wise ones, almighty, am like dust
Under their feet: lift thy heart to the height
Of what I bring. If mortal man offend
The most high gods, death is what springs of it.
Spare me to live, thou faultless lady! Choose
Which of these excellent great gods thou wilt;
Wear the unstainèd robes! bear on thy brows
The wreaths which never fade, of heavenly blooms!
Be, as thou mayest, a goddess, and enjoy
Godlike delights! Him who enfolds the earth,
Creating and consuming, Brightest Power,
Hutâsa, Eater of the Sacrifice,
What woman would not take? Or him whose rod
Herds all the generations forward still
On virtue's path, Red Yama, King of Death,
What woman would affront? Or him, the all-good,
All-wise destroyer of the Demons, first
In heaven, Mahendra—who of womankind
Is there that would not wed? Or, if thy mind
Incline, doubt not to choose Varuna; he
Is of these world-protectors. From a heart
Full friendly cometh what I tell thee now."
    Unto Nishadha's Prince the maid replied—

Tears of distress dimming her lustrous eyes—
" Humbly I reverence these mighty gods;
But thee I choose, and thee I take for lord;
And this I vow!"
                With folded palms she stood,
And trembling lips, while his faint answer fell:—
" Sent on such embassy, how shall I dare
Speak, sweetest Princess, for myself to thee?
Bound by my promise for the gods to sue,
How can I be a suitor for myself?
Silence is here my duty; afterwards,
If I shall come, in mine own name I'll come,
Mine own cause pleading. Ah, might that so be!"
   Checking her tears, Damayanti sadly smiled,
And said full soft: " One way of hope I see,
A blameless way, O Lord of men! wherefrom
No fault shall rise, nor any danger fall.
Thou also, Prince, with Indra and these gods,
Must enter in where my Swayamvara
Is held; then I, in presence of those gods,
Will choose thee, dearest, for my lord; and so
Blame shall not light on thee."
                  With which sweet words
Soft in his ears, Nishadha straight returned
There where the gods were gathered, waiting him;
Whom the world's masters, on his way, perceived,
And, spying, questioned, asking for his news:—
" Saw'st thou her, Prince?   Didst see the sweet-lipped one?
What spake she of us?   Tell us true; tell all!"
   Quoth Nala: " By your worshipful behest
Sent to her house, the great gates entered I,
Though the gray porters watched; but none might spy
My entering, by your power, O radiant Ones,
Saving the Raja's daughter; her I saw
Amid her maidens, and by them was seen.
On me with much amazement they did gaze
Whilst I your high Divinities extolled.
But she that hath the lovely face, with mind
Set upon me, hath chosen me, ye Gods.
For thus she spake, my Princess: ' Let them come,
And come thou, like a lordly tiger, too,

Unto the place of my Swayamvara;
There will I choose thee in their presence, Prince,
To be my lord; and so there will not fall
Blame, thou strong-armed! to thee.' This she did say
Even as I tell it; and what shall be next,
To will is yours, O ye immortal Ones!"
  Soon, when the moon was good, and day and hour
Were found propitious, Bhima, King of men,
Summoned the chiefs to the Swayamvara;
Upon which message all those eager lords
For love of Damayanti hastened there.
Glorious with gilded pillars was the court,
Whereto a gate-house opened, and thereby
Into the square, like lions from the hills,
Paced the proud guests; and there their seats they took,
Each in his rank, the masters of the lands,
With crowns of fragrant blossoms garlanded,
And polished jewels swinging in their ears.
Of some the thews, knitted and rough, stood forth
Like iron maces; some had slender limbs,
Sleek and fine-turned like the five-headed snake;
Lords with long-flowing hair; glittering lords;
High-nosed, and eagle-eyed, and heavy-browed;
The faces of those kings shone in a ring
As shine at night the stars; and that great square
As thronged with Rajas was as Naga-land
Is full of serpents; thick with warlike chiefs
As mountain-caves with panthers. Unto these
Entered, in matchless majesty of form,
The Princess Damayanti. As she came,
The glory of her ravished eyes and hearts,
So that the gaze of all those haughty kings,
Fastening upon her loveliness, grew fixed—
Not moving save with her—step after step
Onward and always following the maid.
  But while the styles and dignities of all
Were cried aloud, (O son of Bhârat!) lo!
The Princess marked five of that throng alike
In form and garb and visage. There they stood,
Each from the next undifferenced, but each
Nala's own self;—yet which might Nala be

In nowise could that doubting maid descry.
Who took her eye seemed Nala while she gazed,
Until she looked upon his like; and so
Pondered the lovely lady, sore-perplexed,
Thinking, " How shall I tell which be the gods,
And which is noble Nala?" Deep-distressed
And meditative waxed she, musing hard
What those signs were, delivered us of old,
Whereby gods may be known: " Of all those signs
Taught by our elders, lo! I see not one
Where stand yon five." So murmured she, and turned
Over and over every mark she knew.
At last, resolved to make the gods themselves
Her help at need, with reverent air and voice
Humbly saluted she those heavenly ones,
And with joined palms and trembling accents spake:—
" As, when I heard the swans, I chose my Prince,
By that sincerity I call ye, Gods,
To show my Love to me and make me know!
As in my heart and soul and speech I stand
True to my choice, by that sincerity
I call the all-knowing gods to make me know!
As the high gods created Nishadha's chief
To be my lord, by their sincerity
I bid them show themselves, and make me know!
As my vow, sealed to him, must be maintained
For his name, and for mine, I call the gods
By such sincerity to make me know!
Let them appear, the masters of the world—
The high gods—each one in his proper shape,
That I may see Nishadha's chief, my choice,
Whom minstrels praise, and Damayanti loves."
    Hearing that earnest speech—so passion-fraught,
So full of truth, of strong resolve, of love,
Of singleness of soul and constancy—
Even as she spake, the gods disclosed themselves.
By well-seen signs the effulgent Ones she knew.
Shadowless stood they, with unwinking eyes,
And skins which never moist with sweat; their feet
Light-gliding o'er the ground, not touching it;
The unfading blossoms on their brows not soiled

By earthly dust, but ever fair and fresh.
Whilst, by their side, garbed so and visaged so,
But doubled by his shadow, stained with dust,
The flower-cups wiltering in his wreath, his skin
Pearly with sweat, his feet upon the earth,
And eyes a-wink, stood Nala.   One by one
Glanced she on those divinities, then bent
Her gaze upon the Prince, and, joyous, said:—
" I know thee, and I name my rightful lord,
Taking Nishadha's chief."   Therewith she drew
Modestly nigh, and held him by the cloth,
With large eyes beaming love, and round his neck
Hung the bright chaplet, love's delicious crown;
So choosing him—him only—whom she named
Before the face of all to be her lord.

    Oh, then brake forth from all those suitors proud,
" Ha!" and " Aho!"   But from the gods and saints,
" Sadhu! well done! well done!"   And all admired
The happy Prince, praising the grace of him;
While Virasena's son, delightedly,
Spake to the slender-waisted these fond words:—
" Fair Princess! since, before all gods and men,
Thou makest me thy choice, right glad am I
Of this thy mind, and true lord will I be.
For so long, loveliest, as my breath endures,
Thine am I!   Thus I plight my troth to thee."
So, with joined palms, unto that beauteous maid
His gentle faith he pledged, rejoicing her;
And, hand in hand, radiant with mutual love,
Before great Agni and the gods they passed,
The world's protectors worshipping.

                      Then those,
The lords of life, the powerful Ones, bestowed—
Being well-pleased—on Nala, chosen so,
Eight noble boons.   The boon which Indra gave
Was grace, at times of sacrifice, to see
The visible god approach, with step divine;
And Agni's boon was this, that he would come
Whenever Nala called—for everywhere
Hutâsa shineth, and all worlds are his;
Yama gave skill in cookery, steadfastness

In virtue; and Varuna, King of Floods,
Bade all the waters ripple at his call.
These boons the high gods doubled by the gift
Of bright wreaths wove with magic blooms of heaven;
And those bestowed, ascended to their seats.
Also with wonder and with joy returned
The Rajas and the Maharajas all,
Full of the marriage-feast; for Bhima made,
In pride and pleasure, stately nuptials;
So Damayanti and the Prince were wed.

    Then, having tarried as is wont, that lord—
Nishadha's chief—took the King's leave, and went
Unto his city, bringing home with him
His jewel of all womanhood, with whom
Blissful he lived, as lives by Sachi's side
The slayer of the Demons.   Like a sun
Shone Nala on his throne, ruling his folk
In strength and virtue, guardian of his state.
Also the Aśwamedha Rite he made
Greatest of rites, the Offering of the Horse,
As did Yayâti; and all other acts
Of worship; and to sages gave rich gifts.

    Many dear days of much delicious love,
In pleasant gardens and in shadowy groves,
Passed they together, sojourning like gods.
And Damayanti bore unto her lord
A boy named Indrasen, and next, a girl
Named Indrasena.   So in happiness
The good Prince governed, seeing all his lands
Wealthy and well, in piety and peace.

    Now at the choosing of Nishadha's chief
By Bhima's daughter, when those lords of life—
The effulgent gods—departed, Dwapara
They saw with Kali, coming.   Indra said—
The Demon-slayer—spying these approach:—
"Whither, with Dwapara, goest thou to-day,
O Kali?"   And the sombre Shade replied:—
"To Damayanti's high Swayamvara
I go, to make her mine, since she hath passed
Into my heart."   But Indra, laughing, said:—
"Ended is that Swayamvara; for she

Hath taken Raja Nala for her lord,
Before us all." But Kali, hearing this,
Breaks into wrath—while he stood worshipping
That band divine—and furiously cries:—
" If she hath set a man above the gods,
To wed with him, for such sin let there fall
Doom, rightful, swift, and terrible, on her!"
" Nay," answered unto him those heavenly ones,
" But Damayanti chose with our good-will;
And what maid but would choose so fair a prince,
Seeing he hath all qualities, and knows
Virtue, and rightly practises the vows,
And reads the four great Vedas, and, what's next,
The Holy Stories, whilst, perpetually,
The gods are honored in his house with gifts?
No hurt he does, kind to all living things;
True of word is he, faithful, liberal, just;
Steadfast and patient, temperate and pure;
A king of men is Nala, like the gods.
He that would curse a prince of such a mould,
Thou foolish Kali, lays upon himself
A sin to crush himself; the curse comes back
And sinks him in the bottomless vast gulf
Of Narak."
        Thus the gods to Kali spake,
And mounted heavenward; whereupon that Shade,
Frowning, to Dwapara burst forth: " My rage
Beareth no curb. Henceforth in Nala I
Will dwell; his kingdom I will make to fall;
His bliss with Damayanti I will mar;
And thou within the dice shalt enter straight,
And help me, Dwapara! to drag him down."
Into which compact entering, those repaired—
Kali and Dwapara—to Nala's house,
And haunted in Nishadha, where he ruled,
Seeking occasion 'gainst the blameless Prince.
Long watched they; twelve years rolled ere Kali saw
The fateful fault arrive; Nishadha's Lord,
Easing himself, and sprinkling hands and lips
With purifying water, passed to prayer,
His feet unwashed, offending. Kali straight

Possessed the heedless Raja, entering him.
  That hour there sat with Nala, Pushkara
His brother; and the evil spirit hissed
Into the ear of Pushkara: "Ehi!
Arise, and challenge Nala at the dice.
Throw with the Prince! it may be thou shalt win
(Luck helping thee, and I) Nishadha's throne,
Town, treasures, palace—thou mayest gain them all."
And Pushkara, hearing Kali's evil voice,
Made near to Nala, with the dice in hand
(A great piece for the "Bull," and little ones
For "Cows," and Kali hiding in the Bull).
So Pushkara came to Nala's side and said:—
"Play with me, brother, at the 'Cows and Bull';"
And, being put off, cried mockingly, "Nay, play!"
Shaming the Prince, whose spirit chafed to leave
A gage unfaced; but when Vidarbha's gem,
The Princess, heard that challenge, Nala rose:
"Yea, Pushkara, I will play!" fiercely he said;
And to the game addressed.
                              His gems he lost,
Armlets and belt and necklet; next the gold
Of the palace and its vessels; then the cars
Yoked with swift steeds; and last, the royal robes:
For, cast by cast, the dice against him fell,
Bewitched by Kali; and, cast after cast,
The passion of the dice kept hold on him,
Until not one of all his faithfullest
Could stay the madman's hand and gamester's heart
Of who was named "Subduer of his Foes."
  The townsmen gathered with the ministers:
Into that palace gate they thronged (my King!)
To see their lord, if so they might abate
This sickness of his soul. The charioteer,
Forth standing from their midst, low worshipping,
Spake thus to Damayanti: "Great Princess,
Before thy door all the grieved city sits.
Say to our lord for us, 'Thy folk are here;
They mourn that evil fortunes hold their liege,
Who was so high and just.'" Then she, deject,
Passed in, and to Nishadha's ruler said,

Her soft voice broken, and her bright eyes dimmed:—
" Raja, the people of thy town are here;
Before our gates they gather, citizens
And counsellors, desiring speech with thee;
In lealty they come. Wilt thou be pleased
We open to them? Wilt thou?" So she asked
Again and yet again; but not one word
To that sad lady with the lovely brows
Did Nala answer, wholly swallowed up
Of Kali and the gaming; so that those—
The citizens and counsellors—cried out,
" Our lord is changed! He is not Nala now!"
And home returned, ashamed and sorrowful;
Whilst ceaselessly endured that foolish play
Moon after moon—the Prince the loser still.
   Then Damayanti, seeing so estranged
Her lord, the praised in song, the chief of men,
Watching, all self-possessed, his fantasy,
And how the gaming held him; sad, and 'feared,
The heavy fortunes pondering of her Prince;
Hating the fault, but to the offender kind;
And fearing Nala should be stripped of all,
This thing devised: Vrihatsenâ she called—
Her foster-nurse and faithful ministrant—
True, skilful at all service, soft of speech,
Kind-hearted; and she said, " Vrihatsenâ,
Go call the ministers to council now,
As though 'twere Nala bade; and make them count
What store is gone of treasure, what abides."
So went Vrihatsenâ, and summoned those;
And when they knew all things, as from the Prince,
" Truly we, too, shall perish!" cried they then;
And all to Nala went, and all the town,
A second time assembling, thronged his gates:—
Which Bhima's daughter told; but not one word
Answered the Prince. And when she saw her lord
Put by her plea, utterly slighting it,
Back to her chamber, full of shame, she goes,
And there still hears the dice are falling ill;
Still hears of Nala daily losing more;
So that again unto her nurse she spake:—

" Send to Varshneya, good Vrihatsenâ;
Say to the charioteer—in Nala's name—
' A great thing is to do.   Come thou!' "   And this—
So soon as Damayanti uttered it—
Vrihatsenâ, by faithful servants, told
Unto the son of Vrishni, who, being come
In fitting time and place, heard the sweet Queen
In mournful music speak these wistful words:—
" Thou knowest how thy Raja trusted thee;
Now he hath fall'n on evil; succor him!
The more that Pushkara conquers in the play,
The wilder rage of gaming takes thy lord—
The more for Pushkara the dice light well,
More contrary they happen to the Prince:
Nor heeds he, as were meet, kindred or friends;
Nay, of myself he putteth by the prayer
Unanswered, being bewitched; for well I deem
This is not noble-minded Nala's sin,
But some ill spell possesseth him to shut
His ears to me.   Thou, therefore, charioteer!
Our refuge be; do what I shall command;
My heart is dark with fear.   Yea, it may fall
Our lord will perish.   Wherefore, harnessing
His chosen steeds, which fly as swift as thought,
Take these our children in the chariot
And drive to Kundina, delivering there
Unto my kin the little ones, and car,
And horses.   Afterwards abide thou there,
Or otherwhere depart."
       Varshneya heard
The words of Damayanti, and forthwith
In Nala's council-hall recounted them,
The chief men being present; who, thus met,
And long debating, gave him leave to go.
So with that royal pair to Bhima's town
Drove he, and at Vidarbha rendered up,
Together with the swift steeds and the car,
That sweet maid Indrasena, and the Prince
Indrasen, and made reverence to the King,
Saddened for sake of Nala.   Afterwards
Taking his leave, unto Ayodhyâ

Varshneya went, exceeding sorrowful,
And with King Rituparna (O my Prince!)
Took service as a charioteer.

     These gone—
The praised-of-poets, Nala, still played on,
Till Pushkara his kingdom's wealth had won,
And whatso was to lose beside. Thereat
With scornful laugh mocked he that beggared Prince,
Saying, " One other throw ; once more !—Yet sooth,
What canst thou stake? Nothing is left for thee
Save Damayanti ; all the rest is mine.
Play we for Damayanti, if thou wilt."
But hearing this from Pushkara, the Prince
So in his heart by grief and shame was torn,
No word he uttered—only glared in wrath
Upon his mocker, upon Pushkara.
Then, his rich robes and jewels stripping off,
Uncovered, with one cloth, 'mid waiting friends
Sorrowful passed he forth, his great state gone ;
The Princess, with one garment, following him,
Piteous to see. And there without the gates
Three nights they lay—Nashadha's King and Queen.
Upon the fourth day Pushkara proclaimed,
Throughout the city, " Whoso yieldeth help
To Nala, dieth ! Let my will be known ! "
 So, for this bitter word of Pushkara's power
(O Yudhisthir !) the townsmen rendered not
Service nor love, but left them outcast there,
Unhelped, whom all the city should have helped.
Yet three nights longer tarried he, his drink
The common pool, his meat such fruits and roots
As miserable hunger plucks from earth :
Then fled they from those walls, the Prince going first,
The Princess following.

     After grievous days,
Pinched ever with sharp famine, Nala saw
A flock of gold-winged birds lighting anigh,
And to himself the famished Raja said :—
" Lo ! here is food ; this day we shall have store ; "
Then lightly cast his cloth and covered them.
But these, fluttering aloft, bore with them there

Nala's one cloth; and, hovering overhead,
Uttered sharp-stinging words, reviling him
Even as he stood, naked to all the airs,
Downcast and desperate: "Thou brain-sick Prince!
We are the dice; we come to ravish hence
Thy last poor cloth; we were not well content
Thou shouldst depart owning a garment still."
And when he saw the dice take wings and fly,
Leaving him bare, to Damayanti spake
This melancholy Prince: "O Blameless One,
They by whose malice I am driven forth,
Finding no sustenance, sad, famine-gaunt—
They whose decree forbade Nishadha's folk
Should succor me, their Raja—these have come—
Demon and dice—and like to wingèd birds
Have borne away my cloth. To such shame fall'n,
Such utmost woe, wretched, demented—I
Thy lord am still, and counsel thee for good.
Attend! Hence be there many roads which go
Southwards: some pass Avanti's walls, and some
Skirt Rikshavan, the forest of the bears;
This wends to Vindhya's lofty peaks, and this
To the green banks where quick Payoshni runs
Seaward, between her hermitages, rich
In fruits and roots; and yon path leadeth thee
Unto Vidarbha; that to Kosala,
And therefrom southward—southward—far away."
    So spake he to the Princess wistfully,
Between his words pointing along the paths,
Which she should take (O King!). But Bhima's child
Made answer, bowed with grief, her soft voice choked
With sobs, these piteous accents uttering:—
    "My heart beats quick; my body's force is gone,
Thinking, dear Prince, on this which thou hast said,
Pointing along the paths. What! robbed of realm,
Stripped of thy wealth, bare, famished, parched with thirst,
Thus shall I leave thee in the untrodden wood?
Ah, no! While thou dost muse on dear days fled,
Hungry and weeping, I in this wild waste
Will charm thy griefs away, solacing thee.
The wisest doctors say, 'In every woe

No better physic is than wifely love.'
And, Nala, I will make it true to thee."
    " Thou mak'st it true," he said; " thou sayest well,
Sweet Damayanti; neither is there friend
To sad men given better than a wife.
I had not thought to leave thee, foolish Love!
Why didst thou fear? Alas, 't is from myself
That I would fly—not thee, thou Faultless One!"
    " Yet, if," the Princess answered, " Maharaja!
Thou hadst no thought to leave me, why by thee
Was the way pointed to Vidarbha's walls?
I know thou wouldst not quit me, noblest Lord,
Being thyself, but only if thy mind
Were sore distraught; and see, thou gazest still
Along the southward road, my dread thereby
Increasing, thou that wert as are the gods!
If it be thy fixed thought, ' 'Twere best she went
Unto her people '—be it so; I go;
But hand in hand with thee.   Thus let us fare
Unto Vidarbha, where the King, my sire,
Will greet thee well, and honor thee; and we
Happy and safe within his gates shall dwell."
    " As is thy father's kingdom," Nala said,
" So, once, was mine.   Be sure, whate'er betide,
Never will I go thither!   How, in sooth,
Should I, who came there glorious, gladdening thee,
Creep back, thy shame and scorn, disconsolate?"
    So to sweet Damayanti spake the Prince,
Beguiling her, whom now one cloth scarce clad—
For but one garb they shared; and thus they strayed
Hither and thither, faint for meat and drink,
Until a little hut they spied; and there,
Nishadha's monarch, entering, sat him down
On the bare ground, the Princess by his side—
Vidarbha's glory, wearing that scant cloth,
Without a mat, soiled by the dust and mire.
At Damayanti's side he sank asleep,
Outworn; and beauteous Damayanti slept,
Spent with strange trials—she so gently reared,
So soft and holy.   But while slumbering thus,
No peaceful rest knew Nala.   Trouble-tossed

He woke, forever thinking of his realm
Lost, lieges estranged, and all the griefs
Of that wild wood.   These on his heart came back,
And, " What if I shall do it?   What, again,
If I shall do it not? "   So murmured he.
" Would death be better, or to leave my Love?
For my sake she endures this woe, my fate
Too fondly sharing;   freed from me, her steps
Would turn unto her people.   At my side,
Sure suffering is her portion;   but apart,
It might be she would somewhere comfort find."
    Thus with himself debating o'er and o'er,
The Prince resolves abandonment were best.
" For how," saith he, " should any in the wood
Harm her, so radiant in her grace, so good,
So noble, virtuous, faithful, famous, pure? "
Thus mused his miserable mind, seduced
By Kali's cursèd mischiefs to betray
His sleeping wife.   Then, seeing his loin-cloth gone,
And Damayanti clad, he drew anigh,
Thinking to take of hers, and muttering,
" May I not rend one fold, and she not know? "
So meditating, round the cabin crept
Prince Nala, feeling up and down its walls;
And, presently, within the purlieus found
A naked knife, keen-tempered;   therewithal
Shred he away a piece, and bound it on;
Then made with desperate steps to seek the waste,
Leaving the Princess sleeping;   but, anon,
Turns back again in changeful mood and glides
Into the hut, and, gazing wistfully
On slumbering Damayanti, moans with tears:—
" Ah, Sweetheart!   whom nor wind nor sun before
Hath ever rudely touched;   thou to be couched
In this poor hut, its floor thy bed, and I,
Thy lord, deserting thee, stealing from thee
Thy last robe!   O my Love with the bright smile,
My slender-waisted Queen!   Will she not wake
To madness?   Yea, and when she wanders lone
In the dark wood, haunted with beasts and snakes,
How will it fare with Bhima's tender child,

The bright and peerless? O my life, my wife!
May the great sun, may the Eight Powers of air,
The Rudras, Maruts, and the Aswins twain,
Guard thee, thou true and dear one, on thy way!"
　　So to his sleeping Queen—on all the earth
Unmatched for beauty—spake he piteously;
Then breaks away once more, by Kali driven.
But yet another and another time
Stole back into the hut, for one last gaze—
That way by Kali dragged, this way by love.
Two hearts he had—the trouble-stricken Prince—
One beating " Go," one throbbing " Stay "; and thus
Backwards and forwards swung his mind between,
Till, mastered by the sorrow and the spell,
Frantic flies Nala, leaving there alone
That tender sleeper, sighing as she slept.
He flies—the soulless prey of Kali flies;
Still, while he hurries through the forest drear,
Thinking upon that sweet face he hath left.
　　Far distant (King!) was Nala, when, refreshed,
The slender-waisted wakened, shuddering
At the wood's silence; but when, seeking him,
She found no Nala, sudden anguish seized
Her frightened heart, and, lifting high her voice,
Loud cries she: " Maharaja! Nishadha's Prince!
Ha, Lord! ha, Maharaja! ha, Master! why
Hast thou abandoned me? Now am I lost,
Am doomed, undone, left in this lonesome gloom.
Wert thou not named, O Nala, true and just?
Yet art thou such, to quit me while I slept?
And hast thou so forsaken me, thy wife—
Thine own fond wife—who never wrought thee wrong
When by all others wrong was wrought on thee?
Mak'st thou it good to me, now, Lord of men,
That love which long ago before the gods
Thou didst proclaim? Alas! Death will not come,
Except at his appointed time to men,
And therefore for a little I shall live,
Whom thou hast lived to leave. Nay, 't is a jest!
Ah, Truant, Runaway, enough thou play'st!
Come forth, my Lord!—I am afraid! Come forth!

Linger not, for I see—I spy thee there;
Thou art within yon thicket! Why not speak
One word, Nishadha? Nala, cruel Prince!
Thou know'st me, lone, and comest not to calm
My terrors, and be with me in my need.
Art gone indeed? Then I'll not mourn myself,
For whatso may befall me; I must think
How desolate thou art, and weep for thee.
What wilt thou do, thirsty and hungry, spent
With wandering, when, at nightfall, 'mid the trees
Thou hast me not, sweet Prince, to comfort thee?"
  Thereat, distracted by her bitter fears,
Like one whose heart is fire, forward and back
She runs, hither and thither, weeping, wild.
One while she sinks to earth, one while she springs
Quick to her feet; now utterly o'ercome
By fear and fasting, now by grief driven mad,
Wailing and sobbing; till anon, with moans
And broken sighs and tears, Bhima's fair child,
The ever-faithful wife, speaks thus again:—
" By whomsoever's spell this harm hath fall'n
On Nishadha's Lord, I pray that evil one
May bear a bitterer plague than Nala doth!
To him, whoever set my guileless Prince
On these ill deeds, I pray some direr might
May bring far darker days, and life to live
More miserable still!"
                              Thus, woe-begone,
Mourned that great-hearted wife her vanished lord,
Seeking him ever in the gloomy shades,
By wild beasts haunted. Roaming everywhere,
Like one possessed, frantic, disconsolate,
Went Bhima's daughter. "Ha, ha! Maharaja!"
So crying runs she, so in every place
Is heard her ceaseless wail, as when is heard
The fish-hawk's cry, which screams, and circling screams,
And will not stint complaining.
                              Suddenly,
Straying too near his den, a serpent's coils
Seized Bhima's daughter. A prodigious snake,
Glittering and strong, and furious for food,

Knitted about the Princess.   She, o'erwhelmed
With horror, and the cold enfolding death,
Spends her last breaths in pitiful laments
For Nala, not herself.   " Ah, Prince!" she cried,
" That would have saved me, who must perish now,
Seized in the lone wood by this hideous snake,
Why art thou not beside me?   What will be
Thy thought, Nishadha! me remembering
In days to come, when, from the curse set free,
Thou hast thy noble mind again, thyself,
Thy wealth—all save thy wife?   Then thou'lt be sad,
Be weary, wilt need food and drink; but I
Shall minister no longer.   Who will tend
My Love, my Lord, my Lion among kings,
My blameless Nala—Damayanti dead?"
     That hour a hunter, roving through the brake,
Heard her bewailing, and with quickened steps
Made nigh, and, spying a woman, almond-eyed,
Lovely, forlorn, by that fell monster knit,
He ran, and, as he came, with keen shaft clove,
Through gaping mouth and crown, th' unwitting worm,
Slaying it.   Then the woodman from its folds
Freed her, and laved the snake's slime from her limbs
With water of the pool, comforting her
And giving food; and afterwards (my King!)
Inquiry made: " What doest, in this wood,
Thou with the fawn's eyes?   And how camest thou,
My mistress, to such pit of misery?"
     And Damayanti, spoken fair by him,
Recounted all which had befallen her.
     But, gazing on her graces, scantly clad
With half a cloth, those smooth, full sides, those breasts
Beauteously swelling, form of faultless mould,
Sweet youthful face, fair as the moon at full,
And dark orbs, by long curving lashes swept;
Hearing her tender sighs and honeyed speech,
The hunter fell to hot desire; he dared
Essay to woo, with whispered words at first,
And next by amorous approach, the Queen;
Who, presently perceiving what he would,
'And all that baseness of him—being so pure,

So chaste, and faithful—like a blazing torch
Took fire of scorn and anger 'gainst the man,
Her true soul burning at him, till the wretch,
Wicked in heart, but impotent of will,
Glared on her, splendidly invincible
In weakness, loftily defying wrong,
A living flame of lighted chastity.
She then—albeit so desolate, so lone,
Abandoned by her lord, stripped of her state—
Like a proud princess stormed, flinging away
All terms of supplication, cursing him
With wrath which scorched: " If I am clean in heart
And true in thought unto Nishadha's King,
Then mayest thou, vile pursuer of the beasts,
Sink to the earth, stone dead! "
                              While she did speak,
The hunter breathless fell to earth, stone dead,
As falls a tree-trunk blasted by the bolt.
   That ravisher destroyed, the lotus-eyed
Fared forward, threading still the fearful wood,
Lonely and dim, with trill of jhillikas [1]
Resounding, and fierce noise of many beasts
Laired in its shade, lions and leopards, deer,
Close-hiding tigers, sullen bisons, wolves,
And shaggy bears.   Also the glades of it
Were filled with fowl which crept, or flew, and cried.
A home for savage men and murderers,
Thick with a world of trees, whereof was sal,
Sharp-seeded, weeping gum; knotted bambus,
Dhavas with twisted roots; smooth aswatthas,
Large-leaved, and creeping through the cloven rocks;
Tindukas, iron-fibred, dark of grain;
Ingudas, yielding oil; and kinsukas,
With scarlet flowerets flaming.   Thronging these
Were arjuns and arishta-clumps, which bear
The scented purple clusters; syandans,
And tall silk-cotton trees, and mango-belts
With silvery spears; and wild rose-apple, blent
'Mid lodhra-tufts and khadirs, interknit
By clinging rattans, climbing everywhere

---

[1] Jhillikas are the large wood-crickets.

From stem to stem. Therewith were intermixed—
Round pools where rocked the lotus—âmalaks,
Plakshas with fluted leaves, kadambas sweet,
Udumbaras; and, on the jungle-edge,
Tangles of reed and jujube, whence there rose
Bel-trees and nyagrodhas, dropping roots
Down from the air; broad-leaved priyâlas, palms
And date-trees, and the gold myrobalan,
With copper-leaved vibhîtikas. All these
Crowded the wood; and many a crag it held,
With precious ore of metals interveined;
And many a creeper-covered cave wherein
The spoken word rolled round; and many a cleft
Where the thick stems were like a wall to see;
And many a winding stream and reedy jheel,
And glassy lakelet, where the woodland beasts
In free peace gathered.
       Wandering onward thus,
The Princess saw far-gliding forms of dread—
Pisâchas, Rakshasas, ill sprites and fiends
Which haunt, with swinging snakes, the undergrowth.
Dark pools she saw, and drinking-holes, and peaks
Wherefrom break down in tumbling cataracts
The wild white waters, marvellous to hear.
Also she passed—this daughter of a king—
Where snorted the fierce buffaloes, and where
The gray boars rooted for their food, and where
The black bears growled, and serpents in the grass
Rustled and hissed. But all along that way
Safe paced she in her majesty of grace,
High fortune, courage, constancy, and right—
Vidarbha's glory—seeking, all alone,
Lost Nala; and less terror at these sights
Came to sad Damayanti for herself—
Threading this dreadful forest—than for him.
Most was her mind on Nala's fate intent.
Bitterly grieving stood the sweet Princess
Upon a rock, her tender limbs a-thrill
With heavy fears for Nala while she spake:—
 "Broad-chested Chief! my long-armed Lord of men!
Nishadha's King! Ah! whither art thou gone,

Leaving me thus in the unpeopled wood?
The Aśwamedha sacrifice thou mad'st,
And all the rites and royal gifts hast given,
A lion-hearted Prince, holy and true
To all save me!   That which thou didst declare,
Hand in hand with me—once so fond and kind—
Recall it now—thy sacred word, thy vow,
Whithersoever, Raja, thou art fled.
Think how the message of the gold-winged swans
Was spoken, by thine own lips, then to me!
True men keep faith; this is the teaching taught
In Vedas, Angas, and Upangas all,
Hear which we may; wilt thou not, therefore, Prince—
Wilt thou not, terror of thy foes, keep faith,
Making thy promise good to cleave to me?
Ha, Nala, Lord!   Am I not surely still
Thy chosen, thy belovèd?   Answerest not
Thy wife in this dark, horror-haunted shade?
The tyrant of the jungle, fierce and fell,
With jaws agape to take me, crouches nigh,
And thou not here to rescue me—not thou,
Who saidst none other in the world was dear
But Damayanti!   Prove the fond speech true,
Uttered so often!   Why repliest not
To me, thy well-belovèd; me, distraught,
Longed for and longing; me, my Prince and pride.
That am so weary, weak, and miserable,
Stained with the mire, in this torn cloth half clad,
Alone and weeping, seeing no help near?
Ah, stag of all the herd! leav'st thou thy hind
Astray, regarding not these tears which roll?
My Nala, Maharaja!   It is I
Who cry, thy Damayanti, true and pure,
Lost in the wood, and still thou answerest not!
High-born, high-hearted, full of grace and strength
In all thy limbs, shall I not find thee soon
On yonder hill?   Shall I not see, at last,
In some track of this grim, beast-peopled wood,
Standing, or seated, or upon the leaves
Lying, or coming, him who is of men
The glory, but for me the grief-maker?

If not, whom shall I question, woe-begone,
Saying, ' In any region of this wood
Hast thou, perchance, seen Nala?' Is there none,
In all the forest, would reply to me
With tidings of my lord, wandered away,
Kingly in mind and form, of hosts of foes
The conqueror? Who will say, with blessed voice,
' That Raja with the lotus-eyes is near,
Whom thou dost seek'?—Nay, here comes one to ask,
The yellow forest-king, his great jaws armed
With fourfold fangs. A tiger standeth now
Face to face on my path; I'll speak with him
Fearlessly: ' Dreadful chief of all this waste,
Thou art the sovereign of the beasts, and I
Am daughter of Vidarbha's King; my name,
The Princess Damayanti; know thou me,
Wife of Nishadha's Lord—of Nala—styled
" Subduer of his Foes "? Him seek I here—
Abandoned, sorrow-stricken, miserable.
Comfort me, mighty beast, if so thou canst,
Saying thou hast seen Nala; but if this
Thou canst not do, then, ah, thou savage lord,
Terrible friend, devour me, setting me
Free from all woes!' The tiger answereth not;
He turns, and quits me in my tears, to stalk
Down where the river glitters through the reeds,
Seeking its seaward way. Then will I pray
Unto yon sacred mount of clustered crags,
Broad-shouldered, shining, lifting high to heaven
Its diverse-colored peaks, where the mind climbs
Its hid heart rich with silver veins, and gold,
And stored with many a precious gem unseen.
Clear towers it o'er the forest, broad and bright
Like a green banner; and the sides of it
House many a living thing—lions and boars,
Tigers and elephants, and bears and deer.
Softly around me from its feathered flocks
The songs ring, perched upon the kinsuk trees,
The asokas, vakuls, and punnâga boughs,
Or hidden in the karnikara leaves,
And tendrils of the dhava or the fig;

Full of great glens it soars, where waters leap
And bright birds lave. This king of hills I sue
For tidings of my lord. O Mountain Lord,
Far-seen and celebrated hill! that cleav'st
The blue of the sky, refuge of living things,
Most noble eminence, I worship thee;
Thee I salute, who am a monarch's child,
The daughter and the consort of a prince,
The high-born Damayanti, unto whom
Bhima, Vidarbha's chief—that puissant lord—
Was sire, renowned o'er earth. Protector he
Of the four castes, performer of the rites
Called Rajasuya and the Aśwamedha—
A bounteous giver, first of rulers, known
For his large shining eyes; holy and just,
Fast to his word, unenvious, sweet of speech,
Gentle and valiant, dutiful and pure;
The guardian of Vidarbha, of his foes
The slayer. Know me, O Majestic Mount!
For that King's daughter, bending low to thee.
In Nishadha lived the father of my lord,
The Maharaja Virasena named,
Wealthy and great; whose son, of regal blood,
High-fortuned, powerful, and noble-souled,
Ruleth by right the realm paternal: he
Is Nala, terror of all enemies;
Dark Nala, praised-in-song; Nala the just,
The pure; deep-seen in scriptures, sweet of speech,
Drinker of Soma-juice, and worshipper
Of Agni; sacrificing, giving gifts;
First in the wars, a perfect, princely lord.
His wife am I, Great Mountain! and come here
Fortuneless, husbandless, and spiritless,
Everywhere seeking him, my best of men.
O Mount, whose doubled ridge stamps on the sky
Yon line, by fivescore splendid pinnacles
Indented! tell me, in this gloomy wood
Hast thou seen Nala? Nala, wise and bold,
Like a tusked elephant for might; long armed,
Indomitable, gallant, glorious, true;
Nala, Nishadha's chief—hast thou seen him?

O Mountain, why consolest thou me not,
Answering one word to sorrowful, distressed,
Lonely, lost Damayanti?"
                        Then she cried:—
"But answer for thyself, Hero and Lord!
If thou art in the forest, show thyself!
Alas! when shall I hear that voice, as low,
As tender as the murmur of the rain
When great clouds gather; sweet as Amrit-drink?
Thy voice, once more, my Nala, calling to me
Full softly, ' Damayanti!'—dearest Prince,
That would be music soothing to these ears
As sound of sacred Veda; that would stay
My pains and comfort me, and bring me peace."
    Thereafter, turning from the mount, she went
Northwards, and journeying on three nights and days
Came to a green incomparable grove
By holy men inhabited; a haunt
Placid as Paradise, whose indwellers
Like to Vaśistha, Bhrigu, Atri, were—
Those ancient saints. Restraining sense they lived,
Heedful in meats, subduing passion, pure,
Breathing within; their food water and herbs;
Ascetics; very holy; seeking still
The heavenward road; clad in the bark of trees
And skins—all gauds of earth being put by.
This hermitage, peopled by gentle ones,
Glad Damayanti spied, circled with herds
Of wild things grazing fearless, and with troops
Of monkey-folk o'erheard; and when she saw,
Her heart was lightened, for its quietness.
So drew she nigh—that lovely wanderer—
Bright-browed, long-tressed, large-hipped, full-bosomed,
        fair,
With pearly teeth and honeyed mouth, in gait
Right queenly still, having those long black eyes—
The wife of Virasena's son, the gem
Of all dear women, glory of her time;
Sad Damayanti entered their abode,
Those holy men saluting reverently,
With modest body bowed. Thus stood she there,

And all the saints spake gently, " *Swâgatam*—
Welcome ! " and gave the greetings which are meet ;
And afterwards, " Repose thyself," they said ;
" What wouldst thou have of us ? "   Then, with soft words
The slender-waisted spake : " Of all these here,
So worshipful in sacrifice and rite—
'Mid gentle beasts and birds—in tasks and toils
And blameless duties—is it well ? "   And they
Answered : " We thank you, noble lady, well.
Tell us, most beauteous one, thy name, and say
What thou desirest.   Seeing thee so fair,
So worthy, yet so sorrowful, our minds
Are lost in wonder.   Weep not.   Comfort take.
Art thou the goddess of the wood ?   Art thou
The Mountain-Yakshi, or, belike, some sprite
Which lives under the river ?   Tell us true,
Gentle and faultless form ! "
                                        Whereat reply
Thus made she to the Rishis : " None of these
Am I, good saints.   No goddess of the wood,
Nor yet a mountain nor a river sprite ;
A woman ye behold, most only ones,
Whose moving story I will tell you true.
The Raja of Vidarbha is my sire,
Bhima his name, and—Best of Twice-born !—know
My husband is Nishadha's Chief, the famed,
The wise and valiant and victorious Prince,
The high and lordly Nala ; of the gods
A steadfast worshipper ; of Bráhmanas
The friend ; his people's shield ; honored and strong,
Truth-speaking, skilled in arms, sagacious, just ;
Terrible to his foes, fortunate, lord
Of many conquered towns ; a godlike man,
Princeliest of princes—Nala—one that hath
A countenance like the full moon's for light,
And eyes of lotus.   This true offerer
Of sacrifices, this close votary
Of Vedas and Vedângas, in the war
Deadly to enemies, like sun and moon
For splendor—by some certain evil ones
Being defied to dice, my virtuous Prince

Was, by their wicked acts, of realm despoiled—
Wealth, jewels, all. I am his woful wife,
The Princess Damayanti. Seeking him
Through thickets have I roamed, over rough hills,
By crag and river and the reedy lake,
By marsh and waterfall and jungle-bush,
In quest of him—my lord, my warrior,
My hero—and still roam, uncomforted.
Worshipful brethren! say if he hath come—
Nishadha's Chief, my Nala, hitherward
Unto your pleasant homes—he, for whose sake
I wander in the dismal pathless wood
With bears and tigers haunted—terrible!
Ah! if I find him not, ere there be passed
Many more nights and days, peace will I win;
For death shall set my mournful spirit free.
What cause have I to live, lacking my Prince?
Why should I longer breathe, whose heart is dead
With sorrow for my lord?"
                                        To Bhima's child,
So in the wood bewailing, made reply
Those holy, truthful men: " Beautiful One!
The future is for thee; fair will it fall!
Our eyes, by long devotions opened, see—
Even now—thy lord; thou shalt behold him soon,
Nishadha's chief, the famous Nala, strong
In battle, loving justice. Yea, this Prince
Thou wilt regain, Bhima's sad daughter! freed
From troubles, purged of sin; and witness him—
With all his gems and glories—governing
Nishadha once again, invincible,
Joy of his friends and terror of his foes.
Yea, Noblest, thou shalt have thy love anew
In days to come."
                                So speaking, from the sight
Of Damayanti, at that instant, passed
Hermits, with hermitage and holy fires,
Evanishing. In wonderment she stood,
Gazing bewildered. Then the Princess cried:—
" Was it in dream I saw them? Whence befell
This unto me? Where are the brethren gone,

The ring of huts, the pleasant stream that ran
With birds upon its crystal banks, the grove
Delightful, with its fruits and flowers?"   Long while
Pondered and wondered Damayanti there,
Her bright smile fled, pale, strengthless, sorrowful;
Then to another region of the wood,
With sighs, and eyes welling great tears, she passed,
Lamenting; till a beauteous tree she spied—
The Asoka, best of trees.   Fair rose it there
Beside the forest, glowing with the flame
Of golden and crimson blossoms, and its boughs
Full of sweet-singing birds.
                              "*Ahovat*—Look!"
She cried: " Ah, lovely tree, that wavest here
Thy crown of countless, shining, clustering blooms
As thou wert woodland king—Asoka tree,
Tree called ' the sorrow-ender,' heart's-ease tree!
Be what thy name saith—end my sorrow now,
Saying, ah, bright Asoka! thou hast seen
My Prince, my dauntless Nala; seen that lord
Whom Damayanti loves and his foes fear;
Seen great Nishadha's Chief, so dear to me,
His tender princely skin in rended cloth
Scantily clad.   Hath he passed wandering
Under thy branches, grievously forlorn?
Answer, Asoka!   ' Sorrow-ender,' speak!
That I go sorrowless, O heart's-ease, be
Truly heart-easing—ease my heart of pain."

   Thus, wild with grief, she spake unto the tree,
Round and round walking, as to reverence it;
And then, unanswered, the sweet lady sped
Through wastes more dreadful, passing many a runn,
Many still-gliding rillets, many a peak
Tree-clad, with beasts and birds of wondrous kind,
In dark ravines, and caves, and lonely glooms.
These things saw Damayanti, Bhima's child,
Seeking her lord.
                        At last, on the long road,
She, whose soft smile was once so beautiful,
A caravan encountered.   Merchantmen
With trampling horses, elephants, and wains,

Made passage of a river, running slow
In cool, clear waves.   The quiet waters gleamed,
Shining and wide outspread, between the canes
Which bordered it, wherefrom echoed the cries
Of fish-hawks, curlews, and red chakravâks,
With sounds of leaping fish and water-snakes,
And tortoises, amid its shoals and flats
Sporting or feeding.

           When she spied that throng—
Heart-maddened with her anguish, weak and wan,
Half clad, bloodless and thin, her long black locks
Matted with dust—breathlessly breaks she in
Upon them—Nala's wife—so beauteous once,
So honored.   Seeing her, some fled in fear;
Some gazed, speechless with wonder; some called out,
Mocking the piteous face by words of scorn;
But some (my King!) had pity of her woe,
And spake her fair, inquiring: "Who art thou?
And whence?   And in this grove what seekest thou,
To come so wild?   Thy mien astonisheth.
Art of our kind, or art thou something strange,
The spirit of the forest, or the hill,
Or river valley?   Tell us true; then we
Will buy thy favor.   If, indeed, thou art
Yakshini, Rakshasi, or she-creature
Haunting this region, be propitious!   Send
Our caravan in safety on its path,
That we may quickly, by thy fortune, go
Homeward, and all fair chances fall to us."

  Hereby accosted, softly gave response
That royal lady—weary for her lord—
Answering the leader of the caravan,
And those that gathered round, a marvelling throng
Of men and boys and elders: "Oh, believe
I am as you, of mortal birth, but born
A Raja's child, and made a Raja's wife.
Him seek I, Chieftain of Nishadha, named
Prince Nala—famous, glorious, first in war.
If ye know aught of him, my king, my joy,
My tiger of the jungle, my lost lord,
Quick, tell me, comfort me!"

Then one who led
Their line—the merchant Śuchi—answering,
Spake to the peerless Princess: " Hear me now.
I am the captain of this caravan,
But nowhere any named by Nala's name
Have I, or these, beheld.   Of evil beasts
The woods were full—cheetahs and bears and cats,
Tigers and elephants, bison and boar;
Those saw we in the brake on every side,
But nowhere nought of human shape, save thee.
May Manibhadra have us in his grace—
The Lord of Yakshas—as I tell thee truth! "
    Then sadly spake she to the trader-chief
And to his band: " Whither wend ye, I pray?
Please ye, acquaint me where this Sârthâ [2] goes."
    Replied the captain: " Unto Chedi's realm,
Where rules the just Subâhu, journey we,
To sell our merchandise, daughter of men! "
    Thus by the chieftain of the band informed,
The peerless Princess journeyed with them, still
Seeking her lord.   And at the first the way
Fared through another forest, dark and deep;
Afterwards came the traders to a pool
Broad, everywhere delightful, odorous
With cups of opened lotus, and its shores
Green with rich grass, and edged with garden trees—
A place of flowers and fruits and singing birds.
So cool and clear and peacefully it gleamed,
That men and cattle, weary with the march,
Clamored to pitch; and, on their chieftain's sign,
The pleasant hollow entered they, and camped—
All the long caravan—at sunset's hour.
    There, in the quiet of the middle night,
Deep slumbered these; when, sudden on them fell
A herd of elephants, thirsting to drink,
In rut, the mada [3] oozing from their heads.
And when those great beasts spied the caravan,
And smelled the tame cows of their kind, they rushed
Headlong, and, mad with must, o'erwhelming all,

[2] A caravan.
[3] This is a secretion which flows by a small orifice from the elephant's tem- ples at certain seasons. It is sweet-smelling, and constantly alluded to in Hindoo poetry.

With onset vast and irresistible.
As when from some tall peak into the plain
Thunder and smoke and crash the rolling rocks,
Through splintered stems and thorns breaking their path,
So swept the herd to where, beside the pool,
Those sleepers lay; and trampled them to earth
Half-risen, helpless, shrieking in the dark,
" Haha! the elephants! "   Of those unslain,
Some in the thickets sought a shelter; some,
Yet dazed with sleep, stood panic-stricken, mute;
Till here with tusks, and there with trunks, the beasts
Gored them, and battered them, and trod them flat
Under their monstrous feet.   Then might be seen
Camels with camel-drivers, perishing,
And men flying in fear, who struck at men—
Terror and death and clamor everywhere:
While some, despairing, cast themselves to earth;
And some, in fleeing, fell and died; and some
Climbed to the tree-tops.   Thus on every side
Scattered and ruined was that caravan—
Cattle and merchants—by the herd assailed.
So hideous was the tumult, all three worlds
Seemed filled with fright; and one was heard to cry:—
" The fire is in the tents! fly for your lives!
Stay not! "   And others cried: " Look where we leave ⁻
Our treasures trodden down; gather them!   Halt!
Why run ye, losing ours and yours?   Nay, stay!
Stand ye, and we will stand! "   And then to these
One voice cried, " Stand! " another, " Fly! we die! "
Answered by those again who shouted, " Stand!
Think what we lose, O cowards! "

       While this rout
Raged, amid dying groans and sounds of fear,
The Princess, waking startled, terror-struck,
Saw such a sight as might the boldest daunt—
Such scene as those great lovely lotus-eyes
Ne' er gazed upon before.   Sick with new dread—
Her breath suspended 'twixt her lips—she rose
And heard, of those surviving, some one moan
Amidst his fellows: " From whose evil act
Is this the fruit?   Hath worship not been paid

To mighty Manibhadra? Gave we not
The reverence due to Vaishravan, that King
Of all the Yakshas? Was not offering made
At outset to the spirits which impede?
Is this the evil portent of the birds?
Were the stars adverse? or what else hath fall'n?"
    And others said, wailing for friends and goods:—
"Who was that woman, with mad eyes, that came
Into our camp, ill-favored, hardly cast
In mortal mould? By her, be sure, was wrought
This direful sorcery. Demon or witch,
Yakshî or Rakshasî, or gliding ghost,
Or something frightful, was she. Hers this deed
Of midnight murders; doubt there can be none.
Ah, if we could espy that hateful one,
The ruin of our march, the woe-maker,
With stones, clods, canes, or clubs, nay, with clenched fists,
We'd strike her dead, the murderess of our band!"
    Trembling the Princess heard those angry words;
And—saddened, maddened, shamed—breathless she fled
Into the thicket, doubtful if such sin
Might not be hers, and with fresh dread distressed.
"Aho!" she weeps, "pitiless grows the wrath
Of Fate against me. Not one gleam of good
Arriveth. Of what fault is this the fruit?
I cannot call to mind a wrong I wrought
To any—even a little thing—in act
Or thought or word; whence then hath come this curse?
Belike from ill deeds done in by-gone lives
It hath befall'n, and what I suffer now
Is payment of old evils undischarged.
Grievous the doom—my palace lost, my lord,
My children, kindred; I am torn away
From home and love and all, to roam accurst
In this plague-haunted waste!"
                              When broke the day,
Those which escaped alive, with grievous cries
Departed, mourning for their fellows slain.
Each one a kinsman or a friend laments—
Father or brother, son, or comrade dear.
    And Damayanti, hearing, weeps anew,

Saying: " What dreadful sin was that I wrought
Long, long ago, which, when I chance to meet
These wayfarers in the unpeopled wood,
Dooms them to perish by the elephants,
In my dark destiny enwrapped?   No doubt
More and more sorrow I shall bear, or bring,
For none dies ere his time; this is the lore
Of ancient sages; this is why—being glad
If I could die—I was not trampled down
Under the elephants.   There haps to man
Nothing unless by destiny.   Why else,
Seeing that never have I wrought one wrong,
From childhood's hours, in thought or word or deed,
Hath this woe chanced?   May be—meseems it may!—
The mighty gods, at my Swayamvara
Slighted by me for Nala's dearest sake,
Are wroth, and by their dread displeasure thus
To loss and loneliness I am consigned! "
    So—woe-begone and wild—this noble wife,
Deserted Damayanti, poured her griefs:
And afterwards, with certain Bráhmanas
Saved from the rout—good men who knew the Veds—
Sadly her road she finished, like the moon
That goeth clouded in the month of rain.
Thus travelling long, the Princess drew at last
Nigh to a city, at the evening hour.
The dwelling-place it was of Chedi's Chief,
The just Subâhu.   Through its lofty gates
Painfully passed she, clad in half a cloth;
And as she entered—sorrow-stricken, wan,
Foot-weary, stained with mire, with unsmoothed hair,
Unbathed, and eyes of madness—those who saw,
Wondered and stared, and watched her as she toiled
Down the long city street.   The children break
From play, and—boys with girls—followed her steps,
So that she came—a crowd encompassing—
Unto the King's door.   On the palace roof
The mother of the Maharaja paced,
And marked the throng, and that sad wayfarer.
Then to her nurse spake the queen-mother this:—
" Go thou, and bring yon woman unto me!

The people trouble her; mournful she walks,
Seeming unfriended, yet bears she a mien
Made for a king's abode, and, all so wild,
Still are her wistful eyes like the great eyes
Of Lakshmi's self." So downwards went the nurse,
Bidding the rude folk back; and to the roof
Of the great palace led that wandering one—
Desolate Damayanti—whom the Queen
Courteous besought: "Though thou art wan of face,
Thou wear'st a noble air, which through thy griefs
Shineth as lightning doth behind its cloud.
Tell me thy name, and whose thou art, and whence.
No lowborn form is thine, albeit thou com'st
Wearing no ornaments; and all alone
Wanderest—not fearing men—by some spell safe."
   Hearing which words, the child of Bhima spake
Gratefully this: "A woful woman I,
And woful wife, but faithful to my vows;
High-born, but like a servant, like a slave,
Lodging where it may hap, and finding food
From the wild roots and fruits wherever night
Brings me my resting-place. Yet is my lord
A prince noble and great, with countless gifts
Endued; and him I followed faithfully
As 't were his shadow, till hard fate decreed
That he should fall into the rage of dice:—
And, worsted in that play, into the wood
He fled, clad in one cloth, frenzied and lone.
And I his steps attended in the wood,
Comforting him, my husband. But it chanced,
Hungry and desperate, he lost his cloth;
And I—one garment bearing—followed still
My unclad lord, despairing, reasonless,
Through many a weary night not slumbering.
But when, at length, a little while I slept,
My Prince abandoned me, rending away
Half of my garment, leaving there his wife,
Who never wrought him wrong. That lord I seek
By day and night, with heart and soul on fire—
Seek, but still find not; though he is to me
Brighter than light which gleams from lotus-cups,

Divine as are the immortals, dear as breath,
The master of my life, my pride, my joy!"
   Whom, grieving so, her sweet eyes blind with tears,
Gently addressed Subâhu's mother—sad
To hear as she to tell. "Stay with us here,
Thou ill-starred lady. Great the friendliness
I have for thee. The people of our court
Shall thy lost husband seek; or, it may be,
He too will wander hither of himself
By devious paths: yea, mournful one, thy lord
Thou wilt regain, abiding with us here."
   And Damayanti, bowing, answered thus
Unto the Queen: "I will abide with thee,
O mother of illustrious sons, if so
They feed me not on orts, nor seek from me
To wash the feet of comers, nor that I
Be set to speak with any stranger-men
Before the curtain; and, if any man
Sue me, that he be punished; and if twice,
Then that he die, guilty of infamy.
This is my earnest prayer; but Bráhmanas
Who seek my husband, or bear news of him,
Such will I speak with. If it may be thus,
Gladly would I abide, great lady, here;
If otherwise, it is not on my mind
To sojourn longer."
               Very tenderly
Quoth the queen-mother: "All that thou dost ask
We will ordain. The gods reward thy love,
Which hath such honor!" Comforting her so,
To the king's daughter, young Sunandâ, spake
The Maharajni: "See, Sunandâ, here
Clad as a handmaid, but in form divine,
One of thy years, gentle and true. Be friends;
Take and give pleasure in glad company
Each with the other, keeping happy hearts."
   So went Sunandâ joyous to her house,
Leading with loving hand the Princess in,
The maidens of the court accompanying.

Part II.

NOT long (O Maharaja!) was Nala fled
 From Damayanti, when, in midmost gloom
 Of the thick wood a flaming fire he spied,
And from the fire's heart heard proceed a voice
Of one imperilled, crying many times:—
" Haste hither, Punyashloka, Nala, haste ! "
" Fear not," the Prince replied; " I come ! " and sprang
Across the burning bushes, where he saw
A snake—a king of serpents—lying curled
In a great ring, which reared its dancing crest
Saluting, and in human accents spoke:—
" Maharaja, kindly lord, I am the snake
Karkôtaka; by me was once betrayed
The famous Rishi Narada; his wrath
Doomed me, thou Chief of men! to bear this spell—
' Coil thy false folds,' said he, ' forever here,
A serpent, motionless upon this spot,
Till it shall chance that Nala passeth by
And bears thee hence; then only from my curse
Canst thou be freed.' And prisoned by that curse
I have no power to stir, though the wood burns;
Nay, not a coil! good fellowship I'll show
If thou wilt succor me. I'll be to thee
A faithful friend, as no snake ever yet.
Lift me, and quickly from the flames bear forth:
For thee I shall grow light." Thereat shrank up
That monstrous reptile to a finger's length;
And grasping this, unto a place secure
From burning, Nala bore it, where the air
Breathed freshly, and the fire's black path was stayed.
 Then made the Prince to lay the serpent down,
But yet again it speaks: " Nishadha's Lord,
Grasp me and slowly go, counting thy steps;
For, Raja, thou shalt have good fortune hence."

So Nala slowly went, counting his steps;
And when the tenth pace came, the serpent turned
And bit the Prince.   No sooner pierced that tooth
Than all the likeness of Nishadha changed;
And, wonder-struck, he gazed upon himself;
While from the dust he saw the snake arise
A man, and, speaking as Karkôtaka,
Comfort him thus:—

                " Thou art by me transformed
That no man know thee: and that evil one
(Possessing, and undoing thee, with grief)
Shall so within thee by my venom smart,
Shall through thy blood so ache, that—till he quit—
He shall endure the woe he did impart.
Thus by my potent spell, most noble Prince!
(Who sufferest too long) thou wilt be freed
From him that haunts thee.   Fear no more the wood,
Thou tiger of all princes! fear thou not
Horned nor fanged beasts, nor any enemies,
Though they be Bráhmans! safe thou goest now,
Guarded from grief and hurt—Chieftain of men!
By this kind poison.   In the fields of war
Henceforth the victory always falls to thee;
Go joyous, therefore, Prince; give thyself forth
For ' Vahûka, the charioteer:' repair
To Rituparna's city, who is skilled
In play, and dwells in fair Ayodhyâ.
Wend thou, Nishadha! thither; he will teach
Great subtlety in numbers unto thee,
Exchanging this for thine own matchless gift
Of taming horses.   From the lordly line
Descended of Ikshvaku, glad and kind
The King will be; and thou, learning of him
His deepest act of dice, wilt win back all,
And clasp again thy Princess.   Therefore waste
No thought on woes.   I tell thee truth! thy realm
Thou shalt regain; and when the time is come
That thou hast need to put thine own form on,
Call me to mind, O Prince, and tie this cloth
Around thy body.   Wearing it, thy shape
Thou shalt resume."

     Therewith the serpent gave
A magic twofold robe, not wove on earth,
Which (O thou son of Kuru!) Nala took;
And so the snake, transformed, vanished away.
  The great snake being gone, Nishadha's Chief
Set forth, and on the tenth day entered in
At Rituparna's town; there he besought
The presence of the Raja, and spake thus:—
" I am the chariot-driver, Vahûka.
There is not on this earth another man
Hath gifts like mine to tame and guide the steed;
Moreover, thou mayest use me in nice needs
And dangerous, where kings lack faithful hearts.
Specially skilful I am in dressing meats;
And whatso other duties may befall,
Though they be weighty, I shall execute,
If, Rituparna, thou wilt take me in."
  " I take thee," quoth the King.　" Dwell here with me.
Such service as thou knowest, render us.
'T is, Vahûka, forever in my heart
To have my steeds the swiftest; be thy task
To train me horses like the wind for speed;
My charioteer I make thee, and thy wage
Ten thousand gold suvernas.　Thou wilt have
For fellows, Varshneya and Jîvala;
With those abiding, lodge thou happy here."
  So entertained and honored of the King,
In Rituparna's city Nala dwelled,
Lodging with Varshneya and Jîvala.
  There sojourned he (my Raja!), thinking still
Of sweet Vidarbha's Princess day by day;
And sunset after sunset one sad strain
He sang: " Where resteth she that roamed the wood
Hungry and parched and worn, but always true?
Doth she remember yet her faultful lord?
Ah, who is near her now? "　So it befell
Jîvala heard him ever sighing thus,
And questioned: " Who is she thou dost lament?
Say, Vahûka! fain would I know her name.
Long life be thine; but tell me who he is,
The faultful man that was the lady's lord."

And Nala answered him: " There lives a man,
Evil and rash, that had a noble wife.
False to his word he was; and thus it fell
That somewhere, for some reason (ask not me!),
He quitted her, this rash one.   And—so wrenched
Apart from hers—his spirit, bad and sad,
Muses and moans, with grief's slow fire consumed
Night-time and day-time.   Thence it is he sings
At every sunset this unchanging verse,
An outcast on the earth, by hazard led
Hither and thither.   Such a man thou seest
Woful, unworthy, holding in his heart
Always that sin.   I was that lady's lord,
Whom she did follow through the dreadful wood,
Living by me abandoned, at this hour;
If yet, in truth, she lives—youthful, alone,
Unpractised in the ways, not meriting
Fortunes so hard.   Ah, if indeed she lives,
Who roamed the thick and boundless forest, full
Of prowling beasts—roamed it, my Jivala,
Unguarded by her guilty lord—forsook,
Betrayed, good friend! "
                              Thus did Nishadha grieve,
Calling sweet Damayanti to his mind.
So tarried he within the Raja's house,
And no man knew his place of sojourning.
   While, stripped of state, the Prince and Princess thus
Were sunk to servitude, Bhima made quest,
Sending his Bráhmans forth to search for them
With straight commands, and for their road-money
Liberal store.   " Seek everywhere," said he
Unto the twice-born, " Nala—everywhere
My daughter Damayanti.   Whoso comes
Successful in this quest, discovering her—
With lost Nishadha's Lord—and bringing them,
A thousand cows to that man will I give,
And village-lands whence shall be revenue
As great as from a city.   If so be
Ye cannot bring me Nala and my child,
To him that learns their refuge I will give
The thousand cows."

                        Thereby rejoiced, they went,
Those Bráhmans, hither and thither, up and down,
Into all regions, rajaships, and towns,
Seeking Nishadha's Chieftain, and his wife.
But Nala nowhere found they; nowhere found
Sweet Damayanti, Bhima's beauteous child—
    Until, straying to pleasant Chedipur,
One day a twice-born came, Sudêva named,
And entered it; and, spying round about
(Upon a feast-day by the King proclaimed),
He saw forth-passing through the palace gate
A woman—Bhima's daughter—side by side
With young Sunanda. Little praise had now
That beauty which in old days shone so bright;
Marred with much grief it was, like sunlight dimmed
By fold on fold of wreathed and creeping mists.
But when Sudêva marked the great dark eyes—
Lustreless though they were, and she so worn,
So listless—" Lo, the Princess!" whispered he;—
" 'T is the King's daughter," quoth he to himself;
And thus mused on:—
                        " Yea! as I used to see,
'T is she! no other woman hath such grace!
My task is done; I gaze on that one form,
Which is like Lakshmi's, whom all worlds adore.
I see the bosoms, rounded, dark, and smooth,
As they were sister-moons; the soft moon-face
Which with its queenly light makes all things bright
Where it doth gleam; the large deep lotus-eyes,
That, like to Rati's own, the Queen of Love,
Beam, each a lovelit star, filling the worlds
With longing. Ah, fair lotus-flower, plucked up
By Fate's hard grasp from far Vidarbha's pool,
How is thy cup muddied and slimed to-day!
Ah, moon, how is thy night like to the eclipse
When Rahu swallows up the silver round!
Ah, tearless eyes, reddened with weeping him,
How are ye like to gentle streams run dry!
Ah, lake of lilies, where grief's elephant
Hath swung his trunk, and turned the crystal black,
And scattered all the blue and crimson cups,

And frightened off the birds! Ah, lily-cup,
Tender, and delicately leaved, and reared
To blossom in a palace built of gems,
How dost thou wither here, wrenched by the root,
Sun-scorched and faded! Noblest, loveliest, best!—
Who bear'st no gems, yet so becomest them—
How like the new moon's silver horn thou art,
When envious black clouds blot it! Lost for thee
Are love, home, children, friends, and kinsmen; lost
All joy of that fair body thou dost wear
Only that it may last to find thy lord.
Truly a woman's ornament is this:—
The husband is her jewel; lacking him
She hath none, though she shines with priceless pearls;
Piteous must be her state! And, torn from her,
Doth Nala cling to life; or, day by day,
Waste with long yearning? Oh, as I behold
Those black locks, and those eyes—dark and long-shaped
As are the hundred-petalled lotus-leaves—
And watch her joyless who deserves all joy,
My heart is sore! When will she overpass
The river of this sorrow, and come safe
Unto its farther shore? When will she meet
Her lord, as moon and moon-star in the sky
Mingle? For, as I think, in winning her,
Nala would win his happy days again,
And—albeit banished now—have back his lands.
Alike in years and graces, and alike
In lordly race these were: no bride could seem
Worthy Nishadha, if it were not she;
Nor husband worthy of Vidarbha's Pride,
Save it were Nala. It is meet I bring
Comfort forthwith to yon despairing one,
The consort of the just and noble Prince,
For whom I see her heart-sick. I will go
And speak good tidings to this moon-faced Queen,
Who once knew nought of sorrows, but to-day
Stands yonder, plunged heart-deep in woful thought."
    So, all those signs and marks considering
Which stamped her Bhima's child, Sudêva drew
Nearer, and said: " Vidarbhi, Nala's wife,

I am the Bráhmana Sudêva, friend
Unto my lord, thy brother, and I come
By royal Bhima's mandate, seeking thee.
That Maharaja, thy father, dwells in health;
Thy mother and thy house are well; and well—
With promise of long years—thy little ones,
Sister and brother. Yet, for thy sake, Queen,
Thy kindred sit as men with spirit gone;
In search of thee a hundred twice-born rove
Over all lands."

             But (O King Yudhisthir!)
Hardly one word she heard before she broke
With question after question on the man,
Asking of this dear friend and that and this;
All mingled with quick tears, and tender sighs,
And hungry gazing on her brother's friend,
Sudêva—best of Bráhmanas—come there.
Which soon Sunandâ marked, watching them speak
Apart, and Damayanti all in tears.
Then came she to her mother, saying: "See,
The handmaid thou didst give me talks below
With one who is a Bráhman, all her words
Watered with weeping; if thou wilt, demand
What this man knows."

            Therewith swept forth amazed
The mother of the Raja, and beheld
How Nala's wife spake with the Bráhmana.
Whom straight she bade them summon; and, being brought,
In this wise questioned: "Knowest thou whose wife,
Whose daughter, this one is; and how she left
Her kin; and wherefore, being heavenly-eyed
And noble-mannered, she hath wandered here?
I am full fain to hear this; tell me all,
No whit withholding; answer faithfully—
Who is our slave-girl with the goddess gait?"

    The Bráhmana Sudêva, so addressed,
Seating himself at ease, unto the Queen
Told Damayanti's story, how all fell.
    Sudêva said: "There reigns in majesty
King Bhima at Vidarbha; and of him
The Princess Damayanti here is child;

And Virasena's son, Nala, is Lord
Over Nishadha, praised-in-song and wise;
And of that Prince this lady is the wife.
In play his brother worsted Nala—stripped
Of lands and wealth the Prince; who fled his realm,
Wandering with Damayanti—where, none knew.
In quest of Damayanti we have roamed
The earth's face o'er, until I found her here
In thy son's house, the King's—the very same,
Since like to her for grace no woman lives
Of all fair women.   Where her eyebrows meet
A pretty mole, born with her, should be seen
A little lotus-bud—not visible
By reason of the dust of toil which clouds
Her face and veils its moon-like beauty—that
The wondrous Maker on the rare work stamped
To be His Mark.   But as the waxing moon
Goes thin and darkling for awhile, then rounds
The crescent's rims with splendors, so this Queen
Hath lost not queenliness.   Being now obscured,
Soiled with the grime of chores, unbeautified,
She shows true gold.   The fire which trieth gold
Denoteth less itself by instant heat
Than Damayanti by her goodlihood.
As first sight knew I her.   She bears that mole."
   Whilst yet Sudêva spake (O King of men!),
Sunandâ from the slave's front washed away
The gathered dust, and forth that mark appeareo
'Twixt Damayanti's brows, as when clouds break,
And in the sky the moon, the night-maker,
Glitters to view.   Seeing the spot awhile,
Sunandâ and the mother of the King
Gazed voiceless; then they clasped her neck and wept
Rejoicing, till the Queen, staying her tears,
Exclaimed: " My sister's daughter, dear! thou art,
By this same mark.   Thy mother and myself
Were sisters by one father—he that rules
Daśarna, King Sudâman.   She was given
To Bhima, and to Virabahu I.
Once at Daśarna, in my father's house,
I saw thee, newly born.   Thy race and mine,

Princess, are one: henceforward, therefore, here
As I am, Damayanti, shalt thou be."
   With gladdened heart did Damayanti bend
Before her mother's sister, answering thus:—
" Peaceful and thankful dwelled I here with thee,
Being unknown, my every need supplied,
My life and honor by thy succor safe,
Yet, Maharajni, even than this dear home
One would be dearer: 't is so many days
Since we were parted.   Suffer me to go
Where those my tender little ones were led;
So long—poor babes!—of me and of their sire
Bereft.   If, lady, thou dost think to show
Kindness to me, this is my wish: to wend
Unto Vidarbha swiftly; wilt thou bid
They bear me thither?"
                    Was no sooner heard
That fond desire, than the queen-mother gave
Willing command; and soon an ample troop,
The King consenting, gathered for her guard.
So was she sent upon a palanquin,
With soldiers, pole-bearers, and meat and drink,
And garments as befitted—happier—home.
   Thus to Vidarbha came its Pride again,
By no long road; and joyously her kin
Brought the sweet Princess in, and welcomed her.
In peace and safety all her house she found;
Her children well;—father and mother, friends.
The gods she worshipped, and to Bráhmanas
Due reverence made, and whatso else was meet
That Damayanti did, regal in all.
To wise Sudêva fell the thousand cows
By Bhima granted, with the village-lands,
And goodly gifts beside.
                But when there passed
One night of rest within the palace-walls,
The wistful Princess to her mother said:—
" If thou wouldst have me live, I tell thee true,
Dear mother, it must be by bringing back
My Nala, my own lord; and only so."
   When this she spake, right sorrowful became

The Rani, weeping silently, nor gave
One word of answer; and the palace-girls,
Seeing this grief, sat round them, weeping too,
And crying: " Haha! where is gone her lord?"
And loud the lamentation was of all.
    Afterwards to the Maharaja his Queen
Told what was said: " Lord! all uncomforted
Thy daughter Damayanti weeps and grieves,
Lacking her husband.   Even to me she spake
Before our damsels, laying shame aside:—
' Find Nala; let the people of the court
Strive day and night to learn where Nala is.'"
    Then Bhima, hearing, called his Bráhmanas
Patient and wise, and issued hest to go
Into all regions, seeking for the Prince.
But first, by mandate of the Maharaja,
To Damayanti all those twice-born came,
Saying: " Now we depart!"   Then Bhima's child
Gave ordinance: " To whatsoever lands
Ye wend, say this—wherever gather men,
Say this—in every place these verses speak:—

    Whither art thou departed, cruel lover,
        Who stole the half of thy belovèd's cloth,
    And left her to awaken, and discover
        The wrong thou wroughtest to the love of both?
    She, as thou didst command, a sad watch keepeth,
        With woful heart wearing the rended dress.
    Prince, hear her cry who thus forever weepeth;
        Be mindful, hero; comfort her distress!

And, furthermore," the Princess said, " since fire
Leaps into flame when the wind fans the spark,
Be this too spoken, that his heart may burn:—

    By every husband nourished and protected
        Should every wife be.   Think upon the wood!
    Why these thy duties hast thou so neglected,
        Prince, that was called noble and true and good?
    Art then become compassionate no longer,
        Shunning, perchance, my fortune's broken way?

Ah, husband, love is most! let love be stronger;
Ahimsa paro dharma,[4] thou didst say.

These verses while ye speak," quoth the Princess,
" Should any man make answer, note him well
In any place; and who he is, and where
He dwells.   And if one listens to these words
Intently, and shall so reply to them,
Good Bráhmans, hold ye fast his speech, and bring,
Breath by breath, all of it unto me here;
But so that he shall know not whence ye speak,
If ye go back.   Do this unweariedly;
And if one answer—be he high or low,
Wealthy or poor—learn all he was and is,
And what he would."
                              Hereby enjoined, they went,
Those twice-born, into all the lands to seek
Prince Nala in his loneliness.   Through towns,
Cities and villages, hamlets and camps,
By shepherds' huts and hermits' caves, they passed,
Searching for Nala; yet they found him not;
Albeit in every region (O my king!)
The words of Damayanti, as she taught,
Spake they again in hearing of all men.
    Suddenly—after many days—there came
A Bráhman back, Parnâda he was called,
Who unto Bhima's child in this wise spake:—
" O Damayanti, seeking Nala still,
Ayodhyâ's streets I entered, where I saw
The Maharaja; he—noble-minded one!—
Heard me thy verses say, as thou hadst said;
Great Rituparna heard those very words,
Excellent Princess; but he answered nought;
And no man answered, out of all the throng
Ofttimes addressed.   But when I had my leave
And was withdrawn, a man accosted me
Privately—one of Rituparna's train,
Vahûka named, the Raja's charioteer
(Something misshapen, with a shrunken arm,
But skilled in driving, very dexterous
In cookery and sweetmeats).   He—with groans,

4 " Gentleness is chief of virtues."

And tears which rolled and rolled—asked of my health,
And then these verses spake full wistfully:—

  ' Even when their loss is largest, noble ladies
    Keep the true treasure of their hearts unspent,
  Attaining heaven through faith, which undismayed is
    By wrong, unaltered by abandonment;
  Such an one guards with virtue's golden shield
    Her name from harm; pious and pure and tender;
  And, though her lord forsook her, will not yield
    To wrath, even against that vile offender—
  Even against the ruined, rash, ungrateful,
    Faithless, fond Prince from whom the birds did steal
  His only cloth, whom now a penance fateful
    Dooms to sad days, that dark-eyed will not feel
  Anger; for if she saw him she should see
    A man consumed with grief and loss and shame;
  Ill or well lodged, ever in misery,
    Her unthroned lord, a slave without a name.'

Such words I heard him speak," Parnâda said,
" And, hastening thence, I tell them to thee, here;
Thou knowest; thou wilt judge; make the King know."
  But Damayanti listened, with great eyes
Welling quick tears, while thus Parnâda spake,
And afterwards crept secretly and said
Unto her mother: " Breathe no word hereof,
Dear mother, to the King, but let me speak
With wise Sudêva in thy presence here;
Nothing should Bhima know of what I plan,
But, if thou lovest me, by thee and me
This shall be wrought. As I was safely led
By good Sudêva home, so let him go—
With not less happy fortune—to bring back,
Ere many days, my Nala; let him seek
Ayodhyâ, mother dear, and fetch my Prince!"
  But first Parnâda, resting from his road—
That best of twice-borns—did the Princess thank
With honorable words and gifts: " If home
My Nala cometh, Bráhman!" so she spake,
" Great guerdon will 1 give. Thou hast well done
For me herein—better than any man;

Helping me find again my wandered lord."
To which fair words made soft reply, and prayers
For " peace and fortune," that high-minded one,
And so passed home, his service being wrought.
  Next to Sudêva spake the sad Princess
This (O my King!), her mother standing by:—
" Good Bráhman, to Ayodhyâ's city go.
Say in the ears of Raja Rituparna,
As though thou cam'st a simple traveller,
' The daughter of King Bhima once again
Maketh to hold her high Swayamvara.
The kings and princes from all lands repair
Thither; the time draws nigh; to-morrow's dawn
Shall bring the day. If thou wouldst be of it,
Speed quickly, conquering King! at sunsetting
Another lord she chooseth for herself;
Since whether Nala liveth or is dead,
None knoweth.' "
                These the words which he should say;
And, learning them, he sped, and thither came—
That Bráhmana Sudêva—and he spake
To Maharaja Rituparna so.
  Now when the Raja Rituparna heard
Sudêva's words, quoth he to Vahûka
Full pleasantly: " Much mind I have to go
Where Damayanti holds Swayamvara,
If to Vidarbha, in a single day,
Thou deemest we might drive, my charioteer! "
  Of Nala, by his Raja thus addressed,
Torn was the heart with anguish; for he thought:—
" Can Damayanti purpose this? Could grief
So change her? Is it not some fine device
For my sake schemed? Or doth my Princess seek,
All holy as she was, this guilty joy,
Being so wronged of me, her rash weak lord?
Frail is a woman's heart, and my fault great!
Thus might she do it, being far from home,
Bereft of friends, desolate with long woes
Of love for me—my slender-waisted one!
Yet no, no, no! she would not—she that is
My children's mother! Be it false or true,

Best shall I know in going; therefore now
The will of Rituparna must I serve."
　　Thus pondering in his mind, the troubled Prince
With joined palms meekly to his master said:—
" I shall thy hest accomplish! I can drive
In one day, Raja, to Vidarbha's gates."
　　Then in the royal stables—steed by steed,
Stallions and mares, Vahûka scanned them all,
By Rituparna prayed quickly to choose.
Slowly he picked four coursers, under-fleshed,
But big of bone and sinew; fetlocked well
For journeying; high-bred, heavy-framed; of blood
To match the best, yet gentle; blemish-free;
Broad in the jaw, with scarlet nostrils spread;
Bearing the *Avarthas*, the ten true marks—
Reared on the banks of Indus, swift as wind.
Which, when the Raja looked upon, he cried,
Half-wrathful: " What thing thinkest thou to do?
Wilt thou betray me? How should sorry beasts,
Lean-ribbed and ragged, take us all that way,
The long road we must swiftly travel hence?"
　　Vahûka answered: " See on all these four
The ten sure marks: one curl upon each crest,
Two on the cheeks, two upon either flank,
Two on the breast, and on each crupper one.*
These to Vidarbha—doubt it not—will go;
Yet, Raja, if thou wilt have others, speak;
And I shall yoke them."
　　　　　　　　　Rituparna said:—
" I know thou hast deep skill in stable-craft;
Yoke therefore such four coursers as thou wilt,
But quickly!"
　　　　　　Thus those horses, two by two,
High-mettled, spare, and strong, Prince Nala put
Under the bars; and when the car was hitched,
And eagerly the Raja made to mount,
At sign the coursers bent their knees, and lay
Along the earth. Then Nala (O my King!),
With kindly voice cheering the gaunt bright steeds,
Loosed them, and grasped the reins, and bade ascend

* These "curls" are the "Arvathas," or marks of good blood and high-breeding.

Varshneya: so he started, headlong, forth.
  At cry of Vahûka the four steeds sprung
Into the air, as they would fly with him;
And when the Raja felt them, fleet as wind,
Whirling along, mute sat he and amazed;
And much Varshneya mused to hear and see
The thundering of those wheels; the fiery four
So lightly held; Vahûka's matchless art.
" Is Mâtali, who driveth Indra's car,
Our charioteer? for all the marks of him
Are here! or Sâlihotra can this be,
The god of horses, knowing all their ways,
Who here in mortal form his greatness hides?
Or is it—can it be—Nala the Prince,
Nala the steed-tamer? " Thus pondered he:—
" Whatever Nala knew this one doth know.
Alike the mastery seems of both; alike
I judge their years. If this man be not he,
Two Nalas are there in the world for skill.
They say there wander mighty powers on earth
In strange disguises, who, divinely sprung,
Veil themselves from us under human mould;
Bewilderment it brings me, this his shape
Misshappen—from conclusion that alone
Withholds me; yet I wist not what to think,
In age and manner like—and so unlike
In form! Else Vahûka I must have deemed
Nala, with Nala's gifts."

                    So in his heart,
Varshneya, watching, wondered—being himself
The second charioteer. But Rituparna
Sat joyous with the speed, delightedly
Marking the driving of the Prince: the eyes
Attent; the hand so firm upon the reins;
The skill so quiet, wise, and masterful;
Great joy the Maharaja had to see.
  By stream and mountain, woodland-path and pool,
Swiftly, like birds that skim in air, they sped;
Till, as the chariot plunged, the Raja saw
His shoulder-mantle falling to the ground;
And—loath to lose the robe—albeit so pressed,

To Nala cried he, " Let me take it up;
Check the swift horses, wondrous charioteer;
And bid Varshneya light, and fetch my cloth."
But Nala answered: " Far it lies behind;
A yojana already we have passed;
We cannot turn again to pick it up."
  A little onward Riturparna saw
Within the wood a tall Myrobolan
Heavy with fruit; hereat, eager he cried:—
" Now, Vahûka, my skill thou mayest behold
In the Arithmic. All arts no man knows;
Each hath his wisdom, but in one man's wit
Is perfect gift of one thing, and not more.
From yonder tree how many leaves and fruits,
Think'st thou, lie fall'n there upon the earth?
Just one above a thousand of the leaves,
And one above a hundred of the fruits;
And on those two limbs hang, of dancing leaves,
Five crores exact; and shouldst thou pluck yon boughs
Together with their shoots, on those twain boughs
Swing twice a thousand nuts and ninety-five!"
  Vahûka checked the chariot wonderingly,
And answered: " Imperceptible to me
Is what thou boastest, slayer of thy foes!
But I to proof will put it, hewing down
The tree, and, having counted, I shall know.
Before thine eyes the branches twain I'll lop:
How prove thee, Maharaja, otherwise,
Whether this be or be not? I will count
One by one—fruits and leaves—before thee, King;
Varshneya, for a space, can rein the steeds."
  To him replied the Raja: " Time is none
Now to delay."
          Vahûka answered quick
(His own set purpose serving): " Stay this space,
Or by thyself drive on! The road is good,
The son of Vrishni will be charioteer!"
  On that the Raja answered soothingly:—
" There is not in the earth another man
That hath thy skill; and by thy skill I look
To reach Vidarbha, O thou steed-tamer!

Thou art my trust; make thou not hindrance now!
Yet would I suffer, too, what thou dost ask,
If thou couldst surely reach Vidarbha's gate
Before yon sun hath sunk."

                              Nala replied:—
"When I have counted those vibhítak boughs,
Vidarbha I will reach; now keep thy word."

    Ill pleased, the Raja said: "Halt then, and count!
Take one bough from the branch which I shall show,
And tell its fruits, and satisfy thy soul."

    So leaping from the car—eager he shore
The boughs, and counted; and all wonder-struck
To Rituparna spake: "Lo, as thou saidst
So many fruits there be upon this bough!
Exceeding marvellous is this thy gift,
I burn to know such learning, how it comes."

    Answered the Raja, for his journey fain:—
"My mind is quick with numbers, skilled to count;
I have the science."

                    "Give it me, dear Lord!"
Vahûka cried: "teach me, I pray, this lore,
And take from me my skill in horse-taming."

    Quoth Rituparna—impatient to proceed—
Yet of such skill desirous: "Be it so!
As thou hast prayed, receive my secret art,
Exchanging with me here thy mastery
Of horses."
                    Thereupon did he impart
His rules of numbers, taking Nala's too.

    But wonderful! So soon as Nala knew
That hidden gift, the accursed Kali leapt
Forth from his breast, the evil spirit's mouth
Spewing the poison of Karkôtaka
Even as he issued. From the afflicted Prince
That bitter plague of Kali passed away;
And for a space Prince Nala lost himself,
Rent by the agony. But when he saw
The evil one take visible shape again—
Free from the serpent's poison—Nishadha's Lord
Had thought to curse him then; but Kali stood
With clasped palms trembling, and besought the Prince,

Saying: "Thy wrath restrain, Sovereign of men!
I will repay thee well.   Thy virtuous wife,
Indrasen's angered mother, laid her ban
Upon me when thou didst forsake her; since
Within thee have I dwelled in anguish sore,
Tortured and tossed and burning, night and day,
With venom from the great snake's fang, which passed
Into me by thy blood.   Be pitiful!
I take my refuge in thy mercy!   Hear
My promise, Prince!   Wherever men henceforth
Shall name thee before people, praising thee,
This shall protect them from the dread of me;
Nala shall guard from Kali, if so now
Thou spare to curse me, seeking grace of thee."

Thus supplicated, Nala stayed his wrath,
Acceding; and the direful Kali fled
Into the wounded tree, possessing it.
But of no eyes, save Nala's, was he seen,
Nor heard of any other; and the Prince,
His sorrows shaking off, when Kali passed,
After that numbering of the leaves, in joy
Unspeakable, and glowing with new hope,
Mounted the car again, and urged his steeds.
But from that hour the tall Myrobolan,
Possessed by Kali, stood there, sear and dead.

Then onward, onward, speeding like the birds,
Those coursers flew; and fast and faster still
The glad Prince cheered them forward, all elate:
And proudly rode the Raja towards the walls
Of high Vidarbha.   Thus did journey down
Exultant Nala, free of trouble now,
Quit of the evil spell, but bearing still
His form misshapen, and the shrunken limb.

At sunset in Vidarbha (O great King!)
The watchers on the walls proclaimed, "There comes
The Raja Rituparna!" Bhima bade
Open the gates; and thus they entered in,
Making all quarters of the city shake
With rattling of the chariot-wheels.   But when
The horses of Prince Nala heard that sound,
For joy they neighed, as when of old their lord

Drew nigh.   And Damayanti, in her bower,
Far off that rattling of the chariot heard,
As when at time of rains is heard the voice
Of clouds low thundering; and her bosom thrilled
At echo of that ringing sound.   It came
Loud and more loud, like Nala's, when of old,
Gripping the reins, he cheered his mares along.
It seemed like Nala to the Princess then—
That clatter of the trampling of the hoofs;
It seemed like Nala to the stabled steeds:
Upon the palace-roof the peacocks heard
And screamed; the elephants within their stalls
Heard it and trumpeted; the coursers, tied,
Snorted for joy to hear that leaping car;

Peacocks and elephants and cattle stalled
All called and clamored with uplifted heads,
As wild things do at noise of coming rain.

Then to herself the Princess spake: " This car,
The rolling of it, echoing all around,
Gladdens my heart.   It must be Nala comes,
My King of men!   If I see not, this day,
My Prince that hath the bright and moon-like face,
My hero of unnumbered gifts, my lord,
Ah, I shall die!   If this day fall I not
Into his opening arms—at last, at last—
And feel his close embrace, oh, beyond doubt,
I cannot live!   If—ending all—to-day
Nishadha cometh not, with this deep sound
Like far-off thunder, then to-night I'll leap
Into the golden, flickering, fiery flames!
If now, now, now, my lion draws not nigh,
My warrior-love, like the wild elephant,
My Prince of princes—I shall surely die!
Nought call I now to mind he said or did
That was not rightly said and justly done.
No idle word he spake, even in free speech;
Patient and lordly; generous to bestow
Beyond all givers; scorning to be base,
Yea, even in secret—such Nishadha was.
Alas! when, day and night, I think of him,
How is my heart consumed, reft of its joy!"

So meditating, like one torn by thoughts,
She mounted to the palace-roof to see;
And thence, in the mid-court, the car beheld
Arriving. Rituparna and Vahûka
She saw, with Vrishni's son, descend and loose
The panting horses, wheeling back the car.
   Then Rituparna, alighting, sought the King,
Bhima the Maharaja, far-renowned—
Whom Bhima with fair courtesies received;
Since well he deemed such breathless visit made
With deep cause, knowing not the women's plots.
" *Swâgatam!* " cried he; " what hath brought thee,
      Prince? "
For nothing wist he that the Raja came
Suitor of Damayanti. Questioned so,
This Raja Rituparna, wise and brave,
Seeing no kings nor princes in the court,
Nor noise of the Swayamvara, nor crowd
Of Bráhmans gathering—weighing all those things,
Answered in this wise: " I am come, great Lord,
To make thee salutations! " But the King
Laughed in his beard at Rituparna's word—
That this of many weary yojanas
Should be the mark. " *Ahoswid!* Hath he passed
Through twenty towns," thought he, " and hither flown
To bid good-morrow? Nay, it is not that.
Good! I shall know it when he bids me know."
   Thereat, with friendly speech his noble guest
The King to rest dismissed. " Repose thyself,"
He said; " the road was long; weary thou art."
And Rituparna, with sentences of grace
Replying to this graciousness, was led
By slaves to the allotted sleeping-room;
And after Rituparna, Varshneya went.
Vahûka, left alone, the chariot ran
Into its shed, and from the foamy steeds
Unbuckled all the harness, thong by thong,
Speaking soft words to them; then sat him down,
Alone, forgotten, on the driving-seat.
   But Damayanti, seeing Rituparna,
And Vrishni's son, and him called Vahûka,

Spake sorrowful: " Whose was the thunder, then,
Of that fleet car? It seemed like Nala's own;
Yet here I see no Nala! Hath yon man
My lord's art learned, or th' other one, that thus
Their car should thunder as when Nala comes?
Could Rituparna drive as Nala doth,
So that those chariot-wheels should sound like his?"
And, after having pondered (O my King!),
The beauteous Princess sent her handmaiden
To Vahûka, that she might question him.

" Go, Keshinî," the Princess said; " inquire
Who is that man upon the driving-seat,
Misshapen, with the shrunken arm. Approach
Composedly, question him winningly
With greetings kind, and bid him answer thee
According to the truth. I feel at heart
A doubt—a hope—that this, perchance, may be
My Lord and Prince; there is some new-born joy
Fluttering within my breast. Accost him, girl;
And, ere thou partest, what Parnâda said,
Say thou, and hear him answer, blameless one,
And bring it on thy lips!"
                                    Then went the maid
Demurely, and accosted Vahûka,
While Damayanti watched them from the roof.

" *Kushalam tê bravîmi*—health and peace
I wish thee!" said she. " Wilt thou answer true
What Damayanti asks? She sends to ask
Whence set ye forth, and wherefore are ye come
Hither? Vidarbha's Princess fain would know."

" 'T was told my Raja," Vahûka replied,
" That Damayanti for the second turn
Holds her Swayamvara: the Bráhman's word
Was, " This shall be to-morrow." So he sped,
Hearing that news, with steeds which in one day
Fly fifty yojanas, swift as the winds,
Exceeding fleet. His charioteer am I."

" Who, then," Keshinî asked, " is he that rode
The third? whence cometh he, and what his race?
And thou thyself whence sprung? and tell me why
Thou servest thus?"

Then Vahûka replied:—
" Varshneya is the third who rode with us,
The famous charioteer of Nala he:
When thy Prince fled, he went to Koshala
And took our service. I in horse-taming
And dressing meat have skill; so am I made
King Rituparna's driver and his cook."
" Knoweth Varshneya, then, where Nala fled?"
Inquired the maid; " and did he tell thee this,
Or what spake he?"
                    " Of that unhappy Prince
He brought the children hither, and then went
Even where he would, of Nala wotting nought;
Nor wotteth any man, fair damsel! more.
Hidden from mortal eyes Nishadha lives,
Wandering the world, his very body changed.
Of Nala only Nala's own heart knows,
And by no sign doth he bewray himself."
Keshinî said: " That Bráhman who did wend
First to Ayodhyâ bore a verse to say
Over and over, everywhere—strange words,
Wove by a woman's wit. Listen to these:—

' Whither art thou departed, cruel lover,
    Who stole the half of thy belovèd's cloth,
And left her to awaken, and discover
    The wrong thou wroughtest to the love of both?
She, as thou didst command, a sad watch keepeth,
    With woful heart wearing the rended dress.
Prince, hear her cry who thus forever weepeth;
    Be mindful, hero; comfort her distress!'

What was it thou didst utter, hearing this?
Some gentle speech! Say it again—the Queen,
My peerless mistress, fain would know from me.
Nay, on thy faith, when thou didst hear that man,
What was it thou replied? She would know."
(Descendant of the Kurus!) Nala's heart,
While so the maid spoke, well-nigh burst with grief,
And from his eyes fast flowed the rolling tears;
But, mastering his anguish, holding down
The passion of his pain, with voice which strove
To speak through sobs, the Prince repeated this:—

" Even against the ruined, rash, ungrateful,
    Faithless, fond Prince, from whom the birds did steal
His only cloth, whom now a penance fateful
    Dooms to sad days, that dark-eyed will not feel
Anger; for if she saw him she should see
    A man consumed with grief and loss and shame;
Ill or well lodged, ever in misery,
    Her unthroned lord, a slave without a name."

Speaking these verses, woful Nala moaned,
And, overcome by thought, restrained no more
His trickling tears; fast broke they forth (O King!).
But Keshini, returning, told his words
To Damayanti, and the grief of him.
    When Damayanti heard, sore-troubled still,
Yet in her heart supposing him her Prince,
Again she spake: " Go, Kashini, and watch
Whatever this man doeth; near him stand,
Holding thy peace, and mark the ways of him
And all his acts, going and coming; note
If aught there be of strange in any deed.
Let them not give him fire, my girl—not though
This hindereth sore; nor water, though he ask
Even with beseeching.   Afterwards observe,
And bring me what befalls, and every sign
Of earthly or unearthly power he shows;
And whatsoever else Vahûka doth,
See it, and say."
          Thereon Keshinî sped,
Obeying Damayanti and—at hand—
Whatever by that horse-tamer was wrought,
The damsel watched, and all his ways; and came
Back to the Princess, unto whom she told
Each thing Vahûka did, as it befell,
And what the signs were, and the wondrous works
Of earthly and unearthly gifts in him.
    " *Subhê!* " [5] quoth she, " the man is magical,
But high and holy mannered; never yet
Saw I another such, nor heard of him.
Passing the low door of the inner court,
Where one must stoop, he did not bow his head,

         [5] " O Beautiful One! "

But as he came the lintel lifted up
And gave him space. Bhima the King had sent
Many and diverse meats for Rituparna,
Of beast and bird and fish—great store of food—
The which to cleanse some chatties stood hard by,
All empty; yet he did but look on them,
Wishful, and lo! the water brimmed the pots.
Then, having washed the meats, he hastened forth
In quest of fire, and, holding towards the sun
A knot of withered grass, the bright flame blazed
Instant amidst it. Wonderstruck was I
This miracle to see, and hither ran
With other strangest marvels to impart:—
For, Princess, when he touched the blazing grass
He was not burned, and water flows for him
At will, or ceases flowing; and this, too,
The strangest thing of all, did I behold—
He took some faded leaves and flowers up,
And idly handled them; but while his hands
Toyed with them, lo! they blossomed forth again
With lovelier life than ever, and fresh scent,
Straight on their stalks. These marvels have I seen,
And fly back now to tell thee, mistress dear!"

But when she knew such wonders of the man,
More certainly she deemed those acts and gifts
Betokened Nala; and so-minded, full
Of trust to find her lord in Vahûka,
With happier tears and softening voice she said
To Keshinî: "Speed yet again, my girl;
And, while he wots not, from the kitchen take
Meat he hath dressed, and bring it here to me."
So went the maid, and, waiting secretly,
Broke from the mess a morsel, hot and spiced,
And, bearing it with faithful swiftness, gave
To Damayanti. She (O Kuru King!)—
That knew so well the dishes dressed by him—
Touched, tasted it, and, laughing—weeping—cried,
Beside herself with joy: "Yes, yes; 't is he!
That charioteer is Nala!" then, a-pant,
Even while she washed her mouth, she bade the maid
Go with the children twain to Vahûka;

Who, when he saw his little Indrasen
And Indrasena, started up, and ran,
And caught, and folded them upon his breast;
Holding them there, his darlings, each as fair
As children of the gods. Then, quite undone
With love and yearning, loudly sobbed the Prince.

   Until, perceiving Keshinî, who watched,
Shamed to be known, he set his children down,
And said: " In sooth, good friend, this lovely pair
So like mine own are, that at seeing them
I am surprised into these foolish tears.
Thou comest here too often; men will think
Thee light, or me; remember, we are here,
Strangers and guests, girl! Go thy ways in peace! "

   But seeing that great trouble of his soul,
Lightly came Keshinî, and pictured all
To Damayanti. She, burning to know
If truly this were Nala, bade the girl
Seek the Queen's presence, saying thus for her:—
" Mother! long watching Vahûka, I deem
The charioteer is Nala. One doubt lives—
His altered form. I must myself have speech
With Vahûka; thou, therefore, bid him come,
Or suffer me to seek him. Be this done
Forthwith, good mother!—whether known or not
Unto the Maharaja."

                   When she heard,
The Queen told Bhima what the Princess prayed,
Who gave consent; and having this good leave
From father and from mother (O my King!),
Command was sent that Vahûka be brought
Where the court ladies lodged.

                So met those twain;
And when Prince Nala's gaze fell on his wife,
He stood with beating heart and tearful eyes.
And when sweet Damayanti looked on him,
She could not speak for anguish of keen joy
To have him close; but sat there, mute and wan,
Wearing a sad-hued cloth, her lustrous hair
Falling unbanded, and the mourning-mark
Stamped in gray ashes on her lovely brow.

And, when she found a voice, these were the words
That came from her: "Didst ever, Vahûka—
If Vahûka thy name be, as thou say'st—
Know one of noble nature, honorable,
Who in the wild woods left his wife asleep—
His innocent, fond wife—weary and worn?
Know'st thou the man. I'll say his name to thee;
'Twas Nala, Raja Nala! Ah, and when
In any thoughtless hour had I once wrought
The smallest wrong, that he should leave me so,
There in the wood, by slumber overcome?
Before the gods I chose him for my lord,
The gods themselves rejecting; tell me how
This Prince could so abandon, in her need,
His true, his loving wife, she who did bear
His babes—abandon her to whom he swore—
My hand clasped, in the sight of all the gods,
And Agni's self—' Thy true lord I will be!'
Thou saidst it!—where is now that promise fled?"
   While thus she spake (O Victor of thy foes!),
Fast from her eyes the woe-sprung waters ran.
And Nala, seeing those night-black, loving eyes
Reddened with weeping, seeing her falling tears;
Broke forth: "Ah! that I lost my throne and realm
In dicing, was not done by fault of mine;
'T was Kali wrought it; Kali, O my wife,
Drove me to leave thee. Therefore, long ago
That evil one was stricken by the curse
Which thou didst utter, wandering in the wood,
Desolate, night and day, grieving for me.
Possessing me he dwelt; but, cursed by thee,
Tortured he dwelt, consuming with thy words
In fierce and fiercer pain, as when is piled
Brand upon burning brand. But he is gone;
Patience and penance have o'ermastered him.
Princess, the end is reached of our long woes.
That evil one being fled, freeing my will,
See, I am here; and wherefore would I come,
Fairest, except for thee? Yet, answer this:—
How should a wife, right-minded to her lord—
Her own and lawful lord—compass to choose

Another love, as thou, that tremblest, didst?
Thy messengers over all regions ran,
By the King's name proclaiming: 'Bhima's child
A second husband chooseth for herself,
Whomso she will—as pleaseth—being free.'
Those shameless tidings brought the Raja here
At headlong speed—and me!"
                                        Tenderly smiled
Damayanti through her tears, with quivering lips,
And joined palms, answering her aggrievèd Prince:—
"Judgest thou me guilty of such a sin?
When for thy sake I put the gods aside—
Thee did I choose, Nishadha, my one lord.
In quest of thee did all those Bráhmans range
In all ten regions, telling all one tale
Taught them by me; and so Parnâda came
To Koshala, where Rituparna dwells,
And found thee in his house, and spake to thee
Those words, and had thy gentle answer back.
Mine the device was, Prince, to bring thee quick;
For well I wist no man in all this world
Could in one day the fleetest coursers urge
So many yojanas, save thou, dear Prince!
I touch thy feet, and tell thee this in truth;
And true it is that never any wrong
Against thee, even in fancy, have I dreamed.
Witness for me, as I am loyal and pure,
The ever-shifting, all-beholding Air,
Who wanders o'er the earth; let him withdraw
My breath and slay me, if I sinned in aught!
Witness for me, yon golden Sun who goes
With bright eye over us; let him withhold
Warm life and kill me, if I sinned in aught!
Witness for me the white Moon, whose pale spell
Lies on all flesh and spirit; let that orb
Deny me peace and end me, if I sinned!
These be the watchers and the testifiers,
The three chief gods that rule the three wide worlds;
I cry unto them; let them speak for me;
And thou shalt hear them answer for my faith,
Or once again, this day, abandon me."

Then Vayu showed—the all-enfolding Air—
And spake: "Not one wrong hath she wrought thee,
        Prince,
I tell thee sooth.   The treasure of her truth
Faultless and undefiled she hath kept
By us regarded, and sustained by us,
These many days.   Her tender plot it was,
Planned for thy sake, which brought thee; since who else
Could in one day drive threescore yojanas?
Nala, thou hast thy noble wife again;
Thou, Damayanti, hast thy Nala back.
Away with doubting; take her to thy breast,
Thrice happy Prince!"
                              And while God Vayu spake,
Look! there showered flowers down out of the sky[6]
Upon them; and the drums of heaven beat
Beautiful music, and a gentle wind,
Fragrant, propitious, floated, kissing them.
But Nala, when he saw these things befall—
Wonderful, gracious—when he heard that voice
Called the great snake to memory:—whereupon
His proper self returned.   Bhima's fair child
Divinely sounding (Lord of Bhârat's line!)—
Yielded all doubt of his delightful Love.
Then cast he round about his neck the cloth—
Unstained by earth, enchanted—and (O King!)
Saw her dear lord his beauteous form resume.
"Ah, Nala! Nala!" cried she, while her arms
Clasped him and clung; and Nala to his heart
Pressed that bright lady, glowing, as of old,
With princely majesty.   Their children twain
Next he caressed; while she—at happy peace—
Her beautiful glad face laid on his breast,
Sighing with too much joy.   And Nala stood
A great space silent, gazing on her face,
Sorrow-stamped yet, her long, deep-lidded eyes,
Her melting smile—himself 'twixt joy and woe.

    Afterwards, all that story of the Prince,
And all of Damayanti, Bhima's Queen

[6] This raining down of heavenly flowers on auspicious occasions is a frequent
incident in ancient Indian poetry.

Told to the Maharaja joyously.
And Bhima said: "To-morrow will I see—
When Nala hath his needful offerings made—
Our daughter and this wandering lord well knit."
 But all that night they sat, hand clasped in hand,
Rejoicing, and relating what befell
In the wild wood, and of the woful times.
 That night being spent, Prince Nala in his state
Led forth Vidarbha's Pride before the court.
And Bhima—in an hour found fortunate—
Re-wed those married lovers. Dutifully
Nala paid homage to the Maharaja,
And reverently did Damayanti bow
Before her father. He the Prince received
With grace and gladness, as a son restored,
Making fair welcome, and with words of praise
Exalting Damayanti, tried and true;
Which in all dignity Prince Nala took,
Returning, as was meet, words honorable.
Therewith unto the city spread the noise
Of that rejoicing. All the townspeople,
Learning of Nala joyously returned,
Made all their quarters gay with float of flags,
Flutter of cloths, and garlands; sprinkled free
The King's-ways with fresh water, and the cups
Of fragrant flowers; and hung long wreaths of flowers
From door to door the white street-fronts before;
And decked each temple-porch, and went about
The altar-gods.
And afterwards, in Bhima's royal house
Serenely dwelled the Princess and the Prince,
Each making for the other peaceful joy.
So in the fourth year Nala was rejoined
To Damayanti, comforted and free,
Restful, attained, tasting delights again.
Also the glad Princess, gaining her lord,
Laid sorrows by, and blossomed forth anew,
As doth the laughing earth when the rain falls,
And brings her unseen, waiting wonders forth
Of blade and flower and fruit. The ache was gone,
The loneliness and load. Heart-full of ease,

Lovelier she grew and brighter, like the moon
Mounting at midnight in the cloudless blue.
                      When Rituparna heard
How Vahûka is Nala in disguise,
And of the meeting, right rejoiced at heart
That Raja grew.   And, being softly prayed
By Nala favorable thought, the King
Made royal and gentle answer, with like grace
By Nala met.   To whom spake Rituparna:—
" Joy go with thee and her, happily joined.
But say, Nishadha, wrought I any jot
Wrongful to thee, whilst sojourning unknown
Within my walls?   If any word or deed,
Purposed or purposeless, hath vexed thee, friend,
For one and all thy pardon grant to me ! "
    And Nala answered: " Never act or word,
The smallest, Raja, lingers to excuse!
If this were otherwise, thy slave was I,
And might not question, but must pardon thee.
Yet good to me thou wert, princely and just,
And kind thou art; and friendly from this time
Deign thou to be.   Happily was I lodged,
Well-tended, well-befriended in thy house;
In mine own palace never better stead.
The skill in steeds which pleased thee, that is **mine,**
And, Raja, I will give it all to thee,
If thou art minded."
                      So Nishadha gave
All his great gift in horses to the King,
Who learned each rule approved, and ordinance;
And, having all this knowledge, gave in turn
His deepest lore of numbers and the dice
To Nala, afterwards departing home
To his own place, another charioteer
Driving his steeds; and, Rituparna gone,
Not long did Nala dwell in Bhima's town.
    When one moon he had tarried, taking **leave,**
Nishadha to his city started forth
With chosen train.   A shining car he drove;
And elephants sixteen, and fifty horse,
And footmen thirty-score came in the rear.

Swiftly did Nala journey, making earth
Quake 'neath his flying car; and wrathfully
With quick steps entered he his palace doors.
The son of Virasena, Nala, stood
Once more before that gamester Pushkara!
Spake he: " Play yet again; much wealth is mine,
And that, and all I have—yea, my Princess—
Set I for stakes: set thou this realm, and throw!
My mind is fixed a second chance to try,
Where, Pushkara, we will play for all or none.
Who wins his throne and treasures from a prince,
Must stand the hazard of the counter-cast—
This is the accepted law.   If thou dost blench,
The next game we will play is ' life or death,' ·
In chariot-fight; when, or of thee or me
One shall lie satisfied: ' Descended realms,
By whatsoever means, are to be sought,'
The sages say, ' by whatsoever won.'
Choose, therefore, Pushkara, which way of these
Shall please thee; either meet me with the dice,
Or with thy bow confront me in the field."

   When Pushkara this heard, lightly he smiled,
Concluding victory sure; and to the Prince
Answered, exulting: " *Dishtya!* hast thou gained
Stakes for a counter-game, Nishadha, now?
Dishtya! shall I have my hard-won prize,
Sweet Damayanti? *Dishtya!* didst thou come
In kissing-reach again of thy fair wife?
Soon, in thy new gold splendid, she shall shine
Before all men beside me, as in heaven
On Sakra waits the loveliest Apsarâ.
See, now, I thought on thee, I looked for thee,
Ever and ever, Prince.   There is no joy   ·
Like casting in the game with such as thee.
And when to-day I win thy blameless one—
The smooth-limbed Damayanti—then shall be
What was to be: and I can rest content,
For always in my heart her beauty burns."

   Listening the idle talk that babbler poured,
Angry Prince Nala fain had lopped away
His head with vengeful *khudga;*[7] but, unmoved,

---

[7] A short, broad-bladed sword.

Albeit the wrath blazed in his bloodshot eyes,
He made reply: " Play! mock me not with jests;
Thou wilt not jest when I have cast with thee!"
  So was the game set, and the Princes threw
Nala and Pushkara, and—the numbers named—
By Nala was the hazard gained: he swept
His brother's stake, gems, treasure, kingdom, off;
At one stroke all that mighty venture won.
  Then quoth the conquering Prince to Pushkara,
Scornfully smiling: " Mine is now once more
Nishadha's throne; mine is the realm again,
Its curse plucked forth; Vidarbha's glory thou,
Outcast, shalt ne'er so much as look upon!
Fool! who to-day becom'st her bond and slave.
Not by thy gifts that evil stroke was wrought
Wherefrom I fled before; 't was Kali's spell—
Albeit thou knew'st nought, fool—o'ermastered me;
Yet will I visit not in wrathful wise
My wrong on thee; live as thou wilt; I grant
Wherewith to live, and set apart henceforth
Thy proper goods and substance, and fit food.
Nay, doubt not I shall show thee favor, too,
And be in friendship with thee, if thou wilt,
Who art my brother. Peace abide with thee!"
  Thus all-victorious Nala comforted
His brother, and embraced him, sending him
In honor to his town; and Pushkara—
Gently entreated—to Nishadha spake,
With folded palms and humbled face, these words:—
" Unending be thy glory. May thy bliss
Last and increase for twice five thousand years,
Who grantest me wherewith to live, just Lord!
And where to dwell." Thereafter, well bested,
Pushkara sojourned with the Prince one moon;
So to his town departed—heart-content—
With slaves and foot-soldiers and followers,
Gay as a rising sun (O Bhârat's glory!).
Thus sent he Pushkara, rich and safe, away.
Then, with flags and drums and jewels, robed and royally
        arrayed,
Nala into fair Nishadha entry high and dazzling made;

At the gates the Raja, halting, spake his people words of
    love;
Gathered were they from the city, gathered from the field
    and grove;
From the mountain and the maidan, all a-thrill with joy
    to see
Nala come to guard his children. " Happy now our days
    will be,"
Said the townsfolk, said the elders, said the villagers, " O
    King ! "
Standing all with palms upfolded: " Peace and fortune
    thou wilt bring
To thy city, to thy country! Boundless welcome do we
    give,
As the gods in heaven to Indra, when with them he comes
    to live."
After, when the show was ended, and the city, calm and
    glad,
Rest from tumult of rejoicing and rich flood of feasting
    had,
Girt with shining squadrons, Nala fetched his pearl of
    women home.
Like a queen did Damayanti back unto her palace come,
By the Maharaja Bhima, by that mighty monarch sent
Royally, with countless blessings, to her kingdom, in con-
    tent.
There, beside his peerless Princess, and his children, bore
    he sway,
Godlike, even as Indra ruling 'mid the bliss of Nandana.[8]
Bore he sway—my noble Nala—princeliest of all lords—
    who reign
In the lands of Jambudwipa;[9] winning power and fame
    again;
Ruling well his realm reconquered, like a just and perfect
    king,
All the appointed gifts bestowing, all the rites remem-
    bering.

[8] Nandana is the Paradise of Indra.
[9] Ancient name of India: " The Land of the Rose-apple Tree."

اُسے ہونے مطابق ہر اس و خوشی

ہی بنیاد توحید کی بس یہی

حکمت

بادشاہ دفع کرتا ہی ستم کارو نکو اور کو توال

خوشخوار و نکو ۔ قاضی اصلاح چاہتا ہی چور و نکی

اور جیب کترو نکی ۔ ہرگز وہ دشمن راضی ہو کر

قاضی کے پاس نہیں جاتے بلکہ اُس وقت وہاں بھی

اسکانہیں لاتے

جو حق معاینہ ہو جاے فحجکو دینے کا

نو دے گذر نو اُسے عیش جنگ و دل تنگی

جو کوئی دیوے نہ محصول کو خوشی بخوشی

نو اُسے لیویں بزور آوری و سرہنگی

CHOICE EXAMPLES OF ORIENTAL PRINTING AND
ENGRAVING.

A PAGE OF HINDOSTANEE.

This engraving is a fac-simile of a page from Sa'di's Gulistan, which was translated from the Persian into Hindostanee, and printed at Calcutta in 1802.

SELECTIONS FROM THE RÁMÁYANA

—

BY

VÁLMÍKI

[Metrical translation by R. T. H. Griffiths]

INTRODUCTION

THE ideas of the human family are few, as is apparent from the study of the literature of widely different nations. Thus the "Rámáyana" ranks in Hindoo with the "Iliad" and the "Odyssey" in Greek literature. The character of Ráma corresponds with that of Menelaus, for both the European and the Asiatic heroes have had their wives carried off from them—although Sítá, the bride of Ráma, is chaste as an icicle from Diana's temple, while Helen is the infamous type of wanton wives, ancient and modern. The Hindoo Lanka is Troy, and Ayodhyá is Sparta. The material civilization of the cities in the Hindoo epic is more luxurious and gorgeous than that which Homer attributes to Greece in the heroic age. Such splendor and refinement as invests social life at Lanka and Ayodhyá never appear amid the severe simplicity of Argos or Troy. The moral tone seems perhaps higher in India than in Greece during the periods described in their several epics—at least as far as mutual love and forbearance go—and the ideas of marriage and conjugal fidelity are equally exalted.

As to the literary quality of the Hindoo epic in comparison with Homer's work, we are at once impressed with the immense superiority of the Greek poem in artistic proportion, point, and precision. The Hindoo poet flounders along, amid a maze of prolix description and wearisome simile. Trifles are amplified and repeated, and the whole poem resembles a wild forest abounding in rich tropical vegetation, palms and flowers, but without paths, roads, or limits. Or rather, we are reminded of one of the highly painted and richly decorated idols of India, with their many heads and many hands: but when we turn to the Greek epic we stand before a statue of pure outline, flawless proportions, and more than human beauty.

It is difficult to fix the date of the "Rámáyana." Scholars

167

generally agree that it belongs to the third century before
Christ, in its original form, but that some recent portions were
added even during the Christian era. It is reckoned as one of
the sacred books, and the study of it is supposed to bring forgiveness of sin, and prosperity. Its author is thought to have
been the famous poet Válmíki, but the work has evidently been
rehandled several times, and there are three versions of the
poems still extant. The poem consists of twenty-four thousand
verses, and the story of it—now overlaid as it is with extrava-
gant and fabulous accretions—is evidently founded on fact.
The scene of the poem is laid in the city of Ayodhyá, the modern Oudh, which is described in glowing colors as a place of
health, beauty, and prosperity—

> " In by-gone ages built and planned
> By sainted Manu's princely hand."

In the splendid palace of the Rajah, at Oudh, lives Daśaratha,
mourning in childlessness. He is one of the princes descended
from the sun, and his line now threatens to become extinct.
He determines to appeal to the Gods by the Asva-medha, the
great sacrifice in which a horse is the victim. The rites accordingly are performed with unparalleled magnificence, and,
at the close of the ceremony, the high priest declares to the
king—

> " Four sons, O Monarch, shall be thine,
> Upholders of the royal line."

Among the offspring duly granted to Daśaratha is Ráma,
who is a typical Hindoo of the heroic type. His fair wife, Sítá,
is carried off by the demon Ravana, who had assumed the form
of a humble priest, or ascetic, in order to gain access to her.
He carries her in his chariot to Lanka, the fair city built on an
island of the sea. By the assistance of a large army of monkeys, Ráma marches against Lanka, and when they stand helpless—for the water separates them from Ceylon—he then in-
vokes the goddess of the sea, as Achilles did Thetis, and she
comes in radiant beauty, telling them how to bridge the waves.
The monkeys bring timber and stones, the bridge is built,
Lanka reached, and the battle begins. Indra sends his own
chariot down from heaven to Ráma, who mounts it, and van-
quishes Ravana in single combat, upon which Sítá is restored
to her husband.   E. W.

THE RÁMÁYANA

INVOCATION

PRAISE to Válmíki, bird of charming song,
  Who mounts on Poesy's sublimest spray,
  And sweetly sings with accent clear and strong
Ráma, aye Ráma, in his deathless lay.

Where breathes the man can listen to the strain
That flows in music from Válmíki's tongue,
Nor feel his feet the path of bliss attain
When Ráma's glory by the saint is sung?

The stream Rámáyan leaves its sacred fount
The whole wide world from sin and stain to free.
The Prince of Hermits is the parent mount,
The lordly Ráma is the darling sea.

Glory to him whose fame is ever bright!
Glory to him, Prachet's holy son!
Whose pure lips quaff with ever-new delight
The nectar-sea of deeds by Ráma done.

Hail, arch-ascetic, pious, good, and kind!
Hail, Saint Válmíki, lord of every lore!
Hail, holy Hermit, calm and pure of mind!
Hail, First of Bards, Válmíki, hail once more!

BOOK I

CANTO I

NÁRAD

Om.

TO sainted Nárad, prince of those
    Whose lore in words of wisdom flows,
    Whose constant care and chief delight
Were Scripture and ascetic rite,
The good Válmíki, first and best
Of hermit saints, these words addressed:—
" In all this world, I pray thee, who
Is virtuous, heroic, true?
Firm in his vows, of grateful mind,
To every creature good and kind?
Bounteous, and holy, just, and wise,
Alone most fair to all men's eyes?
Devoid of envy, firm, and sage,
Whose tranquil soul ne'er yields to rage?
Whom, when his warrior wrath is high,
Do Gods embattled fear and fly?
Whose noble might and gentle skill
The triple world can guard from ill?
Who is the best of princes, he
Who loves his people's good to see?
The store of bliss, the living mine
Where brightest joys and virtues shine?
Queen Fortune's best and dearest friend,
Whose steps her choicest gifts attend?
Who may with Sun and Moon compare,
With Indra, Vishnu, Fire, and Air?

Grant, Saint divine, the boon I ask,
For thee, I ween, an easy task,
To whom the power is given to know
If such a man breathe here below."

Then Nárad, clear before whose eye
The present, past, and future lie,
Made ready answer: "Hermit, where
Are graces found so high and rare?
Yet listen, and my tongue shall tell
In whom alone these virtues dwell.
From old Ikshváku's line he came,
Known to the world by Ráma's name:—
With soul subdued, a chief of might,
In Scripture versed, in glory bright.
His steps in virtue's paths are bent,
Obedient, pure, and eloquent.
In each emprise he wins success,
And dying foes his power confess.
Tall and broad-shouldered, strong of limb,
Fortune has set her mark on him.
Graced with a conch-shell's triple line,
His throat displays the auspicious sign.
High destiny is clear impressed
On massive jaw and ample chest.
His mighty shafts he truly aims,
And foemen in the battle tames.
Deep in the muscle, scarcely shown,
Embedded lies his collar-bone.
His lordly steps are firm and free,
His strong arms reach below his knee;
All fairest graces join to deck
His head, his brow, his stately neck,
And limbs in fair proportion set:—
The manliest form e'er fashioned yet.
Graced with each high imperial mark,
His skin is soft and lustrous dark.
Large are his eyes that sweetly shine
With majesty almost divine.
His plighted word he ne'er forgets;
On erring sense a watch he sets.

By nature wise, his teacher's skill
Has trained him to subdue his will.
Good, resolute and pure, and strong,
He guards mankind from scathe and wrong,
And lends his aid, and ne'er in vain,
The cause of justice to maintain.
Well has he studied o'er and o'er
The Vedas and their kindred lore.
Well skilled is he the bow to draw,
Well trained in arts and versed in law;
High-souled and meet for happy fate,
Most tender and compassionate;
The noblest of all lordly givers,
Whom good men follow, as the rivers
Follow the King of Floods, the sea:—
So liberal, so just is he.
The joy of Queen Kaušalyá's heart,
In every virtue he has part;
Firm as Himálaya's snowy steep,
Unfathomed like the mighty deep;
The peer of Vishnu's power and might,
And lovely as the Lord of Night;
Patient as Earth, but, roused to ire,
Fierce as the world-destroying fire;
In bounty like the Lord of Gold,
And Justice' self in human mould.
With him, his best and eldest son,
By all his princely virtues won
King Dašaratha willed to share
His kingdom as the Regent Heir.
But when Kaikeyí, youngest queen,
With eyes of envious hate had seen
The solemn pomp and regal state
Prepared the prince to consecrate,
She bade the hapless king bestow
Two gifts he promised long ago,
That Ráma to the woods should flee,
And that her child the heir should be.

By chains of duty firmly tied,
The wretched King perforce complied.

Ráma, to please Kaikeyí went
Obedient forth, to banishment.
Then Lakshman's truth was nobly shown,
Then were his love and courage known,
When for his brother's sake he dared
All perils, and his exile shared.
And Sítá, Ráma's darling wife,
Loved even as he loved his life,
Whom happy marks combined to bless,
A miracle of loveliness,
Of Janak's royal lineage sprung,
Most excellent of women, clung
To her dear lord, like Rohiní
Rejoicing with the Moon to be.
The King and people, sad of mood,
The hero's car awhile pursued.
But when Prince Ráma lighted down
At Śringavera's pleasant town,
Where Gangá's holy waters flow,
He bade his driver turn and go.
Guha, Nishádas' King, he met,
And on the farther bank was set.
Then on from wood to wood they strayed,
O'er many a stream, through constant shade,
As Bharadvája bade them, till
They came to Chitrakúta's hill.
And Ráma there, with Lakshman's aid,
A pleasant little cottage made,
And spent his days with Sítá, dressed
In coat of bark and deerskin vest.
And Chitrakúta grew to be
As bright with those illustrious three
As Meru's sacred peaks that shine
With glory, when the Gods recline
Beneath them: Śiva's self between
The Lord of Gold and Beauty's Queen.

The aged King for Ráma pined,
And for the skies the earth resigned.
Bharat, his son, refused to reign,
Though urged by all the twice-born train.

Forth to the woods he fared to meet
His brother, fell before his feet,
And cried " Thy claim all men allow:—
O come, our lord and King be thou."
But Ráma nobly chose to be
Observant of his sire's decree.
He placed his sandals in his hand,
A pledge that he would rule the land:—
And bade his brother turn again.
Then Bharat, finding prayer was vain,
The sandals took and went away;
Nor in Ayodhyá would he stay,
But turned to Nandigráma, where
He ruled the realm with watchful care,
Still longing eagerly to learn
Tidings of Ráma's safe return.

Then lest the people should repeat
Their visit to his calm retreat,
Away from Chitrakúta's hill
Fared Ráma, ever onward till
Beneath the shady trees he stood
Of Dandaká's primeval wood.
Virádha, giant fiend, he slew,
And then Agastya's friendship knew.
Counselled by him he gained the sword
And bow of Indra, heavenly lord:—
A pair of quivers too, that bore
Of arrows an exhaustless store.
While there he dwelt in greenwood shade,
The trembling hermits sought his aid,
And bade him with his sword and bow
Destroy the fiends who worked them woe:—
To come like Indra strong and brave,
A guardian God to help and save.
And Ráma's falchion left its trace
Deep cut on Śúrpanakhá's face:—
A hideous giantess who came
Burning for him with lawless flame.
Their sister's cries the giants heard,
And vengeance in each bosom stirred;

The monster of the triple head,
And Dúshan to the contest sped.
But they and myriad fiends beside
Beneath the might of Ráma died.

When Rávan, dreaded warrior, knew
The slaughter of his giant crew—
Rávan, the King, whose name of fear
Earth, hell, and heaven all shook to hear—
He bade the fiend Máricha aid
The vengeful plot his fury laid.
In vain the wise Máricha tried
To turn him from his course aside:—
Not Rávan's self, he said, might hope
With Ráma and his strength to cope.
Impelled by fate and blind with rage
He came to Ráma's hermitage.
There, by Máricha's magic art,
He wiled the princely youths apart,
The vulture slew, and bore away
The wife of Ráma as his prey.
The son of Raghu came and found
Jatáyu slain upon the ground.
He rushed within his leafy cot;
He sought his wife, but found her not.
Then, then the hero's senses failed;
In mad despair he wept and wailed.
Upon the pile that bird he laid,
And still in quest of Sítá strayed.
A hideous giant then he saw,
Kabandha named, a shape of awe.

The monstrous fiend he smote and slew,
And in the flame the body threw;
When straight from out the funeral flame
In lovely form Kabandha came,
And bade him seek in his distress
A wise and holy hermitess.
By counsel of this saintly dame
To Pampá's pleasant flood he came,

And there the steadfast friendship won
Of Hanumán the Wind-God's son.
Counselled by him he told his grief
To great Sugríva, Vánar chief,
Who, knowing all the tale, before
The sacred flame alliance swore.
Sugríva to his new-found friend
Told his own story to the end:—
His hate of Báli for the wrong
And insult he had borne so long.
And Ráma lent a willing ear
And promised to allay his fear.
Sugríva warned him of the might
Of Báli, matchless in the fight,
And, credence for his tale to gain,
Showed the huge fiend by Báli slain.
The prostrate corse of mountain size
Seemed nothing in the hero's eyes;
He lightly kicked it, as it lay,
And cast it twenty leagues away.
To prove his might his arrows through
Seven palms in line, uninjured, flew.
He cleft a mighty hill apart,
And down to hell he hurled his dart.
Then high Sugríva's spirit rose,
Assured of conquest o'er his foes.
With his new champion by his side
To vast Kishkindhá's cave he hied.
Then, summoned by his awful shout,
King Báli came in fury out,
First comforted his trembling wife,
Then sought Sugríva in the strife.
One shaft from Ráma's deadly bow
The monarch in the dust laid low.
Then Ráma bade Sugríva reign
In place of royal Báli slain.
Then speedy envoys hurried forth
Eastward and westward, south and north,
Commanded by the grateful King
Tidings of Ráma's spouse to bring.

Then by Sampáti's counsel led,
Brave Hanumán, who mocked at dread,
Sprang at one wild tremendous leap
Two hundred leagues, across the deep.
To Lanká's * town he urged his way,
Where Rávan held his royal sway.
There pensive 'neath Aśoka boughs
He found poor Sítá, Ráma's spouse.
He gave the hapless girl a ring,
A token from her lord and King.
A pledge from her fair hand he bore;
Then battered down the garden door.
Five captains of the host he slew,
Seven sons of councillors o'erthrew;
Crushed youthful Aksha on the field,
Then to his captors chose to yield.
Soon from their bonds his limbs were free,
But honoring the high decree
Which Brahmá had pronounced of yore,
He calmly all their insults bore.
The town he burnt with hostile flame,
And spoke again with Ráma's dame,
Then swiftly back to Ráma flew
With tidings of the interview.

Then with Sugríva for his guide,
Came Ráma to the ocean side.
He smote the sea with shafts as bright
As sunbeams in their summer height,
And quick appeared the River's King
Obedient to the summoning.
A bridge was thrown by Nala o'er
The narrow sea from shore to shore.
They crossed to Lanká's golden town,
Where Ráma's hand smote Rávan down.
Vibhíshan there was left to reign
Over his brother's wide domain.
To meet her husband Sítá came;
But Ráma, stung with ire and shame,
With bitter words his wife addressed
Before the crowd that round her pressed.

* Ceylon.

But Sítá, touched with noble ire,
Gave her fair body to the fire.
Then straight the God of Wind appeared,
And words from heaven her honor cleared.
And Ráma clasped his wife again,
Uninjured, pure from spot and stain,
Obedient to the Lord of Fire
And the high mandate of his sire.
Led by the Lord who rules the sky,
The Gods and heavenly saints drew nigh,
And honored him with worthy meed,
Rejoicing in each glorious deed.
His task achieved, his foe removed,
He triumphed, by the Gods approved.
By grace of Heaven he raised to life
The chieftains slain in mortal strife;
Then in the magic chariot through
The clouds to Nandigráma flew.
Met by his faithful brothers there,
He loosed his votive coil of hair;
Thence fair Ayodhyá's town he gained,
And o'er his father's kingdom reigned.
Disease or famine ne'er oppressed
His happy people, richly blest
With all the joys of ample wealth,
Of sweet content and perfect health.
No widow mourned her well-loved mate,
No sire his son's untimely fate.
They feared not storm or robber's hand,
No fire or flood laid waste the land:
The Golden Age seemed come again
To bless the days of Ráma's reign.
From him the great and glorious King,
Shall many a princely scion spring.
And he shall rule, beloved by men,
Ten thousand years and hundreds ten,
And when his life on earth is past
To Brahmá's world shall go at last.

Whoe'er this noble poem reads
That tells the tale of Ráma's deeds,

Good as the Scriptures, he shall be
From every sin and blemish free.
Whoever reads the saving strain,
With all his kin the heavens shall gain.
Bráhmans who read shall gather hence
The highest praise for eloquence.
The warrior, o'er the land shall reign,
The merchant, luck in trade obtain;
And Súdras, listening, ne'er shall fail
To reap advantage from the tale.

[*Cantos II., III., IV., and V. are omitted.*]

CANTO VI

THE KING

THERE reigned a King of name revered,
    To country and to town endeared,
    Great Daśaratha, good and sage,
Well read in Scripture's holy page:
Upon his kingdom's weal intent,
Mighty and brave and provident;
The pride of old Ikshváku's seed
For lofty thought and righteous deed.
Peer of the saints, for virtues famed,
For foes subdued and passions tamed;
A rival in his wealth untold
Of Indra and the Lord of Gold.
Like Manu first of kings, he reigned,
And worthily his state maintained.
For firm and just and ever true
Love, duty, gain, he kept in view,
And ruled his city rich and free,
Like Indra's Amarávatí.
And worthy of so fair a place
There dwelt a just and happy race
With troops of children blest.
Each man contented sought no more,
Nor longed with envy for the store
By richer friends possessed.
For poverty was there unknown,
And each man counted as his own
Kine, steeds, and gold, and grain.
All dressed in raiment bright and clean,
And every townsman might be seen
With ear-rings, wreath or chain.
None deigned to feed on broken fare,
And none was false or stingy there.

A piece of gold, the smallest pay,
Was earned by labor for a day.
On every arm were bracelets worn,
And none was faithless or forsworn,
A braggart or unkind.
None lived upon another's wealth,
None pined with dread or broken health,
Or dark disease of mind.
High-souled were all. The slanderous word,
The boastful lie, were never heard.
Each man was constant to his vows,
And lived devoted to his spouse.
No other love his fancy knew,
And she was tender, kind, and true.
Her dames were fair of form and face,
With charm of wit and gentle grace,
With modest raiment simply neat,
And winning manners soft and sweet.
The twice-born sages, whose delight
Was Scripture's page and holy rite,
Their calm and settled course pursued,
Nor sought the menial multitude.
In many a Scripture each was versed,
And each the flame of worship nursed,
And gave with lavish hand.
Each paid to Heaven the offerings due,
And none was godless or untrue
In all that holy band.
To Bráhmans, as the laws ordain,
The Warrior caste were ever fain
The reverence due to pay;
And these the Vaiśyas' peaceful crowd,
Who trade and toil for gain, were proud
To honor and obey;
And all were by the Śúdras served,
Who never from their duty swerved.
Their proper worship all addressed
To Bráhman, spirits, God, and guest.
Pure and unmixt their rites remained,
Their race's honor ne'er was stained.
Cheered by his grandsons, sons, and wife,
Each passed a long and happy life.

Thus was that famous city held
By one who all his race excelled,
Blest in his gentle reign,
As the whole land aforetime swayed
By Manu, prince of men, obeyed
Her king from main to main.
And heroes kept h⸱, strong and brave,
As lions guard their mountain cave;
Fierce as devouring flame they burned,
And fought till death, but never turned.
Horses had she of noblest breed,
Like Indra's for their form and speed,
From Váhli's hills and Sindhu's sand,
Vanáyu and Kámboja's land.
Her noble elephants had strayed
Through Vindhyan and Himálayan shade,
Gigantic in their bulk and height,
Yet gentle in their matchless might.
They rivalled well the world-spread fame
Of the great stock from which they came,
Of Váman, vast of size,
Of Mahápadma's glorious line,
Thine, Anjan, and, Airávat, thine,
Upholders of the skies.
With those, enrolled in fourfold class,
Who all their mighty kin surpass,
Whom men Matangas name,
And Mrigas spotted black and white,
And Bhadras of unwearied might,
And Mandras hard to tame.
Thus, worthy of the name she bore,
Ayodhyá for a league or more
Cast a bright glory round,
Where Daśaratha wise and great
Governed his fair ancestral state,
With every virtue crowned.
Like Indra in the skies he reigned
In that good town whose wall contained
High domes and turrets proud,
With gates and arcs of triumph decked,
And sturdy barriers to protect
Her gay and countless crowd.

CANTO VII

THE MINISTERS

TWO sages, holy saints, had he,
  His ministers and priests to be:—
  Vaśishtha, faithful to advise,
And Vámadeva, Scripture-wise.
Eight other lords around him stood,
All skilled to counsel, wise and good:—
Jayanta, Vijay, Dhrishti bold
In fight, affairs of war controlled;
Siddhárth and Arthasádhak true
Watched o'er expense and revenue,
And Dharmapál and wise Aśok
Of right and law and justice spoke.
With these the sage Sumantra, skilled
To urge the car, high station filled.
All these in knowledge duly trained
Each passion and each sense restrained:—
With modest manners, nobly bred,
Each plan and nod and look they read,
Upon their neighbors' good intent,
Most active and benevolent;
As sits the Vasus round their King,
They sate around him counselling.
They ne'er in virtue's loftier pride
Another's lowly gifts decried.
In fair and seemly garb arrayed,
No weak uncertain plans they made.
Well skilled in business, fair and just,
They gained the people's love and trust,
And thus without oppression stored
The swelling treasury of their lord.

Bound in sweet friendship each to each,
They spoke kind thoughts in gentle speech.
They looked alike with equal eye
On every caste, on low and high.
Devoted to their King, they sought,
Ere his tongue spoke, to learn his thought,
And knew, as each occasion rose,
To hide their counsel or disclose.
In foreign lands or in their own
Whatever passed, to them was known.
By secret spies they timely knew
What men were doing or would do.
Skilled in the grounds of war and peace
They saw the monarch's state increase,
Watching his weal with conquering eye
That never let occasion by,
While nature lent her aid to bless
Their labors with unbought success.
Never for anger, lust, or gain,
Would they their lips with falsehood stain.
Inclined to mercy they could scan
The weakness and the strength of man.
They fairly judged both high and low,
And ne'er would wrong a guiltless foe;
Yet if a fault were proved, each one
Would punish e'en his own dear son.
But there and in the kingdom's bound
No thief or man impure was found:—
None of loose life or evil fame,
No tempter of another's dame.
Contented with their lot each caste
Calm days in blissful quiet passed;
And, all in fitting tasks employed,
Country and town deep rest enjoyed.
With these wise lords around his throne
The monarch justly reigned,
And making every heart his own
The love of all men gained.
With trusty agents, as beseems,
Each distant realm he scanned,
As the sun visits with his beams

Each corner of the land.
Ne'er would he on a mightier foe
With hostile troops advance,
Nor at an equal strike a blow
In war's delusive chance.
These lords in council bore their part
With ready brain and faithful heart,
With skill and knowledge, sense and tact,
Good to advise and bold to act.
And high and endless fame he won
With these to guide his schemes—
As, risen in his might, the sun
Wins glory with his beams.

CANTO VIII

SUMANTRA'S SPEECH

BUT splendid, just, and great of mind,
The childless King for offspring pined.
No son had he his name to grace,
Transmitter of his royal race.
Long had his anxious bosom wrought,
And as he pondered rose the thought:—
"A votive steed 'twere good to slay,
So might a son the gift repay."
Before his lords his plans he laid,
And bade them with their wisdom aid;
Then with these words Sumantra, best
Of royal counsellors, addressed:—
"Hither, Vaśishtha at their head,
Let all my priestly guides be led."

To him Sumantra made reply:—
"Hear, sire, a tale of days gone by.
To many a sage in time of old,
Sanatkumár, the saint, foretold
How from thine ancient line, O King,
A son, when years came round, should spring.
'Here dwells,' 'twas thus the seer began,
'Of Kaśyap's race, a holy man,
Vibhándak named: to him shall spring
A son, the famous Rishyaśring.
Bred with the deer that round him roam,
The wood shall be that hermit's home.
To him no mortal shall be known
Except his holy sire alone.
Still by those laws shall he abide
Which lives of youthful Bráhmans guide,

Obedient to the strictest rule
That forms the young ascetic's school:—
And all the wondering world shall hear
Of his stern life and penance drear;
His care to nurse the holy fire
And do the bidding of his sire.
Then, seated on the Angas' throne,
Shall Lomapád to fame be known.
But folly wrought by that great King
A plague upon the land shall bring;
No rain for many a year shall fall
And grievous drought shall ruin all.
The troubled King with many a prayer
Shall bid the priests some cure declare:—
" The lore of Heaven 'tis yours to know,
Nor are ye blind to things below:—
Declare, O holy men, the way
This plague to expiate and stay."
Those best of Bráhmans shall reply:—
" By every art, O Monarch, try,
Hither to bring Vibhándak's child,
Persuaded, captured, or beguiled.
And when the boy is hither led
To him thy daughter duly wed."

But how to bring that wondrous boy
His troubled thoughts will long employ,
And hopeless to achieve the task
He counsel of his lords will ask,
And bid his priests and servants bring
With honor saintly Rishyaśring.
But when they hear the monarch's speech,
All these their master will beseech,
With trembling hearts and looks of woe,
To spare them, for they fear to go.
And many a plan will they declare
And crafty plots will frame,
And promise fair to show him there,
Unforced, with none to blame.
On every word his lords shall say,
The King will meditate,

And on the third returning day
Recall them to debate.
Then this shall be the plan agreed,
That damsels shall be sent
Attired in holy hermits' weed,
And skilled in blandishment,
That they the hermit may beguile
With every art and amorous wile
Whose use they know so well,
And by their witcheries seduce
The unsuspecting young recluse
To leave his father's cell.
Then when the boy with willing feet
Shall wander from his calm retreat
And in that city stand,
The troubles of the King shall end,
And streams of blessed rain descend
Upon the thirsty land.
Thus shall the holy Rishyaśring
To Lomapád, the mighty King,
By wedlock be allied;
For Śántá, fairest of the fair,
In mind and grace beyond compare,
Shall be his royal bride.
He, at the Offering of the Steed,
The flames with holy oil shall feed,
And for King Daśaratha gain
Sons whom his prayers have begged in vain.'
I have repeated, sire, thus far,
The words of old Sanatkumár,
In order as he spoke them then
Amid the crowd of holy men."
Then Daśaratha cried with joy,
" Say how they brought the hermit boy."

CANTO IX

RISHYAŚRING

THE wise Sumantra, thus addressed,
Unfolded at the King's behest
The plan the lords in council laid
To draw the hermit from the shade.
The priest, amid the lordly crowd,
To Lomapád thus spoke aloud :—
" Hear, King, the plot our thoughts have framed,
A harmless trick by all unblamed.
Far from the world that hermit's child
Lives lonely in the distant wild :
A stranger to the joys of sense,
His bliss is pain and abstinence ;
And all unknown are women yet
To him, a holy anchoret.
The gentle passions we will wake
That with resistless influence shake
The hearts of men ; and he
Drawn by enchantment strong and sweet
Shall follow from his lone retreat,
And come and visit thee.
Let ships be formed with utmost care
That artificial trees may bear,
And sweet fruit deftly made ;
Let goodly raiment, rich and rare,
And flowers, and many a bird be there
Beneath the leafy shade.
Upon the ships thus decked a band
Of young and lovely girls shall stand,
Rich in each charm that wakes desire,
And eyes that burn with amorous fire ;
Well skilled to sing, and play, and dance,

And ply their trade with smile and glance.
Let these, attired in hermits' dress,
Betake them to the wilderness,
And bring the boy of life austere
A voluntary captive here."
He ended; and the King agreed,
By the priest's counsel won,
And all the ministers took heed
To see his bidding done.
In ships with wondrous art prepared
Away the lovely women fared,
And soon beneath the shade they stood
Of the wild, lonely, dreary wood.
And there the leafy cot they found
Where dwelt the devotee,
And looked with eager eyes around
The hermit's son to see.
Still, of Vibhándak sore afraid,
They hid behind the creeper's shade.
But when by careful watch they knew
The elder saint was far from view,
With bolder steps they ventured nigh
To catch the youthful hermit's eye.
Then all the damsels blithe and gay,
At various games began to play.
They tossed the flying ball about
With dance and song and merry shout,
And moved, their scented tresses bound
With wreaths, in mazy motions round.
Some girls as if by love possessed,
Sank to the earth in feigned unrest,
Up-starting quickly to pursue
Their intermitted game anew.
It was a lovely sight to see
Those fair ones, as they played,
While fragrant robes were floating free,
And bracelets clashing in their glee
A pleasant tinkling made.
The anklet's chime, the Koïl's cry
With music filled the place,
As 'twere some city in the sky

Which heavenly minstrels grace.
With each voluptuous art they strove
To win the tenant of the grove,
And with their graceful forms inspire
His modest soul with soft desire.
With arch of brow, with beck and smile,
With every passion-waking wile
Of glance and lotus hand,
With all enticements that excite
The longing for unknown delight
Which boys in vain withstand.
Forth came the hermit's son to view
The wondrous sight to him so new,
And gazed in rapt surprise
For from his natal hour till then
On woman or the sons of men
He ne'er had cast his eyes.
He saw them with their waists so slim,
With fairest shape and faultless limb,
In variegated robes arrayed,
And sweetly singing as they played.
Near and more near the hermit drew,
And watched them at their game,
And stronger still the impulse grew
To question whence they came.
They marked the young ascetic gaze
With curious eye and wild amaze,
And sweet the long-eyed damsels sang,
And shrill their merry laughter rang.
Then came they nearer to his side,
And languishing with passion cried:—
"Whose son, O youth, and who art thou,
Come suddenly to join us now?
And why dost thou all lonely dwell
In the wild wood? We pray thee, tell.
We wish to know thee, gentle youth;
Come, tell us, if thou wilt, the truth."
He gazed upon that sight he ne'er
Had seen before, of girls so fair,
And out of love a longing rose
His sire and lineage to disclose:—

"My father," thus he made reply,
"Is Kaśyap's son, a saint most high,
Vibhándak styled; from him I came,
And Rishyaśring he calls my name.
Our hermit cot is near this place:—
Come thither, O ye fair of face;
There be it mine, with honor due,
Ye gentle youths, to welcome you."

They heard his speech, and gave consent,
And gladly to his cottage went.
Vibhándak's son received them well
Beneath the shelter of his cell—
With guest-gift, water for their feet,
And woodland fruit and roots to eat.
They smiled and spoke sweet words like these,
Delighted with his courtesies:—
"We too have goodly fruit in store,
Grown on the trees that shade our door;
Come, if thou wilt, kind Hermit, haste
The produce of our grove to taste;
And let, O good Ascetic, first
This holy water quench thy thirst."
They spoke, and gave him comfits sweet
Prepared ripe fruits to counterfeit;
And many a dainty cate beside,
And luscious mead their stores supplied.
The seeming fruits, in taste and look,
The unsuspecting hermit took,
For, strange to him, their form beguiled
The dweller in the lonely wild.
Then round his neck fair arms were flung,
And there the laughing damsels clung,
And pressing nearer and more near
With sweet lips whispered at his ear;
While rounded limb and swelling breast
The youthful hermit softly pressed.
The pleasing charm of that strange bowl,
The touch of a tender limb,
Over his yielding spirit stole
And sweetly vanquished him—

But vows, they said, must now be paid;
They bade the boy farewell,
And of the aged saint afraid,
Prepared to leave the dell.
With ready guile they told him where
Their hermit dwelling lay;
Then, lest the sire should find them there,
Sped by wild paths away.
They fled and left him there alone
By longing love possessed;
And with a heart no more his own
He roamed about distressed.
The aged saint came home, to find
The hermit boy distraught,
Revolving in his troubled mind
One solitary thought.
" Why dost thou not, my son," he cried,
" Thy due obeisance pay?
Why do I see thee in the tide
Of whelming thought to-day?
A devotee should never wear
A mien so sad and strange.
Come, quickly, dearest child, declare
The reason of the change."
And Rishyaśring, when questioned thus,
Made answer in this wise:—
" O sire, there came to visit us
Some men with lovely eyes.
About my neck soft arms they wound
And kept me tightly held
To tender breasts so soft and round,
That strangely heaved and swelled.
They sing more sweetly as they dance
Than e'er I heard till now,
And play with many a sidelong glance
And arching of the brow."
" My son," said he, " thus giants roam
Where holy hermits are,
And wander round their peaceful home
Their rites austere to mar.
I charge thee, thou must never lay
Thy trust in them, dear boy:—

They seek thee only to betray,
And woo but to destroy."
Thus having warned him of his foes
That night at home he spent,
And when the morrow's sun arose
Forth to the forest went.

But Rishyaśring with eager pace
Sped forth and hurried to the place
Where he those visitants had seen
Of dainty waist and charming mien.
When from afar they saw the son
Of Saint Vibhándak toward them run,
To meet the hermit boy they hied,
And hailed him with a smile, and cried:—
" O come, we pray, dear lord, behold
Our lovely home of which we told:—
Due honor there to thee we'll pay,
And speed thee on thy homeward way."
Pleased with the gracious words they said
He followed where the damsels led.
As with his guides his steps he bent,
That Bráhman high of worth,
A flood of rain from heaven sent
That gladdened all the earth.

Vibhándak took his homeward road,
And wearied by the heavy load
Of roots and woodland fruit he bore
Entered at last his cottage door.
Fain for his son he looked around,
But desolate the cell he found.
He stayed not then to bathe his feet,
Though fainting with the toil and heat,
But hurried forth and roamed about
Calling the boy with cry and shout.
He searched the wood, but all in vain;
Nor tidings of his son could gain.
One day beyond the forest's bound
The wandering saint a village found,
And asked the swains and neatherds there
Who owned the land so rich and fair,

With all the hamlets of the plain,
And herds of kine and fields of grain.
They listened to the hermit's words,
And all the guardians of the herds,
With suppliant hands together pressed,
This answer to the saint addressed:—
" The Angas' lord who bears the name
Of Lomapád, renowned by fame,
Bestowed these hamlets with their kine
And all their riches, as a sign
Of grace, on Rishyaśring; and he
Vibhándak's son is said to be."
The hermit with exulting breast
The mighty will of fate confessed,
By meditation's eye discerned;
And cheerful to his home returned.

A stately ship, at early morn,
The hermit's son away had borne.
Loud roared the clouds, as on he sped,
The sky grew blacker overhead;
Till, as he reached the royal town,
A mighty flood of rain came down.
By the great rain the monarch's mind
The coming of his guest divined.
To meet the honored youth he went,
And low to earth his head he bent.
With his own priest to lead the train,
He gave the gift high guests obtain,
And sought, with all who dwelt within
The city walls, his grace to win.
He fed him with the daintiest fare,
He served him with unceasing care,
And ministered with anxious eyes
Lest anger in his breast should rise;
And gave to be the Bráhman's bride
His own fair daughter, lotus-eyed.

Thus loved and honored by the King,
The glorious Bráhman Rishyaśring
Passed in that royal town his life
With Sántá his beloved wife.

CANTO X

RISHYAŚRING INVITED

" A GAIN, O best of Kings, give ear:—
My saving words attentive hear,
And listen to the tale of old
By that illustrious Bráhman told.
'Of famed Ikshváku's line shall spring
('Twas thus he spoke) a pious king,
Named Daśaratha, good and great,
True to his word and fortunate.
He with the Angas' mighty lord
Shall ever live in sweet accord,
And his a daughter fair shall be,
Sántá of happy destiny.
But Lomapád, the Angas' chief,
Still pining in his childless grief,
To Daśaratha thus shall say:—
" Give me thy daughter, friend, I pray,
Thy Śántá of the tranquil mind,
The noblest one of womankind."

The father, swift to feel for woe,
Shall on his friend his child bestow;
And he shall take her and depart
To his own town with joyous heart.
The maiden home in triumph led,
To Rishyaśring the King shall wed.
And he with loving joy and pride
Shall take her for his honored bride.
And Daśaratha to a rite
That best of Bráhmans shall invite
With supplicating prayer
To celebrate the sacrifice

To win him sons and Paradise,
That he will fain prepare.
From him the lord of men at length
The boon he seeks shall gain,
And see four sons-of boundless strength
His royal line maintain.'
Thus did the godlike saint of old
The will of fate declare,
And all that should befall unfold
Amid the sages there.
O Prince, supreme of men, go thou,
Consult thy holy guide,
And win, to aid thee in thy vow,
This Bráhman to thy side."

Sumantra's counsel, wise and good,
King Daśaratha heard,
Then by Vaśishtha's side he stood
And thus with him conferred:—
" Sumantra counsels thus:—do thou
My priestly guide, the plan allow."
Vaśishtha gave his glad consent,
And forth the happy monarch went
With lords and servants on the road
That led to Rishyaśring's abode.
Forests and rivers duly past,
He reached the distant town at last—
Of Lomapád the Angas' King,
And entered it with welcoming.
On through the crowded streets he came,
And, radiant as the kindled flame,
He saw within the monarch's house
The hermit's son, most glorious.
There Lomapád, with joyful breast,
To him all honor paid,
For friendship for his royal guest
His faithful bosom swayed.
Thus entertained with utmost care
Seven days, or eight, he tarried there,
And then that best of men thus broke
His purpose to the King, and spoke:—

"O King of men, mine ancient friend,
(Thus Daśaratha prayed),
Thy Sántá with her husband send
My sacrifice to aid."
Said he who ruled the Angas, " Yea,"
And his consent was won:—
And then at once he turned away
To warn the hermit's son.
He told him of their ties beyond
Their old affection's faithful bond:—
"This King," he said, "from days of old
A well beloved friend I hold.
To me this pearl of dames he gave
From childless woe mine age to save,
The daughter whom he loved so much,
Moved by compassion's gentle touch.
In him thy Sántá's father see:—
As I am, even so is he.
For sons the childless monarch yearns,
To thee alone for help he turns.
Go thou, the sacred rite ordain
To win the sons he prays to gain:—
Go, with thy wife thy succor lend,
And give his vows a blissful end."

The hermit's son with quick accord
Obeyed the Angas' mighty lord,
And with fair Sántá at his side
To Daśaratha's city hied.
Each king, with suppliant hands upheld,
Gazed on the other's face:—
And then by mutual love impelled
Met in a close embrace.
Then Daśaratha's thoughtful care,
Before he parted thence,
Bade trusty servants homeward bear
The glad intelligence:—
"Let all the town be bright and gay,
With burning incense sweet;
Let banners wave, and water lay
The dust in every street."

Glad were the citizens to learn
The tidings of their lord's return,
And through the city every man
Obediently his task began.
And fair and bright Ayodhyá showed,
As following his guest he rode
Through the full streets, where shell and drum
Proclaimed aloud the King was come.
And all the people with delight
Kept gazing on their king,
Attended by that youth so bright,
The glorious Rishyaśring.
When to his home the King had brought
The hermit's saintly son,
He deemed that all his task was wrought,
And all he prayed for won.
And lords who saw the stranger dame
So beautiful to view,
Rejoiced within their hearts, and came
And paid her honor, too.
There Rishyaśring passed blissful days,
Graced like the King with love and praise,
And shone in glorious light with her,
Sweet Śántá for his minister,
As Brahmá's son Vaśishtha, he
Who wedded Saint Arundhatí.

CANTO XI

THE SACRIFICE DECREED

THE Dewy Season came and went;
   The spring returned again—
   Then would the King, with mind intent,
His sacrifice ordain.
He came to Rishyaśring, and bowed
To him of look divine,
And bade him aid his offering vowed
For heirs, to save his line.
Nor would the youth his aid deny,
He spake the monarch fair,
And prayed him for that rite so high
All requisites prepare.
The King to wise Sumantra cried
Who stood aye ready near;
" Go summon quick, each holy guide,
To counsel and to hear."
Obedient to his lord's behest
Away Sumantra sped,
And brought Vaśishtha and the rest,
In Scripture deeply read.
Suyajña, Vámadeva came,
Jáváli, Kaśyap's son,
And old Vaśishtha, dear to fame,
Obedient, every one.
King Daśaratha met them there
And duly honored each,
And spoke in pleasant words his fair
And salutary speech:—
" In childless longing doomed to pine,
No happiness, O lords, is mine.

So have I for this cause decreed
To slay the sacrificial steed.
Fain would I pay that offering high
Wherein the horse is doomed to die,
With Rishyaśring his aid to lend,
And with your glory to befriend."

With loud applause each holy man
Received his speech, approved the plan,
And, by the wise Vaśishtha led,
Gave praises to the King, and said:—
" The sons thou cravest shalt thou see,
Of fairest glory, born to thee,
Whose holy feelings bid thee take
This righteous course for offspring's sake."
Cheered by the ready praise of those
Whose aid he sought, his spirits rose—
And thus the King his speech renewed
With looks of joy and gratitude:—
" Let what the coming rites require
Be ready, as the priests desire,
And let the horse, ordained to bleed,
With fitting guard and priest, be freed.
Yonder on Sarjú's northern side
The sacrificial ground provide;
And let the saving rites, that nought
Ill-omened may occur, be wrought.
The offering I announce to-day
Each lord of earth may claim to pay,
Provided that his care can guard
The holy rite by flaws unmarred.
For wandering fiends, whose watchful spite
Waits eagerly to spoil each rite—
Hunting with keenest eye detect
The slightest slip, the least neglect;
And when the sacred work is crossed
The workman is that moment lost.
Let preparation due be made,
Your powers the charge can meet,
That so the noble rite be paid
In every point complete."

And all the Bráhmans answered, " Yea,"
His mandate honoring,
And gladly promised to obey
The order of the King.
They cried with voices raised aloud:—
" Success attend thine aim! "
Then bade farewell, and lowly bowed,
And hastened whence they came.
King Daśaratha went within,
His well-loved wives to see—
And said: " Your lustral rites begin,
For these shall prosper me.
A glorious offering I prepare
That precious fruit of sons may bear."
Their lily faces brightened fast
Those pleasant words to hear,
As lilies, when the winter's past,
In lovelier hues appear.

CANTO XII

THE SACRIFICE BEGUN

AGAIN the spring with genial heat
Returning made the year complete.
To win him sons, without delay
His vow the King resolved to pay—
And to Vaśishtha, saintly man,
In modest words this speech began:—
" Prepare the rite with all things fit
As is ordained in Holy Writ,
And keep with utmost care afar
Whate'er its sacred forms might mar.
Thou art, my lord, my trustiest guide,
Kind-hearted, and my friend beside;
So is it meet thou undertake
This heavy task for duty's sake."

Then he, of twice-born men the best,
His glad assent at once expressed:—
" Fain will I do whate'er may be
Desired, O honored King, by thee."
To ancient priests he spoke, who, trained
In holy rites, deep skill had gained:—
" Here guards be stationed, good and sage,
Religious men of trusted age.
And various workmen send and call,
Who frame the door and build the wall—
With men of every art and trade,
Who read the stars and ply the spade,
And mimes and minstrels hither bring,
And damsels trained to dance and sing."
Then to the learned men he said,
In many a page of Scripture read:—

" Be yours each rite performed to see
According to the King's decree.
And stranger Bráhmans quickly call
To this great rite that welcomes all.
Pavilions for the princes, decked
With art and ornament, erect,
And handsome booths by thousands made
The Bráhman visitors to shade—
Arranged in order side by side,
With meat and drink and all supplied.
And ample stables we shall need
For many an elephant and steed—
And chambers where the men may lie,
And vast apartments, broad and high,
Fit to receive the countless bands
Of warriors come from distant lands.
For our own people too provide
Sufficient tents, extended wide,
And stores of meat and drink prepare,
And all that can be needed there.
And food in plenty must be found
For guests from all the country round.
Of various viands presents make,
For honor, not for pity's sake,
That fit regard and worship be
Paid to each caste in due degree.
And let not wish or wrath excite
Your hearts the meanest guest to slight;
But still observe with special grace
Those who obtain the foremost place,
Whether for happier skill in art
Or bearing in the rite their part
Do you, I pray, with friendly mind
Perform the task to you assigned,
And work the rite, as bids the law,
Without omission, slip, or flaw."

They answered: " As thou seest fit
So will we do and nought omit."
The sage Vasíshtha then addressed
Sumantra, called at his behest :—

" The princes of the earth invite,
And famous lords who guard the rite,
Priest, Warrior, Merchant, lowly thrall,
In countless thousands summon all.
Where'er their home be, far or near,
Gather the good with honor here.
And Janak, whose imperial sway
The men of Mithilá obey,
The firm of vow, the dread of foes,
Who all the lore of Scripture knows,
Invite him here with honor high,
King Daśaratha's old ally.
And Káśí's lord of gentle speech,
Who finds a pleasant word for each—
In length of days our monarch's peer,
Illustrious King, invite him here.
The father of our ruler's bride,
Known for his virtues far and wide,
The King whom Kekaya's realms obey,
Him with his son invite, I pray.
And Lomapád, the Angas King,
True to his vows and godlike, bring.
Far be thine invitations sent
To west and south and orient.
Call those who rule Suráshtra's land,
Suvíra's realm and Sindhu's strand,
And all the kings of earth beside
In friendship's bonds with us allied:—
Invite them all to hasten in
With retinue and kith and kin."
Vaśishtha's speech without delay
Sumantra bent him to obey,
And sent his trusty envoys forth
Eastward and westward, south and north.
Obedient to the saint's request
Himself he hurried forth, and pressed
Each nobler chief and lord and king
To hasten to the gathering.
Before the saint Vaśishtha stood
All those who wrought with stone and wood,
And showed the work which every one

In furtherance of the rite had done.
Rejoiced their ready zeal to see,
Thus to the craftsmen all said he:—
" I charge ye, masters, see to this,
That there be nothing done amiss.
And this, I pray, in mind be borne,
That not one gift ye give in scorn;
Whenever scorn a gift attends
Great sin is his who thus offends."

And now some days and nights had passed,
And Kings began to gather fast,
And precious gems in liberal store
As gifts to Daśaratha bore.
Then joy thrilled through Vaśishtha's breast
As thus the monarch he addressed:—
" Obedient to thy high decree
The Kings, my lord, are come to thee.
And it has been my care to greet
And honor all with reverence meet.
Thy servants' task is ended quite,
And all is ready for the rite.
Come forth then to the sacred ground
Where all in order will be found."
Then Rishyaśring confirmed the tale:—
Nor did their words to move him fail.
The stars propitious influence lent
When forth the world's great ruler went.
Then by the sage Vaśishtha led,
The priest began to speed
Those glorious rites wherein is shed
The lifeblood of the steed.

CANTO XIII

THE SACRIFICE FINISHED

THE circling year had filled its course,
 And back was brought the wandering horse:—
 Then upon Sarjú's northern strand
Began the rite the King had planned.
With Rishyasring the forms to guide,
The Bráhmans to their task applied,
At that great offering of the steed
Their lofty-minded King decreed.
The priests, who all the Scripture knew,
Performed their part in order due,
And circled round in solemn train
As precepts of the law ordain.
Pravargya rites were duly sped:—
For Upasads the flames were fed.
Then from the plant the juice was squeezed,
And those high saints, with minds well pleased,
Performed the mystic rites begun
With bathing ere the rise of sun.
They gave the portion, Indra's claim,
And hymned the King whom none can blame.
The mid-day bathing followed next,
Observed as bids the holy text.
Then the good priests with utmost care,
In form that Scripture's rules declare,
For the third time pure water shed
On high-souled Dasaratha's head.
Then Rishyasring and all the rest
To Indra and the Gods addressed
Their sweet-toned hymn of praise and prayer,
And called them in the rite to share.

With sweetest song and hymn intoned
They gave the Gods in heaven enthroned,
As duty bids, the gifts they claim,
The holy oil that feeds the flame.
And many an offering there was paid,
And not one slip in all was made.
For with most careful heed they saw
That all was done by Veda law.
None, all those days, was seen oppressed
By hunger or by toil distressed.
Why speak of human kind? No beast
Was there that lacked an ample feast.
For there was store for all who came,
For orphan child and lonely dame;
The old and young were well supplied,
The poor and hungry satisfied.
Throughout the day ascetics fed,
And those who roam to beg their bread:—
While all around the cry was still,
" Give forth, give forth," and " Eat your fill."
" Give forth with liberal hand the meal,
And various robes in largess deal."

Urged by these cries on every side
Unweariedly their task they plied,
And heaps of food like hills in size
In boundless plenty met the eyes:—
And lakes of sauce, each day renewed,
Refreshed the weary multitude.
And strangers there from distant lands,
And women folk in crowded bands
The best of food and drink obtained
At the great rite the King ordained.
Apart from all, the Bráhmans there,
Thousands on thousands, took their share
Of various dainties sweet to taste,
On plates of gold and silver placed—
All ready set, as, when they willed,
The twice-born men their places filled.
And servants in fair garments dressed
Waited upon each Bráhman guest.

Of cheerful mind and mien were they,
With gold and jewelled ear-rings gay.
The best of Bráhmans praised the fare
Of countless sorts, of flavor rare—
And thus to Raghu's son they cried:—
" We bless thee, and are satisfied."
Between the rites some Bráhmans spent
The time in learned argument,
With ready flow of speech, sedate,
And keen to vanquish in debate.
There day by day the holy train
Performed all rites as rules ordain.
No priest in all that host was found
But kept the vows that held him bound;
None, but the holy Vedas knew,
And all their sixfold science too.
No Bráhman there was found unfit
To speak with eloquence and wit.

And now the appointed time came near
The sacrificial posts to rear.
They brought them, and prepared to fix
Of Bel and Khádir six and six;
Six, made of the Palása-tree,
Of Fig-wood one, apart to be—
Of Sleshmát and of Devadár
One column each, the mightiest far:—
So thick the two the arms of man
Their ample girth would fail to span.
All these with utmost care were wrought
By hand of priests in Scripture taught,
And all with gold were gilded bright
To add new splendor to the rite;
Twenty-and-one those stakes in all,
Each one-and-twenty cubits tall:—
And one-and-twenty ribbons there
Hung on the pillars bright and fair.
Firm in the earth they stood at last,
Where cunning craftsmen fixed them fast;
And there unshaken each remained,
Octagonal and smoothly planed.

Then ribbons over all were hung,
And flowers and scent around them flung.
Thus decked they cast a glory forth
Like the great saints who star the north.
The sacrificial altar then
Was raised by skilful twice-born men—
In shape and figure to behold
An eagle with his wings of gold,
With twice nine pits and formed threefold.
Each for some special God, beside
The pillars were the victims tied;
The birds that roam the wood, the air,
The water, and the land were there,
And snakes and things of reptile birth,
And healing herbs that spring from earth:—
As texts prescribe, in Scripture found,
Three hundred victims there were bound.
The steed devoted to the host
Of Gods, the gem they honor most,
Was duly sprinkled. Then the Queen
Kauśalyá, with delighted mien,
With reverent steps around him paced,
And with sweet wreaths the victim graced;
Then with three swords in order due
She smote the steed with joy, and slew.
That night the queen, a son to gain,
With calm and steady heart was fain
By the dead charger's side to stay
From evening till the break of day.
Then came three priests, their care to lead
The other queens to touch the steed—
Upon Kauśalyá to attend,
Their company and aid to lend.
As by the horse she still reclined,
With happy mien and cheerful mind,
With Rishyaśring the twice-born came
And praised and blessed the royal dame.
The priest who well his duty knew,
And every sense could well subdue,
From out the bony chambers freed
And boiled the marrow of the steed.

Above the steam the monarch bent,
And, as he smelt the fragrant scent,
In time and order drove afar
All error that his hopes could mar.
Then sixteen priests together came,
And cast into the sacred flame
The severed members of the horse,
Made ready all in ordered course.
On piles of holy Fig-tree raised
The meaner victims' bodies blazed:—
The steed, of all the creatures slain,
Alone required a pile of cane.
Three days, as is by law decreed,
Lasted that Offering of the Steed.
The Chatushtom began the rite,
And when the sun renewed his light,
The Ukthya followed—after came
The Atirátra's holy flame.
These were the rites, and many more,
Arranged by light of holy lore,
The Aptoryám of mighty power,
And, each performed in proper hour,
The Abhijit and Viśvajit
With every form and service fit;
And with the sacrifice at night
The Jyotishtom and Áyus rite.

The task was done, as laws prescribe:—
The monarch, glory of his tribe,
Bestowed the land in liberal grants
Upon the sacred ministrants.
He gave the region of the east,
His conquest, to the Hotri priest.
The west the celebrant obtained,
The south the priest presiding gained—
The northern region was the share
Of him who chanted forth the prayer.
Thus did each priest obtain his meed
At the great Slaughter of the Steed,
Ordained, the best of all to be,
By self-existent deity.

Ikshváku's son, with joyful mind,
This noble fee to each assigned—
But all the priests with one accord
Addressed that unpolluted lord:—
" 'Tis thine alone to keep the whole
Of this broad earth in firm control.
No gift of lands from thee we seek,
To guard these realms our hands were weak.
On sacred lore our days are spent,
Let other gifts our wants content."

The chief of old Ikshváku's line
Gave them ten hundred thousand kine,
A hundred millions of fine gold,
The same in silver four times told.
But every priest in presence there
With one accord resigned his share.
To Saint Vaśishtha, high of soul,
And Rishyaśring they gave the whole.
That largess pleased those Bráhmans well,
Who bade the prince his wishes tell.
Then Daśaratha, mighty King,
Made answer thus to Rishyaśring:—
" O holy Hermit, of thy grace,
Vouchsafe the increase of my race."
He spoke; nor was his prayer denied—
The best of Bráhmans thus replied:—
" Four sons, O Monarch, shall be thine,
Upholders of thy royal line."

CANTO XIV

RÁVAN DOOMED

THE saint, well-read in holy lore,
Pondered awhile his answer o'er,
And thus again addressed the King,
His wandering thoughts regathering:—
"Another rite will I begin
Which shall the sons thou cravest win,
Where all things shall be duly sped
And first Atharva texts be read."

Then by Vibhándak's gentle son
Was that high sacrifice begun,
The King's advantage seeking still
And zealous to perform his will.
Now all the Gods had gathered there,
Each one for his allotted share—
Brahmá, the ruler of the sky,
Sthánu, Náráyan, Lord most high,
And holy Indra men might view
With Maruts for his retinue;
The heavenly chorister, and saint,
And spirit pure from earthly taint,
With one accord had sought the place
The high-souled monarch's rite to grace.
Then to the Gods who came to take
Their proper share, the hermit spake:—
"For you has Daśaratha slain
The votive steed, a son to gain;
Stern penance-rites the King has tried,
And in firm faith on you relied,
And now with undiminished care
A second rite would fain prepare.

214

But, O ye Gods, consent to grant
The longing of your supplicant.
For him beseeching hands I lift,
And pray you all to grant the gift,
That four fair sons of high renown
The offerings of the King may crown."
They to the hermit's son replied:—
" His longing shall be gratified.
For, Bráhman, in most high degree
We love the King and honor thee."

These words the Gods in answer said,
And vanished thence, by Indra led.
Thus to the Lord, the worlds who made,
The Immortals all assembled prayed:—
" O Brahmá, mighty by thy grace,
Rávan, who rules the giant race,
Torments us in his senseless pride,
And penance-loving saints beside.
For thou well pleased in days of old
Gavest the boon that makes him bold,
That God nor demon e'er should kill
His charmed life, for so thy will.
We, honoring that high behest,
Bear all his rage though sore distressed.
That lord of giants fierce and fell
Scourges the earth and heaven and hell.
Mad with thy boon, his impious rage
Smites saint and bard and God and sage.
The sun himself withholds his glow,
The wind in fear forbears to blow;
The fire restrains his wonted heat
Where stand the dreaded Rávan's feet,
And, necklaced with the wandering wave,
The sea before him fears to rave.
Kuvera's self in sad defeat
Is driven from his blissful seat.
We see, we feel the giant's might,
And woe comes o'er us and affright.
To thee, O Lord, thy suppliants pray
To find some cure this plague to stay."

Thus by the gathered Gods addressed
He pondered in his secret breast,
And said: "One only way I find
To slay this fiend of evil mind.
He prayed me once his life to guard
From demon, God, and heavenly bard,
And spirits of the earth and air,
And I consenting heard his prayer.
But the proud giant in his scorn
Recked not of man of woman born.
None else may take his life away,
But only man the fiend may slay."

The Gods, with Indra at their head,
Rejoiced to hear the words he said.
Then, crowned with glory like a flame,
Lord Vishnu to the council came;
His hands shell, mace, and discus bore,
And saffron were the robes he wore.
Riding his eagle through the crowd,
As the sun rides upon a cloud,
With bracelets of fine gold, he came,
Loud welcomed by the Gods' acclaim.
His praise they sang with one consent,
And cried, in lowly reverence bent:—
"O Lord whose hand fierce Madhu slew,
Be thou our refuge, firm and true;
Friend of the suffering worlds art thou,
We pray thee help thy suppliants now."
Then Vishnu spake: "Ye Gods, declare,
What may I do to grant your prayer?"

"King Daśaratha," thus cried they,
"Fervent in penance many a day,
The sacrificial steed has slain,
Longing for sons, but all in vain.
Now, at the cry of us forlorn,
Incarnate as his seed be born.
Three queens has he—each lovely dame
Like Beauty, Modesty, or Fame.
Divide thyself in four, and be

His offspring by these noble three.
Man's nature take, and slay in fight
Rávan who laughs at heavenly might—
This common scourge, this rankling thorn
Whom the three worlds too long have borne.
For Rávan, in the senseless pride
Of might unequalled, has defied
The host of heaven, and plagues with woe
Angel and bard and saint below,
Crushing each spirit and each maid
Who plays in Nandan's heavenly shade.
O conquering Lord, to thee we bow;
Our surest hope and trust art thou.
Regard the world of men below,
And slay the God's tremendous foe."

When thus the suppliant Gods had prayed,
His wise reply Náráyan made:—
"What task demands my presence there,
And when this dread, ye Gods declare."
The Gods replied: "We fear, O Lord,
Fierce Rávan, ravener abhorred.
Be thine the glorious task, we pray,
In human form this fiend to slay.
By thee of all the Blest alone
This sinner may be overthrown.
He gained by penance long and dire
The favor of the mighty Sire.
Then He who every gift bestows
Guarded the fiend from heavenly foes,
And gave a pledge his life that kept
From all things living, man except.
On him thus armed no other foe
Than man may deal the deadly blow.
Assume, O King, a mortal birth,
And strike the demon to the earth."

Then Vishnu, God of Gods, the Lord
Supreme by all the worlds adored,
To Brahmá and the suppliants spake:—
"Dismiss your fear: for your dear sake

In battle will I smite him dead,
The cruel fiend, the Immortal's dread.
And lords and ministers and all
His kith and kin with him shall fall.
Then, in the world of mortal men,
Ten thousand years and hundreds ten
I as a human King will reign,
And guard the earth as my domain."
God, saint, and nymph, and minstrel throng
With heavenly voices raised their song
In hymns of triumph to the God
Whose conquering feet on Madhu trod:—

"Champion of Gods, as man appear,
This cruel Rávan slay,
The thorn that saints and hermits fear,
The plague that none can stay.
In savage fury uncontrolled
His pride forever grows—
He dares the Lord of Gods to hold
Among his deadly foes."

CANTO XV

THE NECTAR

WHEN wisest Vishnu thus had given
His promise to the Gods of heaven,
He pondered in his secret mind
A suited place of birth to find.
Then he decreed, the lotus-eyed,
In four his being to divide,
And Daśaratha, gracious King,
He chose as sire from whom to spring.
That childless prince, of high renown,
Who smote in war his foemen down,
At that same time with utmost care
Prepared the rite that wins an heir.
Then Vishnu, fain on earth to dwell,
Bade the Almighty Sire farewell,
And vanished while a reverent crowd
Of Gods and saints in worship bowed.

The monarch watched the sacred rite,
When a vast form of awful might,
Of matchless splendor, strength and size
Was manifest before his eyes.
From forth the sacrificial flame,
Dark, robed in red, the being came.
His voice was drumlike, loud and low,
His face suffused with rosy glow.
Like a huge lion's mane appeared
The long locks of his hair and beard.
He shone with many a lucky sign,
And many an ornament divine;
A towering mountain in his height,
A tiger in his gait and might.

No precious mine more rich could be,
No burning flame more bright than he.
His arms embraced in loving hold,
Like a dear wife, a vase of gold
Whose silver lining held a draught
Of nectar as in heaven is quaffed—
A vase so vast, so bright to view,
They scarce could count the vision true.
Upon the King his eyes he bent,
And said: "The Lord of life has sent
His servant down, O Prince, to be
A messenger from heaven to thee."
The King with all his nobles by
Raised reverent hands and made reply:—
"Welcome, O glorious being! Say
How can my care thy grace repay."
Envoy of Him whom all adore,
Thus to the King he spake once more:—
"The Gods accept thy worship—they
Give thee the blessed fruit to-day.
Approach and take, O glorious King,
This heavenly nectar which I bring,
For it shall give thee sons and wealth,
And bless thee with a store of health.
Give it to those fair queens of thine,
And bid them quaff the drink divine—
And they the princely sons shall bear
Long sought by sacrifice and prayer."

"Yea, O my lord," the monarch said,
And took the vase upon his head,
The gift of Gods, of fine gold wrought,
With store of heavenly liquor fraught.
He honored, filled with transport new,
That wondrous being, fair to view,
As round the envoy of the God
With reverential steps he trod.
His errand done, that form of light
Arose and vanished from the sight.
High rapture filled the monarch's soul,
Possessed of that celestial bowl,

As when a man by want distressed
With unexpected wealth is blest.
And rays of transport seemed to fall
Illuminating bower and hall,
As when the autumn moon rides high,
And floods with lovely light the sky.
Quick to the ladies' bower he sped,
And thus to Queen Kauśalyá said:—
" This genial nectar take and quaff,"
He spoke, and gave the lady half.
Part of the nectar that remained
Sumitrá from his hand obtained.
He gave, to make her fruitful too,
Kaikeyí half the residue.
A portion yet remaining there,
He paused awhile to think,
Then gave Sumitrá, with her share,
The remnant of the drink.
Thus on each queen of those fair three
A part the King bestowed,
And with sweet hope a child to see
Their yearning bosoms glowed.
The heavenly bowl the King supplied
Their longing souls relieved,
And soon, with rapture and with pride,
Each royal dame conceived.
He gazed upon each lady's face,
And triumphed as he gazed,
As Indra in his royal place
By Gods and spirits praised.

CANTO XVI

THE VÁNARS

WHEN Vishnu thus had gone on earth,
From the great King to take his birth,
The self-existent Lord of all
Addressed the Gods who heard his call:—
" For Vishnu's sake, the strong and true,
Who seeks the good of all of you,
Make helps, in war to lend him aid,
In forms that change at will, arrayed,
Of wizard skill and hero might,
Outstrippers of the wind in flight,
Skilled in the arts of counsel, wise,
And Vishnu's peers in bold emprise;
With heavenly arts and prudence fraught,
By no devices to be caught;
Skilled in all weapons' lore and use
As they who drink the immortal juice.
And let the nymphs supreme in grace,
And maidens of the minstrel race,
Monkeys and snakes, and those who rove
Free spirits of the hill and grove,
And wandering Daughters of the Air,
In monkey form brave children bear.
So erst the lord of bears I shaped,
Born from my mouth as wide I gaped."

Thus by the mighty Sire addressed
They all obeyed his high behest,
And thus begot in countless swarms
Brave sons disguised in sylvan forms.
Each God, each sage became a sire,
Each minstrel of the heavenly choir,

Each faun, of children strong and good
Whose feet should roam the hill and wood.
Snakes, bards, and spirits, serpents bold
Had sons too numerous to be told.
Báli, the woodland hosts who led,
High as Mahendra's lofty head,
Was Indra's child. That noblest fire,
The Sun, was great Sugríva's sire.
Tára, the mighty monkey, he
Was offspring of Vrihaspati—
Tára the matchless chieftain, boast
For wisdom of the Vánar host.
Of Gandhamádan brave and bold
The father was the Lord of Gold.
Nala the mighty, dear to fame,
Of skilful Viśvakarmá came.
From Agni, Níla bright as flame,
Who in his splendor, might, and worth,
Surpassed the sire who gave him birth.
The heavenly Aśvins, swift and fair,
Were fathers of a noble pair,
Who, Dwivida and Mainda named,
For beauty like their sires were famed.
Varun was father of Sushen,
Of Sarabh, he who sends the rain.
Hanumán, best of monkey kind,
Was son of him who breathes the wind—
Like thunderbolt in frame was he,
And swift as Garud's self could flee.
These thousands did the Gods create
Endowed with might that none could mate,
In monkey forms that changed at will—
So strong their wish the fiend to kill.
In mountain size, like lions thewed,
Up-sprang the wondrous multitude,
Auxiliar hosts in every shape,
Monkey and bear and highland ape.
In each the strength, the might, the mien
Of his own parent God were seen.
Some chiefs of Vánar mothers came,
Some of she-bear and minstrel dame,

Skilled in all arms in battle's shock,
The brandished tree, the loosened rock;
And prompt, should other weapons fail,
To fight and slay with tooth and nail.
Their strength could shake the hills amain,
And rend the rooted trees in twain,
Disturb with their impetuous sweep
The Rivers' Lord, the Ocean deep,
Rend with their feet the seated ground,
And pass wide floods with airy bound—
Or forcing through the sky their way
The very clouds by force could stay.
Mad elephants that wander through
The forest wilds, could they subdue,
And with their furious shout could scare
Dead upon earth the birds of air.
So were the sylvan chieftains formed;
Thousands on thousands still they swarmed.
These were the leaders honored most,
The captains of the Vánar host,
And to each lord and chief and guide
Was monkey offspring born beside.
Then by the bears' great monarch stood
The other roamers of the wood,
And turned, their pathless homes to seek,
To forest and to mountain peak.
The leaders of the monkey band
By the two brothers took their stand,
Sugríva, offspring of the Sun,
And Báli, Indra's mighty one.
They both endowed with Garud's might,
And skilled in all the arts of fight,
Wandered in arms the forest through,
And lions, snakes, and tigers, slew.
But every monkey, ape, and bear
Ever was Bali's special care;
With his vast strength and mighty arm
He kept them from all scathe and harm.
And so the earth with hill, wood, seas,
Was filled with mighty ones like these—

Of various shape and race and kind,
With proper homes to each assigned.
With Ráma's champions fierce and strong
'The earth was overspread,
High as the hills and clouds, a throng
With bodies vast and dread.

CANTO XVII

RISHYASRING'S RETURN

NOW when the high-souled monarch's rite,
The Aśvamedh, was finished quite,
Their sacrificial dues obtained,
The Gods their heavenly homes regained.
The lofty-minded saints withdrew,
Each to his place, with honor due,
And kings and chieftains, one and all,
Who came to grace the festival.
And Daśaratha, ere they went,
Addressed them thus benevolent:—
" Now may you, each with joyful heart,
To your own realms, O Kings, depart.
Peace and good luck attend you there,
And blessing, is my friendly prayer;
Let cares of state each mind engage
To guard his royal heritage.
A monarch from his throne expelled
No better than the dead is held.
So he who cares for power and might
Must guard his realm and royal right.
Such care a meed in heaven will bring
Better than rites and offering.
Such care a king his country owes
As man upon himself bestows,
When for his body he provides
Raiment and every need besides.
For future days should kings foresee,
And keep the present error-free."
Thus did the King the kings exhort—
They heard, and turned them from the court,
And, each to each in friendship bound,

Went forth to all the realms around.
The rites were o'er, the guests were sped,
The train the best of Bráhmans led—
In which the King with joyful soul,
With his dear wives, and with the whole
Of his imperial host and train
Of cars and servants turned again,
And, as a monarch dear to fame,
Within his royal city came.

Next, Rishyaśring, well-honored sage,
And Sántá, sought their hermitage.
The King himself, of prudent mind,
Attended him, with troops behind,
And all her men the town outpoured
With Saint Vaśishtha and their lord.
High mounted on a car of state,
O'ercanopied fair Sántá sate,
Drawn by white oxen, while a band
Of servants marched on either hand.
Great gifts of countless price she bore,
With sheep and goats and gems in store.
Like Beauty's self the lady shone
With all the jewels she had on,
As, happy in her sweet content,
Peerless amid the fair she went.
Not Queen Paulomí's self could be
More loving to her lord than she.
She who had lived in happy ease,
Honored with all her heart could please,
While dames and kinsfolk ever vied
To see her wishes gratified—
Soon as she knew her husband's will
Again to seek the forest, still
Was ready for the hermit's cot,
Nor murmured at her altered lot.
The King attended to the wild
That hermit and his own dear child,
And in the centre of a throng
Of noble courtiers rode along.
The sage's son had let prepare

A lodge within the wood, and there
Awhile they lingered blithe and gay,
Then, duly honored, went their way.
The glorious hermit Rishyaśring
Drew near and thus besought the King:—
" Return, my honored lord, I pray,
Return, upon thy homeward way."
The monarch, with the waiting crowd,
Lifted his voice and wept aloud,
And with eyes dripping still to each
Of his good queens he spake this speech:—
" Kauśalyá and Sumitrá dear,
And thou, my sweet Kaikeyí, hear—
All upon Śántá feast your gaze,
The last time for a length of days."
To Śántá's side the ladies leapt,
And hung about her neck and wept,
And cried, " O, happy be the life
Of this great Bráhman and his wife.
The Wind, the Fire, the Moon on high,
The Earth, the Streams, the circling Sky,
Preserve thee in the wood, true spouse,
Devoted to thy husband's vows.
And O dear Śántá, ne'er neglect
To pay the dues of meek respect
To the great saint, thy husband's sire,
With all observance and with fire.
And, sweet one, pure of spot and blame,
Forget not thou thy husband's claim;
In every change, in good and ill,
Let thy sweet words delight him still,
And let thy worship constant be—
Her lord is woman's deity.
To learn thy welfare, dearest friend,
The King will many a Bráhman send.
Let happy thoughts thy spirit cheer,
And be not troubled, daughter dear."

These soothing words the ladies said,
And pressed their lips upon her head.
Each gave with sighs her last adieu,

Then at the King's command withdrew.
The King around the hermit went
With circling footsteps reverent,
And placed at Rishyaśring's command
Some soldiers of his royal band.
The Bráhman bowed in turn and cried,
" May fortune never leave thy side.
O mighty King, with justice reign,
And still thy people's love retain."
He spoke, and turned away his face,
And, as the hermit went,
The monarch, rooted to the place,
Pursued with eyes intent.
But when the sage had passed from view
King Daśaratha turned him too,
Still fixing on his friend each thought,
With such deep love his breast was fraught.
Amid his people's loud acclaim
Home to his royal seat he came,
And lived delighted there—
Expecting when each queenly dame,
Upholder of his ancient fame,
Her promised son should bear.
The glorious sage his way pursued
Till close before his eyes he viewed
Sweet Champá, Lomapád's fair town,
Wreathed with her Champac's leafy crown.
Soon as the saint's approach he knew,
The King, to yield him honor due,
Went forth to meet him with a band
Of priests and nobles of the land :—
" Hail, Sage," he cried, " O joy to me!
What bliss it is, my lord, to see
Thee with thy wife and all thy train
Returning to my town again.
Thy father, honored Sage, is well,
Who hither from his woodland cell
Has sent full many a messenger
For tidings both of thee and her."
Then joyfully, for due respect,

The monarch bade the town be decked.
The King and Rishyaśring elate
Entered the royal city's gate—
In front the chaplain rode.
Then, loved and honored with all care
By monarch and by courtier, there
The glorious saint abode.

CANTO XVIII

RISHYAŚRING'S DEPARTURE

THE monarch called a Bráhman near
   And said, " Now speed away
   To Kaśyap's son, the mighty seer,
And with all reverence say—
The holy child he holds so dear,
The hermit of the noble mind,
Whose equal it were hard to find,
Returned, is dwelling here.
Go, and instead of me do thou
Before that best of hermits bow,
That still he may for his dear son,
Show me the favor I have won."
Soon as the King these words had said,
To Kaśyap's son the Bráhman sped.
Before the hermit low he bent
And did obeisance, reverent;
Then with meek words his grace to crave
The message of his lord he gave:—
" The high-souled father of his bride
Had called thy son his rites to guide—
Those rites are o'er, the steed is slain;
Thy noble child is come again."

Soon as the saint that speech had heard
His spirit with desire was stirred
To seek the city of the King
And to his cot his son to bring.
With young disciples at his side
Forth on his way the hermit hied,
While peasants from their hamlets ran
To reverence the holy man.

Each with his little gift of food,
Forth came the village multitude,
And, as they humbly bowed the head,
" What may we do for thee? " they said.
Then he, of Bráhmans first and best,
The gathered people thus addressed:—
" Now tell me, for I fain would know,
Why is it I am honored so? "
They to the high-souled saint replied:—
" Our ruler is with thee allied.
Our master's order we fulfil;
O Bráhman, let thy mind be still."

With joy the saintly hermit heard
Each pleasant and delightful word,
And poured a benediction down
On King and ministers and town.
Glad at the words of that high saint
Some servants hastened to acquaint
Their King, rejoicing to impart
The tidings that would cheer his heart.
Soon as the joyful tale he knew
To meet the saint the monarch flew,
The guest-gift in his hand he brought,
And bowed before him and besought:—
" This day by seeing thee I gain
Not to have lived my life in vain.
Now be not wroth with me, I pray,
Because I wiled thy son away."
The best of Bráhmans answer made:—
" Be not, great lord of Kings, afraid.
Thy virtues have not failed to win
My favor, O thou pure of sin."
Then in the front the saint was placed,
The King came next in joyous haste,
And with him entered his abode,
'Mid glad acclaim as on they rode.
To greet the sage the reverent crowd
Raised suppliant hands and humbly bowed.
Then from the palace many a dame
Following well-dressed Sántá came,

Stood by the mighty saint and cried:—
" See, honor's source, thy son's dear bride."
The saint, who every virtue knew,
His arms around his daughter threw,
And with a father's rapture pressed
The lady to his wondering breast.
Arising from the saint's embrace
She bowed her low before his face,
And then, with palm to palm applied,
Stood by her hermit father's side.
He for his son, as laws ordain,
Performed the rite that frees from stain,
And, honored by the wise and good,
With him departed to the wood.

CANTO XIX

THE BIRTH OF THE PRINCES

THE seasons six, in rapid flight,
    Had circled since that glorious rite.
    Eleven months had passed away—
'Twas Chaitra's ninth returning day.
The moon within that mansion shone
Which Aditi looks so kindly on.
Raised to their apex in the sky
Five brilliant planets beamed on high.
Shone with the moon, in Cancer's sign,
Vrihaspati with light divine.
Kauśalyá bore an infant blest
With heavenly marks of grace impressed;
Ráma, the universe's lord,
A prince by all the worlds adored.
New glory Queen Kauśalyá won
Reflected from her splendid son.
So Aditi shone more and more,
The Mother of the Gods, when she
The King of the Immortals bore,
The thunder-wielding deity.
The lotus-eyed, the beauteous boy,
He came fierce Rávan to destroy;
From half of Vishnu's vigor born,
He came to help the worlds forlorn.
And Queen Kaikeyí bore a child
Of truest valor, Bharat styled,
With every princely virtue blest,
One-fourth of Vishnu manifest.
Sumitrá too a noble pair,
Called Lakshman and Śatrughna, bare,
Of high emprise, devoted, true,

Sharers in Vishnu's essence too.
'Neath Pushya's mansion, Mína's sign,
Was Bharat born, of soul benign.
The sun had reached the Crab at morn
When Queen Sumitrá's babes were born,
What time the moon had gone to make
His nightly dwelling with the Snake.
The high-souled monarch's consorts bore
At different times those glorious four,
Like to himself and virtuous, bright
As Proshthapadá's fourfold light.

Then danced the nymphs' celestial throng,
The minstrels raised their strain;
The drums of heaven pealed loud and long,
And flowers came down in rain.
Within Ayodhyá, blithe and gay,
All kept the joyous holiday.
The spacious square, the ample road
With mimes and dancers overflowed,
And with the voice of music rang
Where minstrels played and singers sang—
And shone, a wonder to behold,
With dazzling show of gems and gold.
Nor did the King his largess spare,
For minstrel, driver, bard, to share;
Much wealth the Bráhmans bore away,
And many thousand kine that day.
Soon as each babe was twelve days old
'Twas time the naming rite to hold,
When Saint Vaśishtha, rapt with joy,
Assigned a name to every boy.
Ráma, to him the high-souled heir,
Bharat, to him Kaikeyí bare—
Of Queen Sumitrá one fair son
Was Lakshman, and Śatrughna one.
Ráma, his sire's supreme delight,
Like some proud banner cheered his sight,
And to all creatures seemed to be
The self-existent deity.
All heroes, versed in holy lore,

To all mankind great love they bore.
Fair stores of wisdom all possessed,
With princely graces all were blest.
But mid those youths of high descent,
With lordly light preëminent,
Like the full moon unclouded shone
Ráma, the world's dear paragon.
He best the elephant could guide,
Urge the fleet car, the charger ride—
A master he of bowman's skill,
Joying to do his father's will.
The world's delight and darling, he
Loved Lakshman best from infancy;
And Lakshman, lord of lofty fate,
Upon his elder joyed to wait,
Striving his second self to please
With friendship's sweet observances.
His limbs the hero ne'er would rest
Unless the couch his brother pressed;
Except beloved Ráma shared
He could not taste the meal prepared.
When Ráma, pride of Raghu's race,
Sprang on his steed to urge the chase,
Behind him Lakshman loved to go
And guard him with his trusty bow.
As Ráma was to Lakshman dear
More than his life and ever near,
So fond Śatrughna prized above
His very life his Bharat's love.
Illustrious heroes, nobly kind
In mutual love they all combined,
And gave their royal sire delight
With modest grace and warrior might;
Supported by the glorious four
Shone Daśaratha more and more,
As though, with every guardian God
Who keeps the land and skies,
The Father of all creatures trod
The earth before men's eyes.

CANTO XX

VIŚVÁMITRA'S VISIT

NOW Daśaratha's pious mind
    Meet wedlock for his sons designed;
    With priests and friends the King began
To counsel and prepare his plan.
Such thoughts engaged his bosom, when,
To see Ayodhyá's lord of men,
A mighty saint of glorious fame,
The hermit Viśvámitra came.
For evil fiends that roam by night
Disturbed him in each holy rite,
And in their strength and frantic rage
Assailed with witcheries the sage.
He came to seek the monarch's aid
To guard the rites the demons stayed,
Unable to a close to bring
One unpolluted offering.
Seeking the King in this dire strait
He said to those who kept the gate:—
"Haste, warders, to your master run,
And say that here stands Gádhi's son."
Soon as they heard the holy man,
To the King's chamber swift they ran
With minds disordered all, and spurred
To wildest zeal by what they heard.
On to the royal hall they sped,
There stood and lowly bowed the head,
And made the lord of men aware
That the great saint was waiting there.
The King with priest and peer arose
And ran the sage to meet,
As Indra from his palace goes

Lord Brahmá's self to greet.
When glowing with celestial light
The pious hermit was in sight,
The King, whose mien his transport showed,
The honored gift for guests bestowed.
Nor did the saint that gift despise,
Offered as holy texts advise;
He kindly asked the earth's great King
How all with him was prospering.
The son of Kusík bade him tell
If all in town and field were well,
All well with friends, and kith and kin,
And royal treasure stored within:—
" Do all thy neighbors own thy sway?
Thy foes confess thee yet?
Dost thou continue still to pay
To Gods and men each debt? "
Then he, of hermits first and best,
Vasishtha with a smile addressed,
And asked him of his welfare too,
Showing him honor as was due.
Then with the sainted hermit all
Went joyous to the monarch's hall,
And sate them down by due degree,
Each one, of rank and dignity.
Joy filled the noble prince's breast
Who thus bespoke the honored guest:—
" As Amrit by a mortal found,
As rain upon the thirsty ground,
As to an heirless man a son
Born to him of his precious one—
As gain of what we sorely miss,
As sudden dawn of mighty bliss,
So is thy coming here to me—
All welcome, mighty Saint, to thee.
What wish within thy heart hast thou?
If I can please thee, tell me how.
Hail, Saint, from whom all honors flow,
Worthy of all I can bestow.
Blest is my birth with fruit to-day,
Nor has my life been thrown away.

I see the best of Bráhman race,
And night to glorious morn gives place.
Thou, holy Sage, in days of old
Among the royal saints enrolled,
Didst, penance-glorified, within
The Bráhman caste high station win.
'Tis meet and right in many a way
That I to thee should honor pay.
This seems a marvel to mine eyes—
All sin thy visit purifies;
And I by seeing thee, O Sage,
Have reaped the fruit of pilgrimage.
Then say what thou wouldst have me do,
That thou hast sought this interview.
Favored by thee, my wish is still,
O Hermit, to perform thy will.
Nor needest thou at length explain
The object that thy heart would gain.
Without reserve I grant it now—
My deity, O Lord, art thou."
The glorious hermit, far renowned,
With highest fame and virtue crowned,
Rejoiced these modest words to hear
Delightful to the mind and ear.

CANTO XXI

VIŚVÁMITRA'S SPEECH

THE hermit heard with high content
    That speech so wondrous eloquent,
    And while each hair with joy arose,
He thus made answer at the close:—
" Good is thy speech, O noble King,
And like thyself in everything.
So should their lips be wisdom-fraught
Whom kings begot, Vaśishtha taught.
The favor which I came to seek
Thou grantest ere my tongue can speak.
But let my tale attention claim,
And hear the need for which I came.
O King, as Scripture texts allow,
A holy rite employs me now.
Two fiends who change their forms at will
Impede that rite with cursed skill.
Oft when the task is nigh complete,
These worst of fiends my toil defeat,
Throw bits of bleeding flesh, and o'er
The altar shed a stream of gore.
When thus the rite is mocked and stayed,
And all my pious hopes delayed,
Cast down in heart the spot I leave,
And spent with fruitless labor grieve.
Nor can I, checked by prudence, dare
Let loose my fury on them there—
The muttered curse, the threatening word,
In such a rite must ne'er be heard.
Thy grace the rite from check can free,
And yield the fruit I long to see.
Thy duty bids thee, King, defend

The suffering guest, the suppliant friend.
Give me thy son, thine eldest born,
Whom locks like raven's wings adorn.
That hero youth, the truly brave,
Of thee, O glorious King, I crave.
For he can lay those demons low
Who mar my rites and work me woe:
My power shall shield the youth from harm,
And heavenly might shall nerve his arm.
And on my champion will I shower
Unnumbered gifts of varied power—
Such gifts as shall ensure his fame
And spread through all the worlds his name.
Be sure those fiends can never stand
Before the might of Ráma's hand,
And mid the best and bravest none
Can slay that pair but Raghu's son.
Entangled in the toils of Fate
Those sinners, proud and obstinate,
Are, in their fury overbold,
No match for Ráma, mighty-souled.
Nor let a father's breast give way
Too far to fond affection's sway.
Count thou the fiends already slain:
My word is pledged, nor pledged in vain.
I know the hero Ráma well
In whom high thoughts and valor dwell;
So does Vaśishtha, so do these
Engaged in long austerities.
If thou would do the righteous deed,
And win high fame, thy virtue's meed,
Fame that on earth shall last and live,
To me, great King, thy Ráma give.
If to the words that I have said,
With Saint Vaśishtha at their head
Thy holy men, O King, agree,
Then let thy Ráma go with me.
Ten nights my sacrifice will last,
And ere the stated time be past
Those wicked fiends, those impious twain,
Must fall by wondrous Ráma slain.

Let not the hours, I warn thee, fly,
Fixt for the rite, unheeded by;
Good luck have thou, O royal Chief,
Nor give thy heart to needless grief."

Thus in fair words with virtue fraught,
The pious glorious saint besought.
But the good speech with poignant sting
Pierced ear and bosom of the King,
Who, stabbed with pangs too sharp to bear,
Fell prostrate and lay fainting there.

CANTO XXII

DAŚARATHA'S SPEECH

HIS tortured senses all astray,
    Awhile the hapless monarch lay,
    Then slowly gathering thought and strength
To Viśvámitra spoke at length:—
" My son is but a child, I ween;
This year he will be just sixteen.
How is he fit for such emprise,
My darling with the lotus eyes?
A mighty army will I bring
That calls me master, lord, and King,
And with its countless squadrons fight
Against these rovers of the night.
My faithful heroes skilled to wield
The arms of war will take the field;
Their skill the demons' might may break:
Ráma, my child, thou must not take.
I, even I, my bow in hand,
Will in the van of battle stand,
And, while my soul is left alive,
With the night-roaming demons strive.
Thy guarded sacrifice shall be
Completed, from all hindrance free.
Thither will I my journey make:
Ráma, my child, thou must not take.
A boy unskilled, he knows not yet
The bounds to strength and weakness set.
No match is he for demon foes
Who magic arts to arms oppose.
O chief of saints, I have no power,
Of Ráma reft, to live one hour—
Mine aged heart at once would break:

243

Ráma, my child, thou must not take.
Nine thousand circling years have fled
With all their seasons o'er my head,
And as a hard-won boon, O Sage,
These sons have come to cheer mine age.
My dearest love amid the four
Is he whom first his mother bore,
Still dearer for his virtue's sake;
Ráma, my child, thou must not take.
But if, unmoved by all I say,
Thou needs must bear my son away,
Let me lead with him, I entreat,
A fourfold army all complete.
What is the demons' might, O Sage?
Who are they? What their parentage?
What is their size? What beings lend
Their power to guard them and befriend?
How can my son their arts withstand?
Or I or all my armed band?
Tell me the whole that I may know
To met in war each evil foe
Whom conscious might inspires with pride."

And Viśvámitra thus replied:—
" Sprung from Pulastya's race there came
A giant known by Rávan's name.
Once favored by the Eternal Sire
He plagues the worlds in ceaseless ire,
For peerless power and might renowned,
By giant bands encompassed round.
Viśravas for his sire they hold,
His brother is the Lord of Gold.
King of the giant hosts is he,
And worst of all in cruelty.
This Rávan's dread commands impel
Two demons who in might excel,
Márícha and Suváhu Light,
To trouble and impede the rite."
Then thus the King addressed the sage:—
" No power have I, my lord, to wage
War with this evil-minded foe;

Now pity on my darling show,
And upon me of hapless fate,
For thee as God I venerate.
Gods, spirits, bards of heavenly birth,
The birds of air, the snakes of earth
Before the might of Rávan quail,
Much less can mortal man avail.
He draws, I hear, from out the breast,
The valor of the mightiest.
No, ne'er can I with him contend,
Or with the forces he may send.
How can I then my darling lend,
Godlike, unskilled in battle? No,
I will not let my young child go.
Foes of thy rite, those mighty ones,
Sunda and Upasunda's sons,
Are fierce as Fate to overthrow:
I will not let my young child go.
Márícha and Suváhu fell
Are valiant and instructed well.
One of the twain I might attack
With all my friends their lord to back."

CANTO XXIII

VAŚISHTHA'S SPEECH

WHILE thus the hapless monarch spoke,
Paternal love his utterance broke.
Then words like these the saint returned,
And fury in his bosom burned:—
" Didst thou, O King, a promise make,
And wishest now thy word to break?
A son of Raghu's line should scorn
To fail in faith, a man forsworn.
But if thy soul can bear the shame
I will return e'en as I came.
Live with thy sons, and joy be thine,
False scion of Kakutstha's line."
As Viśvámitra, mighty sage,
Was moved with this tempestuous rage,
Earth rocked and reeled throughout her frame,
And fear upon the Immortals came.
But Saint Vaśishtha, wisest seer,
Observant of his vows austere,
Saw the whole world convulsed with dread,
And thus unto the monarch said:—
" Thou, born of old Ikshváku's seed,
Art Justice' self in mortal weed.
Constant and pious, blest by fate,
The right thou must not violate.
Thou, Raghu's son, so famous through
The triple world as just and true,
Perform thy bounden duty still,
Nor stain thy race by deed of ill.
If thou have sworn and now refuse
Thou must thy store of merit lose.
Then, Monarch, let thy Ráma go,

Nor fear for him the demon foe.
The fiends shall have no power to hurt
Him trained to war or inexpert—
Nor vanquish him in battle field,
For Kuśik's son the youth will shield.
He is incarnate Justice, he
The best of men for bravery—
Embodied love of penance drear,
Among the wise without a peer.
Full well he knows, great Kuśik's son,
The arms celestial, every one,
Arms from the Gods themselves concealed,
Far less to other men revealed.
These arms to him, when earth he swayed,
Mighty Kriśáśva, pleased, conveyed.
Kriśáśva's sons they are indeed,
Brought forth by Daksha's lovely seed,
Heralds of conquest, strong and bold,
Brilliant, of semblance manifold.
Jayá and Vijayá, most fair,
A hundred splendid weapons bare.
Of Jayá, glorious as the morn,
First fifty noble sons were born,
Boundless in size yet viewless too,
They came the demons to subdue.
And fifty children also came
Of Vijayá the beauteous dame,
Sanháras named, of mighty force,
Hard to assail or check in course.
Of these the hermit knows the use,
And weapons new can he produce.
All these the mighty saint will yield
To Ráma's hand, to own and wield;
And armed with these, beyond a doubt
Shall Ráma put those fiends to rout.
For Ráma and the people's sake,
For thine own good my counsel take,
Nor seek, O King, with fond delay,
The parting of thy son to stay."

CANTO XXIV

THE SPELLS

VASISHTHA thus was speaking still:
 The monarch, of his own free will,
 Bade with quick zeal and joyful cheer
Ráma. and Lakshman hasten near.
Mother and sire in loving care
Sped their dear son with rite and prayer;
Vaśishtha blessed him ere he went,
O'er his loved head the father bent—
And then to Kuśik's son resigned
Ráma with Lakshman close behind.
Standing by Viśvámitra's side,
The youthful hero, lotus-eyed,
The Wind-God saw, and sent a breeze
Whose sweet pure touch just waved the trees.
There fell from heaven a flowery rain,
And with the song and dance the strain
Of shell and tambour sweetly blent
As forth the son of Raghu went.
The hermit led: behind him came
The bow-armed Ráma, dear to fame,
Whose locks were like the raven's wing:—
Then Lakshman, closely following.
The Gods and Indra, filled with joy,
Looked down upon the royal boy,
And much they longed the death to see
Of their ten-headed enemy.
Ráma and Lakshman paced behind
That hermit of the lofty mind,
As the young Aśvins, heavenly pair,
Follow Lord Indra through the air.

On arm and hand the guard they wore,
Quiver and bow and sword they bore;
Two fire-born Gods of War seemed they,
He, Śiva's self who led the way.
Upon fair Sarjú's southern shore
They now had walked a league or more,
When thus the sage in accents mild
To Ráma said: " Beloved child,
This lustral water duly touch:
My counsel will avail thee much.
Forget not all the words I say,
Nor let the occasion slip away.
Lo, with two spells I thee invest,
The mighty and the mightiest.
O'er thee fatigue shall ne'er prevail,
Nor age nor change thy limbs assail.
Thee powers of darkness ne'er shall smite
In tranquil sleep or wild delight.
No one is there in all the land
Thine equal for the vigorous hand.
Thou, when thy lips pronounce the spell,
Shalt have no peer in heaven or hell.
None in the world with thee shall vie,
O sinless one, in apt reply—
In fortune, knowledge, wit, and tact,
Wisdom to plan and skill to act.
This double science take, and gain
Glory that shall for aye remain.
Wisdom and judgment spring from each
Of these fair spells whose use I teach.
Hunger and thirst unknown to thee,
High in the worlds thy rank shall be.
For these two spells with might endued,
Are the Great Father's heavenly brood,
And thee, O Chief, may fitly grace,
Thou glory of Kakutstha's race.
Virtues which none can match are thine,
Lord, from thy birth, of gifts divine—
And now these spells of might shall cast
Fresh radiance o'er the gifts thou hast."
Then Ráma duly touched the wave,

Raised suppliant hands, bowed low his head,
And took the spells the hermit gave,
Whose soul on contemplation fed.
From him whose might these gifts enhanced,
A brighter beam of glory glanced:—
So shines in all his autumn blaze
The Day-God of the thousand rays.
The hermit's wants those youths supplied,
As pupils used to holy guide.
And then the night in sweet content
On Sarjú's pleasant bank they spent.

CANTO XXV

THE HERMITAGE OF LOVE

SOON as appeared the morning light
Up rose the mighty anchorite,
And thus to youthful Ráma said,
Who lay upon his leafy bed :—
" High fate is hers who calls thee son :
Arise, 'tis break of day;
Rise, Chief, and let those rites be done
Due at the morning's ray."
At that great sage's high behest
Up sprang the princely pair,
To bathing rites themselves addressed,
And breathed the holiest prayer.
Their morning task completed, they
To Viśvámitra came,
That store of holy works, to pay
The worship saints may claim.
Then to the hallowed spot they went
Along fair Sarjú's side
Where mix her waters confluent
With three-pathed Gangá's tide.
There was a sacred hermitage
Where saints devout of mind
Their lives through many a lengthened age
To penance had resigned.
That pure abode the princes eyed
With unrestrained delight,
And thus unto the saint they cried,
Rejoicing at the sight :—
" Whose is that hermitage we see?
Who makes his dwelling there?
Full of desire to hear are we :
O Saint, the truth declare."

The hermit, smiling, made reply
To the two boys' request:—
" Hear, Ráma, who in days gone by
This calm retreat possessed—
Kandarpa in apparent form,
(Called Káma by the wise,)
Dared Umá's new-wed lord to storm
And make the God his prize.
'Gainst Sthánu's self, on rites austere
And vows intent, they say,
His bold rash hand he dared to rear,
Though Sthánu cried, Away!
But the God's eye with scornful glare
Fell terrible on him,
Dissolved the shape that was so fair
And burnt up every limb.
Since the great God's terrific rage
Destroyed his form and frame,
Káma in each succeeding age
Has borne Ananga's name.
So, where his lovely form decayed,
This land is Anga styled:—
Sacred to him of old this shade,
And hermits undefiled.
Here Scripture-talking elders sway
Each sense with firm control,
And penance-rites have washed away
All sin from every soul.
One night, fair boy, we here will spend,
A pure stream on each hand,
And with to-morrow's light will bend
Our steps to yonder strand.
Here let us bathe, and free from stain
To that pure grove repair,
Sacred to Káma, and remain
One night in comfort there."
With penance' far-discerning eye
The saintly men beheld
Their coming, and with transport high
Each holy bosom swelled.
To Kuśik's son the gift they gave

That honored guest should greet—
Water they brought his feet to lave,
And showed him honor meet.
Ráma and Lakshman next obtained
In due degree their share—
Then with sweet talk the guests remained,
And charmed each listener there.
The evening prayers were duly said
With voices calm and low:—
Then on the ground each laid his head
And slept till morning's glow.

CANTO XXVI

THE FOREST OF TÁDAKÁ

WHEN the fair light of morning rose
The princely tamers of their foes
Followed, his morning worship o'er,
The hermit to the river's shore.
The high-souled men with thoughtful care
A pretty barge had stationed there.
All cried, " O lord, this barge ascend,
And with thy princely followers bend
To yonder side thy prosperous way—
With nought to check thee or delay."
Nor did the saint their rede reject:
He bade farewell with due respect,
And crossed, attended by the twain,
That river rushing to the main.
When now the bark was half-way o'er,
Ráma and Lakshman heard the roar,
That louder grew and louder yet,
Of waves by dashing waters met.
Then Ráma asked the mighty seer:—
" What is the tumult that I hear
Of waters cleft in mid-career? "
Soon as the speech of Ráma, stirred
By deep desire to know, he heard,
The pious saint began to tell
What caused the waters' roar and swell:—
" On high Kailása's distant hill
There lies a noble lake
Whose waters, born from Brahmá's will,
The name of Mánas take.
Thence, hallowing where'er they flow,
The streams of Sarjú fall,

And wandering through the plains below
Embrace Ayodhyá's wall.
Still, still preserved in Sarjú's name
Sarovar's fame we trace,
The flood of Brahmá whence she came
To run her holy race.
To meet great Gangá here she hies
With tributary wave—
Hence the loud roar ye hear arise,
Of floods that swell and rave.
Here, pride of Raghu's line, do thou
In humble adoration bow."

He spoke. The princes both obeyed,
And reverence to each river paid.
They reached the southern shore at last,
And gayly on their journey passed.
A little space beyond there stood
A gloomy awe-inspiring wood.
The monarch's noble son began
To question thus the holy man:—
"Whose gloomy forest meets mine eye,
Like some vast cloud that fills the sky?
Pathless and dark it seems to be,
Where birds in thousands wander free;
Where shrill cicalas' cries resound,
And fowl of dismal note abound.
Lion, rhinoceros, and bear,
Boar, tiger, elephant, are there,
There shrubs and thorns run wild:
Dháo, Sál, Bignonia, Bel, are found,
And every tree that grows on ground:
How is the forest styled?"
The glorious saint this answer made:—
"Dear child of Raghu, hear
Who dwells within the horrid shade
That looks so dark and drear.
Where now is wood, long ere this day
Two broad and fertile lands,
Malaja and Karúsha lay,
Adorned by heavenly hands.

Here, mourning friendship's broken ties,
Lord Indra of the thousand eyes
Hungered and sorrowed many a day,
His brightness soiled with mud and clay,
When in a storm of passion he
Had slain his dear friend Namuchi.
Then came the Gods and saints who bore
Their golden pitchers brimming o'er
With holy streams that banish stain,
And bathed Lord Indra pure again.
When in this land the God was freed
From spot and stain of impious deed
For that his own dear friend he slew,
High transport thrilled his bosom through.
Then in his joy the lands he blessed,
And gave a boon they long possessed:—
"Because these fertile lands retain
The washings of the blot and stain,
('Twas thus Lord Indra sware,)
Malaja and Karúsha's name
Shall celebrate with deathless fame
My malady and care."
"So be it," all the Immortals cried,
When Indra's speech they heard—
And with acclaim they ratified
The names his lips conferred.
"Long time, O victor of thy foes,
These happy lands had sweet repose,
And higher still in fortune rose.
At length a spirit, loving ill,
Tádaká, wearing shapes at will—
Whose mighty strength, exceeding vast,
A thousand elephants' surpassed,
Was to fierce Sunda, lord and head
Of all the demon armies, wed.
From her, Lord Indra's peer in might
Giant Márícha sprang to light;
And she, a constant plague and pest,
These two fair realms has long distressed.
Now dwelling in her dark abode
A league away she bars the road:

And we, O Ráma, hence must go
Where lies the forest of the foe.
Now on thine own right arm rely,
And my command obey:
Smite the foul monster that she die,
And take the plague away.
To reach this country none may dare,
Fallen from its old estate,
Which she, whose fury nought can bear,
Has left so desolate.
And now my truthful tale is told—
How with accursed sway
The spirit plagued this wood of old,
And ceases not to-day."

CANTO XXVII

THE BIRTH OF TÁDAKÁ

WHEN thus the sage without a peer
Had closed that story strange to hear,
Ráma again the saint addressed,
To set one lingering doubt at rest:—
" O holy man, 'tis said by all
That spirits' strength is weak and small,
How can she match, of power so slight,
A thousand elephants in might? "
And Viśvámitra thus replied
To Raghu's son, the glorified:—
" Listen, and I will tell thee how
She gained the strength that arms her now
A mighty spirit lived of yore;
Suketu was the name he bore.
Childless was he, and free from crime
In rites austere he passed his time.
The mighty Sire was pleased to show
His favor, and a child bestow,
Tádaká named, most fair to see,
A pearl among the maids was she—
And matched, for such was Brahmá's dower,
A thousand elephants in power.
Nor would the Eternal Sire, although
The spirit longed, a son bestow.
That maid in beauty's youthful pride
Was given to Sunda for a bride.
Her son, Márícha was his name,
A giant, through a curse, became.
She, widowed, dared with him molest
Agastya, of all saints the best.
Inflamed with hunger's wildest rage,
Roaring she rushed upon the sage.

258

When the great hermit saw her near,
On-speeding in her fierce career,
He thus pronounced Márícha's doom:—
'A giant's form and shape assume.'
And then, by mighty anger swayed,
On Tádaká this curse he laid:—
'Thy present form and semblance quit,
And wear a shape thy mood to fit;
Changed form and feature by my ban,
A fearful thing that feeds on man.'
She, by his awful curse possessed,
And mad with rage that fills her breast,
Has on this land her fury dealt
Where once the saint Agastya dwelt.
Go, Ráma, smite this monster dead,
The wicked plague, of power so dread,
And further by this deed of thine
The good of Bráhmans and of kine.
Thy hand alone can overthrow,
In all the worlds, this impious foe.
Nor let compassion lead thy mind
To shrink from blood of womankind;
A monarch's son must ever count
The people's welfare paramount—
And whether pain or joy he deal
Dare all things for his subjects' weal;
Yea, if the deed bring praise or guilt,
If life be saved or blood be spilt:—
Such, through all time, should be the care
Of those a kingdom's weight who bear.
Slay, Ráma, slay this impious fiend,
For by no law her life is screened.
So Manthará, as bards have told,
Virochan's child, was slain of old
By Indra, when in furious hate
She longed the earth to devastate.
So Kávya's mother, Bhrigu's wife,
Who loved her husband as her life,
When Indra's throne she sought to gain,
By Vishnu's hand of yore was slain.
By these and high-souled kings beside,
Struck down, have lawless women died."

CANTO XXVIII

THE DEATH OF TÁDAKÁ

THUS spoke the saint. Each vigorous word
The noble monarch's offspring heard—
And, reverent hands together laid,
His answer to the hermit made:—
" My sire and mother bade me aye
Thy word, O mighty Saint, obey.
So will I, O most glorious, kill
This Tádaká who joys in ill—
For such my sire's, and such thy will.
To aid with mine avenging hand
The Bráhmans, kine, and all the land,
Obedient, heart and soul, I stand."
Thus spoke the tamer of the foe,
And by the middle grasped his bow.
Strongly he drew the sounding string
That made the distant welkin ring.
Scared by the mighty clang the deer
That roamed the forest shook with fear.
And Tádaká the echo heard,
And rose in haste from slumber stirred.
In wild amaze, her soul aflame
With fury towards the spot she came.
When that foul shape of evil mien
And stature vast as e'er was seen
The wrathful son of Raghu eyed,
He thus unto his brother cried:—
" Her dreadful shape, O Lakshman, see,
A form to shudder at and flee.
The hideous monster's very view
Would cleave a timid heart in two.
Behold the demon hard to smite,

Defended by her magic might.
My hand shall stay her course to-day,
And shear her nose and ears away.
No heart have I her life to take:
I spare it for her sex's sake.
My will is but—with minished force—
To check her in her evil course."
While thus he spoke, by rage impelled—
Roaring as she came nigh,
The fiend her course at Ráma held
With huge arms tossed on high.
Her, rushing on, the seer assailed
With a loud cry of hate;
And thus the sons of Raghu hailed:—
"Fight, and be fortunate."
Then from the earth a horrid cloud
Of dust the demon raised,
And for awhile in darkling shroud
Wrapt Raghu's sons amazed.
Then calling on her magic power
The fearful fight to wage,
She smote him with a stony shower,
Till Ráma burned with rage.
Then pouring forth his arrowy rain
That stony flood to stay,
With wingèd darts, as she charged amain,
He shore her hands away.
As Tádaká still thundered near
Thus maimed by Ráma's blows,
Lakshman in fury severed sheer
The monster's ears and nose.
Assuming by her magic skill
A fresh and fresh disguise,
She tried a thousand shapes at will,
Then vanished from their eyes.
When Gádhi's son of high renown
Still saw the stony rain pour down
Upon each princely warrior's head,
With words of wisdom thus he said:—
"Enough of mercy, Ráma, lest
This sinful evil-working pest,

Disturber of each holy rite,
Repair by magic arts her might.
Without delay the fiend should die,
For, see, the twilight hour is nigh.
And at the joints of night and day
Such giant foes are hard to slay."
Then Ráma, skilful to direct
His arrow to the sound—
With shafts the mighty demon checked
Who rained her stones around.
She, sore impeded and beset
By Ráma and his arrowy net—
Though skilled in guile and magic lore,
Rushed on the brothers with a roar.
Deformed, terrific, murderous, dread,
Swift as the levin on she sped—
Like cloudy pile in autumn's sky,
Lifting her two vast arms on high:
When Ráma smote her with a dart
Shaped like a crescent, to the heart.
Sore wounded by the shaft that came
With lightning speed and surest aim,
Blood spurting from her mouth and side,
She fell upon the earth and died.
Soon as the Lord who rules the sky
Saw the dread monster lifeless lie,
He called aloud, Well done! well done!
And the Gods honored Raghu's son.
Standing in heaven the Thousand-eyed,
With all the Immortals, joying cried:—
"Lift up thine eyes, O Saint, and see
The Gods and Indra nigh to thee.
This deed of Ráma's boundless might
Has filled our bosoms with delight.
Now, for our will would have it so,
To Raghu's son some favor show.
Invest him with the power which nought
But penance gains, and holy thought.
Those heavenly arms on him bestow—
To thee entrusted long ago
By great Kriśáśva best of kings,

Son of the Lord of living things.
More fit recipient none can be
Than he who joys in following thee;
And for our sakes the monarch's seed
Has yet to do a mighty deed."

He spoke; and all the heavenly train
Rejoicing sought their homes again,
While honor to the saint they paid—
Then came the evening's twilight shade.
The best of hermits overjoyed
To know the monstrous fiend destroyed,
His lips on Ráma's forehead pressed,
And thus the conquering chief addressed:—
" O Ráma, gracious to the sight,
Here will we pass the present night,
And with the morrow's earliest ray
Bend to my hermitage our way."
The son of Daśaratha heard,
Delighted, Viśvámitra's word—
And as he bade, that night he spent
In Tádaká's wild wood, content.
And the grove shone that happy day,
Freed from the curse that on it lay—
Like Chaitraratha fair and gay.

CANTO XXIX

THE· CELESTIAL ARMS

THAT night they slept and took their rest;
And then the mighty saint addressed,
With pleasant smile and accents mild
These words to Raghu's princely child:—
" Well pleased am I. High fate be thine,
Thou scion of a royal line.
Now will I, for I love thee so,
All heavenly arms on thee bestow.
Victor with these, whoe'er oppose,
Thy hand shall conquer all thy foes—
Though Gods and spirits of the air,
Serpents and fiends, the conflict dare.
I'll give thee as a pledge of love
The mystic arms they use above,
For worthy thou to have revealed
The weapons I have learnt to wield.
First, son of Raghu, shall be thine
The arm of Vengeance, strong, divine:
The arm of Fate, the arm of Right,
And Vishnu's arm of awful might:—
That, before which no foe can stand,
The thunderbolt of Indra's hand;
And Śiva's trident, sharp and dread,
And that dire weapon, Brahmá's Head.
And two fair clubs, O royal child,
One Charmer and one Pointed styled—
With flame of lambent fire aglow,
On thee, O Chieftain, I bestow.
And Fate's dread net and Justice' noose
That none may conquer, for thy use:—
And the great cord, renowned of old,

Which Varun ever loves to hold.
Take these two thunderbolts, which I
Have got for thee, the Moist and Dry.
Here Siva's dart to thee I yield,
And that which Vishnu wont to wield.
I give to thee the arm of Fire,
Desired by all and named the Spire.
To thee I grant the Wind-God's dart,
Named Crusher, O thou pure of heart.
This arm, the Horse's Head, accept,
And this, the Curlew's Bill yclept,
And these two spears, the best e'er flew,
Named the Invincible and True.
And arms of fiends I make thine own,
Skull-wreath and mace that smashes bone.
And Joyous, which the spirits bear,
Great weapon of the sons of air.
Brave offspring of the best of lords,
I give thee now the Gem of swords—
And offer next, thine hand to arm,
The heavenly bard's beloved charm.
Now with two arms I thee invest
Of never-ending Sleep and Rest—
With weapons of the Sun and Rain,
And those that dry and burn amain;
And strong Desire with conquering touch,
The dart that Káma prizes much.
I give the arm of shadowy powers
That bleeding flesh of man devours.
I give the arms the God of Gold
And giant fiends exult to hold.
This smites the foe in battle-strife,
And takes his fortune, strength, and life.
I give the arms called False and True,
And great Illusion give I too;
The hero's arm called Strong and Bright
That spoils the foeman's strength in fight.
I give thee as a priceless boon
The Dew, the weapon of the Moon,
And add the weapon, deftly planned,
That strengthens Visvakarmá's hand.

The Mortal dart whose point is chill,
And Slaughter, ever sure to kill;
All these and other arms, for thou
Art very dear, I give thee now.
Receive these weapons from my hand,
Son of the noblest in the land."
Facing the east, the glorious saint
Pure from all spot of earthly taint,
To Ráma, with delighted mind,
That noble host of spells consigned.
He taught the arms, whose lore is won
Hardly by Gods, to Raghu's son.
He muttered low the spell whose call
Summons those arms and rules them all—
And each, in visible form and frame,
Before the monarch's son they came.
They stood and spoke in reverent guise
To Ráma with exulting cries:—
"O noblest child of Raghu, see,
Thy ministers and thralls are we."
With joyful heart and eager hand
Ráma received the wondrous band,
And thus with words of welcome cried:—
"Aye present to my will abide"—
Then hasted to the saint to pay
Due reverence, and pursued his way.

CANTO XXX

THE MYSTERIOUS POWERS

PURE, with glad cheer and joyful breast,
    Of those mysterious arms possessed,
    Ráma, now passing on his way,
Thus to the saint began to say:—
" Lord of these mighty weapons, I
Can scarce be harmed by Gods on high;
Now, best of saints, I long to gain
The powers that can these arms restrain."
Thus spoke the prince. The sage austere,
True to his vows, from evil clear,
Called forth the names of those great charms
Whose powers restrain the deadly arms.
" Receive thou True and Truly-famed,
And Bold and Fleet: the weapons named
Warder and Progress, swift of pace,
Averted-head and Drooping-face;
The Seen, and that which Secret flies—
The weapon of the thousand eyes;
Ten-headed, and the Hundred-faced,
Star-gazer and the Layer-waste;
The Omen-bird, the Pure-from-spot,
The pair that wake and slumber not;
The Fiendish, that which shakes amain,
The Strong-of-Hand, the Rich-in-Gain;
The Guardian, and the Close-allied,
The Gaper, Love, and Golden-side:—
O Raghu's son receive all these,
Bright ones that wear what forms they please;
Kriśáśva's mystic sons are they,
And worthy thou their might to sway."

With joy the pride of Raghu's race
Received the hermit's proffered grace—
Mysterious arms, to check and stay,
Or smite the foeman in the fray.
Then, all with heavenly forms endued,
Nigh came the wondrous multitude.
Celestial in their bright attire
Some shone like coals of burning fire—
Some were like clouds of dusky smoke;
And suppliant thus they sweetly spoke:—
" Thy thralls, O Ráma, here we stand—
Command, we pray, thy faithful band."
" Depart," he cried, " where each may list,
But when I call you to assist,
Be present to my mind with speed,
And aid me in the hour of need."

To Ráma then they lowly bent,
And round him in due reverence went—
To his command they answered, " Yea,"
And as they came so went away.
When thus the arms had homeward flown,
With pleasant words and modest tone,
E'en as he walked, the prince began
To question thus the holy man:—
" What cloudlike wood is that which near
The mountain's side I see appear?
O tell me, for I long to know:
Its pleasant aspect charms me so.
Its glades are full of deer at play,
And sweet birds sing on every spray.
Passed is the hideous wild—I feel
So sweet a tremor o'er me steal—
And hail with transport fresh and new
A land that is so fair to view.
Then tell me all, thou holy Sage,
And whose this pleasant hermitage
In which those wicked ones delight
To mar and kill each holy rite—
And with foul heart and evil deed
Thy sacrifice, great Saint, impede.

To whom, O Sage, belongs this land
In which thine altars ready stand?
'Tis mine to guard them, and to slay
The giants who the rites would stay.
All this, O best of saints, I burn
From thine own lips, my lord, to learn."

CANTO XXXI

THE PERFECT HERMITAGE

THUS spoke the prince of boundless might,
　　And thus replied the anchorite:—
　　" Chief of the mighty arm, of yore
Lord Vishnu, whom the Gods adore
For holy thought and rites austere,
Of penance made his dwelling here.
This ancient wood was called of old
Grove of the Dwarf, the mighty-souled—
And when perfection he attained
The grove the name of Perfect gained.
Bali of yore, Virochan's son,
Dominion over Indra won—
And when with power his proud heart swelled,
O'er the three worlds his empire held.
When Bali then began a rite,
The Gods and Indra in affright
Sought Vishnu in this place of rest,
And thus with prayers the God addressed:—
' Bali, Virochan's mighty son,
His sacrifice has now begun:
Of boundless wealth, that demon king
Is bounteous to each living thing.
Though suppliants flock from every side
The suit of none is e'er denied.
Whate'er, where'er, howe'er the call,
He hears the suit and gives to all.
Now with thine own illusive art
Perform, O Lord, the helper's part:
Assume a dwarfish form, and thus
From fear and danger rescue us.'

Thus in their dread the Immortals sued
The God, a dwarfish shape indued:—
Before Virochan's son he came,
Three steps of land his only claim.
The boon obtained, in wondrous wise
Lord Vishnu's form increased in size;
Through all the worlds, tremendous, vast,
God of the Triple Step, he passed.
The whole broad earth from side to side
He measured with one mighty stride—
Spanned with the next the firmament,
And with the third through heaven he went.
Thus was the king of demons hurled
By Vishnu to the nether world—
And thus the universe restored
To Indra's rule, its ancient lord.
And now because the Immortal God
This spot in dwarflike semblance trod,
The grove has aye been loved by me
For reverence of the devotee.
But demons haunt it, prompt to stay
Each holy offering I would pay.
Be thine, O lion-lord, to kill
These giants that delight in ill.
This day, beloved child, our feet
Shall rest within the calm retreat;
And know, thou chief of Raghu's line,
My hermitage is also thine."
He spoke; and soon the anchorite,
With joyous looks that beamed delight,
With Ráma and his brother stood
Within the consecrated wood.
Soon as they saw the holy man,
With one accord together ran
The dwellers in the sacred shade,
And to the saint their reverence paid—
And offered water for his feet,
The gift of honor, and a seat;
And next with hospitable care
They entertained the princely pair.
The royal tamers of their foes

Rested awhile in sweet repose—
Then to the chief of hermits sued
Standing in suppliant attitude:—
" Begin, O best of saints, we pray,
Initiatory rites to-day.
This Perfect Grove shall be anew
Made perfect, and thy words be true."

Then, thus addressed, the holy man,
The very glorious sage, began
The high preliminary rite,
Restraining sense and appetite.
Calmly the youths that night reposed,
And rose when morn her light disclosed—
Their morning worship paid, and took
Of lustral water from the brook.
Thus purified they breathed the prayer,
Then greeted Viśvámitra where
As celebrant he sate beside
The flame with sacred oil supplied.

CANTO XXXII

VIŚVÁMITRA'S SACRIFICE

THAT conquering pair, of royal race,
    Skilled to observe due time and place—
    To Kúśik's hermit son addressed,
In timely words, their meet request:—
"When must we, lord, we pray thee tell,
Those Rovers of the Night repel?
Speak, lest we let the moment fly,
And pass the due occasion by."
Thus longing for the strife, they prayed,
And thus the hermits answer made:—
" Till the fifth day be come and past,
O Raghu's sons, your watch must last.
The saint his Díkshá has begun,
And all that time will speak to none."
Soon as the steadfast devotees
Had made reply in words like these,
The youths began, disdaining sleep,
Six days and nights their watch to keep—
The warrior pair who tamed the foe,
Unrivalled benders of the bow,
Kept watch and ward unwearied still
To guard the saint from scathe and ill.
'Twas now the sixth returning day,
The hour foretold had passed away.
Then Ráma cried: " O Lakshman, now
Firm, watchful, resolute be thou.
The fiends as yet have kept afar
From the pure grove in which we are;
Yet waits us, ere the day shall close,
Dire battle with the demon foes."
While thus spoke Ráma, borne away

By longing for the deadly fray,
See! bursting from the altar came
The sudden glory of the flame;
Round priest and deacon, and upon
Grass, ladles, flowers, the splendor shone—
And the high rite, in order due,
With sacred texts began anew.
But then a loud and fearful roar
Re-echoed through the sky;
And like vast clouds that shadow o'er
The heavens in dark July,
Involved in gloom of magic might
Two fiends rushed on amain—
Máricha, Rover of the Night,
Suváhu, and their train.
As on they came in wild career
Thick blood in rain they shed;
And Ráma saw those things of fear
Impending overhead.
Then, soon as those accursed two
Who showered down blood he spied,
Thus to his brother brave and true
Spoke Ráma lotus-eyed:—
" Now, Lakshman, thou these fiends shalt see,
Man-eaters, foul of mind,
Before my mortal weapon flee
Like clouds before the wind."
He spoke. An arrow, swift as thought,
Upon his bow he pressed,
And smote, to utmost fury wrought,
Máricha on the breast.
Deep in his flesh the weapon lay
Winged by the mystic spell,
And, hurled a hundred leagues away,
In ocean's flood he fell.
Then Ráma, when he saw the foe
Convulsed and mad with pain
'Neath the chill-pointed weapon's blow,
To Lakshman spoke again:—
" See, Lakshman, see! this mortal dart
That strikes a numbing chill,

Hath struck him senseless with the smart,
But left him breathing still.
But these who love the evil way
And drink the blood they spill,
Rejoicing holy rites to stay,
Fierce plagues, my hand shall kill."
He seized another shaft, the best,
Aglow with living flame;
It struck Suváhu on the chest,
And dead to earth he came.
Again a dart, the Wind-God's own,
Upon his string he laid,
And all the demons were o'erthrown—
The saints no more afraid.
When thus the fiends were slain in fight,
Disturbers of each holy rite,
Due honor by the saints was paid
To Ráma for his wondrous aid:—
So Indra is adored when he
Has won some glorious victory.
Success at last the rite had crowned,
And Viśvámitra gazed around—
And seeing every side at rest,
The son of Raghu thus addressed:—
" My joy, O Prince, is now complete—
Thou hast obeyed my will:
Perfect before, this calm retreat
Is now more perfect still."

CANTO XXXIII

THE SONE

THEIR task achieved, the princes spent
  That night with joy and full content.
  Ere yet the dawn was well displayed
Their morning rites they duly paid—
And sought, while yet the light was faint,
The hermits and the mighty saint.
They greeted first that holy sire
Resplendent like the burning fire,
And then with noble words began
Their sweet speech to the sainted man:—
"Here stand, O lord, thy servants true—
Command what thou wouldst have us do."
The saints, by Viśvámitra led,
To Ráma thus in answer said:—
"Janak, the king who rules the land
Of fertile Mithilá, has planned
A noble sacrifice, and we
Will thither go the rite to see.
Thou, Prince of men, with us shalt go,
And there behold the wondrous bow—
Terrific, vast, of matchless might,
Which, splendid at the famous rite,
The Gods assembled gave the King.
No giant, fiend, or God can string
That gem of bows, no heavenly bard;
Then, sure, for man the task were hard.
When lords of earth have longed to know
The virtue of that wondrous bow,
The strongest sons of kings in vain
Have tried the mighty cord to strain.
This famous bow thou there shalt view,

And wondrous rites shalt witness too.
The high-souled king who lords it o'er
The realm of Mithilá, of yore
Gained from the Gods this bow, the price
Of his imperial sacrifice.
Won by the rite the glorious prize
Still in his royal palace lies—
Laid up in oil of precious scent
With aloes-wood and incense blent."
Then Ráma answering, "Be it so,"
Made ready with the rest to go.
The saint himself was now prepared,
But ere beyond the grove he fared,
He turned him and in words like these
Addressed the sylvan deities:—
"Farewell! each holy rite complete,
I leave the hermits' perfect seat:
To Gangá's northern shore I go
Beneath Himálaya's peaks of snow."
With reverent steps he paced around
The limits of the holy ground—
And then the mighty saint set forth
And took his journey to the north.
His pupils, deep in Scripture's page,
Followed behind the holy sage,
And servants from the sacred grove
A hundred wains for convoy drove.
The very birds that winged that air,
The very deer that harbored there,
Forsook the glade and leafy brake
And followed for the hermits' sake.
They travelled far, till in the west
The sun was speeding to his rest,
And made, their portioned journey o'er,
Their halt on Sona's distant shore.
The hermits bathed when sank the sun,
And every rite was duly done—
Oblations paid to Fire, and then
Sate round their chief the holy men.
Ráma and Lakshman lowly bowed
In reverence to the hermit crowd—

And Ráma, having sate him down
Before the saint of pure renown,
With humble palms together laid
His eager supplication made:—
" What country, O my lord, is this,
Fair-smiling in her wealth and bliss?
Deign fully, O thou mighty Seer,
To tell me, for I long to hear."
Moved by the prayer of Ráma, he
Told forth the country's history.

CANTO XXXIV

BRAHMADATTA

A KING of Brahmá's seed who bore
  The name of Kúsa reigned of yore.
    Just, faithful to his vows, and true,
He held the good in honor due.
His bride, a queen of noble name,
Of old Vidarbha's monarchs came.
Like their own father, children four,
All valiant boys, the lady bore.
In glorious deeds each nerve they strained,
And well their Warrior part sustained.
To them most just, and true, and brave,
Their father thus his counsel gave:—
" Beloved children, ne'er forget
Protection is a prince's debt:
The noble work at once begin,
High virtue and her fruits to win."
The youths, to all the people dear,
Received his speech with willing ear;
And each went forth his several way,
Foundations of a town to lay.
Kuśámba, prince of high renown,
Was builder of Kauśámbí's town,
And Kuśanábha, just and wise,
Bade high Mahodaya's towers arise.
Amúrtarajas chose to dwell
In Dharmáranya's citadel,
And Vasu bade his city fair
The name of Girivraja bear.
This fertile spot whereon we stand
Was once the high-souled Vasu's land.
Behold! as round we turn our eyes,

Five lofty mountain peaks arise.
See! bursting from her parent hill,
Sumágadhí, a lovely rill,
Bright gleaming as she flows between
The mountains, like a wreath is seen—
And then through Magadh's plains and groves
With many a fair meander roves.
And this was Vasu's old domain,
The fertile Magadh's broad champaign,
Which smiling fields of tilth adorn
And diadem with golden corn.
The queen Ghritáchí, nymph most fair,
Married to Kuśanábha, bare
A hundred daughters lovely faced,
With every charm and beauty graced.
It chanced the maidens, bright and gay
As lightning-flashes on a day
Of rain-time, to the garden went
With song and play and merriment—
And there in gay attire they strayed,
And danced, and laughed, and sang, and played.
The God of Wind who roves at will
All places, as he lists, to fill,
Saw the young maidens dancing there,
Of faultless shape and mien most fair—
"I love you all, sweet girls," he cried,
"And each shall be my darling bride.
Forsake, forsake your mortal lot,
And gain a life that withers not.
A fickle thing is youth's brief span,
And more than all is mortal man.
Receive unending youth, and be
Immortal, O my loves, with me."
The hundred girls, to wonder stirred,
The wooing of the Wind-God heard,
Laughed, as a jest, his suit aside,
And with one voice they thus replied:—
"O mighty Wind, free spirit who
All life pervadest, through and through—
Thy wondrous power we maidens know;
Then wherefore wilt thou mock us so?

Our sire is Kuśanábha, King;
And we, forsooth, have charms to bring
A God to woo us from the skies;
But honor first we maidens prize.
Far may the hour, we pray, be hence,
When we, O thou of little sense,
Our truthful father's choice refuse,
And for ourselves our husbands choose.
Our honored sire our lord we deem,
He is to us a God supreme—
And they to whom his high decree
May give us shall our husbands be."

He heard the answer they returned,
And mighty rage within him burned.
On each fair maid a blast he sent—
Each stately form he bowed and bent.
Bent double by the Wind-God's ire
They sought the palace of their sire,
There fell upon the ground with sighs,
While tears and shame were in their eyes.
The King himself, with troubled brow,
Saw his dear girls so fair but now,
A mournful sight all bent and bowed—
And grieving, thus he cried aloud:—
"What fate is this, and what the cause?
What wretch has scorned all heavenly laws?
Who thus your forms could curve and break?
You struggle, but no answer make."
They heard the speech of that wise king
Of their misfortune questioning.
Again the hundred maidens sighed,
Touched with their heads his feet, and cried:—
"The God of Wind, pervading space,
Would bring on us a foul disgrace,
And choosing folly's evil way
From virtue's path in scorn would stray.
But we in words like these reproved
The God of Wind whom passion moved:—
'Farewell, O Lord! A sire have we,
No women uncontrolled and free.

Go, and our sire's consent obtain
If thou our maiden hands wouldst gain.
No self-dependent life we live:
If we offend, our fault forgive,'
But led by folly as a slave,
He would not hear the rede we gave,
And even as we gently spoke
We felt the Wind-God's crushing stroke."
The pious King, with grief distressed,
The noble hundred thus addressed:—
" With patience, daughters, bear your fate,
Yours was a deed supremely great
When with one mind you kept from shame
The honor of your father's name.
Patience, when men their anger vent,
Is woman's praise and ornament;
Yet when the Gods inflict the blow
Hard is it to support the woe.
Patience, my girls, exceeds all price—
'Tis alms, and truth, and sacrifice.
Patience is virtue, patience fame:
Patience upholds this earthly frame.
And now, I think, is come the time
To wed you in your maiden prime.
Now, daughters, go where'er you will:
Thoughts for your good my mind shall fill."
The maidens went, consoled, away:—
The best of kings, that very day,
Summoned his ministers of state
About their marriage to debate.
Since then, because the Wind-God bent
The damsels' forms for punishment,
That royal town is known to fame
By Kanyákubja's borrowed name.

There lived a sage called Chúli then,
Devoutest of the sons of men;
His days in penance rites he spent,
A glorious saint, most continent.
To him absorbed in tasks austere
The child of Urmílá draw near—

Sweet Somadá, the heavenly maid,
And lent the saint her pious aid.
Long time near him the maiden spent,
And served him meek and reverent,
Till the great hermit, pleased with her,
Thus spoke unto his minister:—
"Grateful am I for all thy care—
Blest maiden, speak, thy wish declare."
The sweet-voiced nymph rejoiced to see
The favor of the devotee,
And to that excellent old man,
Most eloquent she thus began:—
"Thou hast, by heavenly grace sustained,
Close union with the Godhead gained.
I long, O Saint, to see a son
By force of holy penance won.
Unwed, a maiden life I live:
A son to me, thy suppliant, give."
The saint with favor heard her prayer,
And gave a son exceeding fair.
Him, Chúli's spiritual child,
His mother Brahmadatta styled.
King Brahmadatta, rich and great,
In Kámpilí maintained his state—
Ruling, like Indra in his bliss,
His fortunate metropolis.
King Kuśanábha planned that he
His hundred daughters' lord should be.
To him, obedient to his call,
The happy monarch gave them all.
Like Indra then he took the hand
Of every maiden of the band.
Soon as the hand of each young maid
In Brahmadatta's palm was laid,
Deformity and cares away,
She shone in beauty bright and gay.
Their freedom from the Wind-God's might
Saw Kuśanábha with delight.
Each glance that on their forms he threw
Filled him with raptures ever new.
Then when the rites were all complete,

With highest marks of honor meet
The bridegroom with his brides he sent
To his great seat of government.
The nymph received with pleasant speech
Her daughters; and, embracing each,
Upon their forms she fondly gazed,
And royal Kuśanábha praised.

CANTO XXXV

VIŚVÁMITRA'S LINEAGE

" THE rites were o'er, the maids were wed,
  The bridegroom to his home was sped.
  The sonless monarch bade prepare
A sacrifice to gain an heir.
Then Kuśa, Brahmá's son, appeared,
And thus King Kuśanábha cheered:—
' Thou shalt, my child, obtain a son
Like thine own self, O holy one.
Through him forever, Gádhi named,
Shalt thou in all the worlds be famed.'
He spoke and vanished from the sight
To Brahmá's world of endless light.
Time fled, and, as the saint foretold,
Gádhi was born, the holy-souled.
My sire was he; through him I trace
My line from royal Kúsa's race.
My sister—elder-born was she—
The pure and good Satyavatí,
Was to the great Richíka wed.
Still faithful to her husband dead,
She followed him, most noble dame,
And, raised to heaven in human frame,
A pure celestial stream became.
Down from Himálaya's snowy height,
In floods forever fair and bright,
My sister's holy waves are hurled
To purify and glad the world.
Now on Himálaya's side I dwell
Because I love my sister well.
She, for her faith and truth renowned,
Most loving to her husband found,

High-fated, firm in each pure vow,
Is queen of all the rivers now.
Bound by a vow I left her side
And to the Perfect convent hied.
There, by the aid 'twas thine to lend,
Made perfect, all my labors end.
Thus, mighty Prince, I now have told
My race and lineage, high and old,
And local tales of long ago
Which thou, O Ráma, fain wouldst know.
As I have sate rehearsing thus
The midnight hour is come on us.
Now, Ráma, sleep, that nothing may
Our journey of to-morrow stay.
No leaf on any tree is stirred—
Hushed in repose are beast and bird:
Where'er you turn, on every side,
Dense shades of night the landscape hide.
The light of eve is fled: the skies,
Thick-studded with their host of eyes,
Seem a star-forest overhead,
Where signs and constellations spread.
Now rises, with his pure cold ray,
The moon that drives the shades away,
And with his gentle influence brings
Joy to the hearts of living things.
Now, stealing from their lairs, appear
The beasts to whom the night is dear.
Now spirits walk, and every power
That revels in the midnight hour."

The mighty hermit's tale was o'er,
He closed his lips and spoke no more.
The holy men on every side,
" Well done! well done," with reverence cried
" The mighty men of Kuśa's seed
Were ever famed for righteous deed.
Like Brahmá's self in glory shine
The high-souled lords of Kuśa's line.
And thy great name is sounded most,
O Saint, amid the noble host.

And thy dear sister—fairest she
Of streams, the high-born Kauśikí—
Diffusing virtue where she flows,
New splendor on thy lineage throws."
Thus by the chief of saints addressed
The son of Gádhi turned to rest;
So, when his daily course is done,
Sinks to his rest the beaming sun.
Ráma, with Lakshman, somewhat stirred
To marvel by the tales they heard,
Turned also to his couch, to close
His eyelids in desired repose.

CANTO XXXVI

THE BIRTH OF GANGÁ

THE hours of night now waning fast
On Śona's pleasant shore they passed.
Then, when the dawn began to break,
To Ráma thus the hermit spake:—
" The light of dawn is breaking clear,
The hour of morning rites is near.
Rise, Ráma, rise, dear son, I pray,
And make thee ready for the way."
Then Ráma rose, and finished all
His duties at the hermit's call—
Prepared with joy the road to take,
And thus again in question spake:—
" Here fair and deep the Śona flows,
And many an isle its bosom shows:
What way, O Saint, will lead us o'er
And land us on the farther shore?"
The saint replied: " The way I choose
Is that which pious hermits use."
For many a league they journeyed on
Till, when the sun of mid-day shone,
The hermit-haunted flood was seen
Of Jáhnaví, the Rivers' Queen.
Soon as the holy stream they viewed,
Thronged with a white-winged multitude
Of sárases and swans, delight
Possessed them at the lovely sight;
And then prepared the hermit band
To halt upon that holy strand.
They bathed as Scripture bids, and paid
Oblations due to God and shade.
To Fire they burnt the offerings meet,

And sipped the oil, like Amrit sweet.
Then pure and pleased they sate around
Saint Viśvámitra, on the ground.
The holy men of lesser note,
In due degree, sate more remote,
While Raghu's sons took nearer place
By virtue of their rank and race.
Then Ráma said: " O Saint, I yearn
The three-pathed Gangá's tale to learn."

Thus urged, the sage recounted both
The birth of Gangá and her growth:—
" The mighty hill with metals stored,
Himálaya, is the mountains' lord,
The father of a lovely pair
Of daughters fairest of the fair—
Their mother, offspring of the will
Of Meru, everlasting hill,
Mená, Himálaya's darling, graced
With beauty of her dainty waist.
Gangá was elder-born:—then came
The fair one known by Umá's name.
Then all the Gods of heaven, in need
Of Gangá's help their vows to speed,
To great Himálaya came and prayed
The Mountain King to yield the maid.
He, not regardless of the weal
Of the three worlds, with holy zeal
His daughter to the Immortals gave,
Gangá whose waters cleanse and save—
Who roams at pleasure, fair and free,
Purging all sinners, to the sea.
The three-pathed Gangá thus obtained,
The Gods their heavenly homes regained.
Long time the sister Umá passed
In vows austere and rigid fast,
And the King gave the devotee
Immortal Rudra's bride to be—
Matching with that unequalled Lord
His Umá through the worlds adored.
So now a glorious station fills

Each daughter of the King of Hills—
One honored as the noblest stream,
One mid the Goddesses supreme.
Thus Gangá, King Himálaya's child,
The heavenly river, undefiled,
Rose bearing with her to the sky
Her waves that bless and purify."

[*Cantos XXXVII and XXXVIII are omitted.*]

CANTO XXXIX

THE SONS OF SAGAR

THE saint in accents sweet and clear
 Thus told his tale for Ráma's ear—
 And thus anew the holy man
A legend to the prince began:—
" There reigned a pious monarch o'er
Ayodhyá in the days of yore:
Sagar his name:—no child had he,
And children much he longed to see.
His honored consort, fair of face,
Sprang from Vidarbha's royal race—
Keśiní, famed from early youth
For piety and love of truth.
Arishtanemi's daughter fair,
With whom no maiden might compare
In beauty, though the earth is wide,
Sumati, was his second bride.
With his two queens afar he went,
And weary days in penance spent,
Fervent, upon Himálaya's hill
Where springs the stream called Bhrigu's rill.
Nor did he fail that saint to please
With his devout austerities,
And, when a hundred years had fled,
Thus the most truthful Bhrigu said:—
' From thee, O Sagar, blameless King,
A mighty host of sons shall spring,
And thou shalt win a glorious name
Which none, O Chief, but thou shall claim.
One of thy queens a son shall bear
Maintainer of thy race and heir;
And of the other there shall be
Sons sixty thousand born to thee.'

Thus as he spake, with one accord,
To win the grace of that high lord,
The queens, with palms together laid,
In humble supplication prayed:—
'Which queen, O Bráhman, of the pair,
The many, or the one shall bear?
Most eager, Lord, are we to know,
And as thou sayest be it so.'
With his sweet speech the saint replied:—
Yourselves, O Queens, the choice decide.
Your own discretion freely use
Which shall the one or many choose:
One shall the race and name uphold,
The host be famous, strong, and bold.
Which will have which?' Then Keśiní
The mother of one heir would be.
Sumati, sister of the King
Of all the birds that ply the wing,
To that illustrious Bráhman sued
That she might bear the multitude—
Whose fame throughout the world should sound
For mighty enterprise renowned.
Around the saint the monarch went,
Bowing his head, most reverent.
Then with his wives, with willing feet,
Resought his own imperial seat.
Time passed. The elder consort bare
A son called Asamanj, the heir.
Then Sumati, the younger, gave
Birth to a gourd, O hero brave,
Whose rind, when burst and cleft in two,
Gave sixty thousand babes to view.
All these with care the nurses laid
In jars of oil; and there they stayed,
Till, youthful age and strength complete,
Forth speeding from each dark retreat—
All peers in valor, years, and might,
The sixty thousand came to light.
Prince Asamanj, brought up with care,
Scourge of his foes, was made the heir.
But liegemen's boys he used to cast

To Sarjú's waves that hurried past—
Laughing the while in cruel glee
Their dying agonies to see.
This wicked prince who aye withstood
The counsel of the wise and good,
Who plagued the people in his hate,
His father banished from the state.
His son, kind-spoken, brave, and tall,
Was Anśumán, beloved of all.
Long years flew by. The King decreed
To slay a sacrificial steed.
Consulting with his priestly band
He vowed the rite his soul had planned,
And, Veda-skilled, by their advice
Made ready for the sacrifice."

CANTO XL

THE CLEAVING OF THE EARTH

THE hermit ceased—the tale was done:—
Then in a transport Raghu's son
Again addressed the ancient sire
Resplendent as a burning fire:—
" O holy man, I fain would hear
The tale repeated full and clear
How he from whom my sires descend
Brought the great rite to happy end."
The hermit answered with a smile:—
" Then listen, son of Raghu, while
My legendary tale proceeds
To tell of high-souled Sagar's deeds.
Within the spacious plain that lies
From where Himálaya's heights arise
To where proud Vindhya's rival chain
Looks down upon the subject plain—
A land the best for rites declared—
His sacrifice the king prepared.
And Anśumán the prince—for so
Sagar advised—with ready bow
Was borne upon a mighty car
To watch the steed who roamed afar.
But Indra, monarch of the skies,
Veiling his form in demon guise,
Came down upon the appointed day
And drove the victim horse away.
Reft of the steed the priests, distressed,
The master of the rite addressed:—
' Upon the sacred day by force
A robber takes the victim horse.

Haste, King! now let the thief be slain;
Bring thou the charger back again:
The sacred rite prevented thus
Brings scathe and woe to all of us.
Rise, Monarch, and provide with speed
That nought its happy course impede.'

King Sagar in his crowded court
Gave ear unto the priests' report.
He summoned straightway to his side
His sixty thousand sons, and cried:—
' Brave sons of mine, I know not how
These demons are so mighty now—
The priests began the rite so well
All sanctified with prayer and spell.
If in the depths of earth he hide,
Or lurk beneath the ocean's tide,
Pursue, dear sons, the robber's track;
Slay him and bring the charger back.
The whole of this broad earth explore,
Sea-garlanded, from shore to shore:
Yea, dig her up with might and main
Until you see the horse again.
Deep let your searching labor reach,
A league in depth dug out by each.
The robber of our horse pursue,
And please your sire who orders you.
My grandson, I, this priestly train,
Till the steed comes, will here remain.'

Their eager hearts with transport burned
As to their task the heroes turned.
Obedient to their father, they
Through earth's recesses forced their way.
With iron arms' unflinching toil
Each dug a league beneath the soil.
Earth, cleft asunder, groaned in pain,
As emulous they plied amain—
Sharp-pointed coulter, pick, and bar,
Hard as the bolts of Indra are.
Then loud the horrid clamor rose

Of monsters dying 'neath their blows,
Giant and demon, fiend and snake,
That in earth's core their dwelling make.
They dug, in ire that nought could stay,
Through sixty thousand leagues their way—
Cleaving the earth with matchless strength
Till hell itself they reached at length.
Thus digging searched they Jambudvíp
With all its hills and mountains steep.
Then a great fear began to shake
The heart of God, bard, fiend, and snake—
And all distressed in spirit went
Before the Sire Omnipotent.
With signs of woe in every face
They sought the mighty Father's grace,
And trembling still and ill at ease
Addressed their Lord in words like these:—
' The sons of Sagar, Sire benign,
Pierce the whole earth with mine on mine,
And as their ruthless work they ply
Innumerable creatures die.'
' This is the thief,' the princes say,
' Who stole our victim steed away.
This marred the rite, and caused us ill.'
And so their guiltless blood they spill.

CANTO XLI

KAPIL

" THE Father lent a gracious ear
And listened to their tale of fear,
And kindly to the Gods replied
Whom woe and death had terrified:—
' The wisest Vásudeva, who
The Immortals' foe, fierce Madhu, slew,
Regards broad Earth with love and pride,
And guards, in Kapil's form, his bride.
His kindled wrath will quickly fall
On the King's sons and burn them all.
This cleaving of the earth his eye
Foresaw in ages long gone by:
He knew with prescient soul the fate
That Sagar's children should await.'
The Three-and-thirty, freed from fear,
Sought their bright homes with hopeful cheer.
Still rose the great tempestuous sound
As Sagar's children pierced the ground.
When thus the whole broad earth was cleft,
And not a spot unsearched was left,
Back to their home the princes sped,
And thus unto their father said:—
' We searched the earth from side to side,
While countless hosts of creatures died.
Our conquering feet in triumph trod
On snake and demon, fiend and God;
But yet we failed, with all our toil,
To find the robber and the spoil.
What can we more? If more we can,
Devise, O King, and tell thy plan.'

His children's speech King Sagar heard,
And answered thus, to anger stirred:—
' Dig on, and ne'er your labor stay
Till through earth's depths you force your way.
Then smite the robber dead, and bring
The charger back with triumphing.'

The sixty thousand chiefs obeyed—
Deep through the earth their way they made.
Deep as they dug and deeper yet
The immortal elephant they met—
Famed Virúpáksha vast of size,
Upon whose head the broad earth lies:·
The mighty beast who earth sustains
With shaggy hills and wooded plains.
When, with the changing moon, distressed,
And longing for a moment's rest,
His mighty head the monster shakes,
Earth to the bottom reels and quakes.
Around that warder strong and vast
With reverential steps they passed—
Nor, when the honor due was paid,
Their downward search through earth delayed.
But turning from the east aside
Southward again their task they plied.
There Mahápadma held his place,
The best of all his mighty race—
Like some huge hill, of monstrous girth,
Upholding on his head the earth.
When the vast beast the princes saw,
They marvelled and were filled with awe.
The sons of high-souled Sagar round
That elephant in reverence wound.
Then in the western region they
With might unwearied cleft their way.
There saw they with astonished eyes
Saumanas, beast of mountain size.
Round him with circling steps they went
With greetings kind and reverent.

On, on—no thought of rest or stay—
They reached the seat of Soma's sway.
There saw they Bhadra, white as snow,
With lucky marks that fortune show,
Bearing the earth upon his head.
Round him they paced with solemn tread,
And honored him with greetings kind;
Then downward yet their way they mined.
They gained the tract 'twixt east and north
Whose fame is ever blazoned forth,
And by a storm of rage impelled,
Digging through earth their course they held.
Then all the princes, lofty-souled,
Of wondrous vigor, strong and bold,
Saw Vásudeva standing there
In Kapil's form he loved to wear,
And near the everlasting God
The victim charger cropped the sod.
They saw with joy and eager eyes
The fancied robber and the prize,
And on him rushed the furious band
Crying aloud, ' Stand, villain! stand!'
' Avaunt! avaunt!' great Kapil cried,
His bosom flushed with passion's tide;
Then by his might that proud array
All scorched to heaps of ashes lay.

CANTO XLII

SAGAR'S SACRIFICE

" THEN to the prince his grandson, bright
With his own fame's unborrowed light,
King Sagar thus began to say,
Marvelling at his sons' delay:—
' Thou art a warrior skilled and bold,
Match for the mighty men of old.
Now follow on thine uncles' course
And track the robber of the horse.
To guard thee take thy sword and bow,
For huge and strong are beasts below.
There to the reverend reverence pay,
And kill the foes who check thy way;
Then turn successful home and see
My sacrifice complete through thee.'

Obedient to the high-souled lord
Grasped Anśumán his bow and sword,
And hurried forth the way to trace
With youth and valor's eager pace.
On sped he by the path he found
Dug by his uncles underground.
The warder elephant he saw
Whose size and strength pass Nature's law—
Who bears the world's tremendous weight,
Whom God, fiend, giant, venerate.
Bird, serpent, and each flitting shade,
To him the honor meet he paid—
With circling steps and greeting due,
And further prayed him, if he knew,
To tell him of his uncles' weal,
And who had dared the horse to steal.

To him in war and council tried
The warder elephant replied:—
' Thou, son of Asamanj, shalt lead
In triumph back the rescued steed.'

As to each warder beast he came
And questioned all, his words the same,
The honored youth with gentle speech
Drew eloquent reply from each—
That fortune should his steps attend,
And with the horse he home should wend.
Cheered with the grateful answer, he
Passed on with step more light and free,
And reached with careless heart the place
Where lay in ashes Sagar's race.
Then sank the spirit of the chief
Beneath that shock of sudden grief—
And with a bitter cry of woe
He mourned his kinsmen fallen so.
He saw, weighed down by woe and care,
The victim charger roaming there.
Yet would the pious chieftain fain
Oblations offer to the slain:
But, needing water for the rite,
He looked and there was none in sight.
His quick eye searching all around
The uncle of his kinsmen found—
King Garud, best beyond compare
Of birds who wing the fields of air.
Then thus unto the weeping man
The son of Vinatá began:—
' Grieve not, O hero, for their fall
Who died a death approved of all.
Of mighty strength, they met their fate
By Kapil's hand whom none can mate.
Pour forth for them no earthly wave,
A holier flood their spirits crave.
If, daughter of the Lord of Snow,
Gangá would turn her stream below,
Her waves that cleanse all mortal stain
Would wash their ashes pure again.

Yea, when her flood whom all revere
Rolls o'er the dust that moulders here,
The sixty thousand, freed from sin,
A home in Indra's heaven shall win.
Go, and with ceaseless labor try
To draw the Goddess from the sky.
Return, and with thee take the steed;
So shall thy grandsire's rite succeed.'

Prince Anśumán the strong and brave
Followed the rede Suparna gave.
The glorious hero took the horse,
And homeward quickly bent his course.
Straight to the anxious King he hied,
Whom lustral rites had purified—
The mournful story to unfold
And all the King of birds had told.
The tale of woe the monarch heard,
No longer was the rite deferred:
With care and just observance he
Accomplished all, as texts decree.
The rites performed, with brighter fame,
Mighty in counsel, home he came.
He longed to bring the river down,
But found no plan his wish to crown.
He pondered long with anxious thought,
But saw no way to what he sought.
Thus thirty thousand years he spent,
And then to heaven the monarch went.

CANTO XLIII

BHAGÍRATH

" WHEN Sagar thus had bowed to fate,
    The lords and commons of the state
    Approved with ready heart and will
Prince Anśumán his throne to fill.
He ruled, a mighty king, unblamed,
Sire of Dilípa justly famed.
To him, his child and worthy heir,
The King resigned his kingdom's care,
And on Himálaya's pleasant side
His task austere of penance plied.
Bright as a God in clear renown
He planned to bring pure Gangá down.
There on his fruitless hope intent
Twice sixteen thousand years he spent,
And in the grove of hermits stayed
Till bliss in heaven his rites repaid.
Dilípa then, the good and great,
Soon as he learnt his kinsmen's fate,
Bowed down by woe, with troubled mind,
Pondering long no cure could find.
' How can I bring,' the mourner sighed,
' To cleanse their dust, the heavenly tide?
How can I give them rest, and save
Their spirits with the offered wave?'
Long with this thought his bosom skilled
In holy discipline was filled.
A son was born, Bhagírath named,
Above all men for virtue famed.
Dilípa many a rite ordained,
And thirty thousand seasons reigned.
But when no hope the king could see

His kinsmen from their woe to free,
The lord of men, by sickness tried,
Obeyed the law of fate, and died;
He left the kingdom to his son,
And gained the heaven his deeds had won.
The good Bhagírath, royal sage,
Had no fair son to cheer his age.
He, great in glory, pure in will,
Longing for sons was childless still.
Then on one wish, one thought intent,
Planning the heavenly stream's descent,
Leaving his ministers the care
And burden of his state to bear—
Dwelling in far Gokarna he
Engaged in long austerity.
With senses checked, with arms upraised,
Five fires around and o'er him blazed.
Each weary month the hermit passed
Breaking but once his awful fast.
In winter's chill the brook his bed,
In rain, the clouds to screen his head.
Thousands of years he thus endured
Till Brahmá's favor was assured—
And the high Lord of living things
Looked kindly on his sufferings.
With trooping Gods the Sire came near
The King who plied his task austere:—
'Blest Monarch, of a glorious race,
Thy fervent rites have won my grace.
Well hast thou wrought thine awful task,
Some boon in turn, O Hermit, ask.'

Bhagírath, rich in glory's light,
The hero with the arm of might,
Thus to the Lord of earth and sky
Raised supplant hands and made reply:—
'If the great God his favor deigns,
And my long toil its fruit obtains,
Let Sagar's sons receive from me
Libations that they long to see.
Let Gangá with her holy wave

The ashes of the heroes lave—
That so my kinsmen may ascend
To heavenly bliss that ne'er shall end.
And give, I pray, O God, a son,
Nor let my house be all undone.
Sire of the worlds! be this the grace
Bestowed upon Ikshváku's race.'
The Sire, when thus the King had prayed,
In sweet kind words his answer made:—
' High, high thy thought and wishes are,
Bhagírath of the mighty car!
Ikshváku's line is blest in thee,
And as thou prayest it shall be.
Gangá, whose waves in Swarga flow,
Is daughter of the Lord of Snow.
Win Śiva that his aid be lent
To hold her in her mid-descent—
For earth alone will never bear
Those torrents hurled from upper air;
And none may hold her weight but He,
The Trident-wielding deity.'
Thus having said, the Lord supreme
Addressed him to the heavenly stream;
And then with Gods and Maruts went
To heaven, above the firmament."

VOL. III.—20

LORD CURZON.

Although Lord Curzon is the Viceroy of India, and practically the monarch of two hundred and fifty millions of people, he is almost youthful in appearance. As he was born in 1859, and is now but forty-one years of age, he is probably the youngest viceroy that England has ever sent to govern India. In addition to his position as a statesman he is also an author of note. In 1895 he married Miss **Mary** Leiter, the daughter of L. Z. Leiter, of Chicago.

ŚAKOONTALÁ

—

BY

KÁLIDÁSA

[*Translation by Sir Monier Monier-Williams*]

INTRODUCTION

THE drama is always the latest development of a national poetry—for the origin of poetry is in the religious rite, where the hymn or the ode is used to celebrate the glories of some divinity, or some hero who has been received into the circle of the gods. This at least is the case in Sanscrit as in Greek literature, where the hymn and ballad precede the epic. The epic poem becomes the stable form of poetry during the middle period in the history of literature, both in India and Greece. The union of the lyric and the epic produces the drama. The speeches uttered by the heroes in such poems as the " Iliad " are put into the mouths of real personages who appear in sight of the audience and represent with fitting gestures and costumes the characters of the story. The dialogue is interspersed with songs or odes, which reach their perfection in the choruses of Sophocles.

The drama is undoubtedly the most intellectual, as it is the most artificial, form of poetry. The construction of the plot, and the arrangement of the action, give room for the most thoughful and deliberate display of genius. In this respect the Greek drama stands forth as most philosophically perfect. The drama, moreover, has always been by far the most popular form of poetry; because it aids, as much as possible, the imagination of the auditor, and for distinctness and clearness of impression stands preëminent above both the epic narrative and the emotional description of the lyric.

The drama in India appears to have been a perfectly indigenous creation, although it was of very late development, and could not have appeared even so early as the Alexandrian pastorals which marked the last phase of Greek poetry. When it did appear, it never took the perfect form of the drama at Athens. It certainly borrowed as little from Greece as it did from China or Japan, and the Persians and Arabians do not appear to have produced any dramatic masterpieces.

The greatest of dramatists in the Sanscrit language is undoubtedly Kálidása, whose date is placed, by different scholars, anywhere from the first to the fifth century of our era. His masterpiece, and indeed the masterpiece of the Indian drama, is the " Śakoontalá," which has all the graces as well as most of the faults of Oriental poetry. There can be no doubt that to most Europeans the charm of it lies in the exquisite description of natural scenery and of that atmosphere of piety and religious calm—almost mediæval in its austere beauty and serenity—which invests the hermit life of India. The abode of the ascetics is depicted with a pathetic grace that we only find paralleled in the " Adr:.etus " of Euripides. But at the same time the construction of the drama is more like such a play as Milton's " Comus," than the closely-knit, symmetrical, and inevitable progress of such a work of consummate skill as the " King Œdipus " of Sophocles. Emotion, and generally the emotion of love, is the motive in the " Śakoontalá " of Kálidása, and different phases of feeling, rather than the struggles of energetic action, lead on to the *denouement* of the play. The introduction of supernatural agencies controlling the life of the personages, leaves very little room for the development and description of human character. As the fate of the hero is dependent altogether upon the caprice of superhuman powers, the moral elements of a drama are but faintly discernible. Thus the central action of Śakoontalá hinges on the fact that the heroine, absorbed in thoughts of love, neglects to welcome with due respect the great saint Durvasas—certainly a trifling and venial fault—but he is represented as blighting her with a curse which results in all the unhappiness of the drama, and which is only ended at last by the intervention of a more powerful being. By this principle of construction the characters are reduced to mere shadow creations: beautiful as arabesques, delicate as a piece of ivory carving, tinted like the flat profiles of an Oriental fan or the pattern of a porcelain vase, but deficient in robustness and vigorous coloring. Humanity is absolutely dwarfed and its powers rendered inoperative by the crowd of supernatural creatures that control its destiny. Even in the " Tempest " of Shakespeare, in which the supernatural plays a greater part than in any other English drama, the strength and nobility of human character are allowed full play—and man in his fortitude, in his intellect and will, even more than

in his emotions, keeps full possession of the stage, and imparts
a reality to every scene which makes the wildest flight of fancy
bear a real relation to the common experiences of human life.

The " Śakoontalá " is divided into seven acts, and is a mixture
of prose and verse;—each character rising in the intensity of
emotional utterance into bursts of lyric poetry.   The first act
introduces the King of India, Dushyanta, armed with bow and
arrows, in a chariot with his driver.   They are passing through
a forest in pursuit of a black antelope, which they fail to over-
take before the voice of some hermit forbids them to slay the
creature as it belongs to the hermitage.   The king piously
desists and reaches the hermitage of the great saint Kanwa,
who has left his companions in charge of his foster-daughter,
Śakoontalá, while he is bound on a pilgrimage.   Following
these hermits the king finds himself within the precincts of a
sacred grove, where rice is strewn on the ground to feed the
parrots that nest in the hollow trunks, and where the unter-
rified antelopes do not start at the human voice.   The king
stops his chariot and alights, so as not to disturb the dwellers
in the holy wood.   He feels a sudden throb in his right arm,
which augurs happy love, and sees hermit maidens approaching to sprinkle the young shrubs, with watering-pots suited
to their strength.   The forms of these hermit maidens eclipse
those found in queenly halls, as the luxuriance of forest vines
excels the trim vineyards of cultivation.   Amongst these
maidens the king, concealed by the trees, observes Śakoontalá,
dressed in the bark garment of a hermit—like a blooming bud
enclosed within a sheა.n of yellow leaves.   When she stands
by the *keśara*-tree, the king is impressed by her beauty, and
regrets that she is, if of a purely Bráhmanic origin, forbidden
to marry one of the warrior class, even though he be a king.
A very pretty description is given of the pursuit of Śakoontalá
by a bee which her sprinkling has startled from a jasmine
flower.   From this bee she is rescued by the king, and is dismayed to find that the sight of the stranger affects her with
an emotion unsuited to the holy grove.   She hurries off with
her two companions, but as she goes she declares that a prickly
kusa-grass has stung her foot; a *kuruvaka*-bush has caught
her garment, and while her companions disentangle it, she
takes a long look at the king, who confesses that he cannot
turn his mind from Śakoontalá.   This is the opening episode
of their love.

The second act introduces the king's jester, a Bráhman on confidential terms with his master, who, while Dushyanta is thinking of love, is longing to get back to the city. He is tired of the hot jungle, the nauseating water of bitter mountain streams, the racket of fowlers at early dawn, and the eternal galloping, by which his joints are bruised. The king is equally tired of hunting, and confesses that he cannot bend his bow against those fawns which dwell near Śakoontalá's abode, and have taught their tender glance to her. He calls back the beaters sent out to surround the forest, takes off his hunting-suit, and talks to the jester about the charms of Śakoontalá— whom the Creator, he says, has formed by gathering in his mind all lovely shapes, so as to make a peerless woman-gem. He recalls the glance which she shot at him as she cried, " a *kusha*-grass has stung my foot." Meanwhile two hermits approach him with the news that the demons have taken advantage of Kanwa's absence to disturb the sacrifices. They request him to take up his abode in the grove for a few days, in order to vanquish the enemies. A messenger arrives to tell him that his mother, in four days, will be offering a solemn sacrifice for her son's welfare, and invites his presence at the rite. But he cannot leave Śakoontalá, and sends the jester Máthavya in his stead, telling him to say nothing about his love for Śakoontalá.

In the third act the love of the king and the hermit girl reaches its climax. The king is found walking in the hermitage, invoking the God of Love, whose shafts are flowers, though the flowery darts are hard as steel. " Mighty God of Love, hast Thou no pity on me?" What better relief, he asks, than the sight of my beloved? He traces Śakoontalá, by the broken tubes which bore the blossoms she had culled, to the arbor, enclosed by the plantation of canes, and shaded by vines, at whose entrance he observes in the sand the track of recent footsteps. Peering through the branches, he perceives her reclining on a stone seat strewn with flowers. Her two companions are with her, and she is sick unto death. The king notices that her cheeks are wasted, her breasts less swelling, her slender waist more slender, her roseate hue has grown pale, and she seems like some poor *madhave* creeper touched by winds that have scorched its leaves. Her companions anxiously inquire the cause of her sickness, and, after much hesitation, she reveals her love by inscribing a poem, with her finger-nail, on a lotus leaf smooth as a parrot's breast. The king hears the avowal of her love, rushes in to her, and declares his passion: adding that daughters of a royal saint have often been wedded by *Gandharva* rites, without ceremonies or parental consent, yet have not forfeited the father's blessing. He thus overcomes her scruples. Gautamí, the matron of the hermitage, afterwards enters, and asks, "My child, is your fever allayed?" "Venerable mother," is the reply, "I feel a grateful change." As the king sits in solitude that evening in the deserted arbor, he hears a voice outside, uttering the verses—"The evening rites have begun; but, dark as the clouds of night, the demons are swarming round the altar fires." With these words of ill-omen the third act comes to an end.

The fourth act describes the fulfilment of this evil omen. The king has now returned to the city, and has given Śakoontalá a signet ring, with an inscription on it, pronouncing that after there have elapsed as many days as there are letters in this inscription he will return. As the two maiden companions of Śakoontalá are culling flowers in the garden of the her-mitage, they hear a voice exclaiming, "It is I! give heed!" This is the great Durvasas, whom Śakoontalá, lost in thoughts of her absent husband, has neglected at once to go forth to welcome. The voice from behind the scenes is soon after heard uttering a curse—"Woe unto her who is thus neglect-ful of a guest," and declaring that Dushyanta, of whom alone she is thinking, regardless of the presence of a pious saint, shall forget her in spite of all his love, as the wine-bibber forgets his delirium. The Hindoo saint is here described in all his arrogance and cruelty. One of the maidens says that he who had uttered the curse is now retiring with great strides, quivering with rage—for his wrath is like a consuming fire. A pretty picture is given of Śakoontalá, who carries on her finger the signet ring, which has the virtue of restoring the king's love, if ever he should forget her. "There sits our beloved friend," cries one of the maidens: "motionless as a picture; her cheek supported by her left hand, so absorbed in thoughts of her absent lover that she is unconscious of her own self—how much more of a passing stranger?"

In the fourth act there is an exquisite description of the

return of Kanwa from his pilgrimage, and the preparations for the start of Śakoontalá for her husband's palace, in the city. The delicate pathos of the scene is worthy of Euripides. "Alas! Alas!" exclaim the two maidens, "Now Śakoontalá has disappeared behind the trees of the forest. Tell us, master, how shall we enter again the sacred grove made desolate by her departure?" But the holy calm, broken for a moment by the excitement of his child's departure, is soon restored to Kanwa's mind. "Now that my child is dismissed to her husband's home, tranquillity regains my soul." The closing reflection is worthy of a Greek dramatist: "Our maids we rear for the happiness of others; and now that I have sent her to her husband I feel the satisfaction that comes from restoring a trust."

In the fifth act, the scene is laid in Dushyanta's palace, where the king is living, under the curse of Durvasas, in complete oblivion of Śakoontalá. The life of the court is happily suggested, with its intrigues and its business. The king has yet a vague impression of restlessness, which, on hearing a song sung behind the scenes, prompts him to say, "Why has this strain flung over me so deep a melancholy, as though I was separated from some loved one; can this be the faint remembrance of affections in some previous existence?" It is here that the hermits, with Gautamí, arrive, bringing Śakoontalá, soon to be made a mother, into the presence of the king; but she has been utterly forgotten by him. He angrily denies his marriage; and when she proposes to bring forth the ring, she finds she has lost it from her finger. "It must have slipped off," suggested Gautamí, "when thou wast offering homage to Sachí's holy lake." The king smiles derisively. Śakoontalá tries to quicken his memory:—"Do you remember how, in the jasmine bower, you poured water from the lotus cup into the hollow of my hand? Do you remember how you said to my little fawn, Drink first, but she shrunk from you—and drank water from my hand, and you said, with a smile, 'Like trusts Like,' for you are two sisters in the same grove." The king calls her words "honeyed falsehoods." Śakoontalá buries her face in her mantle and bursts into tears.

The tenderness of this scene, its grace and delicacy, are quite idyllic, and worthy of the best ages of the pastoral drama. The ring is at length restored to Dushyanta, having been found by a fisherman in the belly of a carp. On its being restored to the king's finger, he is overcome with a flood of recollection: he gives himself over to mourning and forbids the celebration of the Spring festival. He admits that his palsied heart had been slumbering, and that, now it is roused by memories of his fawn-eyed love, he only wakes to agonies of remorse. Meanwhile Śakoontalá had been carried away like a celestial nymph to the sacred grove of Kaśyapa, far removed from earth in the upper air. The king, being summoned by Indra to destroy the brood of giants, descendants of Kalamemi, the monster of a hundred arms and heads, reaches in the celestial car Indra, the grove where dwell his wife and child, an heroic boy whom the hermits call Sarva-damana—the all-tamer. The recognition and reconciliation of husband and wife are delineated with the most delicate skill, and the play concludes with a prayer to Shiva.

E. W.

DRAMATIS PERSONÆ

DUSHYANTA, King of India.

MÁTHAVYA, the Jester, friend and companion of the King.

KANWA, chief of the Hermits, foster-father of Śakoontalá.

ŚÁRNGARAVA, ŚÁRADWATA, two Bráhmans, belonging to the hermitage of Kanwa.

MITRÁVASU, brother-in-law of the King, and Superintendent of the city police.

JÁNUKA, SÚCHAKA, two constables.

VÁTÁYANA, the Chamberlain or attendant on the women's apartments.

SOMARÁTA, the domestic Priest.

KARABHAKA, a messenger of the Queen-mother.

RAIVATAKA, the warder or door-keeper.

MÁTALI, charioteer of Indra.

SARVA-DAMANA, afterwards Bharata, a little boy, son of Dushyanta by Śakoontalá.

KAŚYAPA, a divine sage, progenitor of men and gods, son of Maríchi and grandson of Brahmá.

ŚAKOONTALÁ, daughter of the sage Viśwámitra and the nymph Menaká, foster-child of the hermit Kanwa.

PRIYAMVADÁ and ANASÚYÁ, female attendants, companions of Śakoontalá.

GAUTAMÍ, a holy matron, Superior of the female inhabitants of the hermitage.

VASUMATÍ, the Queen of Dushyanta.

SÁNUMATÍ, a nymph, friend of Śakoontalá.

TARALIKÁ, personal attendant of the King.

CHATURIKÁ, personal attendant of the Queen.

VETRAVATÍ, female warder, or door-keeper.

PARABARITIKÁ and MADHUKARIKÁ, maidens in charge of the royal gardens.

SUVRATÁ, a nurse.

ADITI, wife of Kaśyapa; grand-daughter of Brahmá, through her father, Daksha.

Charioteer, Fisherman, Officers, and Hermits.

RULES FOR PRONUNCIATION OF PROPER NAMES

Observe, that in order to secure the correct pronunciation of the title of this Drama, " Śakuntalá " has been spelt " Śakoontalá," the *u* being pronounced like the *u* in the English word *rule*.

The vowel *a* must invariably be pronounced with a dull sound, like the *a* in *organ*, or the *u* in *fun, sun*. *Dushyanta* must therefore be pronounced as if written *Dooshyunta*. The long vowel *á* is pronounced like the *a* in *last, cart; i* like the *i* in *pin, sin; í* like the *i* in *marine; e* like the *e* in *prey; o* like the *o* in *so; ai* like the *ai* in *aisle; au* like *au* in the German word *baum*, or like the *ou* in *our*.

The consonants are generally pronounced as in English, but *g* has always the sound of *g* in *gun, give*, never of *g* in *gin*. *S* with the accent over it (ś) has the sound of *s* in *sure*, or of the last *s* in *session*.

ŚAKOONTALÁ

PROLOGUE

Benediction

Iśa preserve you! he who is revealed
In these eight forms by man perceptible—
Water, of all creation's works the first;
The fire that bears on high the sacrifice
Presented with solemnity to heaven;
The Priest, the holy offerer of gifts;
The Sun and Moon, those two majestic orbs,
Eternal marshallers of day and night;
The subtle Ether, vehicle of sound,
Diffused throughout the boundless universe;
The Earth, by sages called " The place of birth
Of all material essences and things ";
And Air, which giveth life to all that breathe.

STAGE-MANAGER [*after the recitation of the benediction, looking towards the tiring-room*].—Lady, when you have finished attiring yourself, come this way.

ACTRESS [*entering*].—Here I am, Sir; what are your commands?

STAGE-MANAGER.—We are here before the eyes of an audience of educated and discerning men; and have to represent in their presence a new drama composed by Kálidása, called " Śakoontalá, or the Lost Ring." Let the whole company exert themselves to do justice to their several parts.

ACTRESS.—You, Sir, have so judiciously managed the cast of the characters, that nothing will be defective in the acting.

STAGE-MANAGER.—Lady, I will tell you the exact state of the case.

No skill in acting can I deem complete,
Till from the wise the actor gain applause:
Know that the heart e'en of the truly skilful,
Shrinks from too boastful confidence in self.

ACTRESS [*modestly*].—You judge correctly. And now, what
are your commands?

STAGE-MANAGER.—What can you do better than engage the
attention of the audience by some captivating melody?

ACTRESS.—Which among the seasons shall I select as the subject of my song?

STAGE-MANAGER.—You surely ought to give the preference to
the present Summer season that has but recently commenced, a season so rich in enjoyment. For now

Unceasing are the charms of halcyon days,
When the cool bath exhilarates the frame;
When sylvan gales are laden with the scent
Of fragrant Pátalas; when soothing sleep
Creeps softly on beneath the deepening shade;
And when, at last, the dulcet calm of eve
Entrancing steals o'er every yielding sense.

'ACTRESS.—I will.   [*Sings.*

Fond maids, the chosen of their hearts to please,
Entwine their ears with sweet Sirísha flowers,
Whose fragrant lips attract the kiss of bees
That softly murmur through the summer hours.

STAGE-MANAGER.—Charmingly sung! The audience are motionless as statues, their souls riveted by the enchanting
strain. What subject shall we select for representation,
that we may insure a continuance of their favor?

ACTRESS.—Why not the same, Sir, announced by you at first?
Let the drama called "Sakoontalá, or the Lost Ring," be
the subject of our dramatic performance.

STAGE-MANAGER.—Rightly reminded! For the moment I had
forgotten it.

Your song's transporting melody decoyed
My thoughts, and rapt with ecstasy my soul;
As now the bounding antelope allures
The King Dushyanta on the chase intent.   [*Exeunt.*

ACT FIRST

Scene.—A Forest

Enter King Dushyanta, armed with a bow and arrow, in a chariot, chasing an antelope, attended by his Charioteer.

CHARIOTEER [*looking at the deer, and then at the King*].—
　　Great Prince,
　　When on the antelope I bend my gaze,
　　And on your Majesty, whose mighty bow
　　Has its string firmly braced; before my eyes
　　The god that wields the trident seems revealed,
　　Chasing the deer that flies from him in vain.

KING.—Charioteer, this fleet antelope has drawn us far from
　　my attendants. See! there he runs:—
　　Aye and anon his graceful neck he bends
　　To cast a glance at the pursuing car;
　　And dreading now the swift-descending shaft,
　　Contracts into itself his slender frame:
　　About his path, in scattered fragments strewn,
　　The half-chewed grass falls from his panting mouth;
　　See! in his airy bounds he seems to fly,
　　And leaves no trace upon th' elastic turf.
　　　　　　　　　　　　　[*With astonishment.*
　　How now! swift as is our pursuit, I scarce can see him.

CHARIOTEER.—Sire, the ground here is full of hollows; I have
　　therefore drawn in the reins and checked the speed of the
　　chariot. Hence the deer has somewhat gained upon us.
　　Now that we are passing over level ground, we shall have
　　no difficulty in overtaking him.

KING.—Loosen the reins, then.

CHARIOTEER.—The King is obeyed. [*Drives the chariot at full
　　speed.*] Great Prince, see! see!

Responsive to the slackened rein, the steeds
Chafing with eager rivalry, career
With emulative fleetness o'er the plain;
Their necks outstretched, their waving plumes, that late
Fluttered above their brows, are motionless;
Their sprightly ears, but now erect, bent low;
Themselves unsullied by the circling dust,
That vainly follows on their rapid course.

KING [*joyously*].—In good sooth, the horses seem as if they
would outstrip the steeds of Indra and the Sun.[1]

That which but now showed to my view minute
Quickly assumes dimension; that which seemed
A moment since disjoined in diverse parts,
Looks suddenly like one compacted whole;
That which is really crooked in its shape
In the far distance left, grows regular;
Wondrous the chariot's speed, that in a breath,
Makes the near distant and the distant near.

Now, Charioteer, see me kill the deer.   [*Takes aim.*

A VOICE [*behind the scenes*].—Hold, O King! this deer belongs to our hermitage. Kill it not! kill it not!

CHARIOTEER [*listening and looking*].—Great King, some hermits have stationed themselves so as to screen the antelope
at the very moment of its coming within range of your
arrow.

KING [*hastily*].—Then stop the horses.

CHARIOTEER.—I obey.   [*Stops the chariot.*

Enter a Hermit, and two others with him.

HERMIT [*raising his hand*].—This deer, O King, belongs to
our hermitage. Kill it not! kill it not!

Now heaven forbid this barbèd shaft descend
Upon the fragile body of a fawn,
Like fire upon a heap of tender flowers!
Can thy steel bolts no meeter quarry find
Than the warm life-blood of a harmless deer?
Restore, great Prince, thy weapon to its quiver;

---

[1] The speed of the chariot resembled that of the wind and the sun. Indra was the god of the firmament or atmosphere. The sun, in Hindoo mythology, is represented as seated in a chariot drawn by seven green horses, having before him a lovely youth without legs, who acts as charioteer, and who is Aruna, or the Dawn personified.

More it becomes thy arms to shield the weak,
Than to bring anguish on the innocent.

KING.—'Tis done. [*Replaces the arrow in its quiver.*

HERMIT.—Worthy is this action of a Prince, the light of Puru's race.

Well does this act befit a Prince like thee,
Right worthy is it of thine ancestry.
Thy guerdon be a son of peerless worth,
Whose wide dominion shall embrace the earth.

BOTH THE OTHER HERMITS [*raising their hands*].—May heaven indeed grant thee a son, a sovereign of the earth from sea to sea!

KING [*bowing*].—I accept with gratitude a Bráhman's benediction.

HERMIT.—We came hither, mighty Prince, to collect sacrificial wood. Here on the banks of the Málini you may perceive the hermitage of the great sage Kanwa. If other duties require not your presence, deign to enter and accept our hospitality.

When you behold our penitential rites
Performed without impediment by Saints
Rich only in devotion, then with pride
Will you reflect, Such are the holy men
Who call me Guardian; such the men for whom
To wield the bow I bare my nervous arm,
Scarred by the motion of the glancing string.

KING.—Is the Chief of your Society now at home?

HERMIT.—No; he has gone to Soma-tírtha to propitiate Destiny, which threatens his daughter Śakoontalá with some calamity; but he has commissioned her in his absence to entertain all guests with hospitality.

KING.—Good! I will pay her a visit. She will make me acquainted with the mighty sage's acts of penance and devotion.

HERMIT.—And we will depart on our errand.

[*Exit with his companions.*

KING.—Charioteer, urge on the horses. We will at least purify our souls by a sight of this hallowed retreat.

CHARIOTEER.—Your Majesty is obeyed.

[*Drives the chariot with great velocity.*

KING [*looking all about him*].—Charioteer, even without be-

ing told, I should have known that these were the precincts
of a grove consecrated to penitential rites.

CHARIOTEER.—How so?

KING.—Do not you observe?

    Beneath the trees, whose hollow trunks afford
    Secure retreat to many a nestling brood
    Of parrots, scattered grains of rice lie strewn.
    Lo! here and there are seen the polished slabs
    That serve to bruise the fruit of Ingudí
    The gentle roe-deer, taught to trust in man,
    Unstartled hear our voices. On the paths
    Appear the traces of bark-woven vests
    Borne dripping from the limpid fount of waters.
    And mark!
    Laved are the roots of trees by deep canals,
    Whose glassy waters tremble in the breeze;
    The sprouting verdure of the leaves is dimmed
    By dusky wreaths of upward curling smoke
    From burnt oblations; and on new-mown lawns
    Around our car graze leisurely the fawns.

CHARIOTEER.—I observe it all.

KING [*advancing a little further*].—The inhabitants of this
sacred retreat must not be disturbed. Stay the chariot,
that I may alight.

CHARIOTEER.—The reins are held in. Your Majesty may descend.

KING [*alighting*].—Charioteer, groves devoted to penance
must be entered in humble attire. Take these ornaments.
[*Delivers his ornaments and bow to the Charioteer.*]
Charioteer, see that the horses are watered, and attend to
them until I return from visiting the inhabitants of the
hermitage.

CHARIOTEER.—I will.   [*Exit.*

KING [*walking and looking about*].—Here is the entrance to
the hermitage. I will now go in.

    [*Entering he feels a throbbing sensation in his arm.*
    Serenest peace is in this calm retreat,
    By passion's breath unruffled; what portends
    My throbbing arm? Why should it whisper here
    Of happy love? Yet everywhere around us
    Stand the closed portals of events unknown.

A Voice [*behind the scenes*].—This way, my dear companions; this way.

King [*listening*].—Hark! I hear voices to the right of yonder grove of trees. I will walk in that direction. [*Walking and looking about.*] Ah! here are the maidens of the hermitage coming this way to water the shrubs, carrying watering-pots proportioned to their strength. [*Gazing at them.*] How graceful they look!

In palaces such charms are rarely ours;
The woodland plants outshine the garden flowers.

I will conceal myself in this shade and watch them.

[*Stands gazing at them.*

Enter Śakoontalá, with her two female companions, employed in the manner described.

Śakoontalá.—This way, my dear companions; this way.

Anasúyá.—Dear Śakoontalá. one would think that father Kanwa had more affection for the shrubs of the hermitage even than for you, seeing he assigns to you who are yourself as delicate as the fresh-blown jasmine, the task of filling with water the trenches which encircle their roots.

Śakoontalá.—Dear Anasúyá, although I am charged by my good father with this duty, yet I cannot regard it as a task. I really feel a sisterly love for these plants.

[*Continues watering the shrubs.*

King.—Can this be the daughter of Kanwa? The saintly man, though descended from the great Kaśyapa, must be very deficient in judgment to habituate such a maiden to the life of a recluse.

The sage who would this form of artless grace
Inure to penance—thoughtlessly attempts
To cleave in twain the hard acacia's stem
With the soft edge of a blue lotus leaf.

Well! concealed behind this tree, I will watch her without raising her suspicions. [*Conceals himself.*

Śakoontalá.—Good Anasúyá, Priyamvadá has drawn this bark-dress too tightly about my chest. I pray thee, loosen it a little.

Anasúyá.—I will. [*Loosens it.*

Priyamvadá [*smiling*].—Why do you lay the blame on me?

Blame rather your own blooming youthfulness which imparts fulness to your bosom.

KING.—A most just observation!

This youthful form, whose bosom's swelling charms
By the bark's knotted tissue are concealed,
Like some fair bud close folded in its sheath,
Gives not to view the blooming of its beauty.

But what am I saying? In real truth, this bark-dress, though ill-suited to her figure, sets it off like an ornament.

The lotus with the Saivala entwined
Is not a whit less brilliant: dusky spots
Heighten the lustre of the cold-rayed moon:
This lovely maiden in her dress of bark
Seems all the lovelier. E'en the meanest garb
Gives to true beauty fresh attractiveness.

SAKOONTALÁ [looking before her].—Yon Kesara-tree beckons to me with its young shoots, which, as the breeze waves them to and fro, appear like slender fingers. I will go and attend to it. [Walks towards it.

PRIYAMVADÁ.—Dear Sakoontalá, prithee, rest in that attitude one moment.

SAKOONTALÁ.—Why so?

PRIYAMVADÁ.—The Kesara-tree, whilst your graceful form bends about its stem, appears as if it were wedded to some lovely twining creeper.

SAKOONTALÁ.—Ah! saucy girl, you are most appropriately named Priyamvadá ("Speaker of flattering things").

KING.—What Priyamvadá says, though complimentary, is nevertheless true. Verily,

Her ruddy lip vies with the opening bud;
Her graceful arms are as the twining stalks;
And her whole form is radiant with the glow
Of youthful beauty, as the tree with bloom.

ANASÚYÁ.—See, dear Sakoontalá, here is the young jasmine, which you named "the Moonlight of the Grove," the self-elected wife of the mango-tree. Have you forgotten it?

SAKOONTALÁ.—Rather will I forget myself. [Approaching the plant and looking at it.] How delightful is the season when the jasmine-creeper and the mango-tree seem thus to unite in mutual embraces! The fresh blossoms of the jasmine resemble the bloom of a young bride, and the

newly-formed shoots of the mango appear to make it her
natural protector. [*Continues gazing at it.*

PRIYAMVADÁ [*smiling*].—Do you know, my Anasúyá, why
Śakoontalá gazes so intently at the jasmine?

ANASÚYÁ.—No, indeed, I cannot imagine. I pray thee tell me.

PRIYAMVADÁ.—She is wishing that as the jasmine is united to
a suitable tree, so, in like manner, she may obtain a husband worthy of her.

ŚAKOONTALÁ.—Speak for yourself, girl; this is the thought in
your own mind. [*Continues watering the flowers.*

KING.—Would that my union with her were permissible! and
yet I hardly dare hope that the maiden is sprung from a
caste different from that of the Head of the hermitage.
But away with doubt:—

That she is free to wed a warrior-king
My heart attests. For, in conflicting doubts,
The secret promptings of the good man's soul
Are an unerring index of the truth.

However, come what may, I will ascertain the fact.

ŚAKOONTALÁ [*in a flurry*].—Ah! a bee, disturbed by the
sprinkling of the water, has left the young jasmine, and
is trying to settle on my face. [*Attempts to drive it away.*

KING [*gazing at her ardently*].—Beautiful! there is something
charming even in her repulse.

Where'er the bee his eager onset plies,
Now here, now there, she darts her kindling eyes:
What love hath yet to teach, fear teaches now,
The furtive glances and the frowning brow.
[*In a tone of envy.*

Ah happy bee! how boldly dost thou try
To steal the lustre from her sparkling eye;
And in thy circling movements hover near,
To murmur tender secrets in her ear;
Or, as she coyly waves her hand, to sip
Voluptuous nectar from her lower lip!
While rising doubts my heart's fond hopes destroy,
Thou dost the fulness of her charms enjoy.

ŚAKOONTALÁ.—This impertinent bee will not rest quiet. I
must move elsewhere. [*Moving a few steps off, and casting a glance around.*] How now! he is following me here.
Help! my dear friends, help! deliver me from the attacks
of this troublesome insect.

PRIYAMVADÁ AND ANASÚYÁ.—How can we deliver you? Call Dushyanta to your aid. The sacred groves are under the king's special protection.

KING.—An excellent opportunity for me to show myself. Fear not—[*Checks himself when the words are half-uttered. Aside.*] But stay, if I introduce myself in this manner, they will know me to be the King. Be it so, I will accost them, nevertheless.

SAKOONTALÁ [*moving a step or two further off*].—What! it still persists in following me.

KING [*advancing hastily*].—When mighty Puru's offspring sways the earth,
　And o'er the wayward holds his threatening rod,
　Who dares molest the gentle maids that keep
　Their holy vigils here in Kanwa's grove?
　　　[*All look at the King, and are embarrassed.*

ANASÚYÁ.—Kind Sir, no outrage has been committed; only our dear friend here was teased by the attacks of a troublesome bee. [*Points to Śakoontalá.*

KING [*turning to Śakoontalá*].—I trust all is well with your devotional rites?
　　　[*Śakoontalá stands confused and silent.*

ANASÚYÁ.—All is well, indeed, now that we are honored by the reception of a distinguished guest. Dear Śakoontalá, go, bring from the hermitage an offering of flowers, rice, and fruit. This water that we have brought with us will serve to bathe our guest's feet.

KING.—The rites of hospitality are already performed; your truly kind words are the best offering I can receive.

PRIYAMVADÁ.—At least be good enough, gentle Sir, to sit down awhile, and rest yourself on this seat shaded by the leaves of the Sapta-parna tree.

KING.—You, too, must all be fatigued by your employment.

ANASÚYÁ.—Dear Śakoontalá, there is no impropriety in our sitting by the side of our guest: come, let us sit down here.
　　　[*All sit down together.*

SAKOONTALÁ [*aside*].—How is it that the sight of this man has made me sensible of emotions inconsistent with religious vows?

KING [*gazing at them all by turns*].—How charmingly your friendship is in keeping with the equality of your ages and appearance!

PRIYAMVADÁ [*aside to Anasúyá*].—Who can this person be, whose lively yet dignified manner, and polite conversation, bespeak him a man of high rank?

ANASÚYÁ.—I, too, my dear, am very curious to know. I will ask him myself. [*Aloud.*] Your kind words, noble Sir, fill me with confidence, and prompt me to inquire of what regal family our noble guest is the ornament? what country is now mourning his absence? and what induced a person so delicately nurtured to expose himself to the fatigue of visiting this grove of penance?

ŚAKOONTALÁ [*aside*].—Be not troubled, O my heart, Anasúyá is giving utterance to thy thoughts.

KING [*aside*].—How now shall I reply? shall I make myself known, or shall I still disguise my real rank? I have it; I will answer her thus. [*Aloud.*] I am the person charged by his majesty, the descendant of Puru, with the administration of justice and religion; and am come to this sacred grove to satisfy myself that the rites of the hermits are free from obstruction.

ANASÚYÁ.—The hermits, then, and all the members of our religious society have now a guardian.

[*Śakoontalá gazes bashfully at the King.*

PRIYAMVADÁ AND ANASÚYÁ [*perceiving the state of her feelings, and of the King's. Aside to Śakoontalá*].—Dear Śakoontalá, if father Kanwa were but at home to-day——

ŚAKOONTALÁ [*angrily*].—What if he were?

PRIYAMVADÁ AND ANASÚYÁ.—He would honor this our distinguished guest with an offering of the most precious of his possessions.

ŚAKOONTALÁ.—Go to! you have some silly idea in your minds. I will not listen to such remarks.

KING.—May I be allowed, in my turn, to ask you maidens a few particulars respecting your friend?

PRIYAMVADÁ AND ANASÚYÁ.—Your request, Sir, is an honor.

KING.—The sage Kanwa lives in the constant practice of austerities. How, then, can this friend of yours be called his daughter?

ANASÚYÁ.—I will explain to you, Sir. You have heard of an illustrious sage of regal caste, Viśwámitra, whose family name is Kaúsika.

KING.—I have.

ANASÚYÁ.—Know that he is the real father of our friend. The venerable Kanwa is only her reputed father. He it was who brought her up, when she was deserted by her mother.

KING.—" Deserted by her mother! " My curiosity is excited; pray let me hear the story from the beginning.

ANASÚYÁ.—You shall hear it, Sir. Some time since, this sage of regal caste, while performing a most severe penance on the banks of the river Godávarí, excited the jealousy and alarm of the gods; insomuch that they despatched a lovely nymph named Menaká to interrupt his devotions.

KING.—The inferior gods, I am aware, are jealous of the power which the practice of excessive devotion confers on mortals.

ANASÚYÁ.—Well, then, it happened that Viśwámitra, gazing on the bewitching beauty of that nymph at a season when, spring being in its glory——

[*Stops short, and appears confused.*

KING.—The rest may be easily divined. Śakoontalá, then, is the offspring of the nymph.

ANASÚYÁ.—Just so.

KING.—It is quite intelligible.

How could a mortal to such charms give birth?
The lightning's radiance flashes not from earth.

[*Śakoontalá remains modestly seated with downcast eyes.*
[*Aside.*] And so my desire has really scope for its indulgence. Yet I am still distracted by doubts, remembering the pleasantry of her female companions respecting her wish for a husband.

PRIYAMVADÁ [*looking with a smile at Śakoontalá, and then turning towards the King*].—You seem desirous, Sir, of asking something further.

[*Śakoontalá makes a chiding gesture with her finger.*

KING.—You conjecture truly. I am so eager to hear the particulars of your friend's history, that I have still another question to ask.

PRIYAMVADÁ.—Scruple not to do so. Persons who lead the life of hermits may be questioned unreservedly.

KING.—I wish to ascertain one point respecting your friend—

Will she be bound by solitary vows
Opposed to love, till her espousals only?
Or ever dwell with these her cherished fawns,

Whose eyes, in lustre vieing with her own,
Return her gaze of sisterly affection?

PRIYAMVADÁ.—Hitherto, Sir, she has been engaged in the practice of religious duties, and has lived in subjection to her
foster-father; but it is now his fixed intention to give her
away in marriage to a husband worthy of her.

KING [aside].—His intention may be easily carried into effect.

Be hopeful, O my heart, thy harrowing doubts
Are past and gone; that which thou didst believe
To be as unapproachable as fire,
Is found a glittering gem that may be touched.

ŚAKOONTALÁ [pretending anger].—Anasúyá, I shall leave you.

ANASÚYÁ.—Why so?

ŚAKOONTALÁ.—That I may go and report this impertinent
Priyamvadá to the venerable matron, Gautamí.[2]

ANASÚYÁ.—Surely, dear friend, it would not be right to leave
a distinguished guest before he has received the rights of
hospitality, and quit his presence in this wilful manner.

[Śakoontalá, without answering a word, moves away.

KING [making a movement to arrest her departure, but checking himself. Aside].—Ah! a lover's feelings betray themselves by his gestures.

When I would fain have stayed the maid, a sense
Of due decorum checked my bold design:
Though I have stirred not, yet my mien betrays
My eagerness to follow on her steps.

PRIYAMVADÁ [holding Śakoontalá back].—Dear Śakoontalá,
it does not become you to go away in this manner.

ŚAKOONTALÁ [frowning].—Why not, pray?

PRIYAMVADÁ.—You are under a promise to water two more
shrubs for me. When you have paid your debt, you shall
go, and not before.   [Forces her to turn back.

KING.—Spare her this trouble, gentle maiden. The exertion
of watering the shrubs has already fatigued her.

The water-jar has overtasked the strength
Of her slim arms; her shoulders droop, her hands
Are ruddy with the glow of quickened pulses;
E'en now her agitated breath imparts
Unwonted tremor to her heaving breast;

---

[2] The Matron or Superior of the female part of the society of hermits.
Their authority resembled that of an abbess in a convent of nuns.

The pearly drops that mar the recent bloom
Of the Śirísha pendant in her ear,
Gather in clustering circles on her cheek;
Loosed is the fillet of her hair: her hand
Restrains the locks that struggle to be free.
Suffer me, then, thus to discharge the debt for you.

[*Offers a ring to Priyamvadá. Both the maidens, reading the name Dushyanta on the seal, look at each other with surprise.*

KING.—Nay, think not that I am King Dushyanta. I am only the king's officer, and this is the ring which I have received from him as my credentials.

PRIYAMVADÁ.—The greater the reason you ought not to part with the ring from your finger. I am content to release her from her obligation at your simple request. [*With a smile.*] Now, Śakoontalá my love, you are at liberty to retire, thanks to the intercession of this noble stranger, or rather of this mighty prince.

ŚAKOONTALÁ [*aside*].—My movements are no longer under my own control. [*Aloud.*] Pray, what authority have you over me, either to send me away or keep me back?

KING [*gazing at Śakoontalá. Aside*].—Would I could ascertain whether she is affected towards me as I am towards her! At any rate, my hopes are free to indulge themselves. Because,

Although she mingles not her words with mine,
Yet doth her listening ear drink in my speech;
Although her eye shrinks from my ardent gaze,
No form but mine attracts its timid glances.

A VOICE [*behind the scenes*].—O hermits, be ready to protect the animals belonging to our hermitage. King Dushyanta, amusing himself with hunting, is near at hand.

Lo! by the feet of prancing horses raised,
Thick clouds of moving dust, like glittering swarms
Of locusts in the glow of eventide,
Fall on the branches of our sacred trees;
Where hang the dripping vests of woven bark,
Bleached by the waters of the cleansing fountain.

And see!

Scared by the royal chariot in its course,
With headlong haste an elephant invades

The hallowed precincts of our sacred grove;
Himself the terror of the startled deer,
And an embodied hindrance to our rites.
The hedge of creepers clinging to his feet,
Feeble obstruction to his mad career,
Is dragged behind him in a tangled chain;
And with terrific shock one tusk he drives
Into the riven body of a tree,
Sweeping before him all impediments.

KING [*aside*].—Out upon it! my retinue are looking for me, and are disturbing this holy retreat. Well! there is no help for it; I must go and meet them.

PRIYAMVADÁ AND ANASÚYÁ.—Noble Sir, we are terrified by the accidental disturbance caused by the wild elephant. Permit us to return into the cottage.

KING [*hastily*].—Go, gentle maidens. It shall be our care that no injury happen to the hermitage.   [*All rise up.*

PRIYAMVADÁ AND ANASÚYÁ.—After such poor hospitality we are ashamed to request the honor of a second visit from you.

KING.—Say not so. The mere sight of you, sweet maidens, has been to me the best entertainment.

ŚAKOONTALÁ.—Anasúyá, a pointed blade of Kuśa-grass [3] has pricked my foot; and my bark-mantle is caught in the branch of a Kuruvaka-bush. Be so good as to wait for me until I have disentangled it.

[*Exit with her two companions, after making pretexts for delay, that she may steal glances at the King.*

KING.—I have no longer any desire to return to the city. I will therefore rejoin my attendants, and make them encamp somewhere in the vicinity of this sacred grove. In good truth, Śakoontalá has taken such possession of my thoughts, that I cannot turn myself in any other direction.

My limbs drawn onward leave my heart behind,
Like silken pennon borne against the wind.

---

[3] A grass held sacred by the Hindoos and freely used at their religious ceremonies. Its leaves are very long and taper to a needle-like point.

ACT SECOND

Scene.—A Plain on the Skirts of the Forest

Enter the Jester, Máthavya, in a melancholy mood.

Máthavya [*sighing*].—Heigh-ho! what an unlucky fellow
I am! worn to a shadow by my royal friend's sporting
propensities. "Here's a deer!" "There goes a boar!"
"Yonder's a tiger!" This is the only burden of our talk,
while in the heat of the meridian sun we toil on from
jungle to jungle, wandering about in the paths of the
woods, where the trees afford us no shelter. Are we
thirsty? We have nothing to drink but the foul water
of some mountain stream, filled with dry leaves which
give it a most pungent flavor. Are we hungry? We have
nothing to eat but roast game, which we must swallow
down at odd times, as best we can. Even at night there
is no peace to be had. Sleeping is out of the question,
with joints all strained by dancing attendance upon my
sporting friend; or if I do happen to doze, I am awakened
at the very earliest dawn by the horrible din of a lot of
rascally beaters and huntsmen, who must needs surround
the wood before sunrise, and deafen me with their clatter.
Nor are these my only troubles. Here's a fresh grievance,
like a new boil rising upon an old one! Yesterday, while
we were lagging behind, my royal friend entered yonder
hermitage after a deer; and there, as ill-luck would have
it, caught sight of a beautiful girl, called Śakoontalá, the
hermit's daughter. From that moment, not another
thought about returning to the city! and all last night, not
a wink of sleep did he get for thinking of the damsel.
What is to be done? At any rate, I will be on the watch
for him as soon as he has finished his toilet. [*Walking and
looking about.*] Oh! here he comes, attended by the

334

Yavana women with bows in their hands, and wearing garlands of wild flowers. What shall I do? I have it. I will
pretend to stand in the easiest attitude for resting my
bruised and crippled limbs.   [*Stands leaning on a staff.*

*Enter King Dushyanta, followed by a retinue in the manner
described.*

KING.—True, by no easy conquest may I win her,
   Yet are my hopes encouraged by her mien.
   Love is not yet triumphant; but, methinks,
   The hearts of both are ripe for his delights.
[*Smiling.*] Ah! thus does the lover delude himself;
judging of the state of his loved one's feelings by his own
desires. But yet,
   The stolen glance with half-averted eye,
   The hesitating gait, the quick rebuke
   Addressed to her companion, who would fain
   Have stayed her counterfeit departure; these
   Are signs not unpropitious to my suit.
   So eagerly the lover feeds his hopes,
   Claiming each trivial gesture for his own.
MÁTHAVYA [*still in the same attitude*].—Ah, friend, my hands
   cannot move to greet you with the usual salutation. I can
   only just command my lips to wish your majesty victory.
KING.—Why, what has paralyzed your limbs?
MÁTHAVYA.—You might as well ask me how my eye comes to
   water after you have poked your finger into it.
KING.—I don't understand you; speak more intelligibly.
MÁTHAVYA.—Ah, my dear friend, is yonder upright reed trans-
   formed into a crooked plant by its own act, or by the force
   of the current?
KING.—The current of the river causes it, I suppose.
MÁTHAVYA.—Aye; just as you are the cause of my crippled
   limbs.
KING.—How so?
MÁTHAVYA.—Here are you living the life of a wild man of the
   woods in a savage, unfrequented region, while your state
   affairs are left to shift for themselves; and as for poor me,
   I am no longer master of my own limbs, but have to follow
   you about day after day in your chases after wild animals,

till my bones are all crippled and out of joint. Do, my
dear friend, let me have one day's rest.

KING [aside].—This fellow little knows, while he talks in this
manner, that my mind is wholly engrossed by recollections
of the hermit's daughter, and quite as disinclined to the
chase as his own.

> No longer can I bend my well-braced bow
> Against the timid deer; nor e'er again
> With well-aimed arrows can I think to harm
> These her beloved associates, who enjoy
> The privilege of her companionship;
> Teaching her tender glances in return.

MÁTHAVYA [looking in the King's face].—I may as well speak
to the winds, for any attention you pay to my requests.
I suppose you have something on your mind, and are talking it over to yourself.

KING [smiling].—I was only thinking that I ought not to disregard a friend's request.

MÁTHAVYA.—Then may the King live forever!   [Moves off.

KING.—Stay a moment, my dear friend. I have something
else to say to you.

MÁTHAVYA.—Say on, then.

KING.—When you have rested, you must assist me in another
business, which will give you no fatigue.

MÁTHAVYA.—In eating something nice, I hope.

KING.—You shall know at some future time.

MÁTHAVYA.—No time better than the present.

KING.—What ho! there.

WARDER [entering].—What are your Majesty's commands?

KING.—O Raivataka! bid the General of the forces attend.

WARDER.—I will, Sire. [Exit and reënters with the General.]
Come forward, General; his Majesty is looking towards
you, and has some order to give you.

GENERAL [looking at the King].—Though hunting is known
to produce ill effects, my royal master has derived only
benefit from it. For

> Like the majestic elephant that roams
> O'er mountain wilds, so does the King display
> A stalwart frame, instinct with vigorous life.
> His brawny arms and manly chest are scored
> By frequent passage of the sounding string;

Unharmed he bears the mid-day sun; no toil
His mighty spirit daunts; his sturdy limbs,
Stripped of redundant flesh, relinquish nought
Of their robust proportions, but appear
In muscle, nerve, and sinewy fibre cased.

[*Approaching the King.*] Victory to the King! We have tracked the wild beasts to their lairs in the forest. Why delay, when everything is ready?

KING.—My friend Máthavya here has been disparaging the chase, till he has taken away all my relish for it.

GENERAL [*aside to Máthavya*].—Persevere in your opposition, my good fellow; I will sound the King's real feelings, and humor him accordingly. [*Aloud.*] The blockhead talks nonsense, and your Majesty, in your own person, furnishes the best proof of it. Observe, Sire, the advantage and pleasure the hunter derives from the chase.

Freed from all grosser influences, his frame
Loses its sluggish humors, and becomes
Buoyant, compact, and fit for bold encounter.
'Tis his to mark with joy the varied passions,
Fierce heats of anger, terror, blank dismay,
Of forest animals that cross his path.
Then what a thrill transports the hunter's soul,
When, with unerring course, his driven shaft
Pierces the moving mark! Oh! 't is conceit
In moralists to call the chase a vice;
What recreation can compare with this?

MÁTHAVYA [*angrily*].—Away! tempter, away! The King has recovered his senses, and is himself again. As for you, you may, if you choose, wander about from forest to forest, till some old bear seizes you by the nose, and makes a mouthful of you.

KING.—My good General, as we are just now in the neighborhood of a consecrated grove, your panegyric upon hunting is somewhat ill-timed, and I cannot assent to all you have said. For the present,

All undisturbed the buffaloes shall sport
In yonder pool, and with their ponderous horns
Scatter its tranquil waters, while the deer,
Couched here and there in groups beneath the shade
Of spreading branches, ruminate in peace.

> And all securely shall the herd of boars
> Feed on the marshy sedge; and thou, my bow,
> With slackened string enjoy a long repose.

GENERAL.—So please your Majesty, it shall be as you desire.

KING.—Recall, then, the beaters who were sent in advance to surround the forest. My troops must not be allowed to disturb this sacred retreat, and irritate its pious inhabitants.

> Know that within the calm and cold recluse
> Lurks unperceived a germ of smothered flame,
> All-potent to destroy; a latent fire
> That rashly kindled bursts with fury forth:—
> As in the disc of crystal that remains
> Cool to the touch, until the solar ray
> Falls on its polished surface, and excites
> The burning heat that lies within concealed.

GENERAL.—Your Majesty's commands shall be obeyed.

MÁTHAVYA.—Off with you, you son of a slave! Your nonsense won't go down here, my fine fellow. [*Exit General.*

KING [*looking at his attendants*].—Here, women, take my hunting-dress; and you, Raivataka, keep guard carefully outside.

ATTENDANTS.—We will, sire.   [*Exeunt.*

MÁTHAVYA.—Now that you have got rid of these plagues, who have been buzzing about us like so many flies, sit down, do, on that stone slab, with the shade of the tree as your canopy, and I will seat myself by you quite comfortably.

KING.—Go you, and sit down first.

MÁTHAVYA.—Come along, then.

> [*Both walk on a little way, and seat themselves.*

KING.—Máthavya, it may be said of you that you have never beheld anything worth seeing: for your eyes have not yet looked upon the loveliest object in creation.

MÁTHAVYA.—How can you say so, when I see your Majesty before me at this moment?

KING.—It is very natural that everyone should consider his own friend perfect; but I was alluding to Śakoontalá, the brightest ornament of these hallowed groves.

MÁTHAVYA [*aside*].—I understand well enough, but I am not going to humor him. [*Aloud.*] If, as you intimate, she is a hermit's daughter, you cannot lawfully ask her in

marriage. You may as well, then, dismiss her from your
mind, for any good the mere sight of her can do.

KING.—Think you that a descendant of the mighty Puru could
fix his affections on an unlawful object?

> Though, as men say, the offspring of the sage,
> The maiden to a nymph celestial owes
> Her being, and by her mother left on earth,
> Was found and nurtured by the holy man
> As his own daughter, in this hermitage;—
> So, when dissevered from its parent stalk,
> Some falling blossom of the jasmine, wafted
> Upon the sturdy sunflower, is preserved
> By its support from premature decay.

MÁTHAVYA [smiling].—This passion of yours for a rustic
maiden, when you have so many gems of women at home
in your palace, seems to me very like the fancy of a man
who is tired of sweet dates, and longs for sour tamarinds
as a variety.

KING.—You have not seen her, or you would not talk in this
fashion.

MÁTHAVYA.—I can quite understand it must require something
surpassingly attractive to excite the admiration of such
a great man as you.

KING.—I will describe her, my dear friend, in a few words—

> Man's all-wise Maker, wishing to create
> A faultless form, whose matchless symmetry
> Should far transcend Creation's choicest works,
> Did call together by his mighty will,
> And garner up in his eternal mind,
> A bright assemblage of all lovely things:—
> And then, as in a picture, fashion them
> Into one perfect and ideal form.
> Such the divine, the wondrous prototype,
> Whence her fair shape was moulded into being.

MÁTHAVYA.—If that's the case, she must indeed throw all other
beauties into the shade.

KING.—To my mind she really does.

> This peerless maid is like a fragrant flower,
> Whose perfumed breath has never been diffused;
> A tender bud, that no profaning hand
> Has dared to sever from its parent stalk;

A gem of priceless water, just released
Pure and unblemished from its glittering bed.
Or may the maiden haply be compared
To sweetest honey, that no mortal lip
Has sipped; or, rather to the mellowed fruit
Of virtuous actions in some former birth,
Now brought to full perfection? Lives the man
Whom bounteous heaven has destined to espouse her?

MÁTHAVYA.—Make haste, then, to her aid; you have no time
to lose, if you don't wish this fruit of all the virtues to
drop into the mouth of some greasy-headed rustic of devout habits.

KING.—The lady is not her own mistress, and her foster-
father is not at home.

MÁTHAVYA.—Well, but tell me, did she look at all kindly upon
you?

KING.—Maidens brought up in a hermitage are naturally shy
and reserved; but for all that,

She did look towards me, though she quick withdrew
Her stealthy glances when she met my gaze;
She smiled upon me sweetly, but disguised
With maiden grace the secret of her smiles.
Coy love was half unveiled; then, sudden checked
By modesty, left half to be divined.

MÁTHAVYA.—Why, of course, my dear friend, you never could
seriously expect that at the very first sight she would fall
over head and ears in love with you, and without more
ado come and sit in your lap.

KING.—When we parted from each other, she betrayed her liking for me by clearer indications, but still with the utmost
modesty.

Scarce had the fair one from my presence passed,
When, suddenly, without apparent cause,
She stopped, and counterfeiting pain, exclaimed,
" My foot is wounded by this prickly grass."
Then glancing at me tenderly, she feigned
Another charming pretext for delay,
Pretending that a bush had caught her robe,
And turned as if to disentangle it.

MÁTHAVYA.—I trust you have laid in a good stock of provisions, for I see you intend making this consecrated grove

your game-preserve, and will be roaming here in quest of sport for some time to come.

KING.—You must know, my good fellow, that I have been recognized by some of the inmates of the hermitage. Now I want the assistance of your fertile invention, in devising some excuse for going there again.

MÁTHAVYA.—There is but one expedient that I can suggest. You are the King, are you not?

KING.—What then?

MÁTHAVYA.—Say you have come for the sixth part of their grain, which they owe you for tribute.

KING.—No, no, foolish man; these hermits pay me a very different kind of tribute, which I value more than heaps of gold or jewels; observe,

> The tribute which my other subjects bring
> Must moulder into dust, but holy men
> Present me with a portion of the fruits
> Of penitential services and prayers—
> A precious and imperishable gift.

A VOICE [*behind the scenes*].—We are fortunate; here is the object of our search.

KING [*listening*].—Surely those must be the voices of hermits, to judge by their deep tones.

WARDER [*entering*].—Victory to the King! two young hermits are in waiting outside, and solicit an audience of your Majesty.

KING.—Introduce them immediately.

WARDER.—I will, my liege. [*Goes out, and reënters with two young Hermits.*] This way, Sirs, this way.

[*Both the Hermits look at the King.*

FIRST HERMIT.—How majestic is his mien, and yet what confidence it inspires! But this might be expected in a king whose character and habits have earned for him a title only one degree removed from that of a Saint.

> In this secluded grove, whose sacred joys
> All may participate, he deigns to dwell
> Like one of us; and daily treasures up
> A store of purest merit for himself,
> By the protection of our holy rites.
> In his own person wondrously are joined
> Both majesty and saintlike holiness:—

And often chanted by inspirèd bards,
His hallowed title of " Imperial Sage "
Ascends in joyous accents to the skies.

SECOND HERMIT.—Bear in mind, Gautama, that this is the
great Dushyanta, the friend of Indra.

FIRST HERMIT.—What of that?

SECOND HERMIT.—Where is the wonder if his nervous arm,
Puissant and massive as the iron bar
That binds a castle-gateway, singly sways
The sceptre of the universal earth,
E'en to its dark-green boundary of waters?
Or if the gods, beholden to his aid
In their fierce warfare with the powers of hell,
Should blend his name with Indra's in their songs
Of victory, and gratefully accord
No lower meed of praise to his braced bow,
Than to the thunders of the god of heaven?

BOTH THE HERMITS [approaching].—Victory to the King!

KING [rising from his seat].—Hail to you both!

BOTH THE HERMITS.—Heaven bless your Majesty!
                                        [They offer fruits.

KING [respectfully receiving the offering].—Tell me, I pray
you, the object of your visit.

BOTH THE HERMITS.—The inhabitants of the hermitage having heard of your Majesty's sojourn in our neighborhood,
make this humble petition.

KING.—What are their commands?

BOTH THE HERMITS.—In the absence of our Superior, the great
Sage Kanwa, evil demons are disturbing our sacrificial
rites.[4] Deign, therefore, accompanied by your charioteer,
to take up your abode in our hermitage for a few days.

KING.—I am honored by your invitation.

MÁTHAVYA [aside].—Most opportune and convenient, certainly!

KING [smiling].—Ho! there, Raivataka! Tell the charioteer
from me to bring round the chariot with my bow.

WARDER.—I will, Sire.   [Exit.

BOTH THE HERMITS [joyfully].—Well it becomes the King by
acts of grace

---

⁴ The religious rites of holy men were often disturbed by certain evil spirits
called Rákshasas, who were the determined enemies of piety and devotion.

To emulate the virtues of his race.
Such acts thy lofty destiny attest;
Thy mission is to succor the distressed.

KING [*bowing to the Hermits*].—Go first, reverend Sirs, I will follow you immediately.

BOTH THE HERMITS.—May victory attend you! [*Exeunt.*

KING.—My dear Máthavya, are you not full of longing to see Śakoontalá?

MÁTHAVYA.—To tell you the truth, though I was just now brimful of desire to see her, I have not a drop left since this piece of news about the demons.

KING.—Never fear; you shall keep close to me for protection.

MÁTHAVYA.—Well, you must be my guardian-angel, and act the part of a very Vishnu[5] to me.

WARDER [*entering*].—Sire, the chariot is ready, and only waits to conduct you to victory. But here is a messenger named Karabhaka, just arrived from your capital, with a message from the Queen, your mother.

KING [*respectfully*].—How say you? a messenger from the venerable Queen?

WARDER.—Even so.

KING.—Introduce him at once.

WARDER.—I will, Sire. [*Goes out, and reënters with Karabhaka.*] Behold the King! Approach.

KARABHAKA.—Victory to the King! The Queen-mother bids me say that in four days from the present time she intends celebrating a solemn ceremony for the advancement and preservation of her son. She expects that your Majesty will honor her with your presence on that occasion.

KING.—This places me in a dilemma. Here, on the one hand, is the commission of these holy men to be executed; and, on the other, the command of my revered parent to be obeyed. Both duties are too sacred to be neglected. What is to be done?

MÁTHAVYA.—You will have to take up an intermediate position between the two, like King Triśanku, who was suspended between heaven and earth, because the sage Viśwámitra commanded him to mount up to heaven, and the gods ordered him down again.

KING.—I am certainly very much perplexed. For here,

[5] Vishnu, the Preserver, was one of the three principal gods.

Two different duties are required of me
In widely distant places; how can I
In my own person satisfy them both?
Thus is my mind distracted and impelled
In opposite directions, like a stream
That, driven back by rocks, still rushes on,
Forming two currents in its eddying course.

[*Reflecting.*] Friend Máthavya, as you were my play-fellow in childhood, the Queen has always received you like a second son; go you, then, back to her and tell her of my solemn engagement to assist these holy men. You can supply my place in the ceremony, and act the part of a son to the Queen.

MÁTHAVYA.—With the greatest pleasure in the world; but don't suppose that I am really coward enough to have the slightest fear of those trumpery demons.

KING [*smiling*].—Oh! of course not; a great Bráhman like you could not possibly give way to such weakness.

MÁTHAVYA.—You must let me travel in a manner suitable to the King's younger brother.

KING.—Yes, I shall send my retinue with you, that there may be no further disturbance in this sacred forest.

MÁTHAVYA [*with a strut*].—Already I feel quite like a young prince.

KING [*aside*].—This is a giddy fellow, and in all probability he will let out the truth about my present pursuit to the women of the palace. What is to be done? I must say something to deceive him. [*Aloud to Máthavya, taking him by the hand.*] Dear friend, I am going to the hermit-age wholly and solely out of respect for its pious inhabi-tants, and not because I have really any liking for Śakoon-talá, the hermit's daughter. Observe,

What suitable communion could there be
Between a monarch and a rustic girl?
I did but feign an idle passion, friend,
Take not in earnest what was said in jest.

MÁTHAVYA.—Don't distress yourself; I quite understand.

[*Exeunt.*

PRELUDE TO ACT THIRD

Scene.—The Hermitage

Enter a young Bráhman, carrying bundles of Kuśa-grass for the use of the sacrificing priests.

Young Bráhman.—How wonderful is the power of King Dushyanta! No sooner did he enter our hermitage, than we were able to proceed with our sacrificial rites, unmolested by the evil demons.

No need to fix the arrow to the bow;
The mighty monarch sounds the quivering string,
And, by the thunder of his arms dismayed,
Our demon foes are scattered to the wind.

I must now, therefore, make haste and deliver to the sacrificing priests these bundles of Kuśa-grass, to be strewn round the altar. [*Walking and looking about; then addressing someone off the stage.*] Why, Priyamvadá, for whose use are you carrying that ointment of Usíra-root and those lotus leaves with fibres attached to them? [*Listening for her answer.*] What say you?—that Śakoontalá is suffering from fever produced by exposure to the sun, and that this ointment is to cool her burning frame? Nurse her with care, then, Priyamvadá, for she is cherished by our reverend Superior as the very breath of his nostrils. I, for my part, will contrive that soothing waters, hallowed in the sacrifice, be administered to her by the hands of Gautamí. [*Exit.*

345

ACT THIRD

Scene.—The Sacred Grove

Enter King Dushyanta, with the air of one in love.

KING [*sighing thoughtfully*].—The holy sage possesses magic
  power
  In virtue of his penance; she, his ward,
  Under the shadow of his tutelage
  Rests in security. I know it well;
  Yet sooner shall the rushing cataract
  In foaming eddies re-ascend the steep,
  Than my fond heart turn back from its pursuit.
God of Love! God of the flowery shafts![6] we are all of
us cruelly deceived by thee, and by the Moon, however
deserving of confidence you may both appear.

  For not to us do these thine arrows seem
  Pointed with tender flowerets; not to us
  Doth the pale moon irradiate the earth
  With beams of silver fraught with cooling dews:—
  But on our fevered frames the moon-beams fall
  Like darts of fire, and every flower-tipped shaft
  Of Káma, as it probes our throbbing hearts,
  Seems to be barbed with hardest adamant.
Adorable god of love! hast thou no pity for me? [*In a
tone of anguish.*] How can thy arrows be so sharp when
they are pointed with flowers? Ah! I know the reason:
  E'en now in thine unbodied essence lurks
  The fire of Śiva's anger, like the flame
  That ever hidden in the secret depths
  Of ocean, smoulders there unseen. How else
  Couldst thou, all immaterial as thou art,

---

 [6] Káma, the Hindoo Cupid, or god of love. He has five arrows, each tipped
with the blossom of a flower, which pierce the heart through the five senses.

346

Inflame our hearts thus fiercely?—thou, whose form
Was scorched to ashes by a sudden flash
From the offended god's terrific eye.
Yet, methinks,
Welcome this anguish, welcome to my heart
These rankling wounds inflicted by the god,
Who on his scutcheon bears the monster-fish
Slain by his prowess: welcome death itself,
So that, commissioned by the lord of love,
This fair one be my executioner.

Adorable divinity! Can I by no reproaches excite your commiseration?
Have I not daily offered at thy shrine
Innumerable vows, the only food
Of thine ethereal essence? Are my prayers
Thus to be slighted? Is it meet that thou
Shouldst aim thy shafts at thy true votary's heart,
Drawing thy bow-string even to thy ear?

[*Pacing up and down in a melancholy manner.*] Now that the holy men have completed their rites, and have no more need of my services, how shall I dispel my melancholy? [*Sighing.*] I have but one resource. Oh for another sight of the idol of my soul! I will seek her. [*Glancing at the sun.*] In all probability, as the sun's heat is now at its height, Śakoontalá is passing her time under the shade of the bowers on the banks of the Máliní, attended by her maidens. I will go and look for her there. [*Walking and looking about.*] I suspect the fair one has but just passed by this avenue of young trees.

Here, as she tripped along, her fingers plucked
The opening buds: these lacerated plants,
Shorn of their fairest blossoms by her hand,
Seem like dismembered trunks, whose recent wounds
Are still unclosed; while from the bleeding socket
Of many a severed stalk, the milky juice
Still slowly trickles, and betrays her path.

[*Feeling a breeze.*] What a delicious breeze meets me in this spot!
Here may the zephyr, fragrant with the scent
Of lotuses, and laden with the spray
Caught from the waters of the rippling stream,

Fold in its close embrace my fevered limbs.
[*Walking and looking about.*] She must be somewhere
in the neighborhood of this arbor of overhanging creepers,
enclosed by plantations of cane.   [*Looking down.*
For at the entrance here I plainly see
A line of footsteps printed in the sand.
Here are the fresh impressions of her feet;
Their well-known outline faintly marked in front,
More deeply towards the heel; betokening
The graceful undulation of her gait.
I will peep through those branches. [*Walking and looking. With transport.*] Ah! now my eyes are gratified
by an entrancing sight. Yonder is the beloved of my heart
reclining on a rock strewn with flowers, and attended by
her two friends. How fortunate! Concealed behind the
leaves, I will listen to their conversation, without raising
their suspicions.   [*Stands concealed, and gazes at them.*

*Sakoontalá and her two attendants, holding fans in their hands,
are discovered as described.*

PRIYAMVADÁ AND ANASÚYÁ [*fanning her. In a tone of affection.*]—Dearest Śakoontalá, is the breeze raised by these
broad lotus leaves refreshing to you?
ŚAKOONTALÁ.—Dear friends, why should you trouble your-
selves to fan me?
[*Priyamvadá and Anasúyá look sorrowfully at one another.*
KING.—Śakoontalá seems indeed to be seriously ill. [*Thought-
fully.*] Can it be the intensity of the heat that has af-
fected her? or does my heart suggest the true cause of
her malady? [*Gazing at her passionately.*] Why should
I doubt it?
The maiden's spotless bosom is o'erspread
With cooling balsam; on her slender arm
Her only bracelet, twined with lotus stalks,
Hangs loose and withered; her recumbent form
Expresses languor. Ne'er could noon-day sun
Inflict such fair disorder on a maid—
No, love, and love alone, is here to blame.
PRIYAMVADÁ [*aside to Anasúyá*].—I have observed, Anasúyá,
that Śakoontalá has been indisposed ever since her first

interview with King Dushyanta. Depend upon it, her
ailment is to be traced to this source.

ANASÚYÁ.—The same suspicion, dear Priyamvadá, has crossed
my mind. But I will at once ask her and ascertain the
truth. [*Aloud.*] Dear Śakoontalá, I am about to put a
question to you. Your indisposition is really very serious.

ŚAKOONTALÁ [*half-rising from her couch*].—What were you
going to ask?

ANASÚYÁ.—We know very little about love-matters, dear
Śakoontalá; but for all that, I cannot help suspecting your
present state to be something similar to that of the lovers
we have read about in romances. Tell us frankly what
is the cause of your disorder. It is useless to apply a
remedy, until the disease be understood.

KING.—Anasúyá bears me out in my suspicion.

ŚAKOONTALÁ [*aside*].—I am, indeed, deeply in love; but cannot rashly disclose my passion to these young girls.

PRIYAMVADÁ.—What Anasúyá says, dear Śakoontalá, is very
just. Why give so little heed to your ailment? Every
day you are becoming thinner; though I must confess
your complexion is still as beautiful as ever.

KING.—Priyamvadá speaks most truly.

> Sunk is her velvet cheek; her wasted bosom
> Loses its fulness; e'en her slender waist
> Grows more attenuate; her face is wan,
> Her shoulders droop;—as when the vernal blasts
> Sear the young blossoms of the Mádhaví,
> Blighting their bloom; so mournful is the change,
> Yet in its sadness, fascinating still,
> Inflicted by the mighty lord of love
> On the fair figure of the hermit's daughter.

ŚAKOONTALÁ.—Dear friends, to no one would I rather reveal
the nature of my malady than to you; but I should only
be troubling you.

PRIYAMVADÁ AND ANASÚYÁ.—Nay, this is the very point about
which we are so solicitous. Sorrow shared with affectionate friends is relieved of half its poignancy.

KING.—Pressed by the partners of her joys and griefs,

> Her much beloved companions, to reveal
> The cherished secret locked within her breast,
> She needs must utter it; although her looks

Encourage me to hope, my bosom throbs
As anxiously I listen for her answer.

SAKOONTALÁ.—Know then, dear friends, that from the first
moment the illustrious Prince, who is the guardian of
our sacred grove, presented himself to my sight—
[*Stops short, and appears confused.*

PRIYAMVADÁ AND ANASÚYÁ.—Say on, dear Śakoontalá, say
on.

SAKOONTALÁ.—Ever since that happy moment, my heart's affections have been fixed upon him, and my energies of
mind and body have all deserted me, as you see.

KING [*with rapture*].—Her own lips have uttered the words
I most longed to hear.
Love lit the flame, and Love himself allays
My burning fever, as when gathering clouds
Rise o'er the earth in summer's dazzling noon,
And grateful showers dispel the morning heat.

SAKOONTALÁ.—You must consent, then, dear friends, to contrive some means by which I may find favor with the King,
or you will have ere long to assist at my funeral.

KING [*with rapture*].—Enough! These words remove all my
doubts.

PRIYAMVADÁ [*aside to Anasúyá*].—She is far gone in love,
dear Anasúyá, and no time ought to be lost. Since she
has fixed her affections on a monarch who is the ornament
of Puru's line, we need not hesitate for a moment to ex-
press our approval.

ANASÚYÁ.—I quite agree with you.

PRIYAMVADÁ [*aloud*].—We wish you joy, dear Śakoontalá.
Your affections are fixed on an object in every respect
worthy of you. The noblest river will unite itself to the
ocean, and the lovely Mádhaví-creeper clings naturally to
the Mango, the only tree capable of supporting it.

KING.—Why need we wonder if the beautiful constellation
Viśákhá pines to be united with the Moon.

ANASÚYÁ.—By what stratagem can we best secure to our
friend the accomplishment of her heart's desire, both
speedily and secretly?

PRIYAMVADÁ.—The latter point is all we have to think about.
As to " speedily," I look upon the whole affair as already
settled.

ANASÚYÁ.—How so?

PRIYAMVADÁ.—Did you not observe how the King betrayed his liking by the tender manner in which he gazed upon her, and how thin he has become the last few days, as if he had been lying awake thinking of her?

KING [*looking at himself*].—Quite true! I certainly am becoming thin from want of sleep:—

As night by night in anxious thought I raise
This wasted arm to rest my sleepless head,
My jewelled bracelet, sullied by the tears
That trickle from my eyes in scalding streams,
Slips towards my elbow from my shrivelled wrist.
Oft I replace the bauble, but in vain;
So easily it spans the fleshless limb
That e'en the rough and corrugated skin,
Scarred by the bow-string, will not check its fall.

PRIYAMVADÁ [*thoughtfully*].—An idea strikes me, Anasúyá. Let Śakoontalá write a love-letter; I will conceal it in a flower, and contrive to drop it in the King's path. He will surely mistake it for the remains of some sacred offering, and will, in all probability, pick it up.

ANASÚYÁ.—A very ingenious device! It has my entire approval; but what says Śakoontalá?

ŚAKOONTALÁ.—I must consider before I can consent to it.

PRIYAMVADÁ.—Could you not, dear Śakoontalá, think of some pretty composition in verse, containing a delicate declaration of your love?

ŚAKOONTALÁ.—Well, I will do my best; but my heart trembles when I think of the chances of a refusal.

KING [*with rapture*].—Too timid maid, here stands the man from whom

Thou fearest a repulse; supremely blessed
To call thee all his own. Well might he doubt
His title to thy love; but how couldst thou
Believe thy beauty powerless to subdue him?

PRIYAMVADÁ AND ANASÚYÁ.—You undervalue your own merits, dear Śakoontalá. What man in his senses would intercept with the skirt of his robe the bright rays of the autumnal moon, which alone can allay the fever of his body?

ŚAKOONTALÁ [*smiling*].—Then it seems I must do as I am bid. [*Sits down and appears to be thinking.*

KING.—How charming she looks! My very eyes forget to
wink, jealous of losing even for an instant a sight so enchanting.

> How beautiful the movement of her brow,
> As through her mind love's tender fancies flow!
> And, as she weighs her thoughts, how sweet to trace
> The ardent passion mantling in her face!

SAKOONTALÁ.—Dear girls, I have thought of a verse, but I
have no writing-materials at hand.

PRIYAMVADÁ.—Write the letters with your nail on this lotus
leaf, which is smooth as a parrot's breast.

SAKOONTALÁ [after writing the verse].—Listen, dear friends,
and tell me whether the ideas are appropriately expressed.

PRIYAMVADÁ AND ANASÚYÁ.—We are all attention.

SAKOONTALÁ [reads].—

> I know not the secret thy bosom conceals,
>> Thy form is not near me to gladden my sight;
> But sad is the tale that my fever reveals,
>> Of the love that consumes me by day and by night.

KING [advancing hastily towards her].—

> Nay, Love does but warm thee, fair maiden—thy frame
>> Only droops like the bud in the glare of the noon;
> But me he consumes with a pitiless flame,
>> As the beams of the day-star destroy the pale moon.

PRIYAMVADÁ AND ANASÚYÁ [looking at him joyfully, and
rising to salute him].—Welcome, the desire of our hearts,
that so speedily presents itself!

> [Sakoontalá makes an effort to rise.

KING.—Nay, trouble not thyself, dear maiden,

> Move not to do me homage; let thy limbs
> Still softly rest upon their flowery couch,
> And gather fragrance from the lotus stalks
> Bruised by the fevered contact of thy frame.

ANASÚYÁ.—Deign, gentle Sir, to seat yourself on the rock on
which our friend is reposing.

> [The King sits down. Sakoontalá is confused.

PRIYAMVADÁ.—Anyone may see at a glance that you are
deeply attached to each other. But the affection I have
for my friend prompts me to say something of which you
hardly require to be informed.

KING.—Do not hesitate to speak out, my good girl. If you

omit to say what is in your mind, you may be sorry for it afterwards.

PRIYAMVADÁ.—Is it not your special office as a King to remove the suffering of your subjects who are in trouble?

KING.—Such is my duty, most assuredly.

PRIYAMVADÁ.—Know, then, that our dear friend has been brought to her present state of suffering entirely through love for you. Her life is in your hands; take pity on her and restore her to health.

KING.—Excellent maiden, our attachment is mutual. It is I who am the most honored by it.

ŚAKOONTALÁ [looking at Priyamvadá].—What do you mean by detaining the King, who must be anxious to return to his royal consorts after so long a separation?

KING.—Sweet maiden, banish from thy mind the thought
That I could love another. Thou dost reign
Supreme, without a rival, in my heart,
And I am thine alone: disown me not,
Else must I die a second deadlier death—
Killed by thy words, as erst by Káma's shafts.

ANASÚYÁ.—Kind Sir, we have heard it said that kings have many favorite consorts. You must not, then, by your behavior towards our dear friend, give her relations cause to sorrow for her.

KING.—Listen, gentle maiden, while in a few words I quiet your anxiety.
Though many beauteous forms my palace grace,
Henceforth two things alone will I esteem
The glory of my royal dynasty;—
My sea-girt realm, and this most lovely maid.

PRIYAMVADÁ AND ANASÚYÁ.—We are satisfied by your assurances.

PRIYAMVADÁ [glancing on one side].—See, Anasúyá, there is our favorite little fawn running about in great distress, and turning its eyes in every direction as if looking for its mother; come, let us help the little thing to find her.
[Both move away.

ŚAKOONTALÁ.—Dear friends, dear friends, leave me not alone and unprotected. Why need you both go?

PRIYAMVADÁ AND ANASÚYÁ.—Unprotected! when the Protector of the world is at your side. [Exeunt.

ŚAKOONTALÁ.—What! have they both really left me?

KING.—Distress not thyself, sweet maiden. Thy adorer is
at hand to wait upon thee.

> Oh, let me tend thee, fair one, in the place
> Of thy dear friends; and, with broad lotus fans,
> Raise cooling breezes to refresh thy frame;
> Or shall I rather, with caressing touch,
> Allay the fever of thy limbs, and soothe
> Thy aching feet, beauteous as blushing lilies?

ŚAKOONTALÁ.—Nay, touch me not. I will not incur the cen-
sure of those whom I am bound to respect.

[Rises and attempts to go.

KING.—Fair one, the heat of noon has not yet subsided, and
thy body is still feeble.

> How canst thou quit thy fragrant couch of flowers,
> And from thy throbbing bosom cast aside
> Its covering of lotus leaves, to brave
> With weak and fainting limbs the noon-day heat?

[Forces her to turn back.

ŚAKOONTALÁ.—Infringe not the rules of decorum, mighty descendant of Puru. Remember, though I love you, I have
no power to dispose of myself.

KING.—Why this fear of offending your relations, timid maid?
When your venerable foster-father hears of it, he will not
find fault with you. He knows that the law permits us
to be united without consulting him.

> In Indra's heaven, so at least 'tis said,
> No nuptial rites prevail,[7] nor is the bride
> Led to the altar by her future spouse;
> But all in secret does the bridegroom plight
> His troth, and each unto the other vow
> Mutual allegiance. Such espousals, too,
> Are authorized on earth, and many daughters
> Of royal saints thus wedded to their lords,
> Have still received their father's benison.

ŚAKOONTALÁ.—Leave me, leave me; I must take counsel with
my female friends.

KING.—I will leave thee when——

ŚAKOONTALÁ.—When?

---

[7] A marriage without the usual ceremonies is called Gándharva. It was supposed to be the form of marriage prevalent among the nymphs of Indra's
heaven.

KING.—When I have gently stolen from thy lips
    Their yet untasted nectar, to allay
    The raging of my thirst, e'en as the bee
    Sips the fresh honey from the opening bud.
[*Attempts to raise her face. Śakoontalá tries to prevent him.*
A VOICE [*behind the scenes*].—The loving birds, doomed by
    fate to nightly separation, must bid farewell to each other,
    for evening is at hand.
ŚAKOONTALÁ [*in confusion*].—Great Prince, I hear the voice
    of the matron Gautamí. She is coming this way, to in-
    quire after my health. Hasten and conceal yourself be-
    hind the branches.
KING.—I will.   [*Conceals himself.*

*Enter Gautamí with a vase in her hand, preceded by two
attendants.*

ATTENDANTS.—This way, most venerable Gautamí.
GAUTAMÍ [*approaching Śakoontalá*].—My child, is the fever
    of thy limbs allayed?
ŚAKOONTALÁ.—Venerable mother, there is certainly a change
    for the better.
GAUTAMÍ.—Let me sprinkle you with this holy water, and all
    your ailments will depart. [*Sprinkling Śakoontalá on
    the head.*] The day is closing, my child; come, let us go
    to the cottage.   [*They all move away.*
ŚAKOONTALÁ [*aside*].—Oh my heart! thou didst fear to taste
    of happiness when it was within thy reach. Now that
    the object of thy desires is torn from thee, how bitter will
    be thy remorse, how distracting thine anguish! [*Mov-
    ing on a few steps and stopping. Aloud.*] Farewell!
    bower of creepers, sweet soother of my sufferings, fare-
    well! may I soon again be happy under thy shade.
                    [*Exit reluctantly with the others.*
KING [*returning to his former seat in the arbor. Sighing*].—
    Alas! how many are the obstacles to the accomplishment
    of our wishes!
    Albeit she did coyly turn away
    Her glowing cheek, and with her fingers guard
    Her pouting lips, that murmured a denial
    In faltering accents, she did yield herself

A sweet reluctant captive to my will,
As eagerly I raised her lovely face:
But ere with gentle force I stole the kiss,
Too envious Fate did mar my daring purpose.

Whither now shall I betake myself? I will tarry for a brief space in this bower of creepers, so endeared to me by the presence of my beloved Śakoontalá.

[*Looking round.*

Here printed on the flowery couch I see
The fair impression of her slender limbs;
Here is the sweet confession of her love,
Traced with her nail upon the lotus leaf—
And yonder are the withered lily stalks
That graced her wrist. While all around I view
Things that recall her image, can I quit
This bower, e'en though its living charm be fled?

A VOICE [*in the air*].—Great King,
Scarce is our evening sacrifice begun,
When evil demons, lurid as the clouds
That gather round the dying orb of day,
Cluster in hideous troops, obscene and dread,
About our altars, casting far and near
Terrific shadows, while the sacred fire
Sheds a pale lustre o'er their ghostly shapes.

KING.—I come to the rescue, I come.   [*Exit.*

PRELUDE TO ACT FOURTH

Scene.—The Garden of the Hermitage

Enter Priyamvadá and Anasúyá in the act of gathering flowers.

ANASÚYÁ.—Although, dear Priyamvadá, it rejoices my heart to think that Śakoontalá has been happily united to a husband in every respect worthy of her, by the form of marriage prevalent among Indra's celestial musicians, nevertheless, I cannot help feeling somewhat uneasy in my mind.

PRIYAMVADÁ.—How so?

ANASÚYÁ.—You know that the pious King was gratefully dismissed by the hermits on the successful termination of their sacrificial rites. He has now returned to his capital, leaving Śakoontalá under our care; and it may be doubted whether, in the society of his royal consorts, he will not forget all that has taken place in this hermitage of ours.

PRIYAMVADÁ.—On that score be at ease. Persons of his noble nature are not so destitute of all honorable feeling. I confess, however, that there is one point about which I am rather anxious. What, think you, will father Kanwa say when he hears what has occurred?

ANASÚYÁ.—In my opinion, he will approve the marriage.

PRIYAMVADÁ.—What makes you think so?

ANASÚYÁ.—From the first, it was always his fixed purpose to bestow the maiden on a husband worthy of her; and since heaven has given her such a husband, his wishes have been realized without any trouble to himself.

PRIYAMVADÁ [*looking at the flower-basket*].—We have gathered flowers enough for the sacred offering, dear Anasúyá.

ANASÚYÁ.—Well, then, let us now gather more, that we may

357

have wherewith to propitiate the guardian-deity of our
dear Śakoontalá.

PRIYAMVADÁ.—By all means.   [*They continue gathering.*

A VOICE [*behind the scenes*].—Ho there! See you not that I
am here?

ANASÚYÁ [*listening*].—That must be the voice of a guest announcing his arrival.

PRIYAMVADÁ.—Surely, Śakoontalá is not absent from the cottage. [*Aside.*] Her heart at least is absent, I fear.

ANASÚYÁ.—Come along, come along; we have gathered flowers enough.   [*They move away.*

THE SAME VOICE [*behind the scenes*].—Woe to thee, maiden,
for daring to slight a guest like me!

    Shall I stand here unwelcomed; even I,
    A very mine of penitential merit,
    Worthy of all respect? Shalt thou, rash maid,
    Thus set at nought the ever sacred ties
    Of hospitality? and fix thy thoughts
    Upon the cherished object of thy love,
    While I am present? Thus I curse thee, then—
    He, even he of whom thou thinkest, he
    Shall think no more of thee; nor in his heart
    Retain thine image. Vainly shalt thou strive
    To waken his remembrance of the past;
    He shall disown thee, even as the sot,
    Roused from his midnight drunkenness, denies
    The words he uttered in his revellings.

PRIYAMVADÁ.—Alas! alas! I fear a terrible misfortune has
occurred. Śakoontalá, from absence of mind, must have
offended some guest whom she was bound to treat with
respect. [*Looking behind the scenes.*] Ah! yes; I see,
and no less a person than the great sage Durvasas, who
is known to be most irascible. He it is that has just cursed
her, and is now retiring with hasty strides, trembling with
passion, and looking as if nothing could turn him. His
wrath is like a consuming fire.

ANASÚYÁ.—Go quickly, dear Priyamvadá, throw yourself at
his feet, and persuade him to come back, while I prepare
a propitiatory offering for him, with water and refresh-
ments.

PRIYAMVADÁ.—I will.   [*Exit.*

ANASÚYÁ [*advancing hastily a few steps and stumbling*].—
Alas! alas! this comes of being in a hurry. My foot has
slipped and my basket of flowers has fallen from my hand.
[*Stays to gather them up.*

PRIYAMVADÁ [*reëntering*].—Well, dear Anasúyá, I have done
my best; but what living being could succeed in pacify-
ing such a cross-grained, ill-tempered old fellow? However, I managed to mollify him a little.

ANASÚYÁ [*smiling*].—Even a little was much for him. Say
on.

PRIYAMVADÁ.—When he refused to turn back, I implored his
forgiveness in these words: " Most venerable sage, pardon, I beseech you, this first offence of a young and in-
experienced girl, who was ignorant of the respect due to
your saintly character and exalted rank."

ANASÚYÁ.—And what did he reply?

PRIYAMVADÁ.—" My word must not be falsified; but at the
sight of the ring of recognition the spell shall cease." So
saying, he disappeared.

ANASÚYÁ.—Oh! then we may breathe again; for now I think
of it, the King himself, at his departure, fastened on
Śakoontalá's finger, as a token of remembrance, a ring
on which his own name was engraved. She has, therefore, a remedy for her misfortune at her own command.

PRIYAMVADÁ.—Come, dear Anasúyá, let us proceed with our
religious duties. [*They walk away.*

PRIYAMVADÁ [*looking off the stage*].—See, Anasúyá, there
sits our dear friend, motionless as a statue, resting her
face on her left hand, her whole mind absorbed in thinking of her absent husband. She can pay no attention to
herself, much less to a stranger.

ANASÚYÁ.—Priyamvadá, let this affair never pass our lips.
We must spare our dear friend's feelings. Her constitution is too delicate to bear much emotion.

PRIYAMVADÁ.—I agree with you. Who would think of watering a tender jasmine with hot water?

ACT FOURTH

Scene.—The Neighborhood of the Hermitage

Enter one of Kanwa's pupils, just arisen from his couch at the dawn of day.

PUPIL.—My master, the venerable Kanwa, who is but lately returned from his pilgrimage, has ordered me to ascertain how the time goes. I have therefore come into the open air to see if it be still dark. [*Walking and looking about.*] Oh! the dawn has already broken.

> Lo! in one quarter of the sky, the Moon,
> Lord of the herbs and night-expanding flowers,
> Sinks towards his bed behind the western hills;
> While in the east, preceded by the Dawn,
> His blushing charioteer, the glorious Sun
> Begins his course, and far into the gloom
> Casts the first radiance of his orient beams.
> Hail! co-eternal orbs, that rise to set,
> And set to rise again; symbols divine
> Of man's reverses, life's vicissitudes.

And now,

> While the round Moon withdraws his looming disc
> Beneath the western sky, the full-blown flower
> Of the night-loving lotus sheds her leaves
> In sorrow for his loss, bequeathing nought
> But the sweet memory of her loveliness
> To my bereavèd sight: e'en as the bride
> Disconsolately mourns her absent lord,
> And yields her heart a prey to anxious grief.

ANASÚYÁ [*entering abruptly*].—Little as I know of the ways of the world, I cannot help thinking that King Dushyanta is treating Śakoontalá very improperly.

PUPIL.—Well, I must let my revered preceptor know that it is time to offer the burnt oblation.   [*Exit.*

ANASÚYÁ.—I am broad awake, but what shall I do? I have no energy to go about my usual occupations. My hands and feet seem to have lost their power. Well, Love has gained his object; and Love only is to blame for having induced our dear friend, in the innocence of her heart, to confide in such a perfidious man. Possibly, however, the imprecation of Durvasas may be already taking effect. Indeed, I cannot otherwise account for the King's strange conduct, in allowing so long a time to elapse without even a letter; and that, too, after so many promises and protestations. I cannot think what to do, unless we send him the ring which was to be the token of recognition. But which of these austere hermits could we ask to be the bearer of it? Then, again, Father Kanwa has just returned from his pilgrimage: and how am I to inform him of Śakoontalá's marriage to King Dushyanta, and her expectation of being soon a mother? I never could bring myself to tell him, even if I felt that Śakoontalá had been in fault, which she certainly has not. What is to be done?

PRIYAMVADÁ [*entering; joyfully*].—Quick! quick! Anasúyá! come and assist in the joyful preparations for Śakoontalá's departure to her husband's palace.

ANASÚYÁ.—My dear girl, what can you mean?

PRIYAMVADÁ.—Listen, now, and I will tell you all about it. I went just now to Śakoontalá, to inquire whether she had slept comfortably——

ANASÚYÁ.—Well, well; go on.

PRIYAMVADÁ.—She was sitting with her face bowed down to the very ground with shame, when Father Kanwa entered and, embracing her, of his own accord offered her his congratulations. " I give thee joy, my child," he said, " we have had an auspicious omen. The priest who offered the oblation dropped it into the very centre of the sacred fire, though thick smoke obstructed his vision. Henceforth thou wilt cease to be an object of compassion. This very day I purpose sending thee, under the charge of certain trusty hermits, to the King's palace; and shall deliver thee into the hands of thy husband, as I would commit knowledge to the keeping of a wise and faithful student."

ANASÚYÁ.—Who, then, informed the holy Father of what passed in his absence?

PRIYAMVADÁ.—As he was entering the sanctuary of the consecrated fire, an invisible being chanted a verse in celestial strains.

ANASÚYÁ [*with astonishment*].—Indeed! pray repeat it.

PRIYAMVADÁ [*repeats the verse*].—

> Glows in thy daughter King Dushyanta's glory,
> As in the sacred tree the mystic fire.
> Let worlds rejoice to hear the welcome story;
> And may the son immortalize the sire.

ANASÚYÁ [*embracing Priyamvadá*].—Oh, my dear Priyamvadá, what delightful news! I am pleased beyond measure; yet when I think that we are to lose our dear Sakoontalá this very day, a feeling of melancholy mingles with my joy.

PRIYAMVADÁ.—We shall find means of consoling ourselves after her departure. Let the dear creature only be made happy, at any cost.

ANASÚYÁ.—Yes, yes, Priyamvadá, it shall be so; and now to prepare our bridal array. I have always looked forward to this occasion, and some time since, I deposited a beautiful garland of Keśara flowers in a cocoa-nut box, and suspended it on a bough of yonder mango-tree. Be good enough to stretch out your hand and take it down, while I compound unguents and perfumes with this consecrated paste and these blades of sacred grass.

PRIYAMVADÁ.—Very well.

[*Exit Anasúyá. Priyamvadá takes down the flowers.*

A VOICE [*behind the scenes*].—Gautamí, bid Sárngarava and the others hold themselves in readiness to escort Sakoontalá.

PRIYAMVADÁ [*listening*].—Quick, quick, Anasúyá! They are calling the hermits who are to go with Sakoontalá to Hastinápur.

ANASÚYÁ [*reëntering, with the perfumed unguents in her hand*].—Come along then, Priyamvadá; I am ready to go with you. [*They walk away.*

PRIYAMVADÁ [*looking*].—See! there sits Sakoontalá, her locks arranged even at this early hour of the morning. The holy women of the hermitage are congratulating her, and invoking blessings on her head, while they present her with wedding-gifts and offerings of consecrated wild-rice. Let us join them. [*They approach.*

Śakoontalá is seen seated, with women surrounding her, occupied in the manner described.

FIRST WOMAN [*to Śakoontalá*].—My child, may'st thou receive the title of " Chief-queen," and may thy husband delight to honor thee above all others!

SECOND WOMAN.—My child, may'st thou be the mother of a hero!

THIRD WOMAN.—My child, may'st thou be highly honored by thy lord!

[*Exeunt all the women, excepting Gautami, after blessing Śakoontalá.*

PRIYAMVADÁ AND ANASÚYÁ [*approaching*].—Dear Śakoontalá, we are come to assist you at your toilet, and may a blessing attend it!

ŚAKOONTALÁ.—Welcome, dear friends, welcome. Sit down here.

PRIYAMVADÁ AND ANASÚYÁ [*taking the baskets containing the bridal decorations, and sitting down*].—Now, then, dearest, prepare to let us dress you. We must first rub your limbs with these perfumed unguents.

ŚAKOONTALÁ.—I ought indeed to be grateful for your kind offices, now that I am so soon to be deprived of them. Dear, dear friends, perhaps I shall never be dressed by you again. [*Bursts into tears.*

PRIYAMVADÁ AND ANASÚYÁ.—Weep not, dearest, tears are out of season on such a happy occasion.

[*They wipe away her tears and begin to dress her.*

PRIYAMVADÁ.—Alas! these simple flowers and rude ornaments which our hermitage offers in abundance, do not set off your beauty as it deserves.

Enter two young Hermits, bearing costly presents.

BOTH HERMITS.—Here are ornaments suitable for a queen.

[*The women look at them in astonishment.*

GAUTAMÍ.—Why, Nárada, my son, whence came these?

FIRST HERMIT.—You owe them to the devotion of Father Kanwa.

GAUTAMÍ.—Did he create them by the power of his own mind?

SECOND HERMIT.—Certainly not; but you shall hear. The venerable sage ordered us to collect flowers for Śakoontalá from the forest-trees; and we went to the wood for that purpose, when

> Straightway depending from a neighboring tree
> Appeared a robe of linen tissue, pure
> And spotless as a moon-beam—mystic pledge
> Of bridal happiness; another tree
> Distilled a roseate dye wherewith to stain
> The lady's feet; and other branches near
> Glistened with rare and costly ornaments.
> While, 'midst the leaves, the hands of forest-nymphs,
> Vying in beauty with the opening buds,
> Presented us with sylvan offerings.

PRIYAMVADÁ [*looking at Śakoontalá*].—The wood-nymphs have done you honor, indeed. This favor doubtless signifies that you are soon to be received as a happy wife into your husband's house, and are from this forward to become the partner of his royal fortunes.

[*Śakoontalá appears confused.*

FIRST HERMIT.—Come, Gautama; Father Kanwa has finished his ablutions. Let us go and inform him of the favor we have received from the deities who preside over our trees.

SECOND HERMIT.—By all means. [*Exeunt.*

PRIYAMVADÁ AND ANASÚYÁ.—Alas! what are we to do? We are unused to such splendid decorations, and are at a loss how to arrange them. Our knowledge of painting must be our guide. We will dispose the ornaments as we have seen them in pictures.

ŚAKOONTALÁ.—Whatever pleases you, dear girls, will please me. I have perfect confidence in your taste.

[*They commence dressing her.*

Enter Kanwa, having just finished his ablutions.

KANWA.—This day my loved one leaves me, and my heart
> Is heavy with its grief: the streams of sorrow
> Choked at the source, repress my faltering voice.

I have no words to speak; mine eyes are dimmed
By the dark shadows of the thoughts that rise
Within my soul. If such the force of grief
In an old hermit parted from his nursling,
What anguish must the stricken parent feel—
Bereft forever of an only daughter?

[*Advances towards Śakoontalá.*

PRIYAMVADÁ AND ANASÚYÁ.—Now, dearest Śakoontalá, we have finished decorating you. You have only to put on the two linen mantles.

[*Śakoontalá rises and puts them on.*

GAUTAMÍ.—Daughter, see, here comes thy foster-father; he is eager to fold thee in his arms; his eyes swim with tears of joy. Hasten to do him reverence.

ŚAKOONTALÁ [*reverently*].—My father, I salute you.

KANWA.—My daughter,

May'st thou be highly honored by thy lord,
E'en as Yayáti Śarmishthá adored!
And, as she bore him Puru, so may'st thou
Bring forth a son to whom the world shall bow!

GAUTAMÍ.—Most venerable father, she accepts your benediction as if she already possessed the boon it confers.

KANWA.—Now come this way, my child, and walk reverently round these sacrificial fires. [*They all walk round.*

KANWA [*repeats a prayer in the metre of the Rig-veda*].—

Holy flames, that gleam around
Every altar's hallowed ground;
Holy flames, whose frequent food
Is the consecrated wood,
And for whose encircling bed,
Sacred Kuśa-grass is spread;
Holy flames, that waft to heaven
Sweet oblations daily given,
Mortal guilt to purge away;—
Hear, oh hear me, when I pray—
Purify my child this day!

Now then, my daughter, set out on thy journey. [*Looking on one side.*] Where are thy attendants, Sárngarava and the others?

YOUNG HERMIT [*entering*].—Here we are, most venerable father.

KANWA.—Lead the way for thy sister.

ŚÁRNGARAVA.—Come, Śakoontalá, let us proceed.

[*All move away.*

KANWA.—Hear me, ye trees that surround our hermitage!
Śakoontalá ne'er moistened in the stream
Her own parched lips, till she had fondly poured
Its purest water on your thirsty roots;
And oft, when she would fain have decked her hair
With your thick-clustering blossoms, in her love
She robbed you not e'en of a single flower.
Her highest joy was ever to behold
The early glory of your opening buds:
Oh, then, dismiss her with a kind farewell!
This very day she quits her father's home,
To seek the palace of her wedded lord.

[*The note of a Köil is heard.*

Hark! heard'st thou not the answer of the trees,
Our sylvan sisters, warbled in the note
Of the melodious Köil? they dismiss
Their dear Śakoontalá with loving wishes.

VOICES [*in the air*].—
Fare thee well, journey pleasantly on amid streams
Where the lotuses bloom, and the sun's glowing beams
Never pierce the deep shade of the wide-spreading trees,
While gently around thee shall sport the cool breeze;
Then light be thy footsteps and easy thy tread,
Beneath thee shall carpets of lilies be spread.
Journey on to thy lord, let thy spirit be gay,
For the smiles of all Nature shall gladden thy way.

[*All listen with astonishment.*

GAUTAMÍ.—Daughter! the nymphs of the wood, who love
thee with the affection of a sister, dismiss thee with kind
wishes for thy happiness. Take thou leave of them
reverentially.

ŚAKOONTALÁ [*bowing respectfully and walking on. Aside to
her friend*].—Eager as I am, dear Priyamvadá, to see
my hsuband once more, yet my feet refuse to move, now
that I am quitting forever the home of my girlhood.

PRIYAMVADÁ.—You are not the only one, dearest, to feel the
bitterness of parting. As the time of separation ap-
proaches, the whole grove seems to share your anguish.

In sorrow for thy loss, the herd of deer
Forget to browse; the peacock on the lawn
Ceases its dance; the very trees around us
Shed their pale leaves, like tears, upon the ground.

ŚAKOONTALÁ [*recollecting herself*].—My father, let me, before I go, bid adieu to my pet jasmine, the Moonlight of the Grove. I love the plant almost as a sister.

KANWA.—Yes, yes, my child, I remember thy sisterly affection for the creeper. Here it is on the right.

ŚAKOONTALÁ [*approaching the jasmine*].—My beloved jasmine, most brilliant of climbing plants, how sweet it is to see thee cling thus fondly to thy husband, the mango-tree; yet, prithee, turn thy twining arms for a moment in this direction to embrace thy sister; she is going far away, and may never see thee again.

KANWA.—Daughter, the cherished purpose of my heart
Has ever been to wed thee to a spouse
That should be worthy of thee; such a spouse
Hast thou thyself, by thine own merits, won.
To him thou goest, and about his neck
Soon shalt thou cling confidingly, as now
Thy favorite jasmine twines its loving arms
Around the sturdy mango. Leave thou it
To its protector—e'en as I consign
Thee to thy lord, and henceforth from my mind
Banish all anxious thought on thy behalf.
Proceed on thy journey, my child.

ŚAKOONTALÁ [*to Priyamvadá and Anasúyá*].—To you, my sweet companions, I leave it as a keepsake. Take charge of it when I am gone.

PRIYAMVADÁ AND ANASÚYÁ [*bursting into tears*].—And to whose charge do you leave us, dearest? Who will care for us when you are gone?

KANWA.—For shame, Anasúyá! dry your tears. Is this the way to cheer your friend at a time when she needs your support and consolation?   [*All move on.*

ŚAKOONTALÁ.—My father, see you there my pet deer, grazing close to the hermitage? She expects soon to fawn, and even now the weight of the little one she carries hinders her movements. Do not forget to send me word when she becomes a mother.

KANWA.—I will not forget it.

SAKOONTALÁ [*feeling herself drawn back*].—What can this
    be, fastened to my dress?   [*Turns round.*

KANWA.—My daughter,
    It is the little fawn, thy foster-child.
    Poor helpless orphan! it remembers well
    How with a mother's tenderness and love
    Thou didst protect it, and with grains of rice
    From thine own hand didst daily nourish it;
    And, ever and anon, when some sharp thorn
    Had pierced its mouth, how gently thou didst tend
    The bleeding wound, and pour in healing balm.
    The grateful nursling clings to its protectress,
    Mutely imploring leave to follow her.

SAKOONTALÁ.—My poor little fawn, dost thou ask to follow
    an unhappy woman who hesitates not to desert her com-
    panions? When thy mother died, soon after thy birth,
    I supplied her place, and reared thee with my own hand;
    and now that thy second mother is about to leave thee, who
    will care for thee? My father, be thou a mother to her.
    My child, go back, and be a daughter to my father.
                      [*Moves on, weeping.*

KANWA.—Weep not, my daughter, check the gathering tear
    That lurks beneath thine eyelid, ere it flow
    And weaken thy resolve; be firm and true—
    True to thyself and me; the path of life
    Will lead o'er hill and plain, o'er rough and smooth,
    And all must feel the steepness of the way;
    Though rugged be thy course, press boldly on.

SÁRNGARAVA.—Venerable sire! the sacred precept is—" Ac-
    company thy friend as far as the margin of the first
    stream." Here then, we are arrived at the border of a
    lake. It is time for you to give us your final instructions
    and return.

KANWA.—Be it so; let us tarry for a moment under the shade
    of this fig-tree.   [*They do so.*

KANWA [*aside*].—I must think of some appropriate message
    to send to his majesty King Dushyanta.   [*Reflects.*

SAKOONTALÁ [*aside to Anasúyá*].—See, see, dear Anasúyá, the
    poor female Chakravâka-bird, whom cruel fate dooms to
    nightly separation from her mate, calls to him in mourn-

ful notes from the other side of the stream, though he is
only hidden from her view by the spreading leaves of the
water-lily. Her cry is so piteous that I could almost fancy
she was lamenting her hard lot in intelligible words.

ANASÚYÁ.—Say not so, dearest.

> Fond bird! though sorrow lengthen out her night
> Of widowhood, yet with a cry of joy
> She hails the morning light that brings her mate
> Back to her side. The agony of parting
> Would wound us like a sword, but that its edge
> Is blunted by the hope of future meeting.

KANWA.—Sárngarava, when you have introduced Śakoontalá
into the presence of the King, you must give him this message from me.

SÁRNGARAVA.—Let me hear it, venerable father.

KANWA.—This is it—

> Most puissant prince! we here present before thee
> One thou art bound to cherish and receive
> As thine own wife; yea, even to enthrone
> As thine own queen—worthy of equal love
> With thine imperial consorts. So much, Sire,
> We claim of thee as justice due to us,
> In virtue of our holy character—
> In virtue of thine honorable rank—
> In virtue of the pure spontaneous love
> That secretly grew up 'twixt thee and her,
> Without consent or privity of us.
> We ask no more—the rest we freely leave
> To thy just feeling and to destiny.

SÁRNGARAVA.—A most suitable message. I will take care to
deliver it correctly.

KANWA.—And now, my child, a few words of advice for thee.
We hermits, though we live secluded from the world, are
not ignorant of worldly matters.

SÁRNGARAVA.—No, indeed. Wise men are conversant with all
subjects.

KANWA.—Listen, then, my daughter. When thou reachest
thy husband's palace, and art admitted into his family,

> Honor thy betters; ever be respectful
> To those above thee; and, should others share
> Thy husband's love, ne'er yield thyself a prey

To jealousy; but ever be a friend,
A loving friend, to those who rival thee
In his affections. Should thy wedded lord
Treat thee with harshness, thou must never be
Harsh in return, but patient and submissive.
Be to thy menials courteous, and to all
Placed under thee, considerate and kind:
Be never self-indulgent, but avoid
Excess in pleasure; and, when fortune smiles,
Be not puffed up. Thus to thy husband's house
Wilt thou a blessing prove, and not a curse.
What thinks Gautamí of this advice?

GAUTAMÍ.—An excellent compendium, truly, of every wife's
duties! Lay it well to heart, my daughter.

KANWA.—Come, my beloved child, one parting embrace for
me and for thy companions, and then we leave thee.

ŚAKOONTALÁ.—My father, must Priyamvadá and Anasúyá
really return with you? They are very dear to me.

KANWA.—Yes, my child; they, too, in good time, will be given
in marriage to suitable husbands. It would not be proper
for them to accompany thee to such a public place. But
Gautamí shall be thy companion.

ŚAKOONTALÁ [embracing him].—Removed from thy bosom,
my beloved father, like a young tendril of the sandal-tree
torn from its home in the western mountains,[8] how shall
I be able to support life in a foreign soil?

KANWA.—Daughter, thy fears are groundless:—
Soon shall thy lord prefer thee to the rank
Of his own consort; and unnumbered cares
Befitting his imperial dignity
Shall constantly engross thee. Then the bliss
Of bearing him a son—a noble boy,
Bright as the day-star—shall transport thy soul
With new delights, and little shalt thou reck
Of the light sorrow that afflicts thee now
At parting from thy father and thy friends.
    [Śakoontalá throws herself at her foster-father's feet.

KANWA.—Blessings on thee, my child! May all my hopes of
thee be realized!

---

[8] The sandal-tree is a large kind of myrtle, with pointed leaves. The wood affords many highly esteemed perfumes and is celebrated for its delicious scent. It is chiefly found on the slopes of the Malay mountains or Western Ghants, on the Malabar coast.

ŚAKOONTALÁ [*approaching her friends*].—Come, my two loved companions, embrace me—both of you together.

PRIYAMVADÁ AND ANASÚYÁ [*embracing her*].—Dear Śakoontalá, remember, if the King should by any chance be slow in recognizing you, you have only to show him this ring, on which his own name is engraved.

ŚAKOONTALÁ.—The bare thought of it puts me in a tremor.

PRIYAMVADÁ AND ANASÚYÁ.—There is no real cause for fear, dearest. Excessive affection is too apt to suspect evil where none exists.

ŚÁRNGARAVA.—Come, lady, we must hasten on. The sun is rising in the heavens.

ŚAKOONTALÁ [*looking towards the hermitage*].—Dear father, when shall I ever see this hallowed grove again?

KANWA.—I will tell thee; listen—

When thou hast passed a long and blissful life
As King Dushyanta's queen, and jointly shared
With all the earth his ever-watchful care;
And hast beheld thine own heroic son,
Matchless in arms, united to a spouse
In happy wedlock; when his aged sire,
Thy faithful husband, hath to him resigned
The helm of state; then, weary of the world,
Together with Dushyanta thou shalt seek
The calm seclusion of thy former home:—
There amid holy scenes to be at peace,
Till thy pure spirit gain its last release.

GAUTAMÍ.—Come, my child, the favorable time for our journey is fast passing. Let thy father return. Venerable Sire, be thou the first to move homewards, or these last words will never end.

KANWA.—Daughter, detain me no longer. My religious duties must not be interrupted.

ŚAKOONTALÁ [*again embracing her foster-father*].—Beloved father, thy frame is much enfeebled by penitential exercises. Do not, oh! do not, allow thyself to sorrow too much on my account.

KANWA [*sighing*].—How, O my child, shall my bereavèd heart
Forget its bitterness, when, day by day,
Full in my sight shall grow the tender plants
Reared by thy care, or sprung from hallowed **grain**

Which thy loved hands have strewn around the door—
A frequent offering to our household gods?
Go, my daughter, and may thy journey be prosperous.

                [Exit Sakoontalá with her escort.

PRIYAMVADÁ AND ANASÚYÁ [*gazing after Sakoontalá*].—
Alas! alas! she is gone, and now the trees hide our darling from our view.

KANWA [*sighing*].—Well, Anasúyá, your sister has departed.
Moderate your grief, both of you, and follow me. I go
back to the hermitage.

PRIYAMVADÁ AND ANASÚYÁ.—Holy father, the sacred grove
will be a desert without Sakoontalá. How can we ever
return to it?

KANWA.—It is natural enough that your affection should make
you view it in this light. [*Walking pensively on.*] As
for me, I am quite surprised at myself. Now that I have
fairly dismissed her to her husband's house, my mind is
easy: for indeed,

    A daughter is a loan—a precious jewel
    Lent to a parent till her husband claim her.
    And now that to her rightful lord and master
    I have delivered her, my burdened soul
    Is lightened, and I seem to breathe more freely.

                              [Exeunt.

ACT FIFTH

Scene.—A Room in the Palace

The King Dushyanta and the Jester Máthavya are discovered seated.

MÁTHAVYA [*listening*].—Hark! my dear friend, listen a minute, and you will hear sweet sounds próceeding from the music-room. Someone is singing a charming air. Who can it be? Oh! I know. The queen Hansapadiká is practising her notes, that she may greet you with a new song.

KING.—Hush! Let me listen.

A VOICE [*sings behind the scenes*].—

How often hither didst thou rove,
Sweet bee, to kiss the mango's cheek;
Oh! leave not, then, thy early love,
The lily's honeyed lip to seek.

KING.—A most impassioned strain, truly!

MÁTHAVYA.—Do you understand the meaning of the words?

KING [*smiling*].—She means to reprove me, because I once paid her great attention, and have lately deserted her for the queen Vasumatí. Go, my dear fellow, and tell Hansapadiká from me that I take her delicate reproof as it is intended.

MÁTHAVYA.—Very well. [*Rising from his seat.*] But stay —I don't much relish being sent to bear the brunt of her jealousy. The chances are that she will have me seized by the hair of the head and beaten to a jelly. I would as soon expose myself, after a vow of celibacy, to the seductions of a lovely nymph, as encounter the fury of a jealous woman.

KING.—Go, go; you can disarm her wrath by a civil speech; but give her my message.

MÁTHAVYA.—What must be must be, I suppose. [*Exit.*

KING [*aside*].—Strange! that song has filled me with a most
peculiar sensation. A melancholy feeling has come over
me, and I seem to yearn after some long-forgotten object
of affection. Singular, indeed! but,

Not seldom in our happy hours of ease,
When thought is still, the sight of some fair form,
Or mournful fall of music breathing low,
Will stir strange fancies, thrilling all the soul
With a mysterious sadness, and a sense
Of vague yet earnest longing. Can it be
That the dim memory of events long past,
Or friendships formed in other states of being,
Flits like a passing shadow o'er the spirit?

[*Remains pensive and sad.*

Enter the Chamberlain.

CHAMBERLAIN.—Alas! to what an advanced period of life
have I attained!

Even this wand betrays the lapse of years;
In youthful days 'twas but a useless badge
And symbol of my office; now it serves
As a support to prop my tottering steps.

Ah me! I feel very unwilling to announce to the King
that a deputation of young hermits from the sage Kanwa
has arrived, and craves an immediate audience. Certainly,
his majesty ought not to neglect a matter of sacred duty,
yet I hardly like to trouble him when he has just risen
from the judgment-seat. Well, well; a monarch's business is to sustain the world, and he must not expect much
repose; because—

Onward, forever onward, in his car
The unwearied Sun pursues his daily course,
Nor tarries to unyoke his glittering steeds.
And ever moving speeds the rushing Wind
Through boundless space, filling the universe
With his life-giving breezes. Day and night,
The King of Serpents on his thousand heads
Upholds the incumbent earth; and even so,
Unceasing toil is aye the lot of kings,
Who, in return, draw nurture from their subjects.

I will therefore deliver my message. [*Walking on and looking about.*] Ah! here comes the King:—

His subjects are his children; through the day,
Like a fond father, to supply their wants,
Incessantly he labors; wearied now,
The monarch seeks seclusion and repose—
E'en as the prince of elephants defies
The sun's fierce heat, and leads the fainting herd
To verdant pastures, ere his wayworn limbs
He yields to rest beneath the cooling shade.

[*Approaching.*] Victory to the King! So please your majesty, some hermits who live in a forest near the Snowy Mountains have arrived here, bringing certain women with them. They have a message to deliver from the sage Kanwa, and desire an audience. I await your Majesty's commands.

KING [*respectfully*].—A message from the sage Kanwa, did you say?

CHAMBERLAIN.—Even so, my liege.

KING.—Tell my domestic priest, Somaráta, to receive the hermits with due honor, according to the prescribed form. He may then himself introduce them into my presence. I will await them in a place suitable for the reception of such holy guests.

CHAMBERLAIN.—Your Majesty's commands shall be obeyed.
                                             [*Exit.*

KING [*rising and addressing the Warder*].—Vetravati, lead the way to the chamber of the consecrated fire.

WARDER.—This way, Sire.

KING [*walking on, with the air of one oppressed by the cares of government*].—People are generally contented and happy when they have gained their desires; but kings have no sooner attained the object of their aspirations than all their troubles begin.

'Tis a fond thought that to attain the end
And object of ambition is to rest;
Success doth only mitigate the fever
Of anxious expectation; soon the fear
Of losing what we have, the constant care
Of guarding it doth weary. Ceaseless toil

Must be the lot of him who with his hands
Supports the canopy that shields his subjects.

Two Heralds [*behind the scenes*].—May the King be victorious!

First Herald.—Honor to him who labors day by day
For the world's weal, forgetful of his own.
Like some tall tree that with its stately head
Endures the solar beam, while underneath
It yields refreshing shelter to the weary.

Second Herald.—Let but the monarch wield his threatening rod
And e'en the guilty tremble; at his voice
The rebel spirit cowers; his grateful subjects
Acknowledge him their guardian; rich and poor
Hail him a faithful friend, a loving kinsman.

King.—Weary as I was before, this complimentary address has refreshed me.   [*Walks on.*

Warder.—Here is the terrace of the hallowed fire-chamber, and yonder stands the cow that yields the milk for the oblations. The sacred enclosure has been recently purified, and looks clean and beautiful. Ascend, Sire.

King [*leans on the shoulders of his attendants, and ascends*]. Vetravatí, what can possibly be the message that the venerable Kanwa has sent me by these hermits?—
Perchance their sacred rites have been disturbed
By demons, or some evil has befallen
The innocent herds, their favorites, that graze
Within the precincts of the hermitage;
Or haply, through my sins, some withering blight
Has nipped the creeping plants that spread their arms
Around the hallowed grove. Such troubled thoughts
Crowd through my mind, and fill me with misgiving.

Warder.—If you ask my opinion, Sire, I think the hermits merely wish to take an opportunity of testifying their loyalty, and are therefore come to offer homage to your Majesty.

*Enter the Hermits, leading Śakoontalá, attended by Gautamí;
and, in advance of them, the Chamberlain and the domestic Priest.*

CHAMBERLAIN.—This way, reverend sirs, this way.
ŚÁRNGARAVA.—O Śáradwata,
    'Tis true the monarch lacks no royal grace,
    Nor ever swerves from justice; true, his people,
    Yea such as in life's humblest walks are found,
    Refrain from evil courses; still to me,
    A lonely hermit reared in solitude,
    This throng appears bewildering, and methinks
    I look upon a burning house, whose inmates
    Are running to and fro in wild dismay.
ŚÁRADWATA.—It is natural that the first sight of the King's
capital should affect you in this manner; my own sensa-
tions are very similar.
    As one just bathed beholds the man polluted;
    As one late purified, the yet impure:—
    As one awake looks on the yet unwakened;
    Or as the freeman gazes on the thrall,
    So I regard this crowd of pleasure-seekers.
ŚAKOONTALÁ [*feeling a quivering sensation in her right eye-
lid, and suspecting a bad omen*].—Alas! what means this
throbbing of my right eye-lid?
GAUTAMÍ.—Heaven avert the evil omen, my child! May the
guardian deities of thy husband's family convert it into
a sign of good fortune!   [*Walks on.*
PRIEST [*pointing to the King*].—Most reverend sirs, there
stands the protector of the four classes of the people;
the guardian of the four orders of the priesthood. He
has just left the judgment-seat, and is waiting for you.
Behold him!
ŚÁRNGARAVA.—Great Bráhman, we are happy in thinking that
the King's power is exerted for the protection of all classes
of his subjects. We have not come as petitioners—we
have the fullest confidence in the generosity of his nature.
    The loftiest trees bend humbly to the ground
    Beneath the teeming burden of their fruit;
    High in the vernal sky the pregnant clouds
    Suspend their stately course, and hanging low,

Scatter their sparkling treasures o'er the earth:—
And such is true benevolence; the good
Are never rendered arrogant by riches.

WARDER.—So please your Majesty, I judge from the placid
countenance of the hermits that they have no alarming
message to deliver.

KING [*looking at Sakoontalá*].—But the lady there——
Who can she be, whose form of matchless grace
Is half concealed beneath her flowing veil?
Among the sombre hermits she appears
Like a fresh bud 'mid sear and yellow leaves.

WARDER.—So please your Majesty, my curiosity is also roused,
but no conjecture occurs to my mind. This at least is
certain, that she deserves to be looked at more closely.

KING.—True; but it is not right to gaze at another man's
wife.

SAKOONTALÁ [*placing her hand on her bosom. Aside*].—O
my heart, why this throbbing? Remember thy lord's affection, and take courage.

PRIEST [*advancing*].—These holy men have been received with
all due honor. One of them has now a message to deliver
from his spiritual superior. Will your Majesty deign to
hear it?

KING.—I am all attention.

HERMITS [*extending their hands*].—Victory to the King!

KING.—Accept my respectful greeting.

HERMITS.—May the desires of your soul be accomplished!

KING.—I trust no one is molesting you in the prosecution of
your religious rites.

HERMITS.—Who dares disturb our penitential rites
When thou art our protector? Can the night
Prevail to cast her shadows o'er the earth
While the sun's beams irradiate the sky?

KING.—Such, indeed, is the very meaning of my title—" De-
fender of the Just." I trust the venerable Kanwa is in
good health. The world is interested in his well-being.

HERMITS.—Holy men have health and prosperity in their own
power. He bade us greet your Majesty, and, after kind
inquiries, deliver this message.

KING.—Let me hear his commands.

SÁRNGARAVA.—He bade us say that he feels happy in giving his

sanction to the marriage which your Majesty contracted
with this lady, his daughter, privately and by mutual
agreement. Because

> By us thou art esteemed the most illustrious
> Of noble husbands; and Śakoontalá
> Virtue herself in human form revealed.
> Great Brahmá hath in equal yoke united
> A bride unto a husband worthy of her:—
> Henceforth let none make blasphemous complaint
> That he is pleased with ill-assorted unions.

Since, therefore, she expects soon to be the mother of
thy child, receive her into thy palace, that she may perform, in conjunction with thee, the ceremonies prescribed
by religion on such an occasion.

GAUTAMÍ.—So please your Majesty, I would add a few words:
but why should I intrude my sentiments when an opportunity of speaking my mind has never been allowed me?

> She took no counsel with her kindred; thou
> Didst not confer with thine, but all alone
> Didst solemnize thy nuptials with thy wife.

Together, then, hold converse; let us leave you.

SAKOONTALÁ [aside].—Ah! how I tremble for my lord's reply.

KING.—What strange proposal is this?

SAKOONTALÁ [aside].—His words are fire to me.

SÁRNGARAVA.—What do I hear? Dost thou, then, hesitate?
Monarch, thou art well acquainted with the ways of the
world, and knowest that

> A wife, however virtuous and discreet,
> If she live separate from her wedded lord,
> Though under shelter of her parent's roof,
> Is mark for vile suspicion. Let her dwell
> Beside her husband, though he hold her not
> In his affection. So her kinsmen will it.

KING.—Do you really mean to assert that I ever married this
lady?

SAKOONTALÁ [despondingly. Aside].—O my heart, thy worst
misgivings are confirmed.

SÁRNGARAVA.—Is it becoming in a monarch to depart from the
rules of justice, because he repents of his engagements?

KING.—I cannot answer a question which is based on a mere
fabrication.

SÁRNGARAVA.—Such inconstancy is fortunately not common, excepting in men intoxicated by power.

KING.—Is that remark aimed at me?

GAUTAMÍ.—Be not ashamed, my daughter. Let me remove thy veil for a little space. Thy husband will then recognize thee. [*Removes her veil.*

KING [*gazing at Śakoontalá. Aside*].—What charms are here revealed before mine eyes!

Truly no blemish mars the symmetry
Of that fair form; yet can I ne'er believe
She is my wedded wife; and like a bee
That circles round the flower whose nectared cup
Teems with the dew of morning, I must pause
Ere eagerly I taste the proffered sweetness.

[*Remains wrapped in thought.*

WARDER.—How admirably does our royal master's behavior prove his regard for justice! Who else would hesitate for a moment when good fortune offered for his acceptance a form of such rare beauty?

SÁRNGARAVA.—Great King, why art thou silent?

KING.—Holy men, I have revolved the matter in my mind; but the more I think of it, the less able am I to recollect that I ever contracted an alliance with this lady. What answer, then, can I possibly give you when I do not believe myself to be her husband, and I plainly see that she is soon to become a mother?

SAKOONTALÁ [*aside*].—Woe! woe! Is our very marriage to be called in question by my own husband? Ah me! is this to be the end of all my bright visions of wedded happiness?

SÁRNGARAVA.—Beware!

Beware how thou insult the holy Sage!
Remember how he generously allowed
Thy secret union with his foster-child;
And how, when thou didst rob him of his treasure,
He sought to furnish thee excuse, when rather
He should have cursed thee for a ravisher.

SÁRADWATA.—Sárngarava, speak to him no more. Śakoontalá, our part is performed; we have said all we had to say, and the King has replied in the manner thou hast heard. It is now thy turn to give him convincing evidence of thy marriage.

ŚAKOONTALÁ [*aside*].—Since his feeling towards me has undergone a complete revolution, what will it avail to revive old recollections? One thing is clear—I shall soon have to mourn my own widowhood. [*Aloud.*] My revered husband—— [*Stops short.*] But no—I dare not address thee by this title, since thou hast refused to acknowledge our union. Noble descendant of Puru! It is not worthy of thee to betray an innocent-minded girl, and disown her in such terms, after having so lately and so solemnly plighted thy vows to her in the hermitage.

KING [*stopping his ears*].—I will hear no more. Be such a crime far from my thoughts!

> What evil spirit can possess thee, lady,
> That thou dost seek to sully my good name
> By base aspersions? like a swollen torrent,
> That, leaping from its narrow bed, o'erthrows
> The tree upon its bank, and strives to blend
> Its turbid waters with the crystal stream?

ŚAKOONTALÁ.—If, then, thou really believest me to be the wife of another, and thy present conduct proceeds from some cloud that obscures thy recollection, I will easily convince thee by this token.

KING.—An excellent idea!

ŚAKOONTALÁ [*feeling for the ring*].—Alas! alas! woe is me! There is no ring on my finger!

> [*Looks with anguish at Gautami.*

GAUTAMÍ.—The ring must have slipped off when thou wast in the act of offering homage to the holy water of Śachí's sacred pool, near Śakrávatára.

KING [*smiling*].—People may well talk of the readiness of woman's invention! Here is an instance of it.

ŚAKOONTALÁ.—Say, rather, of the omnipotence of fate. I will mention another circumstance, which may yet convince thee.

KING.—By all means let me hear it at once.

ŚAKOONTALÁ.—One day, while we were seated in a jasmine bower, thou didst pour into the hollow of thine hand some water, sprinkled by a recent shower in the cup of a lotus blossom——

KING.—I am listening; proceed.

ŚAKOONTALÁ.—At that instant, my adopted child, the little

fawn, with soft, long eyes, came running towards us.
Upon which, before tasting the water thyself, thou didst
kindly offer some to the little creature, saying fondly—
"Drink first, gentle fawn." But she could not be induced to drink from the hand of a stranger; though immediately afterwards, when I took the water in my own
hand, she drank with perfect confidence. Then, with a
smile, thou didst say—"Every creature confides naturally
in its own kind. You are both inhabitants of the same
forest, and have learnt to trust each other."

KING.—Voluptuaries may allow themselves to be seduced from
the path of duty by falsehoods such as these, expressed
in honeyed words.

GAUTAMÍ.—Speak not thus, illustrious Prince. This lady was
brought up in a hermitage, and has never learnt deceit.

KING.—Holy matron,

> E'en in untutored brutes, the female sex
> Is marked by inborn subtlety—much more
> In beings gifted with intelligence.
> The wily Köil, ere towards the sky
> She wings her sportive flight, commits her eggs
> To other nests, and artfully consigns
> The rearing of her little ones to strangers.

SAKOONTALÁ [angrily].—Dishonorable man, thou judgest of
others by thine own evil heart. Thou, at least, art unrivalled in perfidy, and standest alone—a base deceiver in
the garb of virtue and religion—like a deep pit whose
yawning mouth is concealed by smiling flowers.

KING [aside].—Her anger, at any rate, appears genuine, and
makes me almost doubt whether I am in the right. For,
indeed,

> When I had vainly searched my memory,
> And so with stern severity denied
> The fabled story of our secret loves,
> Her brows, that met before in graceful curves,
> Like the arched weapon of the god of love,
> Seemed by her frown dissevered; while the fire
> Of sudden anger kindled in her eyes.

[Aloud.] My good lady, Dushyanta's character is well-
known to all. I comprehend not your meaning.

SAKOONTALÁ.—Well do I deserve to be thought a harlot for

having, in the innocence of my heart, and out of the confidence I reposed in a Prince of Puru's race, intrusted my
honor to a man whose mouth distils honey, while his
heart is full of poison.

[*Covers her face with her mantle, and bursts into tears.*

ŚÁRNGARAVA.—Thus is it that burning remorse must ever follow rash actions which might have been avoided, and for
which one has only one's self to blame.

Not hastily should marriage be contracted,
And specially in secret. Many a time,
In hearts that know not each the other's fancies,
Fond love is changed into most bitter hate.

KING.—How now! Do you give credence to this woman
rather than to me, that you heap such accusations on me?

ŚÁRNGARAVA [*sarcastically*].—That would be too absurd, certainly. You have heard the proverb—

Hold in contempt the innocent words of those
Who from their infancy have known no guile:—
But trust the treacherous counsels of the man
Who makes a very science of deceit.

KING.—Most veracious Bráhman, grant that you are in the
right, what end would be gained by betraying this lady?

ŚÁRNGARAVA.—Ruin.

KING.—No one will believe that a Prince of Puru's race would
seek to ruin others or himself.

ŚÁRADWATA.—This altercation is idle, Śárngarava. We have
executed the commission of our preceptor; come, let us
return. [*To the King.*

Śakoontalá is certainly thy bride;
Receive her or reject her, she is thine.
Do with her, King, according to thy pleasure—
The husband o'er the wife is absolute.

Go on before us, Gautamí. [*They move away.*

ŚAKOONTALÁ.—What! is it not enough to have been betrayed
by this perfidious man? Must you also forsake me, regardless of my tears and lamentations?

[*Attempts to follow them.*

GAUTAMÍ [*stopping*].—My son Śárngarava, see, Śakoontalá
is following us, and with tears implores us not to leave
her. Alas! poor child, what will she do here with a cruel
husband who casts her from him?

Śárngarava [*turning angrily towards her*].—Wilful woman, dost thou seek to be independent of thy lord?

[*Sakoontalá trembles with fear.*

Śárngarava.—Sakoontalá!

If thou art really what the King proclaims thee,
How can thy father e'er receive thee back
Into his house and home? but, if thy conscience
Be witness to thy purity of soul,
E'en should thy husband to a handmaid's lot
Condemn thee, thou may'st cheerfully endure it,
When ranked among the number of his household.
Thy duty, therefore, is to stay. As for us, we must return immediately.

King.—Deceive not the lady, my good hermit, by any such expectations.

The moon expands the lotus of the night,
The rising sun awakes the lily; each
Is with his own contented. Even so
The virtuous man is master of his passions,
And from another's wife averts his gaze.

Śárngarava.—Since thy union with another woman has rendered thee oblivious of thy marriage with Śakoontalá, whence this fear of losing thy character for constancy and virtue?

King [*to the Priest*].—You must counsel me, revered sir, as to my course of action. Which of the two evils involves the greater or less sin?

Whether by some dark veil my mind be clouded,
Or this designing woman speak untruly,
I know not. Tell me, must I rather be
The base disowner of my wedded wife,
Or the defiling and defiled adulterer?

Priest [*after deliberation*].—You must take an intermediate course.

King.—What course, revered sir? Tell me at once.

Priest.—I will provide an asylum for the lady in my own house until the birth of her child; and my reason, if you ask me, is this. Soothsayers have predicted that your first-born will have universal dominion. Now, if the hermit's daughter bring forth a son with the discus or mark of empire in the lines of his hand, you must admit her im-

mediately into your royal apartments with great rejoic-
ings; if not, then determine to send her back as soon as
possible to her father.

KING.—I bow to the decision of my spiritual adviser.

PRIEST.—Daughter, follow me.

ŚAKOONTALÁ.—O divine earth, open and receive me into thy
bosom!

[*Exit Sakoontalá weeping, with the Priest and the Hermits.
The King remains absorbed in thinking of her, though
the curse still clouds his recollection.*

A VOICE [*behind the scenes*].—A miracle! a miracle!

KING [*listening*].—What has happened now?

PRIEST [*entering with an air of astonishment*].—Great Prince,
a stupendous prodigy has just occurred!

KING.—What is it?

PRIEST.—May it please your Majesty, so soon as Kanwa's
pupils had departed,
Śakoontalá, her eyes all bathed in tears,
With outstretched arms bewailed her cruel fate——

KING.—Well, well, what happened then?

PRIEST.—When suddenly a shining apparition,
In female shape, descended from the skies,
Near the nymphs' pool, and bore her up to heaven.
[*All remain motionless with astonishment.*

KING.—My good priest, from the very first I declined having
anything to do with this matter. It is now all over, and
we can never, by our conjectures, unravel the mystery;
let it rest; go, seek repose.

PRIEST [*looking at the King*].—Be it so. Victory to the King!
[*Exit.*

KING.—Vetravatí, I am tired out; lead the way to the bed-
chamber.

WARDER.—This way, Sire.   [*They move away.*

KING.—Do what I will, I cannot call to mind
That I did e'er espouse the sage's daughter—
Therefore I have disowned her; yet 'tis strange
How painfully my agitated heart
Bears witness to the truth of her assertion,
And makes me credit her against my judgment.
[*Exeunt.*

PRELUDE TO ACT SIXTH

Scene.—A Street

Enter the King's brother-in-law as Superintendent of the city police; and with him two Constables, dragging a poor fisherman, who has his hands tied behind his back.

BOTH THE CONSTABLES [*striking the prisoner*].—Take that for a rascally thief that you are; and now tell us, sirrah, where you found this ring—aye, the King's own signet-ring. See, here is the royal name engraved on the setting of the jewel.

FISHERMAN [*with a gesture of alarm*].—Mercy! kind sirs, mercy! I did not steal it; indeed I did not.

FIRST CONSTABLE.—Oh! then I suppose the King took you for some fine Bráhman, and made you a present of it?

FISHERMAN.—Only hear me. I am but a poor fisherman, living at Śakrávatára——

SECOND CONSTABLE.—Scoundrel, who ever asked you, pray, for a history of your birth and parentage?

SUPERINTENDENT [*to one of the Constables*].—Súchaka, let the fellow tell his own story from the beginning. Don't interrupt him.

BOTH CONSTABLES.—As you please, master. Go on, then, sirrah, and say what you've got to say.

FISHERMAN.—You see in me a poor man, who supports his family by catching fish with nets, hooks, and the like.

SUPERINTENDENT [*laughing*].—A most refined occupation, certainly!

FISHERMAN.—Blame me not for it, master.
> The father's occupation, though despised
> By others, casts no shame upon the son,
> And he should not forsake it. Is the priest
> Who kills the animal for sacrifice

Therefore deemed cruel? Sure a lowborn man
May, though a fisherman, be tender-hearted.

SUPERINTENDENT.—Well, well; go on with your story.

FISHERMAN.—One day I was cutting open a large carp I had
just hooked, when the sparkle of a jewel caught my eye,
and what should I find in the fish's maw but that ring!
Soon afterwards, when I was offering it for sale, I was
seized by your honors. Now you know everything.
Whether you kill me, or whether you let me go, this is the
true account of how the ring came into my possession.

SUPERINTENDENT [to one of the Constables].—Well, Jánuka,
the rascal emits such a fishy odor that I have no doubt of
his being a fisherman; but we must inquire a little more
closely into this queer story about the finding of the ring.
Come, we'll take him before the King's household.

BOTH CONSTABLES.—Very good, master. Get on with you,
you cutpurse.   [All move on.

SUPERINTENDENT.—Now attend, Súchaka; keep you guard
here at the gate; and hark ye, sirrahs, take good care your
prisoner does not escape, while I go in and lay the whole
story of the discovery of this ring before the King in
person. I will soon return and let you know his commands.

CONSTABLE.—Go in, master, by all means; and may you find
favor in the King's sight!   [Exit Superintendent.

FIRST CONSTABLE [after an interval].—I say, Jánuka, the
Superintendent is a long time away.

SECOND CONSTABLE.—Aye, aye; kings are not to be got at so
easily. Folks must bide the proper opportunity.

FIRST CONSTABLE.—Jánuka, my fingers itch to strike the first
blow at this royal victim here. We must kill him with all
the honors, you know. I long to begin binding the flowers
round his head.

                [Pretends to strike a blow at the fisherman.

FISHERMAN.—Your honor surely will not put an innocent man
to a cruel death.

SECOND CONSTABLE [looking].—There's our Superintendent
at last, I declare. See, he is coming towards us with a
paper in his hand. We shall soon know the King's command; so prepare, my fine fellow, either to become food

for the vultures, or to make acquaintance with some hungry cur.

SUPERINTENDENT [*entering*].—Ho, there, Súchaka! set the fisherman at liberty, I tell you. His story about the ring is all correct.

SÚCHAKÁ.—Oh! very good, sir; as you please.

SECOND CONSTABLE.—The fellow had one foot in hell, and now here he is in the land of the living. [*Releases him.*

FISHERMAN [*bowing to the Superintendent*].—Now, master, what think you of my way of getting a livelihood?

SUPERINTENDENT.—Here, my good man, the King desired me to present you with this purse. It contains a sum of money equal to the full value of the ring. [*Gives him the money.*

FISHERMAN [*taking it and bowing*].—His Majesty does me too great honor.

SÚCHAKÁ.—You may well say so. He might as well have taken you from the gallows to seat you on his state elephant.

JÁNUKA.—Master, the King must value the ring very highly, or he would never have sent such a sum of money to this ragamuffin.

SUPERINTENDENT.—I don't think he prizes it as a costly jewel so much as a memorial of some person he tenderly loves. The moment it was shown to him he became much agitated, though in general he conceals his feelings.

SÚCHAKÁ.—Then you must have done a great service——

JÁNUKA.—Yes, to this husband of a fish-wife.
[*Looks enviously at the fisherman.*

FISHERMAN.—Here's half the money for you, my masters. It will serve to purchase the flowers you spoke of, if not to buy me your good-will.

JÁNUKA.—Well, now, that's just as it should be.

SUPERINTENDENT.—My good fisherman, you are an excellent fellow, and I begin to feel quite a regard for you. Let us seal our first friendship over a glass of good liquor. Come along to the next wine-shop and we'll drink your health.

ALL.—By all means. [*Exeunt.*

ACT SIXTH

Scene.—The Garden of the Palace

The nymph Sánumatí is seen descending in a celestial car.

SÁNUMATÍ.—Behold me just arrived from attending in my proper turn at the nymphs' pool, where I have left the other nymphs to perform their ablutions, whilst I seek to ascertain, with my own eyes, how it fares with King Dushyanta. My connection with the nymph Menaká has made her daughter Śakoontalá dearer to me than my own flesh and blood; and Menaká it was who charged me with this errand on her daughter's behalf. [*Looking round in all directions.*] How is it that I see no preparations in the King's household for celebrating the great vernal festival? I could easily discover the reason by my divine faculty of meditation; but respect must be shown to the wishes of my friend. How then shall I arrive at the truth? I know what I will do. I will become invisible, and place myself near those two maidens who are tending the plants in the garden. [*Descends and takes her station.*

Enter a Maiden, who stops in front of a mango-tree and gazes at the blossom. Another Maiden is seen behind her.

FIRST MAIDEN.—Hail to thee, lovely harbinger of spring!
   The varied radiance of thy opening flowers
   Is welcome to my sight. I bid thee hail,
   Sweet mango, soul of this enchanting season.
SECOND MAIDEN.—Parabaitiká, what are you saying there to yourself?
FIRST MAIDEN.—Dear Madhukariká, am I not named after the Köil?[9] and does not the Köil sing for joy at the first appearance of the mango-blossom?

---

[9] The Köil is the Indian cuckoo. It is sometimes called Parabhrita (nourished by another) because the female is known to leave her eggs in the nest of the crow to be hatched. The bird is a great favorite with the Indian poets, as the nightingale with Europeans.

SECOND MAIDEN [*approaching hastily, with transport*].—
What! is spring really come?

FIRST MAIDEN.—Yes, indeed, Madhukariká, and with it the
season of joy, love, and song.

SECOND MAIDEN.—Let me lean upon you, dear, while I stand
on tip-toe and pluck a blossom of the mango, that I may
present it as an offering to the god of love.

FIRST MAIDEN.—Provided you let me have half the reward
which the god will bestow in return.

SECOND MAIDEN.—To be sure you shall, and that without asking. Are we not one in heart and soul, though divided
in body? [*Leans on her friend and plucks a mango-blossom.*] Ah! here is a bud just bursting into flower. It
diffuses a delicious perfume, though not yet quite expanded.   [*Joining her hands reverentially.*
God of the bow, who with spring's choicest flowers
Dost point thy five unerring shafts; to thee
I dedicate this blossom; let it serve
To barb thy truest arrow; be its mark
Some youthful heart that pines to be beloved.
                    [*Throws down a mango-blossom.*

CHAMBERLAIN [*entering in a hurried manner, angrily*].—
Hold there, thoughtless woman. What are you about,
breaking off those mango-blossoms, when the King has
forbidden the celebration of the spring festival?

BOTH MAIDENS [*alarmed*].—Pardon us, kind sir, we have
heard nothing of it.

CHAMBERLAIN.—You have heard nothing of it? Why, all the
vernal plants and shrubs, and the very birds that lodge
in their branches, show more respect to the King's order
than you do.
Yon mango-blossoms, though long since expanded,
Gather no down upon their tender crests;
The flower still lingers in the amaranth,
Imprisoned in its bud; the tuneful Köil,
Though winter's chilly dews be overpast,
Suspends the liquid volume of his song
Scarce uttered in his throat; e'en Love, dismayed,
Restores the half-drawn arrow to his quiver.

BOTH MAIDENS.—The mighty power of King Dushyanta is
not to be disputed.

FIRST MAIDEN.—It is but a few days since Mitrávasu, the king's brother-in-law, sent us to wait upon his Majesty; and, during the whole of our sojourn here, we have been intrusted with the charge of the royal pleasure-grounds. We are therefore strangers in this place, and heard nothing of the order until you informed us of it.

CHAMBERLAIN.—Well then, now you know it, take care you don't continue your preparations.

BOTH MAIDENS.—But tell us, kind sir, why has the King prohibited the usual festivities? We are curious to hear, if we may.

SÁNUMATÍ [aside].—Men are naturally fond of festive entertainments. There must be some good reason for the prohibition.

CHAMBERLAIN.—The whole affair is now public; why should I not speak of it! Has not the gossip about the King's rejection of Śakoontalá reached your ears yet?

BOTH MAIDENS.—Oh yes, we heard the story from the King's brother-in-law, as far, at least, as the discovery of the ring.

CHAMBERLAIN.—Then there is little more to tell you. As soon as the King's memory was restored by the sight of his own ring, he exclaimed, " Yes, it is all true. I remember now my secret marriage with Śakoontalá. When I repudiated her, I had lost my recollection." Ever since that moment, he has yielded himself a prey to the bitterest remorse.

He loathes his former pleasures; he rejects
The daily homage of his ministers.
On his lone couch he tosses to and fro,
Courting repose in vain. Whene'er he meets
The ladies of his palace, and would fain
Address them with politeness, he confounds
Their names; or, calling them " Śakoontalá,"
Is straightway silent and abashed with shame.

SÁNUMATÍ [aside].—To me this account is delightful.

CHAMBERLAIN.—In short, the King is so completely out of his mind that the festival has been prohibited.

BOTH MAIDENS.—Perfectly right.

A VOICE [behind the scenes].—The King! the King! This way, Sire, this way.

CHAMBERLAIN [*listening*].—Oh! here comes his majesty in
this direction. Pass on, maidens; attend to your duties.
BOTH MAIDENS.—We will, sir. [*Exeunt.*

*Enter King Dushyanta, dressed in deep mourning, attended
by his Jester, Máthavya, and preceded by Vetravatí.*

CHAMBERLAIN [*gazing at the King*].—Well, noble forms are
certainly pleasing, under all varieties of outward circumstances. The King's person is as charming as ever, not-
withstanding his sorrow of mind.

> Though but a single golden bracelet spans
> His wasted arm; though costly ornaments
> Have given place to penitential weeds;
> Though oft-repeated sighs have blanched his lips,
> And robbed them of their bloom; though sleepless care
> And carking thought have dimmed his beaming eye;
> Yet does his form, by its inherent lustre,
> Dazzle the gaze; and, like a priceless gem
> Committed to some cunning polisher,
> Grow more effulgent by the loss of substance.

SÁNUMATÍ [*aside. Looking at the King*].—Now that I have
seen him, I can well understand why Śakoontalá should
pine after such a man, in spite of his disdainful rejection
of her.
KING [*walking slowly up and down, in deep thought*].—

> When fatal lethargy o'erwhelmed my soul,
> My loved one strove to rouse me, but in vain:—
> And now when I would fain in slumber deep
> Forget myself, full soon remorse doth wake me.

SÁNUMATÍ [*aside*].—My poor Śakoontalá's sufferings are very
similar.
MÁTHAVYA [*aside*].—He is taken with another attack of this
odious Śakoontalá fever. How shall we ever cure him?
CHAMBERLAIN [*approaching*].—Victory to the King! Great
Prince, the royal pleasure-grounds have been put in order.
Your Majesty can resort to them for exercise and amuse-
ment whenever you think proper.
KING.—Vetravatí, tell the worthy Piśuna, my prime minister,
from me, that I am so exhausted by want of sleep that I
cannot sit on the judgment-seat to-day. If any case of

importance be brought before the tribunal he must give it his best attention, and inform me of the circumstances by letter.

VETRAVATÍ.—Your Majesty's commands shall be obeyed.
[*Exit.*

KING [*to the Chamberlain*].—And you, Vátáyana, may go about your own affairs.

CHAMBERLAIN.—I will, Sire. [*Exit.*

MÁTHAVYA.—Now that you have rid yourself of these troublesome fellows, you can enjoy the delightful coolness of your pleasure-grounds without interruption.

KING.—Ah! my dear friend, there is an old adage—" When affliction has a mind to enter, she will find a crevice somewhere "—and it is verified in me.

Scarce is my soul delivered from the cloud
That darkened its remembrance of the past,
When lo! the heart-born deity of love
With yonder blossom of the mango barbs
His keenest shaft, and aims it at my breast.

MÁTHAVYA.—Well, then, wait a moment; I will soon demolish Master Káma's arrow with a cut of my cane.
[*Raises his stick and strikes off the mango-blossom.*

KING [*smiling*].—That will do. I see very well the god of Love is not a match for a Bráhman. And now, my dear friend, where shall I sit down, that I may enchant my sight by gazing on the twining plants, which seem to remind me of the graceful shape of my beloved?

MÁTHAVYA.—Do you not remember? you told Chaturiká you should pass the heat of the day in the jasmine bower; and commanded her to bring the likeness of your queen Śakoontalá, sketched with your own hand.

KING.—True. The sight of her picture will refresh my soul. Lead the way to the arbor.

MÁTHAVYA.—This way, Sire.
[*Both move on, followed by Sánumatí.*

MÁTHAVYA.—Here we are at the jasmine bower. Look, it has a marble seat, and seems to bid us welcome with its offerings of delicious flowers. You have only to enter and sit down. [*Both enter and seat themselves.*

SÁNUMATÍ [*aside*].—I will lean against these young jasmines.

I can easily, from behind them, glance at my friend's picture, and will then hasten to inform her of her husband's
ardent affection. [*Stands leaning against the creepers.*

KING.—Oh! my dear friend, how vividly all the circumstances
of my union with Śakoontalá present themselves to my
recollection at this moment! But tell me now how it was
that, between the time of my leaving her in the hermitage
and my subsequent rejection of her, you never breathed
her name to me! True, you were not by my side when
I disowned her; but I had confided to you the story of
my love and you were acquainted with every particular.
Did it pass out of your mind as it did out of mine?

MÁTHAVYA.—No, no; trust me for that. But, if you remember, when you had finished telling me about it, you added
that I was not to take the story in earnest, for that you
were not really in love with a country girl, but were only
jesting; and I was dull and thick-headed enough to believe you. But so fate decreed, and there is no help for it.

SÁNUMATÍ [*aside*].—Exactly.

KING [*after deep thought*].—My dear friend, suggest some
relief for my misery.

MÁTHAVYA.—Come, come, cheer up; why do you give way?
Such weakness is unworthy of you. Great men never
surrender themselves to uncontrolled grief. Do not mountains remain unshaken even in a gale of wind?

KING.—How can I be otherwise than inconsolable, when I call
to mind the agonized demeanor of the dear one on the
occasion of my disowning her?

When cruelly I spurned her from my presence,
She fain had left me; but the young recluse,
Stern as the Sage, and with authority
As from his saintly master, in a voice
That brooked not contradiction, bade her stay.
Then through her pleading eyes, bedimmed with tears,
She cast on me one long reproachful look,
Which like a poisoned shaft torments me still.

SÁNUMATÍ [*aside*].—Alas! such is the force of self-reproach
following a rash action. But his anguish only rejoices me.

MÁTHAVYA.—An idea has just struck me. I should not wonder if some celestial being had carried her off to heaven.

KING.—Very likely. Who else would have dared to lay **a**

finger on a wife, the idol of her husband? It is said that
Menaká, the nymph of heaven, gave her birth. The suspicion has certainly crossed my mind that some of her
celestial companions may have taken her to their own
abode.

SÁNUMATÍ [aside].—His present recollection of every circumstance of her history does not surprise me so much
as his former forgetfulness.

MÁTHAVYA.—If that's the case, you will be certain to meet her
before long.

KING.—Why?

MÁTHAVYA.—No father and mother can endure to see a daughter suffering the pain of separation from her husband.

KING.—Oh! my dear Máthavya,

Was it a dream? or did some magic dire,
Dulling my senses with a strange delusion,
O'ercome my spirit? or did destiny,
Jealous of my good actions, mar their fruit,
And rob me of their guerdon? It is past,
Whate'er the spell that bound me. Once again
Am I awake, but only to behold
The precipice o'er which my hopes have fallen.

MÁTHAVYA.—Do not despair in this manner. Is not this very
ring a proof that what has been lost may be unexpectedly
found?

KING [gazing at the ring].—Ah! this ring, too, has fallen from
a station which it will not easily regain, and deserves all
my sympathy.

O gem, deserved the punishment we suffer,
And equal is the merit of our works,
When such our common doom. Thou didst enjoy
The thrilling contact of those slender fingers,
Bright as the dawn; and now how changed thy lot!

SÁNUMATÍ [aside].—Had it found its way to the hand of any
other person, then indeed its fate would have been deplor-
able.

MÁTHAVYA.—Pray, how did the ring ever come upon her hand
at all?

SÁNUMATÍ.—I myself am curious to know.

KING.—You shall hear. When I was leaving my beloved Sakoontalá that I might return to my own capital, she said

to me, with tears in her eyes, " How long will it be ere my lord send for me to his palace and make me his queen? "

MÁTHAVYA.—Well, what was your reply?

KING.—Then I placed the ring on her finger, and thus addressed her—

Repeat each day one letter of the name
Engraven on this gem; ere thou hast reckoned
The tale of syllables, my minister
Shall come to lead thee to thy husband's palace.

But, hard-hearted man that I was, I forgot to fulfil my promise, owing to the infatuation that took possession of me.

SÁNUMATÍ [aside].—A pleasant arrangement! Fate, however, ordained that the appointment should not be kept.

MÁTHAVYA.—But how did the ring contrive to pass into the stomach of that carp which the fisherman caught and was cutting up?

KING.—It must have slipped from my Śakoontalá's hand, and fallen into the stream of the Ganges, while she was offering homage to the water of Śachí's holy pool.

MÁTHAVYA.—Very likely.

SÁNUMATÍ [aside].—Hence it happened, I suppose, that the King, always fearful of committing the least injustice, came to doubt his marriage with my poor Śakoontalá. But why should affection so strong as his stand in need of any token of recognition?

KING.—Let me now address a few words of reproof to this ring.

MÁTHAVYA [aside].—He is going stark mad, I verily believe.

KING.—Hear me, thou dull and undiscerning bauble!

For so it argues thee, that thou couldst leave
The slender fingers of her hand, to sink
Beneath the waters. Yet what marvel is it
That thou shouldst lack discernment? let me rather
Heap curses on myself, who, though endowed
With reason, yet rejected her I loved.

MÁTHAVYA [aside].—And so, I suppose, I must stand here to be devoured by hunger, whilst he goes on in this sentimental strain.

KING.—O forsaken one, unjustly banished from my presence,

take pity on thy slave, whose heart is consumed by the
fire of remorse, and return to my sight.

Enter Chaturiká hurriedly, with a picture in her hand.

CHATURIKÁ.—Here is the Queen's portrait.
                                        [*Shows the picture.*
MÁTHAVYA.—Excellent, my dear friend, excellent! The imi-
tation of nature is perfect, and the attitude of the figures
is really charming. They stand out in such bold relief that
the eye is quite deceived.
SÁNUMATÍ [*aside*].—A most artistic performance! I admire
the King's skill, and could almost believe that Śakoontalá
herself was before me.
KING.—I own 'tis not amiss, though it portrays
        But feebly her angelic loveliness.
        Aught less than perfect is depicted falsely,
        And fancy must supply the imperfection.
SÁNUMATÍ [*aside*].—A very just remark from a modest man,
whose affection is exaggerated by the keenness of his remorse.
MÁTHAVYA.—Tell me—I see three female figures drawn on
the canvas, and all of them beautiful; which of the three
is her Majesty, Śakoontalá?
SÁNUMATÍ [*aside*].—If he cannot distinguish her from the
others, the simpleton might as well have no eyes in his
head.
KING.—Which should you imagine to be intended for her?
MÁTHAVYA.—She who is leaning, apparently a little tired,
against the stem of that mango-tree, the tender leaves of
which glitter with the water she has poured upon them.
Her arms are gracefully extended; her face is somewhat
flushed with the heat; and a few flowers have escaped
from her hair, which has become unfastened, and hangs
in loose tresses about her neck. That must be the queen
Śakoontalá, and the others, I presume, are her two attendants.
KING.—I congratulate you on your discernment. Behold the
proof of my passion;
        My finger, burning with the glow of love,
        Has left its impress on the painted tablet;

While here and there, alas! a scalding tear
Has fallen on the cheek and dimmed its brightness.
Chaturiká, the garden in the background of the picture is
only half-painted. Go, fetch the brush that I may finish it.

CHATURIKÁ.—Worthy Máthavya, have the kindness to hold
the picture until I return.

KING.—Nay, I will hold it myself.

[*Takes the picture. Exit Chaturiká.*

KING.—My loved one came but lately to my presence
And offered me herself, but in my folly
I spurned the gift, and now I fondly cling
To her mere image; even as a madman
Would pass the waters of the gushing stream,
And thirst for airy vapors of the desert.

MÁTHAVYA [*aside*].—He has been fool enough to forego the
reality for the semblance, the substance for the shadow.
[*Aloud.*] Tell us, I pray, what else remains to be painted.

SÁNUMATÍ [*aside*].—He longs, no doubt, to delineate some
favorite spot where my dear Sakoontalá delighted to
ramble.

KING.—You shall hear——
I wish to see the Málini portrayed,
Its tranquil course by banks of sand impeded—
Upon the brink a pair of swans: beyond,
The hills adjacent to Himálaya,
Studded with deer; and, near the spreading shade
Of some large tree, where 'mid the branches hang
The hermits' vests of bark, a tender doe,
Rubbing its downy forehead on the horn
Of a black antelope, should be depicted.

MÁTHAVYA [*aside*].—Pooh! if I were he, I would fill up the
vacant spaces with a lot of grizzly-bearded old hermits.

KING.—My dear Máthavya, there is still a part of Sakoontalá's
dress which I purposed to draw, but find I have omitted.

MÁTHAVYA.—What is that?

SÁNUMATÍ [*aside*].—Something suitable, I suppose, to the
simple attire of a young and beautiful girl dwelling in a
forest.

KING.—A sweet Sirísha blossom should be twined
Behind her ear, its perfumed crest depending

Towards her cheek; and, resting on her bosom,
A lotus-fibre necklace, soft and bright
As an autumnal moon-beam, should be traced.

MÁTHAVYA.—Pray, why does the Queen cover her lips with the tips of her fingers, bright as the blossom of a lily, as if she were afraid of something? [*Looking more closely.*] Oh! I see; a vagabond bee, intent on thieving the honey of flowers, has mistaken her mouth for a rose-bud, and is trying to settle upon it.

KING.—A bee! drive off the impudent insect, will you?

MÁTHAVYA.—That's your business. Your royal prerogative gives you power over all offenders.

KING.—Very true. Listen to me, thou favorite guest of flowering plants; why give thyself the trouble of hovering here?
See where thy partner sits on yonder flower,
And waits for thee ere she will sip its dew.

SÁNUMATÍ [*aside*].—A most polite way of warning him off!

MÁTHAVYA.—You'll find the obstinate creature is not to be sent about his business so easily as you think.

KING.—Dost thou presume to disobey? Now hear me—
An thou but touch the lips of my beloved,
Sweet as the opening blossom, whence I quaffed
In happier days love's nectar, I will place thee
Within the hollow of yon lotus cup,
And there imprison thee for thy presumption.

MÁTHAVYA.—He must be bold indeed not to show any fear when you threaten him with such an awful punishment. [*Smiling, aside.*] He is stark mad, that's clear; and I believe, by keeping him company, I am beginning to talk almost as wildly. [*Aloud.*] Look, it is only a painted bee.

KING.—Painted? impossible!

SÁNUMATÍ [*aside*].—Even I did not perceive it; how much less should he?

KING.—Oh! my dear friend, why were you so ill-natured as to tell me the truth?
While, all entranced, I gazed upon her picture,
My loved one seemed to live before my eyes,
Till every fibre of my being thrilled
With rapturous emotion. Oh! 'twas cruel

To dissipate the day-dream, and transform
The blissful vision to a lifeless image.   [*Sheds tears.*

SÁNUMATÍ [*aside*].—Separated lovers are very difficult to please; but he seems more difficult than usual.

KING.—Alas! my dear Máthavya, why am I doomed to be the victim of perpetual disappointment?

Vain is the hope of meeting her in dreams,
For slumber night by night forsakes my couch:
And now that I would fain assuage my grief
By gazing on her portrait here before me,
Tears of despairing love obscure my sight.

SÁNUMATÍ [*aside*].—You have made ample amends for the wrong you did Śakoontalá in disowning her.

CHATURIKÁ [*entering*].—Victory to the King! I was coming along with the box of colors in my hand——

KING.—What now?

CHATURIKÁ.—When I met the Queen Vasumatí, attended by Taraliká. She insisted on taking it from me, and declared she would herself deliver it into your Majesty's hands.

MÁTHAVYA.—By what luck did you contrive to escape her?

CHATURIKÁ.—While her maid was disengaging her mantle, which had caught in the branch of a shrub, I ran away.

KING.—Here, my good friend, take the picture and conceal it. My attentions to the Queen have made her presumptuous. She will be here in a minute.

MÁTHAVYA.—Conceal the picture! conceal myself, you mean. [*Getting up and taking the picture.*] The Queen has a bitter draught in store for you, which you will have to swallow as Śiva did the poison at the Deluge. When you are well quit of her, you may send and call me from the Palace of Clouds,[10] where I shall take refuge.
[*Exit, running.*

SÁNUMATÍ [*aside*].—Although the King's affections are transferred to another object, yet he respects his previous attachments. I fear his love must be somewhat fickle.

VETRAVATÍ [*entering with a despatch in her hand*].—Victory to the King!

KING.—Vetravatí, did you observe the Queen Vasumatí coming in this direction?

[10] Palace of King Dushyanta, so-called because it was as lofty as the clouds.

VETRAVATÍ.—I did; but when she saw that I had a despatch in my hand for your Majesty, she turned back.

KING.—The Queen has too much regard for propriety to interrupt me when I am engaged with state-affairs.

VETRAVATÍ.—So please your Majesty, your Prime Minister begs respectfully to inform you that he has devoted much time to the settlement of financial calculations, and only one case of importance has been submitted by the citizens for his consideration. He has made a written report of the facts, and requests your Majesty to cast your eyes over it.

KING.—Hand me the paper.   [*Vetravatí delivers it.*

KING [*reading*].—What have we here? " A merchant named Dhanamitra, trading by sea, was lost in a late shipwreck. Though a wealthy trader, he was childless; and the whole of his immense property becomes by law forfeited to the King." So writes the minister. Alas! alas! for his childlessness. But surely, if he was wealthy, he must have had many wives. Let an inquiry be made whether any one of them is expecting to give birth to a child.

VETRAVATÍ.—They say that his wife, the daughter of the foreman of a guild belonging to Ayodhyá, has just completed the ceremonies usual upon such expectations.

KING.—The unborn child has a title to his father's property. Such is my decree. Go, bid my minister proclaim it so.

VETRAVATÍ.—I will, my liege.   [*Going.*

KING.—Stay a moment.

VETRAVATÍ.—I am at your Majesty's service.

KING.—Let there be no question whether he may or may not have left offspring;

    Rather be it proclaimed that whosoe'er
    Of King Dushyanta's subjects be bereaved
    Of any loved relation, an it be not
    That his estates are forfeited for crimes,
    Dushyanta will himself to them supply
    That kinsman's place in tenderest affection.

VETRAVATÍ.—It shall be so proclaimed.

    [*Exit Vetravatí, and reënter after an interval.*

VETRAVATÍ.—Your Majesty's proclamation was received with acclamations of joy, like grateful rain at the right season.

KING [*drawing a deep sigh*].—So then, the property of rich

men, who have no lineal descendants, passes over to a stranger at their decease. And such, alas! must be the fate of the fortunes of the race of Puru at my death; even as when fertile soil is sown with seed at the wrong season.

VETRAVATÍ.—Heaven forbid!

KING.—Fool that I was to reject such happiness when it offered itself for my acceptance!

SÁNUMATÍ [aside].—He may well blame his own folly when he calls to mind his treatment of my beloved Śakoontalá.

KING.—Ah! woe is me! when I forsook my wife—

My lawful wife—concealed within her breast
There lay my second self, a child unborn,
Hope of my race, e'en as the choicest fruit
Lies hidden in the bosom of the earth.

SÁNUMATÍ [aside].—There is no fear of your race being cut off for want of a son.

CHATURIKÁ [aside to Vetravatí].—The affair of the merchant's death has quite upset our royal master, and caused him sad distress. Had you not better fetch the worthy Máthavya from the Palace of Clouds to comfort him?

VETRAVATÍ.—A very good idea.   [Exit.

KING.—Alas! the shades of my forefathers are even now beginning to be alarmed, lest at my death they may be deprived of their funeral libations.

No son remains in King Dushyanta's place
To offer sacred homage to the dead
Of Puru's noble line: my ancestors
Must drink these glistening tears, the last libation
A childless man can ever hope to make them.

[Falls down in an agony of grief.

CHATURIKÁ [looking at him in consternation].—Great King, compose yourself.

SÁNUMATÍ [aside].—Alas! alas! though a bright light is shining near him, he is involved in the blackest darkness, by reason of the veil that obscures his sight. I will now reveal all, and put an end to his misery. But no; I heard the mother of the great Indra, when she was consoling Śakoontalá, say, that the gods will soon bring about a joyful union between husband and wife, being eager for the sacrifice which will be celebrated in their honor on the occasion. I must not anticipate the happy moment,

but will return at once to my dear friend and cheer her
with an account of what I have seen and heard.

[*Rises aloft and disappears.*

A VOICE [*behind the scenes*].—Help! help! to the rescue!

KING [*recovering himself. Listening*].—Ha! I heard a cry
of distress, and in Máthavya's voice. What ho there!

VETRAVATÍ [*entering*].—Your friend is in danger; save him,
great King.

KING.—Who dares insult the worthy Máthavya?

VETRAVATÍ.—Some evil demon, invisible to human eyes, has
seized him, and carried him to one of the turrets of the
Palace of Clouds.

KING [*rising*].—Impossible! Have evil spirits power over
my subjects, even in my private apartments? Well, well—
Daily I seem less able to avert
Misfortune from myself, and o'er my actions
Less competent to exercise control;
How can I then direct my subjects' ways,
Or shelter them from tyranny and wrong?

A VOICE [*behind the scenes*].—Halloo there! my dear friend;
help! help!

KING [*advancing with rapid strides*].—Fear nothing——

THE SAME VOICE [*behind the scenes*].—Fear nothing, indeed!
How can I help fearing when some monster is twisting
back my neck, and is about to snap it as he would a sugar-
cane?

KING [*looking round*].—What ho there! my bow.

SLAVE [*entering with a bow*].—Behold your bow, Sire, and
your arm-guard.

[*The king snatches up the bow and arrows.*

ANOTHER VOICE [*behind the scenes*].—Here, thirsting for thy
life-blood, will I slay thee,
As a fierce tiger rends his struggling prey.
Call now thy friend Dushyanta to thy aid;
His bow is mighty to defend the weak;
Yet all its vaunted power shall be as nought.

KING [*with fury*].—What! dares he defy me to my face?
Hold there, monster! Prepare to die, for your time is
come. [*Stringing his bow.*] Vetravatí, lead the way to
the terrace.

VETRAVATÍ.—This way, Sire. [*They advance in haste.*

KING [*looking on every side*].—How's this? there is nothing to be seen.

A VOICE [*behind the scenes*].—Help! Save me! I can see you, though you cannot see me. I am like a mouse in the claws of a cat; my life is not worth a moment's purchase.

KING.—Avaunt, monster! You may pride yourself on the magic that renders you invisible, but my arrow shall find you out. Thus do I fix a shaft

That shall discern between an impious demon
And a good Bráhman; bearing death to thee,
To him deliverance—even as the swan
Distinguishes the milk from worthless water.

[*Takes aim.*

Enter Mátali, holding Máthavya, whom he releases.

MÁTALI.—Turn thou thy deadly arrows on the demons;
Such is the will of Indra; let thy bow
Be drawn against the enemies of the gods;
But on thy friends cast only looks of favor.

KING [*putting back his arrow*].—What, Mátali! Welcome, most noble charioteer of the mighty Indra.

MÁTHAVYA.—So, here is a monster who thought as little about slaughtering me as if I had been a bullock for sacrifice, and you must e'en greet him with a welcome.

MÁTALI [*smiling*].—Great Prince, hear on what errand Indra sent me into your presence.

KING.—I am all attention.

MÁTALI.—There is a race of giants, the descendants of Kála-nemi, whom the gods find difficult to subdue.

KING.—So I have already heard from Nárada.

MÁTALI.—Heaven's mighty lord, who deigns to call thee
" friend,"

Appoints thee to the post of highest honor,
As leader of his armies; and commits
The subjugation of this giant brood
To thy resistless arms, e'en as the sun
Leaves the pale moon to dissipate the darkness.

Let your Majesty, therefore, ascend at once the celestial car of Indra; and, grasping your arms, advance to victory.

KING.—The mighty Indra honors me too highly by such a mark of distinction. But tell me, what made you act thus towards my poor friend Máthavya?

MÁTALI.—I will tell you. Perceiving that your Majesty's spirit was completely broken by some distress of mind under which you were laboring, I determined to rouse your energies by moving you to anger. Because

To light a flame, we need but stir the embers;
The cobra, when incensed, extends his head
And springs upon his foe; the bravest men
Display their courage only when provoked.

KING [*aside to Máthavya*].—My dear Máthavya, the commands of the great Indra must not be left unfulfilled. Go you and acquaint my minister, Piśuna, with what has happened, and say to him from me,

Dushyanta to thy care confides his realm—
Protect with all the vigor of thy mind
The interests of my people; while my bow
Is braced against the enemies of heaven.

MÁTHAVYA.—I obey. [*Exit.*

MÁTALI.—Ascend, illustrious Prince.

[*The King ascends the car. Exeunt.*

ACT SEVENTH

Scene.—The Sky

Enter King Dushyanta and Mátali in the car of Indra, moving in the air.

KING.—My good Mátali, it appears to me incredible that I can merit such a mark of distinction for having simply fulfilled the behests of the great Indra.

MÁTALI [*smiling*].—Great Prince, it seems to me that neither of you is satisfied with himself—

> You underrate the service you have rendered,
> And think too highly of the god's reward:
> He deems it scarce sufficient recompense
> For your heroic deeds on his behalf.

KING.—Nay, Mátali, say not so. My most ambitious expectations were more than realized by the honor conferred on me at the moment when I took my leave. For,

> Tinged with celestial sandal, from the breast
> Of the great Indra, where before it hung,
> A garland of the ever-blooming tree
> Of Nandana was cast about my neck
> By his own hand: while, in the very presence
> Of the assembled gods, I was enthroned
> Beside their mighty lord, who smiled to see
> His son Jayanta envious of the honor.

MÁTALI.—There is no mark of distinction which your Majesty does not deserve at the hands of the immortals. See,

> Heaven's hosts acknowledge thee their second saviour;
> For now thy bow's unerring shafts (as erst
> The lion-man's terrific claws) have purged
> The empyreal sphere from taint of demons foul.

KING.—The praise of my victory must be ascribed to the majesty of Indra.

When mighty gods make men their delegates
In martial enterprise, to them belongs
The palm of victory; and not to mortals.
Could the pale Dawn dispel the shades of night,
Did not the god of day, whose diadem
Is jewelled with a thousand beams of light,
Place him in front of his effulgent car?

MÁTALI.—A very just comparison. [*Driving on.*] Great
King, behold! the glory of thy fame has reached even
to the vault of heaven.

Hark! yonder inmates of the starry sphere
Sing anthems worthy of thy martial deeds,
While with celestial colors they depict
The story of thy victories on scrolls
Formed of the leaves of heaven's immortal trees.

KING.—My good Mátali, yesterday, when I ascended the sky,
I was so eager to do battle with the demons, that the road
by which we were travelling towards Indra's heaven escaped my observation. Tell me, in which path of the
seven winds are we now moving?

MÁTALI.—We journey in the path of Parivaha;
The wind that bears along the triple Ganges,
And causes Ursa's seven stars to roll
In their appointed orbits, scattering
Their several rays with equal distribution.
'Tis the same path that once was sanctified
By the divine impression of the foot
Of Vishnu, when, to conquer haughty Bali,
He spanned the heavens in his second stride.

KING.—This is the reason, I suppose, that a sensation of calm
repose pervades all my senses. [*Looking down at the
wheels.*] Ah! Mátali, we are descending towards the
earth's atmosphere.

MÁTALI.—What makes you think so?

KING.—The car itself instructs me; we are moving
O'er pregnant clouds, surcharged with rain; below us
I see the moisture-loving Chátakas
In sportive flight dart through the spokes; the steeds
Of Indra glisten with the lightning's flash;
And a thick mist bedews the circling wheels.

MÁTALI.—You are right; in a little while the chariot will
touch the ground, and you will be in your own dominions.

KING [*looking down*].—How wonderful is the appearance of
the earth as we rapidly descend!

> Stupendous prospect! yonder lofty hills
> Do suddenly uprear their towering heads
> Amid the plain, while from beneath their crests
> The ground receding sinks; the trees, whose stems
> Seemed lately hid within their leafy tresses,
> Rise into elevation, and display
> Their branching shoulders; yonder streams, whose
> waters,
> Like silver threads, but now were scarcely seen,
> Grow into mighty rivers; lo! the earth
> Seems upward hurled by some gigantic power.

MÁTALI.—Well described! [*Looking with awe.*] Grand, indeed, and lovely is the spectacle presented by the earth.

KING.—Tell me, Mátali, what is that range of mountains
which, like a bank of clouds illumined by the setting sun,
pours down a stream of gold? On one side its base dips
into the eastern ocean, and on the other side into the western.

MÁTALI.—Great Prince, it is called " Golden-peak,"[11] and is
the abode of the attendants of the god of Wealth. In
this spot the highest forms of penance are wrought out.

> There Kaśyapa, the great progenitor
> Of demons and of gods, himself the offspring
> Of the divine Maríchi, Brahmá's son,
> With Aditi, his wife, in calm seclusion,
> Does holy penance for the good of mortals.

KING.—Then I must not neglect so good an opportunity of
obtaining his blessing. I should much like to visit this
venerable personage and offer him my homage.

MÁTALI.—By all means! An excellent idea.

> [*Guides the car to the earth.*

KING [*in a tone of wonder*].—How's this?

> Our chariot wheels move noiselessly. Around
> No clouds of dust arise; no shock betokened

---

[11] A sacred range of mountains lying along the Himálaya chain immediately
adjacent to Kailása, the paradise of Kuvera, the god of wealth.

Our contact with the earth; we seem to glide
Above the ground, so lightly do we touch it.

MÁTALI.—Such is the difference between the car of Indra and that of your Majesty.

KING.—In which direction, Mátali, is Kaśyapa's sacred retreat?

MÁTALI [*pointing*].—Where stands yon anchorite, towards the orb
Of the meridian sun, immovable
As a tree's stem, his body half-concealed
By a huge ant-hill. Round about his breast
No sacred cord is twined, but in its stead
A hideous serpent's skin. In place of necklace,
The tendrils of a withered creeper chafe
His wasted neck. His matted hair depends
In thick entanglement about his shoulders,
And birds construct their nests within its folds.

KING.—I salute thee, thou man of austere devotion.

MÁTALI [*holding in the reins of the car*].—Great Prince, we are now in the sacred grove of the holy Kaśyapa—the grove that boasts as its ornament one of the five trees of Indra's heaven, reared by Aditi.

KING.—This sacred retreat is more delightful than heaven itself. I could almost fancy myself bathing in a pool of nectar.

MÁTALI [*stopping the chariot*].—Descend, mighty Prince.

KING [*descending*].—And what will you do, Mátali?

MÁTALI.—The chariot will remain where I have stopped it. We may both descend. [*Doing so.*] This way, great King. [*Walking on*]. You see around you the celebrated region where the holiest sages devote themselves to penitential rites.

KING.—I am filled with awe and wonder as I gaze.
In such a place as this do saints of earth
Long to complete their acts of penance; here,
Beneath the shade of everlasting trees,
Transplanted from the groves of Paradise,
May they inhale the balmy air, and need
No other nourishment; here may they bathe
In fountains sparkling with the golden dust
Of lilies; here, on jewelled slabs of marble,

In meditation rapt, may they recline;
Here, in the presence of celestial nymphs,
E'en passion's voice is powerless to move them.

MÁTALI.—So true is it that the aspirations of the good and great are ever soaring upwards. [*Turning round and speaking off the stage.*] Tell me, Vriddha-śákalya, how is the divine son of Maríchi now engaged? What sayest thou? that he is conversing with Aditi and some of the wives of the great sages, and that they are questioning him respecting the duties of a faithful wife?

KING [*listening*].—Then we must await the holy father's leisure.

MÁTALI [*looking at the King*].—If your Majesty will rest under the shade, at the foot of this Aśoka-tree, I will seek an opportunity of announcing your arrival to Indra's reputed father.

KING.—As you think proper.　　[*Remains under the tree.*

MÁTALI.—Great King, I go.　　　　　　　　[*Exit.*

KING [*feeling his arm throb*].—Wherefore this causeless throbbing, O mine arm?
All hope has fled forever; mock me not
With presages of good, when happiness
Is lost, and nought but misery remains.

A VOICE [*behind the scenes*].—Be not so naughty. Do you begin already to show a refractory spirit?

KING [*listening*].—This is no place for petulance. Who can it be whose behavior calls for such a rebuke? [*Looking in the direction of the sound and smiling.*] A child, is it? closely attended by two holy women. His disposition seems anything but childlike. See,
He braves the fury of yon lioness
Suckling its savage offspring, and compels
The angry whelp to leave the half-sucked dug,
Tearing its tender mane in boisterous sport.

Enter a child, attended by two women of the hermitage, in the manner described.

CHILD.—Open your mouth, my young lion, I want to count your teeth.

FIRST ATTENDANT.—You naughty child, why do you tease the

animals? Know you not that we cherish them in this hermitage as if they were our own children? In good sooth, you have a high spirit of your own, and are beginning already to do justice to the name Sarva-damana (All-taming), given you by the hermits.

KING.—Strange! My heart inclines towards the boy with almost as much affection as if he were my own child. What can be the reason? I suppose my own childlessness makes me yearn towards the sons of others.

SECOND ATTENDANT.—This lioness will certainly attack you if you do not release her whelp.

CHILD [*laughing*].—Oh! indeed! let her come. Much I fear her, to be sure.   [*Pouts his under-lip in defiance.*

KING.—The germ of mighty courage lies concealed
    Within this noble infant, like a spark
    Beneath the fuel, waiting but a breath
    To fan the flame and raise a conflagration.

FIRST ATTENDANT.—Let the young lion go, like a dear child, and I will give you something else to play with.

CHILD.—Where is it? Give it me first.
    [*Stretches out his hand.*

KING [*looking at his hand*].—How's this? His hand exhibits one of those mystic marks which are the sure prognostic of universal empire. See!
    His fingers stretched in eager expectation
    To grasp the wished-for toy, and knit together
    By a close-woven web, in shape resemble
    A lotus-blossom, whose expanding petals
    The early dawn has only half unfolded.

SECOND ATTENDANT.—We shall never pacify him by mere words, dear Suvratá. Be kind enough to go to my cottage, and you will find there a plaything belonging to Márkándeya, one of the hermit's children. It is a peacock made of China-ware, painted in many colors. Bring it here for the child.

FIRST ATTENDANT.—Very well.   [*Exit.*

CHILD.—No, no; I shall go on playing with the young lion.
    [*Looks at the female attendant and laughs.*

KING.—I feel an unaccountable affection for this wayward child.
    How blessed the virtuous parents whose attire

Is soiled with dust, by raising from the ground
The child that asks a refuge in their arms!
And happy are they while with lisping prattle,
In accents sweetly inarticulate,
He charms their ears; and with his artless smiles
Gladdens their hearts, revealing to their gaze
His tiny teeth, just budding into view.

ATTENDANT.—I see how it is. He pays me no manner of attention. [*Looking off the stage.*] I wonder whether any of the hermits are about here. [*Seeing the King.*] Kind Sir, could you come hither a moment and help me to release the young lion from the clutch of this child, who is teasing him in boyish play?

KING [*approaching and smiling*].—Listen to me, thou child of a mighty saint.

Dost thou dare show a wayward spirit here?
Here, in this hallowed region? Take thou heed
Lest, as the serpent's young defiles the sandal,
.Thou bring dishonor on the holy sage,
Thy tender-hearted parent, who delights
To shield from harm the tenants of the wood.

ATTENDANT.—Gentle Sir, I thank you; but he is not the saint's son.

KING.—His behavior and whole bearing would have led me to doubt it, had not the place of his abode encouraged the idea.

[*Follows the child, and takes him by the hand, according to the request of the attendant. Speaking aside.*

I marvel that the touch of this strange child
Should thrill me with delight; if so it be,
How must the fond caresses of a son
Transport the father's soul who gave him being!

ATTENDANT [*looking at them both*].—Wonderful! Prodigious!

KING.—What excites your surprise, my good woman?

ATTENDANT.—I am astonished at the striking resemblance between the child and yourself; and, what is still more extraordinary, he seems to have taken to you kindly and submissively, though you are a stranger to him.

KING [*fondling the child*].—If he be not the son of the great sage, of what family does he come, may I ask?

ATTENDANT.—Of the race of Puru.

KING [*aside*].—What! are we, then, descended from the
same ancestry? This, no doubt, accounts for the resemblance she traces between the child and me. Certainly it
has always been an established usage among the princes
of Puru's race,

> To dedicate the morning of their days
> To the world's weal, in palaces and halls,
> 'Mid luxury and regal pomp abiding;
> Then, in the wane of life, to seek release
> From kingly cares, and make the hallowed shade
> Of sacred trees their last asylum, where
> As hermits they may practise self-abasement,
> And bind themselves by rigid vows of penance.

[*Aloud.*] But how could mortals by their own power
gain admission to this sacred region?

ATTENDANT.—Your remark is just; but your wonder will
cease when I tell you that his mother is the offspring of a
celestial nymph, and gave him birth in the hallowed grove
of Kaśyapa.

KING [*aside*].—Strange that my hopes should be again excited! [*Aloud.*] But what, let me ask, was the name of
the prince whom she deigned to honor with her hand?

ATTENDANT.—How could I think of polluting my lips by the
mention of a wretch who had the cruelty to desert his
lawful wife?

KING [*aside*].—Ha! the description suits me exactly. Would
I could bring myself to inquire the name of the child's
mother! [*Reflecting.*] But it is against propriety to
make too minute inquiries about the wife of another man.

FIRST ATTENDANT [*entering with the china peacock in her
hand*].—Sarva-damana, Sarva-damana, see, see, what a
beautiful Śakoonta (bird).

CHILD [*looking round*].—My mother! Where? Let me go
to her.

BOTH ATTENDANTS.—He mistook the word Śakoonta for Śakoontalá. The boy dotes upon his mother, and she is ever
uppermost in his thoughts.

SECOND ATTENDANT.—Nay, my dear child, I said, Look at
the beauty of this Śakoonta.

KING [*aside*].—What! is his mother's name Śakoontalá? But

the name is not uncommon among women. Alas! I fear
the mere similarity of a name, like the deceitful vapor of
the desert, has once more raised my hopes only to dash
them to the ground.

CHILD [*takes the toy*].—Dear nurse, what a beautiful peacock!

FIRST ATTENDANT [*looking at the child. In great distress*].—
Alas! alas! I do not see the amulet on his wrist.

KING.—Don't distress yourself. Here it is. It fell off while
he was struggling with the young lion.

                                        [*Stoops to pick it up.*

BOTH ATTENDANTS.—Hold! hold! Touch it not, for your
life. How marvellous! He has actually taken it up without the slightest hesitation.

[*Both raise their hands to their breasts and look at each other
in astonishment.*

KING.—Why did you try to prevent my touching it?

FIRST ATTENDANT.—Listen, great Monarch. This amulet,
known as "The Invincible," was given to the boy by the
divine son of Maríchi, soon after his birth, when the natal
ceremony was performed. Its peculiar virtue is, that
when it falls on the ground, no one excepting the father
or mother of the child can touch it unhurt.

KING.—And suppose another person touches it?

FIRST ATTENDANT.—Then it instantly becomes a serpent, and
bites him.

KING.—Have you ever witnessed the transformation with your
own eyes?

BOTH ATTENDANTS.—Over and over again.

KING [*with rapture. Aside*].—Joy! joy! Are then my dearest hopes to be fulfilled?   [*Embraces the child.*

SECOND ATTENDANT.—Come, my dear Suvratá, we must inform Śakoontalá immediately of this wonderful event,
though we have to interrupt her in the performance of her
religious vows.   [*Exeunt.*

CHILD [*to the King*].—Do not hold me. I want to go to my
mother.

KING.—We will go to her together, and give her joy, my son.

CHILD.—Dushyanta is my father, not you.

KING [*smiling*].—His contradiction convinces me only the
more.

*Enter Śakoontalá, in widow's apparel, with her long hair
twisted into a single braid.*

ŚAKOONTALÁ [*aside*].—I have just heard that Sarva-damana's
amulet has retained its form, though a stranger raised
it from the ground. I can hardly believe in my good
fortune. Yet why should not Sánumatí's prediction be
verified?

KING [*gazing at Śakoontalá*].—Alas! can this indeed be my
Śakoontalá?
  Clad in the weeds of widowhood, her face
  Emaciate with fasting, her long hair
  Twined in a single braid, her whole demeanor
  Expressive of her purity of soul:
  With patient constancy she thus prolongs
  The vow to which my cruelty condemned her.

ŚAKOONTALÁ [*gazing at the King, who is pale with remorse*].
  Surely this is not like my husband; yet who can it be
  that dares pollute by the pressure of his hand my child,
  whose amulet should protect him from a stranger's touch?

CHILD [*going to his mother*].—Mother, who is this man that
  has been kissing me and calling me his son?

KING.—My best beloved, I have indeed treated thee most
  cruelly, but am now once more thy fond and affectionate
  lover. Refuse not to acknowledge me as thy husband.

ŚAKOONTALÁ [*aside*].—Be of good cheer, my heart. The
  anger of Destiny is at last appeased. Heaven regards
  thee with compassion. But is he in very truth my husband?

KING.—Behold me, best and loveliest of women,
  Delivered from the cloud of fatal darkness
  That erst oppressed my memory. Again
  Behold us brought together by the grace
  Of the great lord of Heaven. So the moon
  Shines forth from dim eclipse, to blend his rays
  With the soft lustre of his Rohiní.

ŚAKOONTALÁ.—May my husband be victorious——
                [*She stops short, her voice choked with tears.*

KING.—O fair one, though the utterance of thy prayer
  Be lost amid the torrent of thy tears,
  Yet does the sight of thy fair countenance,

And of thy pallid lips, all unadorned
And colorless in sorrow for my absence,
Make me already more than conqueror.

CHILD.—Mother, who is this man?

SAKOONTALÁ.—My child, ask the deity that presides over thy destiny.

KING [*falling at Sakoontalá's feet*].—Fairest of women, banish from thy mind
The memory of my cruelty; reproach
The fell delusion that o'erpowered my soul,
And blame not me, thy husband; 'tis the curse
Of him in whom the power of darkness reigns,
That he mistakes the gifts of those he loves
For deadly evils. Even though a friend
Should wreathe a garland on a blind man's brow,
Will he not cast it from him as a serpent?

SAKOONTALÁ.—Rise, my own husband, rise. Thou wast not to blame. My own evil deeds, committed in a former state of being, brought down this judgment upon me. How else could my husband, who was ever of a compassionate disposition, have acted so unfeelingly? [*The King rises.*] But tell me, my husband, how did the remembrance of thine unfortunate wife return to thy mind?

KING.—As soon as my heart's anguish is removed, and its wounds are healed, I will tell thee all.
Oh! let me, fair one, chase away the drop
That still bedews the fringes of thine eye;
And let me thus efface the memory
Of every tear that stained thy velvet cheek,
Unnoticed and unheeded by thy lord,
When in his madness he rejected thee.
[*Wipes away the tear.*

SAKOONTALÁ [*seeing the signet-ring on his finger*].—Ah! my dear husband, is that the Lost Ring?

KING.—Yes; the moment I recovered it, my memory was restored.

SAKOONTALÁ.—The ring was to blame in allowing itself to be lost at the very time when I was anxious to convince my noble husband of the reality of my marriage.

KING.—Receive it back, as the beautiful twining plant receives again its blossom in token of its reunion with the spring.

ŚAKOONTALÁ.—Nay; I can never more place confidence in it. Let my husband retain it.

Enter Mátali.

MÁTALI.—I congratulate your Majesty. Happy are you in your reunion with your wife: happy are you in beholding the face of your son.

KING.—Yes, indeed. My heart's dearest wish has borne sweet fruit. But tell me, Mátali, is this joyful event known to the great Indra?

MÁTALI [*smiling*].—What is unknown to the gods? But come with me, noble Prince, the divine Kaśyapa graciously permits thee to be presented to him.

KING.—Śakoontalá, take our child and lead the way. We will together go into the presence of the holy Sage.

ŚAKOONTALÁ.—I shrink from entering the august presence of the great Saint, even with my husband at my side.

KING.—Nay; on such a joyous occasion it is highly proper. Come, come; I entreat thee. [*All advance.*

Kaśyapa is discovered seated on a throne with his wife Aditi.

KAŚYAPA [*gazing at Dushyanta. To his wife*].—O Aditi,
This is the mighty hero, King Dushyanta,
Protector of the earth; who, at the head
Of the celestial armies of thy son,
Does battle with the enemies of heaven.
Thanks to his bow, the thunderbolt of Indra
Rests from its work, no more the minister
Of death and desolation to the world,
But a mere symbol of divinity.

ADITI.—He bears in his noble form all the marks of dignity.

MÁTALI [*to Dushyanta*].—Sire, the venerable progenitors of the celestials are gazing at your Majesty with as much affection as if you were their son. You may advance towards them.

KING.—Are these, O Mátali, the holy pair,
Offspring of Daksha and divine Maríchi,
Children of Brahmá's sons, by sages deemed
Sole fountain of celestial light, diffused
Through twelve effulgent orbs? Are these the pair
VOL. III.—27

From whom the ruler of the triple world,
Sovereign of gods and lord of sacrifice,
Sprang into being? That immortal pair
Whom Vishnu, greater than the self-existent,
Chose for his parents, when, to save mankind,
He took upon himself the shape of mortals?

MÁTALI.—Even so.

KING [*prostrating himself*].—Most august of beings, Dushyanta, content to have fulfilled the commands of your son Indra, offers you his adoration.

KAŚYAPA.—My son, long may'st thou live, and happily may'st thou reign over the earth!

ADITI.—My son, may'st thou ever be invincible in the field of battle!

ŚAKOONTALÁ.—I also prostrate myself before you, most adorable beings, and my child with me.

KAŚYAPA.—My daughter,

Thy lord resembles Indra, and thy child
Is noble as Jayanta, Indra's son;
I have no worthier blessing left for thee,
May'st thou be faithful as the god's own wife!

ADITI.—My daughter, may'st thou be always the object of thy husband's fondest love; and may thy son live long to be the joy of both his parents! Be seated.

[*All sit down in the presence of Kaśyapa.*

KAŚYAPA [*regarding each of them by turns*].—Hail to the beautiful Śakoontalá!

Hail to her noble son! and hail to thee,
Illustrious Prince! Rare triple combination
Of virtue, wealth, and energy united!

KING.—Most venerable Kaśyapa, by your favor all my desires were accomplished even before I was admitted to your presence. Never was mortal so honored that his boon should be granted ere it was solicited. Because,

Bloom before fruit, the clouds before the rain—
Cause first and then effect, in endless sequence,
Is the unchanging law of constant nature;
But, ere the blessing issued from thy lips,
The wishes of my heart were all fulfilled.

MÁTALI.—It is thus that the great progenitors of the world confer favors.

KING.—Most reverend Sage, this thy handmaid was married to me by the Gandharva ceremony, and after a time was conducted to my palace by her relations. Meanwhile a fatal delusion seized me; I lost my memory and rejected her, thus committing a grievous offence against the venerable Kanwa, who is of thy divine race. Afterwards the sight of this ring restored my faculties, and brought back to my mind all the circumstances of my union with his daughter. But my conduct still seems to me incomprehensible;

As foolish as the fancies of a man
Who, when he sees an elephant, denies
That 'tis an elephant, yet afterwards,
When its huge bulk moves onward, hesitates,
Yet will not be convinced till it has passed
Forever from his sight, and left behind
No vestige of its presence save its footsteps.

KASYAPA.—My son, cease to think thyself in fault. Even the delusion that possessed thy mind was not brought about by any act of thine. Listen to me.

KING.—I am attentive.

KASYAPA.—Know that when the nymph Menaká, the mother of Śakoontalá, became aware of her daughter's anguish in consequence of the loss of the ring at the nymphs' pool, and of thy subsequent rejection of her, she brought her and confided her to the care of Aditi. And I no sooner saw her than I ascertained by my divine power of meditation, that thy repudiation of thy poor faithful wife had been caused entirely by the curse of Durvásas—not by thine own fault—and that the spell would terminate on the discovery of the ring.

KING [drawing a deep breath].—Oh! what a weight is taken off my mind, now that my character is cleared of reproach.

ŚAKOONTALÁ [aside].—Joy! joy! My revered husband did not, then, reject me without good reason, though I have no recollection of the curse pronounced upon me. But, in all probability, I unconsciously brought it upon myself, when I was so distracted on being separated from my husband soon after our marriage. For I now remember that my two friends advised me not to fail to show the ring in case he should have forgotten me.

KAŚYAPA.—At last, my daughter, thou art happy, and hast
gained thy heart's desire. Indulge, then, no feeling of
resentment against thy partner. See, now,
> Though he repulsed thee, 'twas the sage's curse
> That clouded his remembrance; 'twas the curse
> That made thy tender husband harsh towards thee.
> Soon as the spell was broken, and his soul
> Delivered from its darkness, in a moment
> Thou didst gain thine empire o'er his heart.
> So on the tarnished surface of a mirror
> No image is reflected, till the dust
> That dimmed its wonted lustre is removed.

KING.—Holy father, see here the hope of my royal race.
> [*Takes his child by the hand.*

KAŚYAPA.—Know that he, too, will become the monarch of
the whole earth. Observe,
> Soon, a resistless hero, shall he cross
> The trackless ocean, borne above the waves
> In an aerial car; and shall subdue
> The earth's seven sea-girt isles.[12] Now has he gained,
> As the brave tamer of the forest-beasts,
> The title Sarva-damana; but then
> Mankind shall hail him as King Bharata,
> And call him the supporter of the world.

KING.—We cannot but entertain the highest hopes of a child
for whom your highness performed the natal rites.

ADITI.—My revered husband, should not the intelligence be
conveyed to Kanwa, that his daughter's wishes are fulfilled, and her happiness complete? He is Śakoontalá's
foster-father. Menaká, who is one of my attendants, is
her mother, and dearly does she love her daughter.

ŚAKOONTALÁ [*aside*].—The venerable matron has given utterance to the very wish that was in my mind.

KAŚYAPA.—His penances have gained for him the faculty of
omniscience, and the whole scene is already present to his
mind's eye.

KING.—Then most assuredly he cannot be very angry with
me.

---

[12] According to the mythical geography of the Hindoos the earth consisted of
seven islands surrounded by seven seas.

KAŚYAPA.—Nevertheless it becomes us to send him intelligence
of this happy event, and hear his reply. What, ho there!

PUPIL [*entering*].—Holy father, what are your commands?

KAŚYAPA.—My good Gálava, delay not an instant, but hasten
through the air and convey to the venerable Kanwa, from
me, the happy news that the fatal spell has ceased, that
Dushyanta's memory is restored, that his daughter Śakoontalá has a son, and that she is once more tenderly
acknowledged by her husband.

PUPIL.—Your highness's commands shall be obeyed.   [*Exit.*

KAŚYAPA.—And now, my dear son, take thy consort and thy
child, re-ascend the car of Indra, and return to thy imperial capital.

KING.—Most holy father, I obey.

KAŚYAPA.—And accept this blessing—

> For countless ages may the god of gods,
> Lord of the atmosphere, by copious showers
> Secure abundant harvest to thy subjects;
> And thou by frequent offerings preserve
> The Thunderer's friendship! Thus, by interchange
> Of kindly actions, may you both confer
> Unnumbered benefits on earth and heaven!

KING.—Holy father, I will strive, as far as I am able, to attain
this happiness.

KAŚYAPA.—What other favor can I bestow on thee, my son?

KING.—What other can I desire? If, however, you permit
me to form another wish, I would humbly beg that the
saying of the sage Bharata be fulfilled:—

> May kings reign only for their subjects' weal!
> May the divine Saraswati, the source
> Of speech, and goddess of dramatic art,
> Be ever honored by the great and wise!
> And may the purple self-existent god,
> Whose vital Energy pervades all space,
> From future transmigrations save my soul!

                    [*Exeunt omnes.*

BALLADS OF HINDOSTAN

—

MISCELLANEOUS POEMS

—

BY

TORU DUTT

INTRODUCTION

I F Toru Dutt were alive, she would still be younger than any recognized European writer, and yet her fame, which is already considerable, has been entirely posthumous. Within the brief space of four years which now divides us from the date of her decease, her genius has been revealed to the world under many phases, and has been recognized throughout France and England. Her name, at least, is no longer unfamiliar in the ear of any well-read man or woman. But at the hour of her death she had published but one book, and that book had found but two reviewers in Europe. One of these, M. André Theuriet, the well-known poet and novelist, gave the " Sheaf gleaned in French Fields " adequate praise in the " Revue des Deux Mondes "; but the other, the writer of the present notice, has a melancholy satisfaction in having been a little earlier still in sounding the only note of welcome which reached the dying poetess from England. It was while Professor W. Minto was editor of the " Examiner," that one day in August, 1876, in the very heart of the dead season for books, I happened to be in the office of that newspaper, and was upbraiding the whole body of publishers for issuing no books worth reviewing. At that moment the postman brought in a thin and sallow packet with a wonderful Indian postmark on it, and containing a most unattractive orange pamphlet of verse, printed at Bhowanipore, and entitled " A Sheaf gleaned in French Fields, by Toru Dutt." This shabby little book of some two hundred pages, without preface or introduction, seemed specially destined by its particular providence to find its way hastily into the waste-paper basket. I remember that Mr. Minto thrust it into my unwilling hands, and said " There! see whether you can't make something of that." A hopeless volume it seemed, with its queer type, published at Bhowanipore, printed at the Saptahiksambad Press! But when at last

I took it out of my pocket, what was my surprise and almost
rapture to open at such verse as this:—

> " Still barred thy doors! The far East glows,
>   The morning wind blows fresh and free.
> Should not the hour that wakes the rose
>   Awaken also thee?

> " All look for thee, Love, Light, and Song,
>   Light in the sky deep red above,
> Song, in the lark of pinions strong,
>   And in my heart, true Love.

> " Apart we miss our nature's goal,
>   Why strive to cheat our destinies?
> Was not my love made for thy soul?
>   Thy beauty for mine eyes?
>   No longer sleep,
>   Oh, listen now!
>   I wait and weep,
>   But where art thou? "

When poetry is as good as this it does not much matter
whether Rouveyre prints it upon Whatman paper, or whether
it steals to light in blurred type from some press in Bhowanipore.

Toru Dutt was the youngest of the three children of a high-
caste Hindoo couple in Bengal. Her father, who survives
them all, the Baboo Govin Chunder Dutt, is himself distinguished among his countrymen for the width of his views and
the vigor of his intelligence. His only son, Abju, died in
1865, at the age of fourteen, and left his two younger sisters to
console their parents. Aru, the elder daughter, born in 1854,
was eighteen months senior to Toru, the subject of this mem-
oir, who was born in Calcutta on March 4, 1856. With the
exception of one year's visit to Bombay, the childhood of these
girls was spent in Calcutta, at their father's garden-house. In
a poem now printed for the first time, Toru refers to the scene
of her earliest memories, the circling wilderness of foliage, the
shining tank with the round leaves of the lilies, the murmuring
dusk under the vast branches of the central casuarina-tree.
Here, in a mystical retirement more irksome to a European
in fancy than to an Oriental in reality, the brain of this wonderful child was moulded. She was pure Hindoo, full of the
typical qualities of her race and blood, and, as the present vol-

ume shows us for the first time, preserving to the last her appreciation of the poetic side of her ancient religion, though faith itself in Vishnu and Siva had been cast aside with childish things and been replaced by a purer faith. Her mother fed her imagination with the old songs and legends of their people, stories which it was the last labor of her life to weave into English verse; but it would seem that the marvellous faculties of Toru's mind still slumbered, when, in her thirteenth year, her father decided to take his daughters to Europe to learn English and French. To the end of her days Toru was a better French than English scholar. She loved France best, she knew its literature best, she wrote its language with more perfect elegance. The Dutts arrived in Europe at the close of 1869, and the girls went to school, for the first and last time, at a French pension. They did not remain there very many months; their father took them to Italy and England with him, and finally they attended for a short time, but with great zeal and application, the lectures for women at Cambridge. In November, 1873, they went back to Bengal, and the four remaining years of Toru's life were spent in the old garden-house at Calcutta, in a feverish dream of intellectual effort and imaginative production. When we consider what she achieved in these forty-five months of seclusion, it is impossible to wonder that the frail and hectic body succumbed under so excessive a strain.

She brought with her from Europe a store of knowledge that would have sufficed to make an English or French girl seem learned, but which in her case was simply miraculous. Immediately on her return she began to study Sanscrit with the same intense application which she gave to all her work, and mastering the language with extraordinary swiftness, she plunged into its mysterious literature. But she was born to write, and despairing of an audience in her own language, she began to adopt ours as a medium for her thought. Her first essay, published when she was eighteen, was a monograph, in the " Bengal Magazine," on Leconte de Lisle, a writer with whom she had a sympathy which is very easy to comprehend. The austere poet of " La Mort de Valmiki " was, obviously, a figure to whom the poet of " Sindhu " must needs be attracted on approaching European literature. This study, which was illustrated by translations into English verse, was followed

by another on Joséphin Soulary, in whom she saw more than
her maturer judgment might have justified. There is something very interesting and now, alas! still more pathetic in
these sturdy and workmanlike essays in unaided criticism.
Still more solitary her work became, in July, 1874, when her
only sister, Aru, died, at the age of twenty. She seems to have
been no less amiable than her sister, and if gifted with less originality and a less forcible ambition, to have been finely accomplished. Both sisters were well-trained musicians, with full
contralto voices, and Aru had a faculty for design which promised well. The romance of " Mlle. D'Arvers " was originally
projected for Aru to illustrate, but no page of this book did
Aru ever see.

In 1876, as we have said, appeared that obscure first volume
at Bhowanipore. The " Sheaf gleaned in French Fields " is
certainly the most imperfect of Toru's writings, but it is not
the least interesting. It is a wonderful mixture of strength
and weakness, of genius overriding great obstacles, and of
talent succumbing to ignorance and inexperience. That it
should have been performed at all is so extraordinary that we
forget to be surprised at its inequality. The English verse is
sometimes exquisite; at other times the rules of our prosody are
absolutely ignored, and it is obvious that the Hindoo poetess
was chanting to herself a music that is discord in an English
ear. The notes are no less curious, and to a stranger no less
bewildering. Nothing could be more naïve than the writer's
ignorance at some points, or more startling than her learning
at others. On the whole, the attainment of the book was simply astounding. It consisted of a selection of translations
from nearly one hundred French poets, chosen by the poetess
herself on a principle of her own which gradually dawned
upon the careful reader. She eschewed the Classicist writers
as though they had never existed. For her André Chenier
was the next name in chronological order after Du Bartas.
Occasionally she showed a profundity of research that would
have done no discredit to Mr. Saintsbury or " le doux Asselli-
neau." She was ready to pronounce an opinion on Napol le
Pyrénéan or detect a plagiarism in Baudelaire. But she
thought that Alexander Smith was still alive, and she was curi-
ously vague about the career of Sainte-Beuve. This inequality of equipment was a thing inevitable to her isolation, and

hardly worthy recording, except to show how laborious her mind was, and how quick to make the best of small resources.

We have already seen that the " Sheaf gleaned in French Fields" attracted the very minimum of attention in England. In France it was talked about a little more. M. Garcin de Tassy, the famous Orientalist, who scarcely survived Toru by twelve months, spoke of it to Mlle. Clarisse Bader, author of a somewhat remarkable book on the position of women in ancient Indian society. Almost simultaneously this volume fell into the hands of Toru, and she was moved to translate it into English, for the use of Hindoos less instructed than herself. In January, 1877, she accordingly wrote to Mlle. Bader requesting her authorization, and received a prompt and kind reply. On the 18th of March Toru wrote again to this, her solitary correspondent in the world of European literature, and her letter, which has been preserved, shows that she had already descended into the valley of the shadow of death :—

" Ma constitution n'est pas forte; j'ai contracté une toux opiniâtre, il y a plus de deux ans, qui ne me quitte point. Cependant j'espère mettre la main à l'œuvre bientôt. Je ne peux dire, mademoiselle, combien votre affection—car vous les aimez, votre livre et votre lettre en témoignent assez—pour mes compatriotes et mon pays me touche; et je suis fière de pouvoir le dire que les héroïnes de nos grandes épopées sont dignes de tout honneur et de tout amour. Y a-t-il d'héroïne plus touchante, plus aimable que Sita? Je ne le crois pas. *Quand j'entends ma mère chanter, le soir, les vieux chants de notre pays, je pleure presque toujours.* La plainte de Sita, quand, bannie pour la séconde fois, elle erre dans la vaste forêt, seule, le désespoir et l'effroi dans l'âme, est si pathétique qu'il n'y a personne, je crois, qui puisse l'entendre sans verser des larmes. Je vous envois sous ce pli deux petites traductions du Sanscrit, cette belle langue antique. Malheureusement j'ai été obligée de faire cesser mes traductions de Sanscrit, il y a six mois. Ma santé ne me permet pas de les continuer."

These simple and pathetic words, in which the dying poetess pours out her heart to the one friend she had, and that one gained too late, seem as touching and as beautiful as any strain of Marceline Valmore's immortal verse. In English poetry I do not remember anything that exactly parallels their resigned melancholy. Before the month of March was over, Toru had taken to her bed. Unable to write, she continued to read, strewing her sick-room with the latest European books, and entering with interest into the questions raised by the Société Asiatique of Paris, in its printed Transactions. On the 30th of July she wrote her last letter to Mlle. Clarisse Bader, and a month later, on August 30, 1877, at the age of twenty-one years six months and twenty-six days, she breathed her last in her father's house in Maniktollah street, Calcutta.

In the first distraction of grief it seemed as though her un-equalled promise had been entirely blighted, and as though she would be remembered only by her single book. But as her father examined her papers, one completed work after an-other revealed itself. First a selection from the sonnets of the Comte de Grammont, translated into English, turned up, and was printed in a Calcutta magazine; then some fragments of an English story, which were printed in another Calcutta magazine. Much more important, however, than any of thsee was a complete romance, written in French, being the identical story for which her sister Aru had proposed to make the illustrations. In the meantime Toru was no sooner dead than she began to be famous. In May, 1878, there appeared a second edition of the " Sheaf gleaned in French Fields," with a touching sketch of her death, by her father; and in 1879 was published, under the editorial care of Mlle. Clarisse Bader, the romance of " Le Journal de Mlle. D'Arvers," form-ing a handsome volume of 259 pages. This book, begun, as it appears, before the family returned from Europe, and finished nobody knows when, is an attempt to describe scenes from modern French society, but it is less interesting as an experi-ment of the fancy, than as a revelation of the mind of a young Hindoo woman of genius. The story is simple, clearly told, and interesting; the studies of character have nothing French about them, but they are full of vigor and originality. The description of the hero is most characteristically Indian:—

" Il est beau en effet. Sa taille est haute, mais quelques-uns la trou-veraient mince; sa chevelure noire est bouclée et tombe jusqu'à la nuque; ses yeux noirs sont profonds et bien fendus; le front est noble; la lèvre supérieure, couverte par une moustache naissante et noire, est parfaitement modelée; son menton a quelque chose de sévère; son teint est d'un blanc presque féminin, ce qui dénote sa haute naissance."

In this description we seem to recognize some Surya or Soma of Hindoo mythology, and the final touch, meaningless as applied to a European, reminds us that in India whiteness of skin has always been a sign of aristocratic birth, from the days when it originally distinguished the conquering Aryas from the indigenous race of the Dasyous.

As a literary composition " Mlle. D'Arvers " deserves high commendation. It deals with the ungovernable passion of two brothers for one placid and beautiful girl, a passion which leads to fratricide and madness. That it is a very melancholy and tragical story is obvious from this brief sketch of its con-tents, but it is remarkable for coherence and self-restraint no less than for vigor of treatment. Toru Dutt never sinks to melodrama in the course of her extraordinary tale, and the wonder is that she is not more often fantastic and unreal.

But we believe that the original English poems will be ulti-mately found to constitute Toru's chief legacy to posterity. These ballads form the last and most matured of her writings, and were left so far fragmentary at her death that the fourth and fifth in her projected series of nine were not to be discovered in any form among her papers. It is probable that she had not even commenced them. Her father, therefore, to give a certain continuity to the series, has filled up these blanks with two stories from the " Vishnupurana," which originally ap-peared respectively in the " Calcutta Review " and in the " Bengal Magazine." These are interesting, but a little rude in form, and they have not the same peculiar value as the rhymed octo-syllabic ballads. In these last we see Toru no longer attempting vainly, though heroically, to compete with European literature on its own ground, but turning to the legends of her own race and country for inspiration. No mod-ern Oriental has given us so strange an insight into the con-science of the Asiatic as is presented in the story of " Prehlad," or so quaint a piece of religious fancy as the ballad of " Joga-dhya Uma." The poetess seems in these verses to be chanting to herself those songs of her mother's race to which she always turned with tears of pleasure. They breathe a Vedic solemnity and simplicity of temper, and are singularly devoid of that littleness and frivolity which seem, if we may judge by a slight experience, to be the bane of modern India.

As to the merely technical character of these poems, it may be suggested that in spite of much in them that is rough and inchoate, they show that Toru was advancing in her mastery of English verse. Such a stanza as this, selected out of many

no less skilful, could hardly be recognized as the work of one
by whom the language was a late acquirement:—

> " What glorious trees! The sombre saul,
>   On which the eye delights to rest—
> The betel-nut, a pillar tall,
>   With feathery branches for a crest—
> The light-leaved tamarind spreading wide—
>   The pale faint-scented bitter neem,
> The seemul, gorgeous as a bride,
>   With flowers that have the ruby's gleam.'

In other passages, of course, the text reads like a translation
from some stirring ballad, and we feel that it gives but a faint
and dicordant echo of the music welling in Toru's brain. For
it must frankly be confessed that in the brief May-day of her
existence she had not time to master our language as Blanco
White did, or as Chamisso mastered German. To the end of
her days, fluent and graceful as she was, she was not entirely
conversant with English, especially with the colloquial turns
of modern speech. Often a very fine thought is spoiled for
hypercritical ears by the queer turn of expression which she
has innocently given to it. These faults are found to a much
smaller degree in her miscellaneous poems. Her sonnets seem
to me to be of great beauty, and her longer piece entitled " Our
Casuarina Tree," needs no apology for its rich and mellifluous
numbers.

It is difficult to exaggerate when we try to estimate what we
have lost in the premature death of Toru Dutt. Literature
has no honors which need have been beyond the grasp of a
girl who at the age of twenty-one, and in languages separated
from her own by so deep a chasm, had produced so much of
lasting worth. And her courage and fortitude were worthy
of her intelligence. Among " last words " of celebrated people, that which her father has recorded, " It is only the physical
pain that makes me cry," is not the least remarkable, or the
least significant of strong character. It was to a native of our
island, and to one ten years senior to Toru, to whom it was
said, in words more appropriate, surely, to her than to Oldham,

> " Thy generous fruits, though gathered ere their prime,
>   Still showed a quickness, and maturing time
> But mellows what we write to the dull sweets of Rime."

That mellow sweetness was all that Toru lacked to perfect her as an English poet, and of no other Oriental who has ever lived can the same be said. When the history of the literature of our country comes to be written, there is sure to be a page in it dedicated to this fragile exotic blossom of song.

EDMUND W. GOSSE.

London, 1881.

BALLADS OF HINDOSTAN

JOGADHYA UMA

" SHELL-BRACELETS ho! Shell-bracelets ho!
      Fair maids and matrons come and buy!"
    Along the road, in morning's glow,
  The pedler raised his wonted cry.
The road ran straight, a red, red line,
    To Khirogram, for cream renowned,
Through pasture-meadows where the kine,
    In knee-deep grass, stood magic bound
And half awake, involved in mist,
    That floated in dun coils profound,
Till by the sudden sunbeams kissed
    Rich rainbow hues broke all around.

" Shell-bracelets ho! Shell-bracelets ho!"
    The roadside trees still dripped with dew,
And hung their blossoms like a show.
    Who heard the cry? 'Twas but a few,
A ragged herd-boy, here and there,
    With his long stick and naked feet;
A ploughman wending to his care,
    The field from which he hopes the wheat;
An early traveller, hurrying fast
    To the next town; an urchin slow
Bound for the school; these heard and passed,
    Unheeding all—" Shell-bracelets ho!"

Pellucid spread a lake-like tank
    Beside the road now lonelier still,
High on three sides arose the bank
    Which fruit-trees shadowed at their will;

Upon the fourth side was the Ghat,
    With its broad stairs of marble white,
And at the entrance-arch there sat,
    Full face against the morning light,
A fair young woman with large eyes,
    And dark hair falling to her zone,
She heard the pedler's cry arise,
    And eager seemed his ware to own.

" Shell-bracelets ho!   See, maiden see!
    The rich enamel sunbeam kissed!
Happy, oh happy, shalt thou be,
    Let them but clasp that slender wrist;
These bracelets are a mighty charm,
    They keep a lover ever true,
And widowhood avert, and harm,
    Buy them, and thou shalt never rue.
Just try them on! "—She stretched her hand,
    " Oh what a nice and lovely fit!
No fairer hand, in all the land,
    And lo! the bracelet matches it."

Dazzled the pedler on her gazed
    Till came the shadow of a fear,
While she the bracelet arm upraised
    Against the sun to view more clear.
Oh she was lovely, but her look
    Had something of a high command
That filled with awe.   Aside she shook
    Intruding curls by breezes fanned
And blown across her brows and face,
    And asked the price, which when she heard
She nodded, and with quiet grace
    For payment to her home referred.

" And where, O maiden, is thy house?
    But no, that wrist-ring has a tongue,
No maiden art thou, but a spouse,
    Happy, and rich, and fair, and young."
" Far otherwise, my lord is poor,
    And him at home thou shalt not find;

Ask for my father; at the door
　Knock loudly; he is deaf, but kind.
Seest thou that lofty gilded spire
　Above these tufts of foliage green.?
That is our place; its point of fire
　Will guide thee o'er the tract between."

" That is the temple spire."—" Yes, there
　We live; my father is the priest,
The manse is near, a building fair
　But lowly, to the temple's east.
When thou hast knocked, and seen him, say,
　His daughter, at Dhamaser Ghat,
Shell-bracelets bought from thee to-day,
　And he must pay so much for that.
Be sure, he will not let thee pass
　Without the value, and a meal.
If he demur, or cry alas!
　No money hath he—then reveal,

Within the small box, marked with streaks
　Of bright vermilion, by the shrine,
The key whereof has lain for weeks
　Untouched, he'll find some coin—'tis mine.
That will enable him to pay
　The bracelet's price, now fare thee well!"
She spoke, the pedler went away,
　Charmed with her voice, as by some spell;
While she left lonely there, prepared
　To plunge into the water pure,
And like a rose her beauty bared,
　From all observance quite secure.

Not weak she seemed, nor delicate,
　Strong was each limb of flexile grace,
And full the bust; the mien elate,
　Like hers, the goddess of the chase
On Latmos hill—and oh, the face
　Framed in its cloud of floating hair,
No painter's hand might hope to trace
　The beauty and the glory there!

Well might the pedler look with awe,
  For though her eyes were soft, a ray
Lit them at times, which kings who saw
  Would never dare to disobey.

Onwards through groves the pedler sped
  Till full in front the sunlit spire
Arose before him. Paths which led
  To gardens trim in gay attire
Lay all around. And lo! the manse,
  Humble but neat with open door!
He paused, and blest the lucky chance
  That brought his bark to such a shore.
Huge straw ricks, log huts full of grain,
  Sleek cattle, flowers, a tinkling bell,
Spoke in a language sweet and plain,
  " Here smiling Peace and Plenty dwell."

Unconsciously he raised his cry,
  " Shell-bracelets ho! " And at his voice
Looked out the priest, with eager eye,
  And made his heart at once rejoice.
" Ho, *Sankha* pedler! Pass not by,
  But step thou in, and share the food
Just offered on our altar high,
  If thou art in a hungry mood.
Welcome are all to this repast!
  The rich and poor, the high and low!
Come, wash thy feet, and break thy fast,
  Then on thy journey strengthened go."

" Oh thanks, good priest! Observance due
  And greetings! May thy name be blest!
I came on business, but I knew,
  Here might be had both food and rest
Without a charge; for all the poor
  Ten miles around thy sacred shrine
Know that thou keepest open door,
  And praise that generous hand of thine:
But let my errand first be told,
  For bracelets sold to thine this day,

So much thou owest me in gold,
　　Hast thou the ready cash to pay?

The bracelets were enamelled—so
　　The price is high."—" How! Sold to mine?
Who bought them, I should like to know."
　　" Thy daughter, with the large black eyne,
Now bathing at the marble ghat."
　　Loud laughed the priest at this reply,
" I shall not put up, friend, with that;
　　No daughter in the world have I,
An only son is all my stay;
　　Some minx has played a trick, no doubt,
But cheer up, let thy heart be gay.
　　Be sure that I shall find her out."

" Nay, nay, good father, such a face
　　Could not deceive, I must aver;
At all events, she knows thy place,
　　' And if my father should demur
To pay thee '—thus she said—' or cry
　　He has no money, tell him straight
The box vermilion-streaked to try,
　　That's near the shrine.' " " Well, wait, friend, wait! "
The priest said thoughtful, and he ran
　　And with the open box came back,
" Here is the price exact, my man,
　　No surplus over, and no lack.

How strange! how strange!　Oh blest art thou
　　To have beheld her, touched her hand,
Before whom Vishnu's self must bow,
　　And Brahma and his heavenly band!
Here have I worshipped her for years
　　And never seen the vision bright;
Vigils and fasts and secret tears
　　Have almost quenched my outward sight;
And yet that dazzling form and face
　　I have not seen, and thou, dear friend,
To thee, unsought for, comes the grace,
　　What may its purport be, and end?

How strange! How strange! Oh happy thou!
    And couldst thou ask no other boon
Than thy poor bracelet's price? That brow
    Resplendent as the autumn moon
Must have bewildered thee, I trow,
    And made thee lose thy senses all."
A dim light on the pedler now
    Began to dawn; and he let fall
His bracelet basket in his haste,
    And backward ran the way he came;
What meant the vision fair and chaste,
    Whose eyes were they—those eyes of flame?

Swift ran the pedler as a hind,
    The old priest followed on his trace,
They reached the Ghat but could not find
    The lady of the noble face.
The birds were silent in the wood,
    The lotus flowers exhaled a smell
Faint, over all the solitude,
    A heron as a sentinel
Stood by the bank. They called—in vain,
    No answer came from hill or fell,
The landscape lay in slumber's chain,
    E'en Echo slept within her cell.

Broad sunshine, yet a hush profound!
    They turned with saddened hearts to go;
Then from afar there came a sound
    Of silver bells;—the priest said low,
" O Mother, Mother, deign to hear,
    The worship-hour has rung; we wait
In meek humility and fear.
    Must we return home desolate?
Oh come, as late thou cam'st unsought,
    Or was it but an idle dream?
Give us some sign if it was not,
    A word, a breath, or passing gleam."

Sudden from out the water sprung
    A rounded arm, on which they saw

As high the lotus buds among
   It rose, the bracelet white, with awe.
Then a wide ripple tost and swung
   The blossoms on that liquid plain,
And lo! the arm so fair and young
   Sank in the waters down again.
They bowed before the mystic Power,
   And as they home returned in thought,
Each took from thence a lotus flower
   In memory of the day and spot.

Years, centuries, have passed away,
   And still before the temple shrine
Descendants of the pedler pay
   Shell-bracelets of the old design
As annual tribute.   Much they own
   In lands and gold—but they confess
From that eventful day alone
   Dawned on their industry—success.
Absurd may be the tale I tell,
   Ill-suited to the marching times,
I loved the lips from which it fell,
   So let it stand among my rhymes.

BUTTOO

" HO! Master of the wondrous art!
    Instruct me in fair archery,
      And buy for aye—a grateful heart
That will not grudge to give thy fee."
Thus spoke a lad with kindling eyes,
A hunter's lowborn son was he—
To Dronacharjya, great and wise,
Who sat with princes round his knee.

Up Time's fair stream far back—oh far,
The great wise teacher must be sought!
The Kurus had not yet in war
With the Pandava brethren fought.
In peace, at Dronacharjya's feet,
Magic and archery they learned,
A complex science, which we meet
No more, with ages past inurned.

" And who art thou," the teacher said,
" My science brave to learn so fain?
Which many kings who wear the thread
Have asked to learn of me in vain."
" My name is Buttoo," said the youth,
" A hunter's son, I know not Fear; "
The teacher answered, smiling smooth,
" Then know him from this time, my dear."

Unseen the magic arrow came,
Amidst the laughter and the scorn
Of royal youths—like lightning flame
Sudden and sharp.   They blew the horn,

442

As down upon the ground he fell,
Not hurt, but made a jest and game;—
He rose—and waved a proud farewell,
But cheek and brow grew red with shame.

And lo—a single, single tear
Dropped from his eyelash as he past,
" My place I gather is not here;
No matter—what is rank or caste?
In us is honor, or disgrace,
Not out of us," 'twas thus he mused,
" The question is—not wealth or place,
But gifts well used, or gifts abused."

" And I shall do my best to gain
The science that man will not teach,
For life is as a shadow vain,
Until the utmost goal we reach
To which the soul points. I shall try
To realize my waking dream,
And what if I should chance to die?
None miss one bubble from a stream."

So thinking, on and on he went,
Till he attained the forest's verge,
The garish day was well-nigh spent,
Birds had already raised its dirge.
Oh what a scene! How sweet and calm!
It soothed at once his wounded pride,
And on his spirit shed a balm
That all its yearnings purified.

What glorious trees! The sombre saul
On which the eye delights to rest,
The betel-nut—a pillar tall,
With feathery branches for a crest,
The light-leaved tamarind spreading wide,
The pale faint-scented bitter neem,
The seemul, gorgeous as a bride,
With flowers that have the ruby's gleam,

The Indian fig's pavilion tent
In which whole armies might repose,
With here and there a little rent,
The sunset's beauty to disclose,
The bamboo boughs that sway and swing
'Neath bulbuls as the south wind blows,
The mango-tope, a close dark ring,
Home of the rooks and clamorous crows,

The champac, bok, and South-sea pine,
The nagessur with pendant flowers
Like ear-rings—and the forest vine
That clinging over all, embowers,
The sirish famed in Sanscrit song
Which rural maidens love to wear,
The peepul giant-like and strong,
The bramble with its matted hair,

All these, and thousands, thousands more,
With helmet red, or golden crown,
Or green tiara, rose before
The youth in evening's shadows brown.
He passed into the forest—there
New sights of wonder met his view,
A waving Pampas green and fair
All glistening with the evening dew.

How vivid was the breast-high grass!
Here waved in patches, forest corn—
Here intervened a deep morass—
Here arid spots of verdure shorn
Lay open—rock or barren sand—
And here again the trees arose
Thick clustering—a glorious band
Their tops still bright with sunset glows.—

Stirred in the breeze the crowding boughs,
And seemed to welcome him with signs,
Onwards and on—till Buttoo's brows
Are gemmed with pearls, and day declines.

Then in a grassy open space
He sits and leans against a tree,
To let the wind blow on his face
And look around him leisurely.

Herds, and still herds, of timid deer
Were feeding in the solitude,
They knew not man, and felt no fear,
And heeded not his neighborhood,
Some young ones with large eyes and sweet
Came close, and rubbed their foreheads smooth
Against his arms, and licked his feet,
As if they wished his cares to soothe.

" They touch me," he exclaimed with joy,
" They have no pride of caste like men,
They shrink not from the hunter-boy,
Should not my home be with them then?
Here in this forest let me dwell,
With these companions innocent,
And learn each science and each spell
All by myself in banishment.

A calm, calm life, and it shall be
Its own exceeding great reward!
No thoughts to vex in all I see,
No jeers to bear or disregard;—
All creatures and inanimate things
Shall be my tutors; I shall learn
From beast, and fish, and bird with wings,
And rock, and stream, and tree, and fern.

With this resolve, he soon began
To build a hut, of reeds and leaves,
And when that needful work was done
He gathered in his store, the sheaves
Of forest corn, and all the fruit,
Date, plum, guava, he could find,
And every pleasant nut and root
By Providence for man designed,

A statue next of earth he made,
An image of the teacher wise,
So deft he laid, the light and shade,
On figure, forehead, face and eyes,
That any one who chanced to view
That image tall might soothly swear,
If he great Dronacharjya knew,
The teacher in his flesh was there.

Then at the statue's feet he placed
A bow, and arrows tipped with steel,
With wild-flower garlands interlaced,
And hailed the figure in his zeal
As Master, and his head he bowed,
A pupil reverent from that hour
Of one who late had disallowed
The claim, in pride of place and power.

By strainèd sense, by constant prayer,
By steadfastness of heart and will,
By courage to confront and dare,
All obstacles he conquered still;
A conscience clear—a ready hand,
Joined to a meek humility,
Success must everywhere command,
How could he fail who had all three!

And now, by tests assured, he knows
His own God-gifted wondrous might,
Nothing to any man he owes,
Unaided he has won the fight;
Equal to gods themselves—above
Wishmo and Drona—for his worth
His name, he feels, shall be with love
Reckoned with great names of the earth.

Yet lacks he not, in reverence
To Dronacharjya, who declined
To teach him—nay, with e'en offence
That well might wound a noble mind,

Drove him away;—for in his heart
Meek, placable, and ever kind,
Resentment had not any part,
And Malice never was enshrined.

One evening, on his work intent,
Alone he practised Archery,
When lo! the bow proved false and sent
The arrow from its mark awry;
Again he tried—and failed again;
Why was it? Hark!—A wild dog's bark!
An evil omen:—it was plain
Some evil on his path hung dark!

Thus many times he tried and failed,
And still that lean, persistent dog
At distance, like some spirit wailed,
Safe in the cover of a fog.
His nerves unstrung, with many a shout
He strove to frighten it away,
It would not go—but roamed about,
Howling, as wolves howl for their prey.

Worried and almost in a rage,
One magic shaft at last he sent,
A sample of his science sage,
To quiet but the noises meant.
Unerring to its goal it flew,
No death ensued, no blood was dropped,
But by the hush the young man knew
At last that howling noise had stopped.

It happened on this very day
That the Pandava princes came
With all the Kuru princes gay
To beat the woods and hunt the game.
Parted from others in the chase,
Arjuna brave the wild dog found—
Stuck still the shaft—but not a trace
Of hurt, though tongue and lip were bound.

"Wonder of wonders! Didst not thou
O Dronacharjya, promise me
Thy crown in time should deck my brow
And I be first in archery?
Lo! here, some other thou hast taught
A magic spell—to all unknown;
Who has in secret from thee bought
The knowledge, in this arrow shown!"

Indignant thus Arjuna spake
To his great Master when they met—
"My word, my honor, is at stake,
Judge not, Arjuna, judge not yet.
Come, let us see the dog"—and straight
They followed up the creature's trace.
They found it, in the self-same state,
Dumb, yet unhurt—near Buttoo's place.

A hut—a statue—and a youth
In the dim forest—what mean these?
They gazed in wonder, for in sooth
The thing seemed full of mysteries.
"Now who art thou that dar'st to raise
Mine image in the wilderness?
Is it for worship and for praise?
What is thine object? speak, confess."

"Oh Master, unto thee I came
To learn thy science. Name or pelf
I had not, so was driven with shame,
And here I learn all by myself.
But still as Master thee revere,
For who so great in archery!
Lo, all my inspiration here,
And all my knowledge is from thee."

"If I am Master, now thou hast
Finished thy course, give me my due.
Let all the past, be dead and past,
Henceforth be ties between us new."

" All that I have, O Master mine,
All I shall conquer by my skill,
Gladly shall I to thee resign,
Let me but know thy gracious will."

" Is it a promise? "   " Yea, I swear
So long as I have breath and life
To give thee all thou wilt."   " Beware!
Rash promise ever ends in strife."
" Thou art my Master—ask! oh ask!
From thee my inspiration came,
Thou canst not set too hard a task,
Nor aught refuse I, free from blame."

" If it be so—Arjuna hear! "
Arjuna and the youth were dumb,
" For thy sake, loud I ask and clear,
Give me, O youth, thy right-hand thumb.
I promised in my faithfulness
No equal ever shall there be
To thee, Arjuna—and I press
For this sad recompense—for thee."

Glanced the sharp knife one moment high,
The severed thumb was on the sod,
There was no tear in Buttoo's eye,
He left the matter with his God.
" For this "—said Dronacharjya—" Fame
Shall sound thy praise from sea to sea,
And men shall ever link thy name
With Self-help, Truth, and Modesty."

SINDHU

Part I

DEEP in the forest shades there dwelt
 A *Muni* and his wife,
  Blind, gray-haired, weak, they hourly felt
 Their slender hold on life.

No friends had they, no help or stay,
 Except an only boy,
A bright-eyed child, his laughter gay,
 Their leaf-hut filled with joy.

Attentive, duteous, loving, kind,
 Thoughtful, sedate, and calm,
He waited on his parents blind,
 Whose days were like a psalm.

He roamed the woods for luscious fruits,
 He brought them water pure,
He cooked their simple mess of roots,
 Content to live obscure.

To fretful questions, answers mild
 He meekly ever gave,
If they reproved, he only smiled,
 He loved to be their slave.

Not that to him they were austere,
 But age is peevish still,
Dear to their hearts he was—so dear,
 That none his place might fill.

They called him Sindhu, and his name
  Was ever on their tongue,
And he, nor cared for wealth nor fame,
  Who dwelt his own among.

A belt of *Bela*-trees hemmed round
  The cottage small and rude,
If peace on earth was ever found
  'Twas in that solitude.

PART II

GREAT Dasarath, the King of Oudh,
    Whom all men love and fear,
    With elephants and horses proud
Went forth to hunt the deer.

O gallant was the long array!
    Pennons and plumes were seen,
And swords that mirrored back the day,
    And spears and axes keen.

Rang trump, and conch, and piercing fife,
    Woke Echo from her bed!
The solemn woods with sounds were rife
    As on the pageant sped.

Hundreds, nay thousands, on they went!
    The wild beasts fled away!
Deer ran in herds, and wild boars spent
    Became an easy prey.

Whirring the peacocks from the brake
    With Argus wings arose,
Wild swans abandoned pool and lake
    For climes beyond the snows.

From tree to tree the monkeys sprung,
    Unharmed and unpursued,
As louder still the trumpets rung
    And startled all the wood.

The porcupines and such small game
    Unnoted fled at will,
The weasel only caught to tame
    From fissures in the hill.

Slunk light the tiger from the bank,
    But sudden turned to bay!
When he beheld the serried rank
    That barred his tangled way.

Uprooting fig-trees on their path,
   And trampling shrubs and flowers,
Wild elephants, in fear and wrath,
   Burst through, like moving towers.

Lowering their horns in crescents grim
   Whene'er they turned about,
Retreated into coverts dim
   The bisons' fiercer rout.

And in this mimic game of war
   In bands dispersed and passed
The royal train—some near, some far,
   As day closed in at last.

Where was the king? He left his friends
   At mid-day, it was known,
And now that evening fast descends
   Where was he? All alone.

Curving, the river formed a lake,
' Upon whose bank he stood,
No noise the silence there to break,
   Or mar the solitude.

Upon the glassy surface fell
   The last beams of the day,
Like fiery darts, that lengthening swell,
   As breezes wake and play.

Osiers and willows on the edge
   And purple buds and red,
Leant down—and 'mid the pale green sedge
   The lotus raised its head.

And softly, softly, hour by hour
   Light faded, and a veil
Fell over tree, and wave, and flower,
   On came the twilight pale.

Deeper and deeper grew the shades,
   Stars glimmered in the sky,
The nightingale along the glades
   Raised her preluding cry.

What is that momentary flash?
  A gleam of silver scales
Reveals the *Mahseer;*—then a splash,
  And calm again prevails.

As darkness settled like a pall
  The eye would pierce in vain,
The fireflies gemmed the bushes all,
  Like fiery drops of rain.

Pleased with the scene—and knowing not
  Which way, alas! to go,
The monarch lingered on the spot—
  The lake spread bright below.

He lingered, when—oh hark! oh hark
  What sound salutes his ear!
A roebuck drinking in the dark,
  Not hunted, nor in fear.

Straight to the stretch his bow he drew,
  That bow ne'er missed its aim,
Whizzing the deadly arrow flew,
  Ear-guided, on the game!

Ah me! What means this?—Hark, a cry,
  A feeble human wail,
"Oh God!" it said—"I die—I die,
  Who'll carry home the pail?"

Startled, the monarch forward ran,
  And then there met his view
A sight to freeze in any man
  The warm blood coursing true.

A child lay dying on the grass,
  A pitcher by his side,
Poor Sindhu was the child, alas!
  His parents' stay and pride.

His bow and quiver down to fling,
  And lift the wounded boy,
A moment's work was with the king.
  Not dead—that was a joy!

He placed the child's head on his lap,
   And 'ranged the blinding hair,
The blood welled fearful from the gap
   On neck and bosom fair.

He dashed cold water on the face,
   He chafed the hands, with sighs,
Till sense revived, and he could trace
   Expression in the eyes.

Then mingled with his pity, fear—
   In all this universe
What is so dreadful as to hear
   A Brahman's dying curse!

So thought the king, and on his brow
   The beads of anguish spread,
And Sindhu, fully conscious now,
   The anguish plainly read.

" What dost thou fear, O mighty king?
   For sure a king thou art!
Why should thy bosom anguish wring?
   No crime was in thine heart!

Unwittingly the deed was done;
   It is my destiny,
O fear not thou, but pity one
   Whose fate is thus to die.

No curses, no!—I bear no grudge,
   Not thou my blood hast spilt,
Lo! here before the unseen Judge,
   Thee I absolve from guilt.

The iron, red-hot as it burns,
   Burns those that touch it too,
Not such my nature—for it spurns,
   Thank God, the like to do.

Because I suffer, should I give
   Thee, king, a needless pain?
Ah, no! I die, but may'st thou live,
   And cleansed from every stain! "

Struck with these words, and doubly grieved
　　At what his hands had done,
The monarch wept, as weeps bereaved
　　A man his only son.

" Nay, weep not so," resumed the child,
　　" But rather let me say
My own sad story, sin-defiled,
　　And why I die to-day!

Picking a living in our sheaves,
　　And happy in their loves,
Near, 'mid a peepul's quivering leaves,
　　There lived a pair of doves.

Never were they two separate,
　　And lo, in idle mood,
I took a sling and ball, elate
　　In wicked sport and rude—

And killed one bird—it was the male,
　　Oh cruel deed and base!
The female gave a plaintive wail
　　And looked me in the face!

The wail and sad reproachful look
　　In plain words seemed to say,
A widowed life I cannot brook,
　　The forfeit thou must pay.

What was my darling's crime that thou
　　Him wantonly shouldst kill?
The curse of blood is on thee now,
　　Blood calls for red blood still.

'And so I die—a bloody death—
　　But not for this I mourn,
To feel the world pass with my breath
　　I gladly could have borne,

But for my parents, who are blind,
　　And have no other stay—
This, this, weighs sore upon my mind,
　　And fills me with dismay.

Upon the eleventh day of the moon
  They keep a rigorous fast,
All yesterday they fasted; soon
  For water and repast

They shall upon me feebly call!
  Ah, must they call in vain?
Bear thou the pitcher, friend—'tis all
  I ask—down that steep lane."

He pointed—ceased—then sudden died!
  The king took up the corpse,
And with the pitcher slowly hied,
  Attended by Remorse,

Down the steep lane—unto the hut
  Girt round with *Bela*-trees;
Gleamed far a light—the door not shut
  Was open to the breeze.

Part III

" O H why does not our child return?
　　Too long he surely stays."—
　Thus to the *Muni*, blind and stern,
His partner gently says.

" For fruits and water when he goes
　He never stays so long,
Oh can it be, beset by foes,
　He suffers cruel wrong?

Some distance he has gone, I fear,
　A more circuitous round—
Yet why should he? The fruits are near,
　The river near our bound.

I die of thirst—it matters not
　If Sindhu be but safe,
What if he leave us, and this spot,
　Poor birds in cages chafe.

Peevish and fretful oft we are—
　Ah, no—that cannot be:
Of our blind eyes he is the star,
　Without him, what were we?

Too much he loves us to forsake,
　But something ominous,
Here in my heart, a dreadful ache,
　Says, he is gone from us.

Why do my bowels for him yearn,
　What ill has crossed his path?
Blind, helpless, whither shall we turn,
　Or how avert the wrath?

Lord of my soul—what means my pain?
　This horrid terror—like
Some cloud that hides a hurricane;
　Hang not, O lightning—strike!"

Thus while she spake, the king drew near
  With haggard look and wild,
Weighed down with grief, and pale with fear,
  Bearing the lifeless child.

Rustled the dry leaves 'neath his foot,
  And made an eerie sound,
A neighboring owl began to hoot,
  All else was still around.

At the first rustle of the leaves
  The *Muni* answered clear,
" Lo, here he is—oh wherefore grieves
  Thy soul, my partner dear? "

The words distinct, the monarch heard,
  He could no further go,
His nature to its depths was stirred,
  He stopped in speechless woe.

No steps advanced—the sudden pause
  Attention quickly drew,
Rolled sightless orbs to learn the cause,
  But, hark!—the steps renew.

" Where art thou, darling—why so long
  Hast thou delayed to-night?
We die of thirst—we are not strong,
  This fasting kills outright.

Speak to us, dear one—only speak,
  And calm our idle fears,
Where hast thou been, and what to seek?
  Have pity on these tears."

With head bent low the monarch heard,
  Then came a cruel throb
That tore his heart—still not a word,
  Only a stifled sob!

" It is not Sindhu—who art thou?
  And where is Sindhu gone?
There's blood upon thy hands—avow! "
  " There is."—" Speak on, speak on."

The dead child in their arms he placed,
    And briefly told his tale,
The parents their dead child embraced,
    And kissed his forehead pale.

" Our hearts are broken.   Come, dear wife,
    On earth no more we dwell;
Now welcome Death, and farewell Life,
    And thou, O king, farewell!

We do not curse thee, God forbid
    But to my inner eye
The future is no longer hid,
    Thou too shalt like us die.

Die—for a son's untimely loss!
    Die—with a broken heart!
Now help us to our bed of moss,
    And let us both depart."

Upon the moss he laid them down,
    And watched beside the bed;
Death gently came and placed a crown
    Upon each reverend head.

Where the Sarayu's waves dash free
    Against a rocky bank,
The monarch had the corpses three
    Conveyed by men of rank;

There honored he with royal pomp
    Their funeral obsequies—
Incense and sandal, drum and tromp,
    And solemn sacrifice.

What is the sequel of the tale?
    How died the king?—Oh man,
A prophet's words can never fail—
    Go, read the Ramayan.

MISCELLANEOUS POEMS

NEAR HASTINGS

Near Hastings, on the shingle-beach,
   We loitered at the time
When ripens on the wall the peach,
   The autumn's lovely prime.
Far off—the sea and sky seemed blent,
   The day was wholly done,
The distant town its murmurs sent,
   Strangers—we were alone.

We wandered slow; sick, weary, faint,
   'Then one of us sat down,
No nature hers, to make complaint;—
   The shadows deepened brown.
A lady past—she was not young,
   But oh! her gentle face
No painter-poet ever sung,
   Or saw such saintlike grace.

She passed us—then she came again,
   Observing at a glance
That we were strangers; one, in pain—
   Then asked—Were we from France?
We talked awhile—some roses red
   That seemed as wet with tears,
She gave my sister, and she said,
   God bless you both, my dears!"

Sweet were the roses—sweet and full,
   And large as lotus flowers
That in our own wide tanks we cull
   To deck our Indian bowers.

But sweeter was the love that gave
    Those flowers to one unknown,
I think that He who came to save
    The gift a debt will own.

The lady's name I do not know,
    Her face no more may see,
But yet, oh yet I love her so!
    Blest, happy, may she be!
Her memory will not depart,
    Though grief my years should shade,
Still bloom her roses in my heart!
    And they shall never fade!

FRANCE

1870

Not dead—oh no—she cannot die!
    Only a swoon, from loss of blood!
Levite England passes her by,
Help, Samaritan!   None is nigh;
    Who shall staunch me this sanguine flood?

'Range the brown hair, it blinds her eyne,
    Dash cold water over her face!
Drowned in her blood, she makes no sign,
Give her a draught of generous wine.
    None heed, none hear, to do this grace.

Head of the human column, thus
    Ever in swoon wilt thou remain?
Thought, Freedom, Truth, quenched ominous
Whence then shall Hope arise for us,
    Plunged in the darkness all again.

No, she stirs!—There's a fire in her glance,
    Ware, oh ware of that broken sword!
What, dare ye for an hour's mischance,
Gather around her, jeering France,
    Attila's own exultant horde?

Lo, she stands up—stands up e'en now,
   Strong once more for the battle-fray,
Gleams bright the star, that from her brow
Lightens the world. Bow, nations, bow,
   Let her again lead on the way!

THE TREE OF LIFE

Broad daylight, with a sense of weariness!
Mine eyes were closed, but I was not asleep,
My hand was in my father's, and I felt
His presence near me. Thus we often passed
In silence, hour by hour. What was the need
Of interchanging words when every thought
That in our hearts arose, was known to each,
And every pulse kept time? Suddenly there shone
A strange light, and the scene as sudden changed.
I was awake:—It was an open plain
Illimitable—stretching, stretching—oh, so far!
And o'er it that strange light—a glorious light
Like that the stars shed over fields of snow
In a clear, cloudless, frosty winter night,
Only intenser in its brilliance calm.
And in the midst of that vast plain, I saw,
For I was wide awake—it was no dream,
A tree with spreading branches and with leaves
Of divers kinds—dead silver and live gold,
Shimmering in radiance that no words may tell!
Beside the tree an Angel stood; he plucked
A few small sprays, and bound them round my head.
Oh, the delicious touch of those strange leaves!
No longer throbbed my brows, no more I felt
The fever in my limbs—" And oh," I cried,
" Bind too my father's forehead with these leaves."
One leaf the Angel took and therewith touched
His forehead, and then gently whispered " Nay! "
Never, oh never had I seen a face
More beautiful than that Angel's, or more full
Of holy pity and of love divine.

Wondering I looked awhile—then, all at once
Opened my tear-dimmed eyes—When lo! the light
Was gone—the light as of the stars when snow
Lies deep upon the ground. No more, no more,
Was seen the Angel's face. I only found
My father watching patient by my bed,
And holding in his own, close-prest, my hand.

MADAME THÉRÈSE

*Written on the fly-leaf of Erckmann-Chatrian's novel, entitled,
" Madame Thérèse."*

Wavered the foremost soldiers—then fell back.
Fallen was their leader, and loomed right before
The sullen Prussian cannon, grim and black,
With lighted matches waving. Now, once more,
Patriots and veterans!—Ah! 'Tis in vain!
Back they recoil, though bravest of the brave;
No human troops may stand that murderous rain;
But who is this—that rushes to a grave?

It is a woman—slender, tall, and brown!
She snatches up the standard as it falls—
In her hot haste tumbles her dark hair down,
And to the drummer-boy aloud she calls
To beat the charge; then forwards on the *pont*
They dash together;—who could bear to see
A woman and a child, thus Death confront,
Nor burn to follow them to victory?

I read the story and my heart beats fast!
Well might all Europe quail before thee, France,
Battling against oppression! Years have passed,
Yet of that time men speak with moistened glance.
Va-nu-pieds! When rose high your Marseillaise
Man knew his rights to earth's remotest bound,
And tyrants trembled. Yours alone the praise!
Ah, had a Washington but then been found!

SONNET

A sea of foliage girds our garden round,
  But not a sea of dull unvaried green,
  Sharp contrasts of all colors here are seen;
The light-green graceful tamarinds abound
Amid the mango clumps of green profound,
  And palms arise, like pillars gray, between;
  And o'er the quiet pools the seemuls lean,
Red—red, and startling like a trumpet's sound.
But nothing can be lovelier than the ranges
  Of bamboos to the eastward, when the moon
Looks through their gaps, and the white lotus changes
  Into a cup of silver. One might swoon
    Drunken with beauty then, or gaze and gaze
    On a primeval Eden, in amaze.

SONNET

Love came to Flora asking for a flower
  That would of flowers be undisputed queen,
  The lily and the rose, long, long had been
Rivals for that high honor. Bards of power
Had sung their claims. " The rose can never tower
  Like the pale lily with her Juno mien "—
  " But is the lily lovelier? " Thus between
Flower-factions rang the strife in Psyche's bower.
" Give me a flower delicious as the rose
  And stately as the lily in her pride "—
" But of what color? "—" Rose-red," Love first chose,
  Then prayed—" No, lily-white—or, both provide; "
    And Flora gave the lotus, " rose-red " dyed,
    And " lily-white "—the queenliest flower that blows.

OUR CASUARINA-TREE

Like a huge Python, winding round and round
  The rugged trunk, indented deep with scars
    Up to its very summit near the stars,
A creeper climbs, in whose embraces bound
  No other tree could live. But gallantly
The giant wears the scarf, and flowers are hung
In crimson clusters all the boughs among,
    Whereon all day are gathered bird and bee;
And oft at nights the garden overflows
With one sweet song that seems to have no close,
Sung darkling from our tree, while men repose,

When first my casement is wide open thrown
  At dawn, my eyes delighted on it rest;
    Sometimes, and most in winter—on its crest
A gray baboon sits statue-like alone
  Watching the sunrise; while on lower boughs
His puny offspring leap about and play;
And far and near kokilas hail the day;
    And to their pastures wend our sleepy cows;
And in the shadow, on the broad tank cast
By that hoar tree, so beautiful and vast,
The water-lilies spring, like snow enmassed.

But not because of its magnificence
  Dear is the Casuarina to my soul:
    Beneath it we have played; though years may roll,
O sweet companions, loved with love intense,
  For your sakes, shall the tree be ever dear!
Blent with your images, it shall arise
In memory, till the hot tears blind mine eyes!
    What is that dirge-like murmur that I hear
Like the sea breaking on a shingle-beach?
It is the tree's lament, an eerie speech,
That haply to the unknown land may reach.

Unknown, yet well-known to the eye of faith!
  Ah, I have heard that wail far, far away

In distant lands, by many a sheltered bay,
When slumbered in his cave the water-wraith
And the waves gently kissed the classic shore
Of France or Italy, beneath the moon,
When earth lay trancèd in a dreamless swoon:
And every time the music rose—before
Mine inner vision rose a form sublime,
Thy form, O Tree, as in my happy prime
I saw thee, in my own loved native clime.

Therefore I fain would consecrate a lay
Unto thy honor, Tree, beloved of those
Who now in blessed sleep, for aye, repose,
Dearer than life to me, alas! were they!
May'st thou be numbered when my days are done
With deathless trees—like those in Borrowdale,
Under whose awful branches lingered pale
"Fear, trembling Hope, and Death, the skeleton,
And Time, the shadow;" and though weak the verse
That would thy beauty fain, oh fain rehearse,
May Love defend thee from Oblivion's curse.